LIVING ABROAD IN
PANAMA

MIRIAM BUTTERMAN

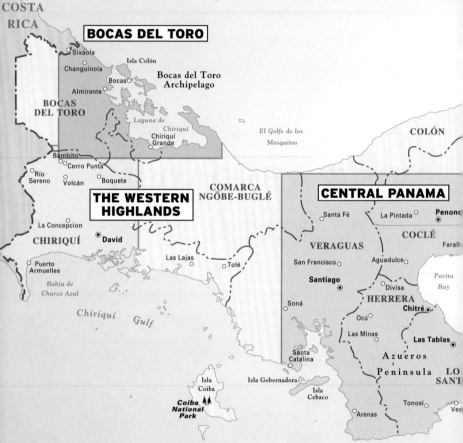

COSTA
RICA

BOCAS DEL TORO

Caribbean Sea

Sixaola

Changuinola

Isla Colón

Bocas

Bocas del Toro
Archipelago

Almirante

**BOCAS
DEL TORO**

Laguna de
Chiriquí
Grande

Chiriquí

El Golfo de los
Mosquitos

COLÓN

Bambito

Cerro Punta

Río
Sereno

Volcán

Boquete

**COMARCA
NGÖBE-BUGLÉ**

CENTRAL PANAMA

Santa Fé

La Pintada

Penonc

**THE WESTERN
HIGHLANDS**

COCLÉ

La Concepcion

CHIRIQUÍ

●**David**

Las Lajas

Tolé

VERAGUAS

San Francisco

Aguadulce

Farall

Puerto
Armuelles

Bahía de
Charco Azul

Chiriquí Gulf

Santa
Catalina

Soná

●**Santiago**

Divisa

Ocú

Las Minas

Parita
Bay

HERRERA

●**Chitré**

●**Las Tablas**

Azueros
Peninsula

**LO
SANT**

Isla
Coiba

**Coiba
National
Park**

Isla Gobernadora

Isla
Cebaco

Arenas

Tonosí

Ver

PACIFIC OCEAN

© AVALON TRAVEL

PRIME LIVING LOCATIONS IN PANAMA

Isla Grande
Palenque
Portobelo
Nombre de Diós
Miramár
El Porvenir
Cartí
Colón
Lago Alajuela
PANAMA CITY
Chepo
Lago Bayano
COMARCA KUNA YALA
Lago Gatún
Gamboa
Cerro Azul
PANAMA
Arriján
Panama Canal
PANAMA CITY
Puerto Obaldía
La Chorrera
Playa Veracruz
Santa Fé
COMARCA EMBERÁ
Isla Taboga
Punta Chame
Las Perlas Archipelago
La Palma
Río Tuira
Nuevo Gorgona
San Miguel
Yaviza
Playa Coronado
El Real de Santa María
San Carlos
Isla del Rey
COMARCA EMBERÁ
DARIÉN
crí
Isla Iguana
Gulf of Panama
Pedasí
Azuero
Puerto Piña
Jaqué
COLOMBIA
Juradó
Cupica
Cupica Gulf

0   25 mi
0   25 km

Contents

At Home in Panama

When the late ex-President and dictator of Panama Omar Torrijos called his country *"El Puente del Mundo, El Corazón del Universo"* (Bridge of the World, Heart of the Universe), he was referring to the pride of the Panama Canal and the importance of his negotiating its return to the operating hands of its national administration. He was not talking directly to the foreign wave of satisfied expats, who decades later would be reclining in the seat of this ideally situated country. Regardless, his words have since been used by transients and expats to communicate the mysterious attachment one feels living in a foreign land that, as Panama's indigenous people have said, "fills your basket with fish and butterflies."

What initially draws us to Panama may not necessarily be the reason we end up staying here. We might be brought here for work, sunshine, or family, but most of us stay because we feel this mysterious connection to Panama. My life in Panama began when I moved to a verdant, calm hilltop just above the urban streets of Panama City. I spent my evenings grading papers, with a fresh breeze blowing through the house and the sweet smell of the tropics wafting through my high-tech mosquito screens. I got to know my neighborhood, visited with new friends, took nature hikes in the morning and trips to the beach in the afternoon. I became an expert at "hammocking" while winding down on my balcony, watching the steady movement of traffic on the Panama Canal and the Bridge of the Americas. These were very small tokens of everyday Panamanian life, yet they obliged me to recognize nuances of the deeper peace that was here. A tropical sunset I had previously seen only in photographs or on a postcard was now in front of me, with the sound of toucans calling in the distance.

Geckos mocked me at night, and I laughed back while I tried to chase their harmless shadows out the door.

If your experience is like mine, living here will open your senses to new sights, smells, and feelings, fill your mouth with savory tropical flavors, and probably teach you about things in the natural world you never knew existed. But it may also leave you exhausted and confused. The more I read from outside sources about Panama's ideal retirement communities and first-world conveniences, the more I find that Panama is still somewhat off the beaten path for the average foreigner. It could be a blessing in disguise because the truth about Panama is not going to be found on a real-estate website or in the Lifestyles section of your favorite cosmopolitan magazine. Discovering Panama's mystery, whether by accident or by intent, calls for sensibility and patience.

Omar Torrijos touched bravely upon Panama's mysterious graces, and those of us who let Panama into our lives attempt to identify exactly what it is that keeps us here. Some say it's Panama's geography, sandwiched between the open borders of two giant oceans. Others say it is the history of thousands of transients who came to Panama between leaving their hardships behind and finding their future dreams.

No matter the true force, those who find the real Panama leave with the desire to come back. With one deep breath, life so vividly defined by lush sensibilities can fill you with wonder and mystery. Maybe no one can say for sure what it is about Panama that pulls us here. The real mystery is yours to discover.

▶ WHAT I LOVE ABOUT PANAMA

- Hammocking
- Early morning walks through Cerro Ancon's jungle foliage while glimpsing Panama City breathing below
- Sunsets along the Panama Canal
- The decadence of Avenida Central and the real people who live, work, and thrive on it daily
- The rustic beauty of a Caribbean coastal town
- Hearing three to four languages spoken on a given day
- Women walking with umbrellas to shade them from the sun

- The quiet return to the old days of Bocas Town in off-season
- Going to El Valle to feel the air of early autumn
- Crossing the Bridge of the Americas, leaving the city skyline behind, and driving over one of the world's most amazing engineering feats, the Panama Canal
- *Pulpo al ajillo* (octopus in garlic sauce)
- Discovering a new tropical fruit every day
- The jovial and laidback Panamanian spirit

WELCOME TO PANAMA

INTRODUCTION

Like the many passages its transcontinental figure has hosted since Pre-Colombian days, Panama is a country in a constant state of motion. Evidence of this lies in everything from the ocean air mixing trade winds from Pacific and Caribbean coasts to the rapidly changing skyline in Panama City, a proud symbol of change and development for this nation, but also a challenge in the making for this tropical environment. A recent boom in the country's real estate and construction sector has propped For Sale signs in every developed area, from Panama City to the western towns of Bocas del Toro, and called for investment brochures to be translated into a myriad of languages for wide-eyed international investors. However, these new developments—five-star hotels and apartment buildings with luxurious penthouses and beach access—say nothing of the real Panama. The real Panama is found in the rainforest fragrances and ocean settings, the indigenous populations, and the familiar transit buses called "Red Devils " (old U.S. school buses painted in wild colors and packed to the brim with daily commuters) that frantically rush through

© SKY GILBAR

the streets while playing loud salsa and reggaeton music. Not to mention the charming mystique of old versus new in Panama City's Old Town, the diversity of flora and fauna that serves as a fountain of knowledge for research scientists, and a history of immigration from across the world as wide-ranging as the layers of the surrounding rainforest. To discover the real Panama is to discover a country pulsating with life and energy and to find peace amid the constantly changing tides.

Many expats, it appears, have been able to do just that. Immigrants from all over the world come to Panama, whether for work, study, navigation, or leisure; many end up finding their roots in the isthmus. Looking at Panama from the inside out, its character is clearly forged by its people. Dichotomies of cultures spiral around one another: Afro-Antillean in Colón's Atlantic and Spanish "white tails" in the Pacific Capital City; Swiss chalet architecture in the Chiriquí highlands and French as the new unofficial second language in Bocas del Toro islands; Panama City's original Chinatown sits side by side with San Felipe de Neri, a community whose founding was dedicated to the Italian priest, Filipo de Neri. The Bahia temple that sits proudly above one of the hilltops of the Capital city is one of just nine in the world, the Jewish community is said to be one of the strongest in Latin America, and new in 2008 is a Mormon Temple, exclusive to only a handful of similar gold-laden Mormon houses of worship found around the world. The United States Canal Zone that opened to Panamanians in 2000 has re-emerged with new character. Panama may be a very young nation, gaining independence only about 100 years ago, but its people have been here in spirit for centuries.

Nine degrees north and 80 degrees west of the equator, Panama is primarily characterized by its heat factor. The seasons are traditionally divided into "dry" or "rainy," but thanks to *"Los Niños"* climate changes, the divisions are becoming more ambiguous, and perhaps "hot" and "hotter" are more appropriate titles. Despite the unpredictability of the day's rainfall, Panamanians have a special ability to truly enjoy the details of their lives and the fruits of their labors. Beaches are the urban weekender's most popular destination, and residents flock to the Pacific and Caribbean coasts to ward off the humidity and the workweek. Rain or shine, "hammocking" is a national pastime for rural dwellers and urbanites alike; another favorite activity is large family meals, not quite vegetarian friendly, and fully stocked bars, especially around payday.

While foreign corporations are often occupied raising Panama's bustling cities and tourist destinations to developed-nation standards, the rest of the country remains vastly unexplored, untouched by tourism, and blessed by Mother Nature. With more than 900 bird species found in Panama, it is impossible for even casual nature lovers to resist the magical aura of a Disney movie come alive in your own backyard. Each province of Panama hosts a special flavor of flora and fauna, such as superfluous orchid farming in the highlands or nesting sea turtles on the islands. The elusive Harpy Eagle—scientists have estimated that fewer than 50 remain in the world—also makes its home in Panama's rainforests. Is it no wonder that Smithsonian Institute of Tropical Research set up headquarters here?

Panama is a generally underestimated country. Its historical significance as a U.S.-run Canal way remains its most advertised feature. While foreigners and "Zonian" characters are prevalent on the isthmus, it is in no way the only marker of what Panama is.

The Lay of the Land

COUNTRY DIVISIONS

Panama is made up of nine provinces, and five indigenous regions, called *comarcas*. Panama's indigenous communities maintain their independence from the central government. All regions share the tropical climate, and no area is more than an hour from the coast. Each region, however, has an independent air, and Panamanians carry their province's culture proudly.

Provinces

DARIÉN

Certainly not the most populated, Darién is however the largest province, measuring 11,896.5 square kilometers. It is located at the southeast side of the country and is infamous as the mysterious jungle connecting Colombia and Panama. The Darién should only be explored with an experienced guide who knows the safer routes, but if you go you will find hidden cultures of refugee villages, special artisans, and amazing coastal scenes. Unfortunately, its vast jungles are becoming scarcer due to quick development and deforestation.

PANAMA

Bordering the Darien to its northwest is Panama Province. It is the second-largest province, with an area of 11,671 square kilometers, resting along the Pacific waters. The Panama Canal runs through the Panama province from Panama City on the Pacific side to Colón on the Atlantic side. Nearly one-third of the population lives here; Panama province is dense with industry, economics, government, and social culture, and the capital and surrounding beaches extending toward the interior continue to develop at rapid paces. It is clearly the most urban area in the country. Even if one decides to live in the interior or another large city, it is almost impossible to escape the need to come to Panama City to tend to some responsibility at least every couple of months.

COLÓN

The province of Colón rests to the north of Panama province and completes the inter-oceanic Canal route at the Atlantic city of Colón. Rains are more common in Colón, and the population is largely descendent of the Afro-Antillean community. It was in this province, in the district of Portobelo, that Christopher Columbus arrived when discovering the Americas. The coastal communities, such as Nombre de Dios and Portobelo, still re-enact traditional stories of confrontations between the Spanish colonists and the African slaves, which can be seen at certain holiday celebrations such as the Festival de Diablo or Carnival. These villages are small, remote beaches populated by locals. Colón City is the bustling city of this area, run down by years of neglect yet a necessity for Canal businesses and activity. It hosts the famous Free Zone for tax-free commerce. Most everything—the food, the language, the people, and the music—deriving from this province are original from the rest of Panama but at the same time have an important influence on the rest of the country.

LOS SANTOS, COCLE, HERRERA, AND VERAGUAS

The Central provinces of Los Santos, Cocle, and Herrera lie to the south of Panama, going west along the Pacific coastline. And moving farther west bordering both the Atlantic and Pacific oceans is the province of Veraguas (To See Waters). These provinces feature an array of terrain ranging from some of the highest elevations in the country, such as in Santa Fe de Veraguas or Cocle, to flat desert land in Herrera, known as the Sarigua Desert. Most people are of mixed Spanish-indigenous descent and are now dedicated to dairy farming. Cocle is known for producing sugarcane, tomato, rice, and salt fields. Cocle, Herrera, and the neighboring central area of Veraguas tend to have a dryer tropical climate. The temperatures here can rise extremely high throughout the year. The northern and southern regions of Veraguas, as well as Coiba Island and parts of the Azueros Peninsula in Los Santos, are a more humid tropical climate, where beach breezes may cool down and delight. Some foreigners have set up homes in the coastal areas of Herrera, Azueros Peninsula and the highlands of Cocle; these are less popular since they are more remote and challenging areas in which to live.

BOCAS DEL TORO

To the northwest is the province of Bocas del Toro, which consists of a mainland and an archipelago of islands by the same name on the Caribbean Atlantic. This area is very popular with foreign tourists and new residents coming to set up in a uniquely Afro-Caribbean culture filled with "island life" personality. Not many foreigners occupy the mainland, where rolling, green landscapes with wild curvy roads give way to indigenous farming communities or border towns along the Costa Rican frontier. The mainland of Bocas del Toro, abutting Costa Rica's Atlantic border, was once known for its thriving role in the Banana Republic, as the production area for Chiquita Banana Company. Today, the banana fields are plenty, but the industry cooperatives have fallen to lesser successes. The La Amistad National Park, a UNESCO World Heritage Site since 1990, is shared by neighboring Costa Rica and lies mainly in Bocas del Toro.

CHIRIQUÍ

Chiriquí is the southwesternmost province in Panama. David, the western capital city of Panama, makes its home here and is only a 20-minute drive from one of Panama's most popular areas with foreign retirees: Boquete and the surrounding towns of Volcán Barú. It is said that Chiricanos are the most proud of their region, usually displaying a spirit of competition with Panamanians from other areas. They are proud of the diversity of their land, their mountainous terrain, and the fresh, mountain air and mild year-round temperatures of 18–21°C (65–70°F), which have lured northerners to relocate here. Volcán Barú, Panama's highest peak, is the focus of Boquete, Cerro Punta, and other small towns such as Bambino and Volcán. The area is crawling with birders, mountaineers, flowing rivers, and thermal baths. Foreign influence is prevalent by way of Swiss-style Chalets. Chiriquí is the coffee-growing region in Panama, and many of the owners of the *fincas* or farms are foreign families who have decided to become agriculturalists in their home away from home.

Comarcas

KUNA YALA

The first region to gain its autonomy was Kuna Yala, known as San Blas to the rest of the world, in 1938. Kuna Yala is in the northeast parcel of the country, made up of 356 small islands of the Caribbean coast, extending east from Colón. The Kuna have opened up their mainland and archipelago of islands to tourism but are strict about keeping their heritage unmixed; hence, they absolutely will not sell land to anyone. They speak the Kuna language and are only just beginning to incorporate Spanish language instruction in their schools. There are many package trips out to Kuna Yala: It is possible to drive there from the Atlantic side and take a boat, or fly to the islands from Panama City.

KUNA DE MADUNGANDI AND KUNA WARGANDI

Two of the other *comarcas,* Kuna de Madungandi and Kuna Wargandi, established their autonomy in 1996 and 2000 respectively and lie on the mainland. Kuna de Madungandi is south of Kuna Yala province, in the area of Chepo, and consists of fourteen Kuna communities with a total population of about 3,300. Kuna Wargandi lies just east of Kuna de Madungandi and has just three communities. Neither are considered provinces but are *corregimientos* (districts).

EMBERA-WOUNAN

In 1983, in the province of Darien, the Embera-Wounan *comarca* was established. The Embera people live in about 500 square miles of the Chagres National Park, and they survive mostly off ecotourism and artistry, inviting travelers to experience their culture as they present their daily lives in a showcase format set up exclusively for tourists.

NGÖBE BUGLÉ

The largest of the five *comarcas* is Ngöbe Buglé, set between the western provinces of Panama, with Veraguas to its east, Chiriquí to the west, and Bocas del Toro to the northwest. The land area encompasses up to 6,680 square kilometers, and there are about 170,000 indigenous Guayami (the Ngöbe and the Buglé) who make their living from agriculture. Current circumstances involving hydroelectric installations are displacing the Guayami, but now that the issue has come to light, many activists are helping the Ngöbe Buglé fight for their right to stay in their land and ensure that no foreign investors displace them further.

GEOGRAPHY

Panama's global position as the land that links the Americas is its geographic claim to fame. It is located in the Northern Hemisphere, west of the Greenwich Meridian. Located between the tropical limits of the Americas, Panama has always had a tough time finding its true belonging on the map. Some say it is part of the Caribbean, which it is, and others say it is part of Central America, which also is a fact.

It encompasses an area of 75,517 square kilometers (29,157 square miles), 772 kilometers in length and 60–177 kilometers at its widest point. The country, shaped like an S set horizontally, borders Colombia to the east and Costa Rica to the west. With thousands of miles of coastline along its borders, the country is gaining tourist interest for the black sands on its Pacific (south) border and its sandy white beaches along the Caribbean waters.

Going west along the curvy terrain, flat interiors give way to the Cordillera Central, part of the Continental Divide, formed from volcanic intrusions. The country's main peaks, also known as the highlands, break the coastal atmosphere from east to west. Volcán Barú, an inactive volcano for over a thousand years, is the highest peak, rising up to 3,500 meters, but there are at least 20 other peaks rising 950–3300 meters above sea level, offering vast views of the Pacific to Atlantic coastlines.

Circling Panama's mainland are some 1,000 islands. The Atlantic archipelago of San Blas, in the east, and the Archipelago of Bocas del Toro in the Northwest raise the number to 550 more islands, which lie in the nautical jurisdiction of Panama.

There are two vitally important rivers in Panama. The first, Rio Chagres, is one of the most important rivers in the Americas. It is only navigable for six to eight miles from the mouth. It was used as the route for Spanish trade, and later for the stream of Gold Rushers from California. It flows into the Atlantic waters and its dams are used for hydroelectric power at Lake Gatun, the man-made lake that allows for ships to climb to the level of the Panama Canal. Rio Chepo, which has also been dammed to create hydroelectric power in the Darien province, empties its water into the Pacific. Panama has about 30 other rivers of importance for flow and drainage, land markers, and water sources for locals. The largest river is the Tuira, which is 171 kilometers (106 miles) long and flows into the Darien province and out to the Pacific. It is another important transit way, since it can be navigated for up to 120 kilometers (75 miles) by ships, allowing access to other local communities.

The vast jungles of Panama's East, in the Darien Province, are the largest forested land in the Western Hemisphere after the Amazon basin. They host a magical, natural world, giving life to a bevy of animal and plant species. For most people, the Darien is known as the forbidden jungle that connects the mainland to Colombia.

CLIMATE

It is odd to describe a climate where the only outstanding factor on a daily basis is that it is *hot*. It is tropical and hot, rainy and hot, dry and hot, and beautiful and hot at any given moment and at any given geographic point. Temperatures in the lowlands stay between 26°C (79°F) at dawn or dusk and build up to 35°C (96°F) during peak daylight hours. Even in the valleys of the some highland areas, the sun remains strong with temperatures reaching up to 24–26°C (75 or 80°F) during the day, though the lows in these areas do offer respite from flaming thermometers. Perhaps the only place to consistently find a spot of cold is the top of the Volcán Barú at 3,500 meters (11,483 feet) above sea level with temperatures of 10–18°C (50–65°F).

Speaking by the book, Panama is classified by a tropical humid climate and tropical savannah. The rainy season exists for 8–9 months a year, but tropical rains tend to be a welcome cooling fix, after which the sun breaks through and sizzles up the concrete or bakes up the sands. Dry season, from the end of December to the beginning of April, bests the verdant vegetation, and the landscape becomes brown and bare. But, the dry season brings a delicious breeze and mild humidity that invites people outside from the air-conditioned, concrete structures.

FLORA

Panama's vegetation is a sprawling domino effect of green flower bulbs popping up indiscriminately through the vast terrain of the country and cityscapes— something uncontrollable, shocking, and beautiful all the same. The unique biodiversity found here has made it a world headquarters for the Smithsonian Tropical Research Institute for more than 85 years. There are several botanists who believe that Panama should be the international center of good health, as most of the natural cures for disease can often be found in your own backyard.

There are more than 10,000 plant species found in Panama's land and island territories. The wooded-timber forests are rich with oak, mahogany, laurel, cedar, and exotic woods like the cuipo, espavé, corotu, cativo, and a rich display of others. Unfortunately, so much wooded area has lured in the timber-vampires; the Panamanian forests have been

© MIRIAM BUTTERMAN

Colorful vegetation like this *flor de pina* sprout up naturally throughout Panama.

suffering the consequences of deforestation since the 1940s. Still, 40 percent of Panama remains wooded area.

Living in a country so replete with biodiversity is a new experience every day. One morning you are planting a seedling, and only a few days later the sprouts are two inches high; life is literally bursting here. Ferns are an example of that, with 953 types classified on the isthmus so far. One thousand species of orchids run wild throughout the highlands and savannahs in Panama. In fact, the national flower is an orchid variety called the *Flor del Espiritu Santo* (Holy Ghost Orchid).

FAUNA

Thanks to the international recognition of Panama's unique biodiversity, scientists have been able to identify upwards of 179 species of amphibians, 229 reptiles, 957 bird species, and 259 mammal species.

Mammals

Panama, its official slogan suggests, is "the route to discover." It is not as developed as neighboring Costa Rica—an advantage that many hope will remain— and therefore if quietly and respectfully trekking across through the vast rainforest landscapes, you may easily discover anteaters, armadillo, sloth, or even deer. I've never heard anyone claim to glimpse a puma or jaguar, but it has always been said that they do live deep in the black holes of the Darien Jungle and out in Bocas del Toro's mainland. Monkeys of all kinds—howlers, titi,

This jaguar nests in his home at the Summit Zoo outside Panama City.

spider monkeys, and capuchins—leap across the treetops from urban parks to islands to deeper wooded areas. The neque, a small rodent-like animal the size of a jackrabbit (without the puffy tail), nervously traverses the open fields. It is something *campesinos* have learned to hunt and eat when other meat is not available.

Reptiles and Amphibians

I am not fond of snakes, and although they are fond of Panama, I have not let that scare me out of my home yet. In fact, although they make me squirm in my seat just thinking about them, I have to admit the colors and classes of reptiles that I have seen slither across

© SKY GILBAR

Monkeys, especially mono titi, are as common in Panama as squirrels or chipmunks in the United States.

the humid fields are absolute eye-candy, not to mention the incredible "live Discovery Channel" interludes between a tree boa and a bird I've witnessed from my home's second-floor window. Boa constrictors, coral snakes, garter snakes, and other harmless (to humans) snakes are prevalent in the wet season. Bushmasters, the world's largest pit viper, are dangerous but mainly stay confined to the rainforests in Panama. Fer-de-lance snakes pose perhaps the biggest danger, as they are often found near people on farms and cultivated land, their poison is highly toxic, and they tend to be bad-tempered, striking with little provocation.

Iguanas and other lizards lazily stray through the green treetops, soaking in the hot sun and eating off the thousands of insects that mosey around them. Six of the world's eight turtle species are found throughout the isthmus's many waterways.

Marinelife

Marinelife in Panama is extraordinarily rich. In particular, Coiba National Park, a protected area, contains 80 percent of the fish species found in the entire planet as well as 1,700 hectares of coral reef and coral communities. Sharks, whales, and dolphins have been are spotted in the deep Pacific waters, and the depths of both oceans hosts all kinds of tropical sea life, including squid, octopus, sponges, and unique species of sea turtles. Learning to spot barracuda in the Atlantic side, and getting over the fear of swimming alongside them, is part of the initiation of living within Panama's wilder side.

Enjoying the ocean in Panama requires great care and consciousness. The survival of much of Panama's marinelife is endangered. Atlantic coast mangroves are unfortunately at great risk due to increased development in the region. The ocean's reefs are deteriorating, leaving the intricate weave of aquatic plantlife and the many sea animals within vulnerable to extinction.

Birds

During the months of November to February, bird migration is at its peak, and it is virtually impossible to ignore the sounds and colors that flutter outside your window. Approximately 950 bird species have been discovered in Panama, 122 of which are migrant birds. Bird-watcher or no, you'll quickly discover that an interest in birds is a Panama-inflicted characteristic, and soon you will be stopping to note the quick sounds of a nearby toucan or falcon flying low over a flycatcher's nest.

The Harpy Eagle is Panama's national bird, and together with international birding organizations such as the Peregrine Fund, the government is doing all it can to save this endangered animal. Harpies can measure over one meter (41 inches) in length, with a wingspan of nearly two meters (6.5 feet). They are large predators who feed off animals such as monkeys, sloths, and occasionally reptiles or other birds. With hind talons the size of grizzly bear claws, adults weigh up to nine kilograms (20 pounds) but only carry half their weight while flying with prey. They prefer to dwell in the provinces of Darien and Bocas del Toro, and some have been captured for breeding and tracking so as to avoid total extinction.

Guatemala's national bird, the resplendent quetzal, a spectacular and rarely sighted bird, can also be spotted in concentration in the highlands of Volcán Barú across The Quetzal Trail from Cero Punta to Boquete. The quetzal's bright green crown mixed with blue-feathered coat and crimson-colored chest leaves bird-watchers gaping at the sky. Its survival, at risk due to development in the jungles from Mexico to Panama, has led conservationists from Panama and its neighbors to join with La Amistad National Park of Chiriquí in a perseveration campaign.

ENVIRONMENTAL ISSUES

One of the hardest adjustments for foreigners arriving in Panama is the delay in setting up infrastructure that supports "green" living. While there are efforts in the private and public sector, they are minimal compared to other countries. Panama's vibrant backdrop of plantlife, marinelife, and wildlife has yet to provoke an innate sense of environmental responsibility in the people who reside here. Of course, environmental groups and conservationists recognize Panama's resplendent ecosystem for the treasure it is and have been here for decades sounding important warnings, doing research, and providing education on the ecological dangers in this region of the world.

But money talks. Due to its sudden popularity in real estate, business

---

AN INSPIRING WILL TO SAVE PANAMA'S TRAILS

The group TransPanama comprises nature conservationists who love their homeland Panama, care to celebrate one of the oldest passageways in the Americas, and send a message to fellow Panamanians: Go out and experience your country, but learn to love it the way it is, the way it has been given to us by nature. The group's goal is to mark 900 kilometers of already native and unaffected trails from the Colombian border to Costa Rica.

Panamanian law, *la ley del servidumbres*, says that Panamanians have access to all their natural jewels, but TransPanama founder Mike Esquevil claims it is not happening. "Panama is on sale right now, and looking from the outside in, there are many people who are doing wonderful things for us, but there are others that are coming in as if the land belongs to them. Some historical paths are being taken away from us. Without marking them first, we can't defend nature the way we want to. We plan to go to the government, eventually, to ask for help in really protecting these trails." But for now they want to prove it can be done without money or the Ministry as long as the desire is strong enough.

The first group outing was in January 2008 and consisted of 20 people, including support groups who don't necessarily hike or camp. The support they have found since is truly inspiring. Members have received transportation, GPS equipment, food, graphic design, print media – almost anything they could possibly need – donated to them.

Today the group has marked 17 percent of its 900-kilometer goal, connecting the trails from the Panama province at the trails of Sora, through Cocle La Laguna in Veraguas. Working on weekends only and with volunteers separated into groups, they can mark up to 70 kilometers in one excursion.

The group now boasts 150 volunteers, working professionals during the week, many of whom sacrifice a few days of freshwater and electricity to receive the luxury of breathing clean air and living by the ocean, in nature, sleeping under the stars.

investment, and tourism, Panama as we know it will soon change drastically if responsible development and waste management tactics are not implemented. As of late much discussion is under way between developers, environmental consultants, and community leaders; hopefully the outcome is one where high-rises, if they must go up, will be constructed with green materials, architectural design will promote tropic-friendly structures, and coastal zoning laws will be enforced to avoid the destruction of ocean life.

Deforestation

There are 65 official protected areas designated throughout Panama, 34 percent of the total land area. UNESCO declared the following areas World Heritage Sites: Coiba National Park, consisting of Coiba Island and 38 smaller islands; the Darien jungle; and the Parque la Amistad touching the western provinces of Bocas del Toro and Chiriquí. The support is meant to deter mining companies and hydroelectric plants from bulldozing rainforest and threatening rare plant and animal species, not to mention the sustainable lifestyles of the indigenous communities living there.

Air Quality and Waste Management

Traffic congestion and industrial contamination in Panama City has raised public awareness about air quality. In the past, breezes sweeping through from two oceans was enough to clean out the airborne toxins, but new development eliminating open spaces and public parks has foiled nature's self-cleaning system. Thankfully, the city is working to restructure open spaces and alleviate the damage being done.

Waste dumped into the Panama Canal bay has added to a sewage smell along the main Balboa Avenue in Panama City, but government agencies are teaming with the Japanese embassy and committing to a "Save the Bay" project, beginning construction of a new waste management system under way in 2009. Other promises include widening the avenue and constructing new open spaces.

Coastal Destruction

According to Dr. Stanley Heckadon of the Smithsonian Tropical Institute, "Destruction of coastal habitats through port development is currently one of the most pressing environmental issues in Colón," a region north of Panama City which is host to the largest mangrove forest in Central America. Because Panama stands apart from the Caribbean hurricane belt, the Atlantic mangrove forest is a primary reserve for marinelife important to local fisheries and birds that dwell in the lush mangroves. *Manglares,* as they are called in Spanish, are also natural buffers or anchors, providing protection from erosion and floods. However, the local population does not recognize their importance, and developers have found their way in, destroying these important natural barriers. The Smithsonian Institute claims that if development of these coastal ways keeps up at the current rate, Colón City will find itself underwater within 50 years.

Social Climate

As expected from a country that draws people and traditions from across the Americas, Panama wears the many shades of a multicultural society. However, segues between these cultural waves have managed to form solid and uniquely "Panamanian" nuances that bond the social structure as well. Most Panamanians are jovial and charismatic. They are always willing to talk about their culture and their origins, and they are proud of what they have accomplished as a society and whom they have connected with, as individuals or as a community, to get where they are today. Networking is a social survival skill and Panamanians are so accustomed to it, they demonstrate how it can be done with tact.

A Panamanian from the metropolitan area defines himself by his provincial origins, family name, and the network he belongs to within the society. The indigenous people are characterized differently: by their language, dress, and pure genetic traits, usually untouched by the outside world. Panamanians are learning to respect this more, the special attributes that create a longer history than just the 100 plus years of independence they now call the Republic of Panama.

"Panamix" is perhaps a more accurate description of the social makeup than anything else. Two Panamanian artists, Abner Benaim and Gustavo Araujo, published a book by that name in 2006. In their publication, through a series of vivid portrait photographs, Panama's social definition is expressed by individuals and families with diverse characteristics, at first shown through physical traits but later revealing a melting pot of ideologies and a future of heterogeneous, open-minded generations. By the end of the photo essay, one interprets Panama as a confused but proud society originating from many starting points and many social classes.

Others describe Panama as two nations within one country. The influence of a U.S. social dynamic has created comforts; people are used to high fashion, technology-driven lives, and international fare. Panama City is filled with shopping malls, global brands, and cinemas showing Hollywood motion pictures, as well as food chains like Dunkin' Donuts, Baskin Robbins, and KFC. South American chains also have a major presence in Panama, and middle to upper class South Americans who have migrated here find a comfortable nostalgia indulging in the familiarity from south of the isthmus. International fashion and food are in abundant representation, brought in by families who long ago settled from Spain, Germany, Italy, Japan, Peru, Colombia, the Middle East, France, and the United States and have never let go of their roots.

DEMOGRAPHICS

Panama has a very diverse population. According to demographic studies published in the *CIA Factbook,* the majority of Panamanians—70 percent—are *mestizos,* a mix of European and indigenous American ancestry, and mulatto, a mix of indigenous American and African ancestry. Most Africans in Panama are descendants of slaves that were brought to Panama as a result of the African Slave Trade during the Spanish Colonial period, and of the Afro-Antillean population who came to work on the Canal in the 19th century. Fourteen percent of Panama's population is black, 10 percent is white, and 6 percent is indigenous. Panamanians tend to simplify their demographics, however, and according to local school books, three-quarters of the population is made up of mestizo and African descendents, and the other one-quarter is indigenous— Kuna, Chocoe, Ngobe-bugle, Bokota, Embera, and Teribe.

Christianity is the principal religion practiced in Panama, with 85 percent of Panamanians as practicing Roman Catholics. Panama is also known to have various religious groups who have established well-founded and active communities. Protestant, Greek-Orthodox, Jewish, Muslim, and Hindu groups all have frequent community events as well as their own institutions of

© SKY GILBAR

The Festival de Diablo is an important tradition for the Afro-Antillean culture.

worship throughout Panama City, if not also in the western provinces of the country.

The population of Panama is roughly 3.4 million and nearly one-third of that number lives in and around Panama City. The literacy rate is 91 percent of adults age 15 or higher. The majority of the population is young, between the ages of 14 and 25 years old. And according to the United Nation's Department of Economic Status and Immigration, the number of foreigners residing in Panama is said to be 102,000, or about three percent of the population. The immigration department in Panama was unable to produce records giving any accurate number.

ATTITUDE TOWARD FOREIGNERS

Panamanians' encounters with foreigners have been a story in the making for the last 150 years, and the storyline is a jagged one of ups and downs when it comes to tolerance and appreciation. The California Gold Rush, the Panama Railroad, construction of the Panama Canal, and a present-day expansion inviting major foreign investment are only some of the major rungs on this ladder of international relationships. Throughout all these phases, Panamanians have constructed interesting attitudes about foreigners, usually stereotyping them by what they have offered or taken away from the community, developing markets that might or might not have been otherwise developed by a Panamanian. Sometimes they are bitter attitudes, such as the undertones of loss due to the U.S. invasion in 1989 or European colonialism in the 16th century. Other times they are nostalgic, recalling the simplicity of a thriving economy when the United States occupied the Canal Zone, and the vast support of the French embassy in Panama's contemporary arts.

Panamanians are otherwise used to North Americans, from the 100 years of occupation in the Canal Zone and the benefits it had on their economy. In 1999, when the U.S. administration was officially closed down in the "Zone," many Panamanians lamented over the decline in the job market and goods available. Still, there is an undercurrent of resentment that the Canal Zone had so much to offer but Panamanians could not enter or take advantage of the movie houses, libraries, and even some open land and parks that were only for the Zonians.

Another major point of contention is Operation Just Cause, the 1989 invasion by George Bush Sr., which ejected Noriega out of dictatorship and into a Miami jail cell. Generally Panamanians wanted Noriega out, but they are even today still discovering the large number of innocent people who died during the invasion, a number disputed between hundreds and thousands.

Panamanian families in the city neighborhoods that were bombed have not gotten over the havoc caused that one time in this small and peaceful country, and in many of these places, the mess is still literally left to pick up. So visitors and expats must be knowledgeable of this history and sensitive to these wounds before they speak about politics or critique Panamanian ways. In addition, regardless of what you hear them say, you should be mindful of what you refer to as "American" and not use it to differentiate from Panamanians and deny them this same heritage. In fact, it is a birthright they are clearly entitled to by geography and the fact that Christopher Columbus walked these sides of the continent before any other.

Present-day foreign investment is something many Panamanians enjoy because it is helping the economy once again. Job standards are getting tougher, and Panamanians are challenged to study harder or learn a second or third language. They are rewarded by openings in business and other industries that were never before here. While many Panamanians have developed an "if you can't beat 'em, join 'em" attitude, others resent the real estate boom that is causing housing prices to skyrocket and knocking down old, historical neighborhoods. Essentially, prices are good for foreigners, but Panamanians who are interested in investing in that first "starter home" or a final destination are struggling. Many of them are kicking themselves for not buying years ago, but given the familial tradition of inheriting land or real estate, many just rent until they are ready to reside on their families' longtime property—something these same families are now realizing can be sold for a shinier penny.

Getting to know a Panamanian may seem rather hard, as *bochinche* (gossip) and lack of trust are generally part of the first hurdles to get over. But once you do form relationships with them, you will find they are solid, sweet, and *tranquilo* (easygoing). You may also find Panamanians talkative and energetic, but always with a mission to please. They love to learn from foreigners, copying styles and especially borrowing language later implemented into Panamanian Spanish. You will do well to observe for a while and, with any luck, let the locals' originality and diversity fill you with a fond sentiment to contribute— respectfully and wisely—to the tapestry that is Panama.

HISTORY, GOVERNMENT, AND ECONOMY

The history of Panama, since the first diminutive yet fierce Spanish conquistadors landed on its Caribbean shores in 1501, reads like a Robert Louis Stevenson or Patrick O'Brian adventure story. Few nations can boast a history as dramatic as Panama's—replete with swashbuckling pirates, fearless privateers, and vengeful, cruel, and corrupt imperial governors. Treasure that crossed the steaming jungles, through the rapid rivers and over the tranquil bays of the Isthmus of Panama during the 16th century was so great the worldwide price of gold actually bottomed out for over 50 years. Understanding Panama's history, allowing for distinct interpretations at many levels, is vital to understanding not only Panama's current global character but also its national identity.

History

PRE-COLUMBIAN PERIOD

Prior to European arrival, Panama was settled by Paleolithic hunter-gatherer groups and tribal clans that crossed the Asian land bridge and migrated south through the North American continent. This settlement took 11,000 years. Traces of the Chibchan, who had come south from what is today Honduras; the Chocoan, the present-day Embera people, who came north from Colombia, and the Cueva, an indigenous people that lived in the Darién region of eastern Panama are found in the fluted projectile points used for their spears and arrows.

Pre-Columbians were diverse and vibrant native groups that exhibited cultural variety, as suggested by their ornamental jewelry and pottery. They used distinctive and intricate designs on ceramics such as beautiful black-on-red polychrome pottery known as Coclé style. Europeans noted that all three tribal groups were highly adaptive to their seemingly inhospitable surroundings, whether living in the volcanic-cragged Cordillera or the impenetrable Darien jungle. While the indigenous population at the time of the European discovery is unknown, scholarly estimates range from 200,000 to an unlikely high of two million.

CHRISTOPHER COLUMBUS

While the name Cristóbal Colón may not be a household word within North America, few can mistake the Anglicized version of his name: Christopher Columbus. Much interest and confusion surrounds this fellow, who reportedly charmed the Queen of Spain into funding his expedition to the Orient. He was a man on a mission, going so far as to modify his name when it suited his task. Leaving his native Genoa in 1470 he was Cristoforo Colombo; when proposing his Oriental expedition to the Portuguese court he was known as Cristováo Colón. When obtaining funding from the Spanish Crown, he permanently changed his name to Cristóbal Colón.

Colón's four expeditions to the New World occupied every waking hour of his life for over 12 years, 1492–1504. On October 5, 1502, Colón anchored in Almirante Bay within the territory of modern-day Panama. Colón noted that natives wore large breast medals made of pure gold and used the name of the area, Cipangu. This convinced Columbus that he had finally reached China. Natives waved the ecstatic Columbus through channels he believed made up the final passage to the riches of China, but, as Panama has done with many

© SKY GILBAR

The town of Portobelo in Colón was a marking point for Spanish gold trade and exploration in the Americas.

travelers over time, he ended up disappointed in a dead-end lagoon. Colón's fourth voyage was a Panamanian odyssey, sailing the entire Panamanian Caribbean coast. He named one area lacking a good harbor and populated with unwelcome insects El Golfo de los Mosquitos. He took refuge from a violent storm in a beautiful bay he named Porto Bello. By any name, however, the celebrated sailor was not the first to visit Panama. It was Rodrigo de Bastides with the then rookie soldier, Vasco de Nunez de Balboa, who sailed through an expedition just one year prior to Colón's famous voyage. Bastides led his ship along South American coastlines into the Caribbean waters of what is today Kuna Yala. Moving northwest to Nombre de Dios and Portobelo, they touched the same grounds and met with indigenous people who would later tell Colón they had met his countrymen one year earlier.

VASCO NUÑEZ DE BALBOA

Vasco Nuñez de Balboa, Spanish Conquistador and the first European to see the eastern Pacific Ocean in 1513, remains an enigma. Balboa mastered contemporary weapons of war in early military training and excelled in the use of the sword. He was also instructed in history, mathematics, science, religion, and the fine art of being a Hidalgo—in other words, a haughty, insufferable, aristocratic gentleman. In 1501, he joined the expedition of Bastidas, which was going to explore the *Tierra Firme*. Off the Colombian coast, Balboa fought aggressive natives in possession of poisonous arrows and darts that killed several of the crew.

In four months Balboa traveled 200 miles along the coast. When the expedition ended in Haiti, the new governor of the Indies and Española granted Balboa a 30-acre farm on the western side of the island. But, he found farming Haiti both a tropical nightmare and a financial disaster.

In 1510 the destitute Balboa stowed away on a voyage to Panama to escape his creditors. Since 1498, some 800 Spaniards had lived there, but by the time Balboa's ship landed, malaria and yellow fever and the many things that can kill in the jungle had eliminated all but 60 men. Not receiving much support from Española, the settlers at Antigua del Darién, the first city constituted by the Spanish crown in Panama, deposed the crown's representative and elected the newly arrived Balboa as a co-mayor.

With no municipal management experience, Balboa proved a competent town administrator. His insistence that all settlers become subsistence farmers rather than depend on supply ships allowed Antigua to become a sustainable if not prosperous community. Friendly Indians told him of some fine villages along a great sea just a few days' travel to the south and a land of gold called Biru (Peru) that could be reached from this sea. Talk of finding gold was all it took to get a conquistador moving. On September 1, 1513, Balboa set out with 190 Spaniards including Francisco Pizarro, a pack of dogs, and 1,000 Indian slaves.

After 25 days of hacking their way through jungle, the party came upon on the wide vista of the Pacific Ocean near present-day Panama City. Balboa, clad in full armor, waded into the water and claimed the sea and all the shores on which it washed for his god and his king. Balboa gave the ocean he discovered the name of Mar del Sur (South Sea), because he had traveled south across the isthmus to find it. It was Portuguese explorer Ferdinand Magalhaes (Magellan) who named it Mar Pacifica because, after crossing the very rough waters of the southern tip of South America, the sea became relatively calm.

Balboa emerged from the jungle in January 1514 with all 190 soldiers he had set out with. Meanwhile, Balboa's enemies had denounced him for usurping municipal power in the Spanish court. King Ferdinand appointed a new colonial governor, Pedro Arias de Avila, a senior citizen farming a small holding in the Caribbean. Panamanian historians dubbed him "Pedrarias the Cruel."

His appointment as governor in 1514 of the regions recently discovered by Balboa, and subsequent arrival with troops, gave rise to trouble. Pedrarias was a man of mediocre talent, jealous and vindictive. Balboa, on the other hand, was careless and over-confident in the merits of his achievements. He was no match for the wily Pedrarias. Arias was complimentary and promised his youngest daughter, still safely in Spain, to Balboa in marriage. Balboa continued his explorations while Arias gathered secret testimony against him

THE SILENT PARTNER: RODRIGO DE BASTIDAS

Rodrigo de Bastidas was the wealthy and well-educated Notary of Triana, a suburb of Seville. A Spanish imperial notary was the equivalent of a modern small claims court judge. Position and education made him quite different in nature and temperament than the ambitious Spanish military explorers who came after him. In June 1500, Bastidas secured a license from the Crown that allowed him to outfit two ships at his own cost and risk and, according to legal documents that approved his expedition, "cross the Ocean Sea to discover island or lands not previously discovered by the Admiral Don Cristóbal Colón, or belonging to the king of Portugal." The license specifically granted him the right to secure all the treasures he could find. Bastidas's charter, which is still preserved in the *Archivo de Inidas,* in Seville, is written in excruciating legalistic detail. This document allows Bastidas to acquire "gold, silver, copper, lead, tin, quicksilver (mercury), and any other metal whatever; as well as pearls, precious stones, and jewels; and slaves, negroes and mixed breeds; monsters, serpents, fishes, and birds; spices and drugs, and every other thing of whatsoever name or quality or value it might be." After deducting the cost of outfitting ships and crew, he was to give the king one-fourth of the net profits. Bastidas was no novice to outfitting a seafaring expedition or the intricacies of obtaining a Royal commission, having accompanied Colón on his second voyage in 1493.

Sailing from Cádiz in October 1500, he took the standard route to the New World, first stopping at the Canary Islands, taking fresh provisions for the two-month voyage. Accompanying Bastidas on this voyage was a young soldier named Vasco Nuñez de Balboa, in charge of the expedition's company of soldiers. Reaching the Antilles, the ships filled their casks with freshwater and continued until they reached the coast of present-day Venezuela. The expedition continued west, exploring the northern coast of what they called *Tierra Firme* (South America), along the Colombian coast. They traded with the natives for gold and pearls, giving them trinkets and mirrors.

Sailing into the Gulf of Darién along the coast of present-day Panama around Cabo Tiburon, they resumed their exploration, heading west in an area now called the Comarca de Kuna Yala. Bastidas sailed along the northern coast perhaps as far as the site of Nombre de Diós or even as far as Portobelo. Bastidas continued to trade with the natives and map the coastal terrain. The port he named El Escribano is still on the Panamanian coast. When Columbus sailed from the eastern coast of Central America past this port to Nombre de Diós, he learned from natives that Bastidas had been there the year before. It is therefore Bastidas, with young Vasco Nuñez de Balboa among his crew, whom historians credit the discovery of Panama in 1501.

regarding the removal of the lawful governor of Antigua. Receiving Balboa's report of the discovery of the Pacific, the Crown, always appreciative of acquiring new oceans, bestowed upon Balboa the title of Adelantado of the South Sea, Governor of Coiba and what subsequently became the district of Panama. But Arias and his agents were only biding their time in order to discredit this young upstart.

While Balboa and 300 of his men were busy planning for the voyage to locate Biru, the jealous Pedrarias was determined to judicially murder him. Arrested, Balboa denied charges of treason and pleaded innocent. The judge, predictably, found Balboa guilty and the penalty was pronounced: death. Balboa was beheaded for high treason in January 1517 at Darien.

Though his life was destined to be adventurous and short, Vasco Nuñez de Balboa's exploits in Panama, his discovery of the South Sea, and his preparations for the expedition to fabled Biru, paved the way for many more Spanish adventure- and treasure-seekers.

THE BRETHREN OF THE COAST: HENRY MORGAN

In the 17th century, a modest population of impoverished European multinationals inhabited the Caribbean and eked out a subsistence living on the few small fever-ridden islands that the Spaniards had not seen fit to take. Casting covetous glances at the treasure ships outbound from Mexico and Panama, a Welshman named Henry Morgan, a one-time destitute indentured servant living in Barbados, was recruited by a criminal gang with a boat—known then as today as pirates.

Morgan prospered in his new profession and made a good impression on his companions. Morgan's power and prestige were sufficient to assemble 12 vessels and nearly 700 men for an attack on Portobelo, the eastern terminus for Panamanian trade, as well the warehouse for all Peruvian gold subsequently shipped to Spain. Portobelo's harbor entrance was flanked by two imposing fortresses manned by at least 300 soldiers, making frontal assault unthinkable. Morgan, therefore, landed at Puerto Pontin, 25 miles west of Portobelo. Some 500 pirates slashed their way through the jungle and attacked Portobelo from the landward side, achieving complete surprise. The pirates took possession of the town, a terrific blow to the prestige of Spain. Morgan sent a ransom demand to the governor of Panama: 100,000 gold pieces for the town and its inhabitants. With a piratical flair for the dramatic, Morgan sent along his pistol as a symbol of how easily he had taken Portobelo and declared within a year he would return and take his pistol back. The governor of Panama paid the ransom.

© SKY GILBAR

The Golden Altar in the San Jose Church of Casco Viejo was saved by Jesuit priests during Henry Morgan's attack.

Morgan's prestige as new pirate "godfather" was such that, the next time he called for recruits, no less than 2,000 men and 37 ships answered. The fleet rendezvoused at Tortuga on October 24, 1670, and the captains learned that the next target was to be the heavily defended city of Panama.

Morgan determined the best route into Panama was up the Chagres River just west of present-day Colón. The Spanish were tipped off and prepared. Morgan was driven back with heavy casualties. An untimely explosion of the fort's magazine devastated the place and gave the pirates their opportunity to storm its walls. More than 100 of Morgan's men were killed and 70 wounded. Morgan now personally marched at the head of the 1,200 remaining pirates into the steamy jungle toward Panama City. After nine hellish days they emerged from the bush. On the morning of January 18, 1671, 3,600 Spanish troops marched out of the city of Panama to face one of the strangest armies ever assembled—a 1,200 strong multinational criminal gang of heavily armed Englishmen, Dutch, French, blacks, Indians and even a few Spaniards. Their leader had come to fetch his pistol back from the governor of Panama. After two hours, most of the Spanish cavalry was cut down and Spanish infantry melted into the jungle. Spanish dead totaled 600, with scores more wounded and taken prisoner.

Panama, second-largest city in the Western Hemisphere and a thriving community of 7,000 homes, fell into Morgan's hands. It was thoroughly pillaged. The pirates returned through the jungle with 175 pack animals laden with treasure. Once safely back at Chagres, the greedy pirates tried to extort a ransom for the town. However, the treasury was empty; Morgan had stolen it all. So, the town and its fortifications were ordered demolished. While his men were busy at work, Morgan quietly slipped out of port with all the loot, leaving his former companions at the mercy of the Spanish. Most of the marooned pirates, now split into smaller groups for their own survival, were eventually tracked down and killed by vengeful Spaniards. Those who survived swore revenge on Henry Morgan.

In 1672, to the delight of Spaniards everywhere, Morgan was arrested and transported back to England in chains to be tried for piracy. However, like a modern-day John Gotti, his public image was more a romantic hero than a ruthless criminal, and Morgan received the King's Pardon. Returning to Jamaica as Lieutenant Governor Sir Henry Morgan, he served as governor from 1680 to 1682. His first order of business was to hang his shipmates from the Panama expedition of 1671. Their crime? Piracy, of course. Morgan died a rich respectable aristocrat in 1688. While earning the enmity of all patriotic Panamanians to this day, his story forever contradicts the old saying "Crime doesn't pay."

© SKY GILBAR

Panama Viejo was founded in 1519 and was the original capital until Henry Morgan attacked it.

COLOMBIA AND INDEPENDENCE

What is today Panama was once part of a larger geographic area that used the name Granada or Colombia. During the colonial period, 1538-1819, Panama was included in the New Kingdom of Granada. After Spain withdrew in 1821, a couple of different versions of Granada existed as well, such as the United Provinces of New Granada and The Granadine Confederation. The Granadine Confederation came to an end in 1863 with the signing of the Constitution, which officially changed the name of the country to the United States of Colombia. By the mid-19th century, with the glory days of the Spanish

Conquista and the era of the buccaneers long since faded, Panama became a little-noticed, politically isolated, and economically poor backwater province within a greater Colombia.

THE PANAMA RAILROAD

During the first half of the 19th century there were only two ways of reaching the Pacific Coast. Either way was dangerous and long. One route was by ship around perilous Cape Horn, a distance of some 12,000 miles, and the other by prairie schooners, buckboards, or on foot from the Missouri River across 3,000 miles of Great Plains and Rocky Mountains. After the war with Mexico in 1848, some folks from the eastern states and a new European immigrant wave headed westward.

Crossing the Isthmus of Panama made sense. When a ship left the American eastern seaboard and made the 2,000-mile journey down to Panama, the next leg was a 54-mile overland trip through the dense mosquito- and malaria-infested jungles from Atlantic to Pacific. The old Spanish trail, though mercifully short, still took the better part of a week. Once in Panama City, another ship made the 3,500-mile trip north to San Francisco.

Figuring all this out in the 1840s, a treaty between the United States and New Granada (Colombia) guaranteed the right of way across the Isthmus of Panama to the highest contracting parties. Three New York speculators, Henry Chauncey, William Aspinwall, and John Stephens often met to discuss the possibility of running a profitable trade route to California. Aspinwall already held a government franchise to deliver mail to California. However, carrying cargo and passengers was an entirely different matter. The three theorized that if that 54-mile jungle track could be replaced with a rail link, the route would not only become popular but profitable. The gold strike at Sutter's Mill and the subsequent 1849 California Gold Rush made the link imperative and the need immediate.

The triumvirate's railroad was designed as a publicly traded corporation based in New York City, which bought exclusive rights to build across the isthmus from the government of New Granada (Colombia). The railway cost nearly eight times more than the original estimate in 1850—almost a million dollars per mile in today's money. It was the most expensive railway per unit length of track ever built, with incredible engineering challenges going over mountains and through dense jungle and crocodile- and snake-infested swamps. Over 300 bridges and culverts were built along the route. Some swamps required fill over 100 feet deep before any solid roadbed could be constructed.

The construction took a heavy toll in human lives. More than 12,000 people probably died during the railroad's construction; the railroad company kept no official count. Cholera, yellow fever, and malaria killed most of the workers, while accidents and the jungle claimed others. When a large military detachment, several hundred men of the 4th US Infantry and their dependents, made the crossing in July 1852 en route to garrison duty in California, the tragic consequence was 150 dead soldiers, women, and children. "The horrors of the road in the rainy season are beyond description," wrote Captain Ulysses S. Grant, the officer in charge of the expedition.

When completed, the railway was proclaimed THE engineering marvel of the era. The first train ran from ocean to ocean on January 28, 1855. Until the opening of the Panama Canal in 1914, the railroad carried the heaviest volume of freight of any railroad in the world. The existence of the railway was the key factor in the selection of Panama, rather than Nicaragua, as the site of the canal. In 1881 the French Compagnie Universelle du Canal Interoceanque purchased controlling interest in the Panama Railway Company. In 1904, the United States government purchased the railway from the French canal company. The rebuilt and improved Panama Railway that now runs beside the canal was completed in 1912.

After World War II few additional improvements were made to the Panama Railway, and it declined in the late 20th century even after the U.S. government handed over control of the railway to the government of Panama. In 1998 the government of Panama turned over control to the private Panama Canal Railway Company (PCRC) for 50 years, with majority shares owned by the Kansas City Southern Railroad. In 2001 a large project upgraded the railway to handle 20- and 40-foot intermodal shipping containers crossing the isthmus using former Amtrak diesel engines. The passenger train's refurbished elegant Pullman cars of the 1930s make the hour-long crossing through the jungle an air-conditioned adventure not to be missed. Although no one is catching ships in Panama City bound for San Francisco anymore, the railroad is as its founders envisioned it back in 1850, "an iron Railroad between the two oceans across the Isthmus of Panama."

CULTURAL ATTITUDES

The history behind Panama's separation from Colombia, the canal occupation, and invasion to oust Noriega from power in 1989 is a moot point depending on who is telling the story. While almost all agree that foreign countries have had a major hand in creating today's Panama, politics and history alone cannot define Panama's ever-fascinating cultural desire for something of their own,

A PIECE OF PANAMA'S IMMIGRANT HISTORY

In mid-1854 it was reported that more than 9,000 workers were busy on the 18-mile stretch of railroad between the Obispo River and Panama City. The dire warnings of the perils to be faced in Panama from climate and tropical disease in U.S. newspapers kept many Americans from coming, but other nationalities such as Irish, Chinese, French, Germans, and Indians came in a flood and died in large numbers.

The railroad company purchased the services of Chinese laborers from a Canton labor contractor under a system similar to that of the British who were building railroads in India. The company paid $25 a month for each man sent. The contractor then made his own arrangements with the individual worker, normally paying him $4-8 a month in wages and retaining the remainder as payment for ocean passage and food.

Under the terms of the labor contract the Chinese contractor agreed to furnish cooks and mess facilities for the workers, and the railroad company was to maintain in its commissary such Chinese food as "dried oysters, cuttlefish, bamboo sprouts, sweet rice crackers, salted cabbage, and tea." The contract also specified that the Chinese would have "joss houses" (opium dens) and opium. The railroad recruiters had agreed to stock the drug in the company commissary along with the Chinese food. The laborers had brought with them priests to staff the dens and set up racks of pipes and the necessary scraper tools. On weekends, after the compulsory 80-hour workweek, entire Chinese labor gangs crew staggered blindly in the sickly sweet smoke from the pipes.

not dependent upon outsiders. Panamanians are a proud people, and given the importance of their country, they have every right. Be careful when imposing your perspective—not everyone believes U.S. occupation of the Canal was the best thing to happen to the country. Certainly with the number of casualties for Operation Just Cause (the December 20, 1989 U.S invasion in Panama), there are many heartbroken nationalists who don't believe that U.S. did a favor to Panama. The country is young, and many political parties that began their ideologies in the late 1950s are still intact today. These days, the political parties are still influential in writing revisionist history; school textbooks reflect their handiwork. In 2009, many details in Panama's history books are still tweaked, while others are...well, simply omitted. For example, Panamanian school history books make no mention of names like Theodore Roosevelt, John Hay, Philippe Bunau-Varilla, John Sullivan, or Manuel Noriega.

PANAMA'S INDEPENDENCE

Political leaders on the isthmus tried no less than 50 times between 1826 and 1902, to gain independence. Simon Bolivar convened a unity conference of former Spanish colonies in 1826. Panamanian nationalists believed their time had come. But Bolivar was disappointed by the number of countries participating in the conference with only Colombia, Peru, and Mexico represented. With his personal prestige on the line, he needed no more divisions. Panamanian representatives were told that secession from Colombia could not be allowed. Panama was where it should rightfully be, at least for the time being.

In the late 1890s, the United States determined that a transoceanic canal in Central America had to be built. After a close vote in the House of Representatives, it was decided that the takeover of the failed French effort in Panama was the most expedient and economical option. In 1902, the United States reached an agreement with Colombia to buy rights to the French canal property, not to exceed $40 million. The French, glad to be rid of the worst scandal since the days of the Bourbon monarchy, agreed to terms. The Colombian government in power in 1902 was not the party that had entered into an agreement with the French in 1881. Colombian politicians felt that the former government could have held out for more money. A rare second chance suddenly offered itself in negotiating with the wealthy gringos. The original French canal concession expired in 1904. If the Colombian Senate could delay action until then, the low contracted price could be modified.

Following the French failure, former French engineer Phillipe Bunau-Varilla untiringly promoted American canal construction in Panama. Bunau-Varilla persuaded undecided congressmen to select Panama as the canal site, as opposed to the alternative route in Nicaragua. Lobbying business, government, and the American public, Bunau-Varilla successfully convinced the U.S. Senate to enact the Spooner Act of 1902, which appropriated $40 million to the New Panama Canal Company.

A Revolution and a Canal

With the clock ticking down to the end of the French concession and Colombia obviously stalling in its negotiations, Theodore Roosevelt and key Panamanian business interests collaborated on a revolution. Their go-between was Bunau-Varilla. Five hundred crack Colombian soldiers landed in Colón to prevent revolution in Panama City but surprisingly found no railroad cars on the Panama Railroad to carry them. The Superintendent of the railway, John Sullivan, had all the rail cars conveniently dispatched to the other side of the isthmus, with the exception of a lone passenger coach and engine. Sullivan handed a telegram to the commander of the newly landed troops from the general in Panama City, ordering him and his staff, but none of his troops, to board the coach and proceed to Panama City for an official reception. Smelling a rat, but following orders, the young officer obeyed, made the trip, was met by his commander and immediately disarmed and arrested. His commander had accepted a $35,000 bribe and a comfortable hacienda in the Panamanian interior to lure his staff for capture and betray his country. When the 500 men (about 30 companies) had disembarked and arrived on the docks, they found that all the railway rolling stock had been sent from Colón to Panama City, so any attack by Colombian forces on the capital, that day or any day, would have to be done on foot. So while the troops waited on the docks in Colón, the brigade staff was lured to Panama City with hopes of sorting out the transportation issue, as well as obeying an order from their commanding officer to meet him in Panama City. But as deceit ensued, the staff was captured there. Once the men were captured, the *USS Nashville* got between the transports riding at anchor and the docks, so that no more troops could be put ashore. These were unescorted and unarmed troop transports, easy targets for the cruiser *Nashville*. The 500 or so soldiers, marooned on the docks, now leaderless, waited for orders. When none came, they returned to their vessels under the watchful eye of the *Nashville,* and after the "revolution" in Panama City the following day, they sailed home on those same vessels. The date was November 2, 1903. On November 3, the nation of Panama was born. Roosevelt approved the payment of $10 million, which secured a canal zone and rights to build a canal. Prepared for a war for Panamanian independence, the wily French engineer handed a former doctor for the Panama Railroad Company, and now the nation's first president, Manuel Amador Guerrero, a conveniently drafted constitution and ready-made flag while promising to act as the national treasury by using his own checkbook. The death toll for the entire revolution against Colombia amounted to the incidental killing of one Chinese civilian and the unfortunate death of a donkey.

The indomitable Bunau-Varilla, as Panama's ambassador to the United States invested with plenipotentiary powers by President Amador, later entered into negotiations with John Hay, Lincoln's former personal secretary and now secretary of state. The Hay-Bunau-Varilla Treaty was signed in Washington without a Panamanian present. This event long gave rise to the charge that the treaty gave unlawful control of the Panama Canal to the United States, though no record of Amador or his government's disapproval has ever been found.

THE PANAMA CANAL AND THE U.S. CANAL ZONE

The United States Governor of the Panama Canal Zone officially proclaimed occupation of the Isthmus of Panama. On May 19, 1904, following in the illustrious steps of that famous soldier, Vasco Nuñez de Balboa, a forgotten U.S.

Army lieutenant by the name of Mark Brooke received the keys to the Canal Zone and formally took possession of it on behalf of the United States.

The year 1904, the Americans' first year in Panama, mirrored the French disaster. The administration failed to effectively organize the canal effort. Living conditions were appalling. Food was available sporadically and was often rancid. There was a stranglehold on appropriations with needless red tape. When yellow fever struck, three out of four American engineers and technicians went home. The United States, in one year, poured $128,000,000 into the swamps of Panama, with no result.

But, the arrival of John Stevens marked a fortunate turn for the struggling canal. Stevens had built the Great Northern Railroad across the Pacific Northwest. Stevens had proven that he was a tenacious and competent engineer. His prompt action saved the canal from the French fate.

Stevens immediately stopped all work and began cleaning. Dr. William Gorgas, who had helped to eradicate yellow fever in Havana by identifying and killing the mosquitoes that carried it, directed sanitation efforts. Workers drained swamps, improved drainage ditches, paved roads, and collected garbage. Sewage treatment and clean water systems in Panama City and Colón were built. Towns appeared in the jungle, along the canal's path, complete with housing, schools, churches, commissaries, ball fields, and social halls.

Stevens then began construction on a scale never before seen in modern times. Behemoth Bucyrus steam shovels scooped tons of earth and rock. Railroad cars ran continuously on a double track, dumping the soil and rock to form the Chagres dam.

By December 1905, yellow fever had been eradicated. Malaria was under control. Fewer workers were involved in accidents, and improvements in living conditions made life almost comfortable. In November 1906, Theodore Roosevelt himself visited the canal. It seemed that the project was destined for success. Then, on February 12, 1907, for reasons never revealed and never understood, Chief Engineer Stevens suddenly resigned. Roosevelt was furious.

Lieutenant Colonel George Washington Goethals, a professional Army engineer who could not quit on Roosevelt, was summoned to the White House. Goethals, who had built the locks at Sault Ste. Marie connecting the Great Lakes, was briefed on his assignment and appointed to the chief engineer's post. Goethals, demanding and rigidly organized, quickly picked up where Stevens left off.

The work continued unabated. His forces moved as much as 200 trainloads of rock and dirt per day. Progress was being made and the statistics were staggering. To construct the Gatun Locks on the Atlantic side, workers poured

© SKY GILBAR

The Panama Canal Administration Building is one of Panama's defining landmarks.

enough concrete to build a wall 2.5 meters (8 feet) wide, 3.5 meters (12 feet) high, and 214 kilometers (133 miles) long. Culverts the size of railroad tunnels were built to channel freshwater from Gatun Lake to power the locks.

In May 1913, steam shovel whistles blew as crews broke through the opposite ends of the Culebra Cut. At the same time, the last ton of cement was poured at the Gatun locks. The Chagres River filled Gatun Lake, and engineers prepared for the canal's first trial run. The little tugboat *Gatun* traveled through the first set of locks on September 26, 1913, and out onto the lake. The locks worked flawlessly. After nine years, the Canal officially opened on August 15, 1914. Amazingly, the world hardly noticed. The greatest engineering achievement in the history of mankind had been dwarfed by the greatest futility of mankind, known as the First World War.

Life in the Zone

The Panama Canal Zone was a strip of land eight kilometers (five miles) wide on either side of the canal. The Zone was administered by the U.S. Department of Civil Administration, under the auspices of the War Department, with a mission of canal defense. Those who lived within the Zone lived with the same basic rights as any other U.S. citizen living in the United States. But living within the Canal Zone was like living within a National Park: It was well cared for, regularly and strictly maintained, well administered, and guarded and patrolled by a Zone police force, though entrance was restricted. Only those connected with the administration, operation, maintenance, or defense of the canal were allowed to live there. You couldn't move to the Zone just because you were a U.S. citizen, perhaps retired, and you liked the climate.

Life for an American (of the U.S.) child born and raised in the Zone was very different from what other American children experienced. It was a constrained world. A world contained in hierarchies. Whether you were civilian or military determined how you lived in the Zone—in the kind of home you lived in, in the benefits and services you were allowed to receive, as well as the parties and affairs you could attend, and the access you had to certain neighborhoods and job duties. These hierarchies were further exploited with the Gold and Silver Roll system, which was the Canal Zone version of the Jim Crow laws that segregated black and white Americans. The Gold and Silver Roll maintained a separate society of workers in the Panama Canal Zone and paid workers based on their race. The system granted higher pay and greater privileges to white Americans in the Zone, and remained in place between 1904 and 1914. It was phased out in the 1960s. There were no school lessons about civics and American ways of life—these were not applicable to Zone students. For example, private ownership of land within the Canal Zone was prohibited; this land belonged to the United States government. Never in the history of the Zone did anyone vote in a local election.

Housing was provided for authorized personnel with free or subsidized electricity and other utilities. A Zonian's home size was based upon rank within the Canal Zone hierarchy. During the early Canal construction era, housing conditions mirrored the accepted social order. White Americans lived in airy wooden structures with screened verandas; unmarried European and black laborers were assigned to barracks. Black families could choose between American-built barracks or shacks within their segregated communities.

While food was shipped to the Zone from the United States, plantations and farms within the Zone provided fresh fruits and vegetables, pork, beef, and poultry, all under the supervision of the local USDA inspector, just like in the United States. Independence of the food supply was part of an overall plan to never rely on outside sources in case the Zone was besieged. Commissaries provided everything possible, and prices were most of the time lower than they were in the United States. Electricity was on an independent grid, and not a watt escaped over the fence into Panama.

The Zone provided recreational facilities including Olympic-size swimming pools, gymnasiums, golf courses, and tennis courts. Several of these facilities are still operated by the Kiwanis and Lions Clubs today. The Zone also administered sports leagues, athletic competitions, and equestrian facilities. For getaway weekends there was the Hotel Aspinwall, located on Taboga Island.

The government staffed medical facilities, police and fire stations, churches, and post offices. Schools of all levels were in nearly every Zone community.

U.S. Canal Occupation

During the early 20th century, Panamanians complained they did not receive a fair share of revenues generated by the canal, and they resented the United States' intention to operate the canal in perpetuity. Because civil unrest was common in the two canal entrance cities of Panama City and Colón, the United States exercised its 1903 treaty obligation to keep the peace so that rioting did not endanger canal property or personnel. American military police were often dispatched by Panamanian civil authorities to quell labor disputes and student demonstrations, saving Panamanian authorities from having to perform these politically unpopular actions. In 1936, the 1903 treaty was amended to increase the annual annuity paid to Panama to $430,000, and the United States gave up its right to intervene in Panama to maintain public order. In 1955, the annual annuity was increased to $1.93 million, a single pay scale for the Panama Canal Company established, and Spanish joined English as an official language within the Canal Zone.

The State Department took little notice of growing nationalist dissatisfaction and in December 1946 proposed a 20-year extension of the leases on 13 U.S occupied facilities. When the National Assembly met to consider ratification, a mob of 10,000 Panamanians armed with stones, machetes, and guns expressed their opposition. The deputies voted unanimously to reject the treaty.

© SKY GILBAR

The Canal Zone was occupied by the United States military until 1999.

Tension continued to mount in the ensuing years. In May 1958 and in November 1959, anti-U.S. demonstrations occurred during the two Panamanian independence holidays. Aroused by the media, Panamanians threatened a "peaceful invasion" of the Canal Zone. Newspapers urged them to march in and raise the flag of the republic as de facto evidence of Panama's sovereignty. Fearful that Panamanian mobs might actually force entry into the Canal Zone, the United States deployed troops. Several hundred Panamanians crossed barbed-wire fences and clashed with Canal Zone police and U.S. troops.

Widespread disorder had a sobering effect on the Panamanian political elite. The United States announced that it was willing to begin flying the republic's flag at a special site in the Canal Zone if it would serve to ease tensions. For a short time, serious disorder was averted. An agreement was reached that both nations' flags would be flown side by side. However, on two consecutive days in January 1964, students at Balboa High School, the high school for Canal Zone residents, provocatively hoisted the American flag alone in front of their school.

Word soon spread, and on the evening of January 9, 1964, nearly 200 passionate Panamanian students marched into the Canal Zone with their flag. A struggle ensued, and the Panamanian flag was torn. Soon thousands of Panamanians stormed the border fence. Rioting lasted three days and resulted in more than 20 deaths and several hundred injuries. More than $2 million of property damage occurred. Most historians agree that 1964 was the beginning of the end for the Canal Zone.

THE MAKING OF MODERN PANAMA

A three-month suspension of diplomatic relations followed. Tension in the mid-1960s gave weight to the Johnson administration views that a new Canal Treaty was needed in order to establish a new relationship with Panama. Negotiations commenced in 1965.

President Nixon's negotiators offered proposals for the continued presence of United States military bases in the Canal Zone, and the right of the United States to deploy troops anywhere in the republic to defend the canal. These proposals failed to take into account both earlier events and Panamanian nationalist sentiment. While Panamanian President Robles initially defended the proposals, he failed to obtain ratification. Robles was not besieged by a mob wielding machetes and guns, but within months he was impeached by an opposition-controlled National Assembly. Despite the Panamanian Supreme Court ruling 8-1 that Robles was still the president; the National Assembly ignored the court and called for new elections.

The new president, the colorful Dr. Arnulfo Arias Madrid, was no stranger to the office, having been elected and overthrown on two prior occasions. Born in Penonomé, Arias was educated by the French Christian Brothers and studied medicine and general surgery at Harvard University. He later specialized in psychiatry, obstetrics, and endocrinology. Arias could at times be an enlightened reformer and at other times a xenophobic despot. Soon after taking the presidency in 1941, Arias enacted a new constitution that granted women the right to vote for the first time, no small feat in the machismo culture of Latin America. However, he also summarily jailed political dissidents, disenfranchised the non-Spanish-speaking population on the Caribbean coast, enacted anti-Chinese immigration legislation, and expressed sympathy with the Axis powers of World War II (he was ousted in October 1941 in a coup applauded by the Roosevelt administration). In order to retake the presidency in October 1968, he had out-maneuvered Robles to gain control of the legislature and the Supreme Court. He went too far, however, when in the euphoria of finally gaining the elusive office, he announced plans to restructure the command of the National Guard. After only 11 days as president, he was ousted by the military for the third time and fled into exile to Miami. By January 1969, power rested in the hands of General Omar Torrijos, commander of the National Guard. By 1971, the negotiation of new Panama Canal treaties had reemerged as the primary goal of the new Torrijos regime.

That same year Secretary of State Henry Kissinger and Panamanian foreign minister Juan Antonio Tack announced their agreement on eight principles. The principles included recognition of Panamanian sovereignty in the Canal Zone and a fixed expiration date for the United States' control of the canal.

After Watergate, progress on negotiations with Panama became deadlocked on the four recurring central issues that dogged Panamanian and U.S. relations: the duration of the treaty; the amount of canal revenues to go to Panama; the amount of territory United States military bases would occupy during the life of the treaty; and the United States' demand for a renewable multi-decade lease of bases to defend the canal. Panama bitterly opposed the "perpetuity provision" of the 1903 treaty, and the United States continued to underestimate the sensitivity of the issue. During negotiations in September 1975, Dr. Kissinger stated "the United States must maintain the right, unilaterally, to defend the Panama Canal for an indefinite future." The words "indefinite future" provoked a furor in Panama. Even while Panamanian and U.S. negotiators were meeting, a group of some 600 rioters, mostly students and labor activists, attacked and stoned the United States Embassy.

THE TORRIJOS-CARTER TREATIES: PANAMA'S NEW DAY

Within a few months of the embassy attack, Torrijos replaced his negotiators in Washington and settled in for what was expected to be some tough discussions. The proposed treaties were the source of controversy in the United States, particularly among the icons of latter 20th century American conservatism. Strom Thurmond, William F. Buckley Jr., and the ranking member of the Senate Foreign Relations Committee, Senator Jesse Helms regarded any treaty with Panama as the surrender of a strategic American asset to a hostile government. American public opinion was unfavorable to giving up the Canal and the Zone. But the new Panamanian negotiating team was encouraged by the high priority that the new president, Jimmy Carter, had placed on rapidly concluding a new treaty with Panama. Carter held that United States possessed "an assured capacity or capability" to guarantee that the canal would remain open and neutral after Panama assumed control. This view contrasted with previous administrations' demands for an ongoing physical military presence to protect the canal and led to the negotiation of two separate treaties.

The first treaty, commonly referred to as the Neutrality Treaty, had the U.S. giving up bases and American military presence in exchange for perpetuity, because it retains the permanent right to defend the canal from any threat that might interfere with its continued neutral service to ships of all nations. The second treaty, entitled The Panama Canal Treaty, provided that from midnight, December 31, 1999, Panama would assume full control of all canal operations and become primarily responsible for its defense.

On September 7, 1977, President Carter and General Omar Torrijos signed the Panama Canal Treaties at the headquarters of the Organization of American States in Washington. Panamanians approved the new treaties in a national plebiscite held on October 23, 1977. The United States Senate ratified the treaties after lengthy debate. Back in Panama, events in Washington were beamed to cheering crowds throughout Panama City. It was a proud day for Panamanians and the Panamanian military, whose leader had accomplished the unimaginable. All eyes were on Omar Torrijos, especially the keen eyes of his deputy Manuel Antonio Noriega.

PANAMA'S DARK DAYS: MANUEL NORIEGA

No name evokes more animated discussion among expats and more change-the-subject jitters among Panamanians than Manuel Antonio Noriega. To expats, he was either a ruthless dictator with an ego the size of Brazil or a poor CIA stooge who was eliminated after he went too far for his masters in

OMAR TORRIJOS

The military in Panama traditionally had an uneasy relationship with political parties. Throughout the decades it allowed political parties to function, subject to their approval. In Panama, General Omar Torrijos was an extremely popular figure. In the late 1960s the Democratic Revolutionary Party (PRD) became associated with Omar Torrijos. It still uses his image today. His son, Martín, was the winning PRD candidate for the presidency in 2004-2009. But his son is not the only legacy left by the general: Some credit Torrijos with being the first Panamanian leader to represent the majority population of Panama, which is poor and of mixed race. He championed ambitious rural school-building projects to improve literacy and instituted a range of social and economic reforms that sought to improve conditions for the poor, such as redistributing agricultural land taken from the richest and most powerful families in the country. Ambitious public works programs, financed by foreign banks, accompanied his reforms. Government-subsidized bus transportation concessions were given to friends of the party. Soon thereafter, anyone who was a card-carrying PRD member, and who had a bus to drive, could pick up passengers. The day of the *Diablo Rojo* (Red Devil), the name given to colorfully painted former U.S. school buses, was born. At the time, the move was a popular concession to the people. The down side was fleets of often unlicensed, uninsured, and reckless speeding bus drivers with loads of passengers.

Torrijos was extremely popular even after his death, but not everyone was cheering. Panamanians seldom hear that General Torrijos was intolerant of political opposition and that many opponents, students and labor organizers were imprisoned, exiled, killed, or simply vanished. He is criticized by some for being a womanizer with a penchant for strong drink. His public works program was plagued by corruption and nepotism. Under Torrijos, Panama became one of the top five countries with the highest public indebtedness. The poverty rate was always near 45 percent. However, before he stepped down as head of the government, he restored some civil liberties; President Carter had warned Torrijos that the U.S. Senate would never ratify the Panama Canal treaties unless he made some effort to liberalize his regime. Before he could return the country to full civilian rule, planned for 1984, General Torrijos died when his aircraft mysteriously exploded in flight on July 31, 1981. Some say it was an accident; some say it was a bomb. Some say the CIA did it. A former associate of Manuel Noriega, Torrijos's partner in the coup against Arias, Colonel Roberto Díaz, claimed that it was indeed a bomb and that Manuel Noriega was behind the incident. However it occurred, Torrijos's death allowed Manuel Noriega to come to power.

Washington. He is still unable to return to his native land because "he knows where the bodies are buried." Among Panamanians, the discussion is much more pragmatic: "He is gone, forget about it, let's have lunch."

Born in Panama City, Manuel Noriega was a career soldier, receiving his education at the Military School of Chorrillos in Peru. He was involved in several military exchange officer programs between the United States and Panama. Noriega worked with the Central Intelligence Agency from the early 1970s through the 1980s and was on the payroll during that time. He was the key player in the arrest and removal of the elected president, Arnulfo Arias, and the installation of his chief, Omar Torrijos, in Arias' place. After the death of Torrijos, Noriega succeeded the general's chief of staff Rubén Darío Paredes; the two men made a deal in which Paredes would retire from the Panamanian National Guard and run as the Democratic Revolutionary Party's (PRD) candidate for president. Noriega would then succeed him as Commander of the National Guard. But Noriega double-crossed him, and after ensuring Paredes was elected, Noriega forced him to resign, arrested him, and took power.

In October 1984, reacting to public criticism and mounting international pressure, Noriega allowed the first presidential elections in 16 years. When the initial returns showed the indomitable Arnulfo Arias on his way to a landslide victory, Noriega stopped the count. Manipulating the results, the government announced that the PRD's candidate, Nicolás Ardito Barletta, had won by less than 2,000 votes. Independent estimates suggested that Arias won by as many as 50,000 votes. Barletta would forever be known as "Ardito Fraudito."

When a popular, vocal critic of Noriega, Hugo Spadafora, who had been living abroad, accused Noriega of having connections to Colombian drug traffickers, he was forcibly removed from a bus by a death squad near the Costa Rican border. Later, his decapitated body was found, showing evidence of torture. When the group National Civic Crusade and the murdered man's family called for an investigation, Noriega blocked any attempts for inquiry.

When a former member of Noriega's inner circle told Panama's main opposition newspaper, *La Prensa,* that Noriega was behind the Spadafora murder, the revelation resulted in a public outcry. On June 8, 1987, nearly 100,000 people—a quarter of the population of Panama City—demonstrated in the streets against Noriega. The opposition formed a new coalition and demanded his immediate resignation. When President Barletta unexpectedly promised an investigation in the Spadafora case, he was summoned to military headquarters and told by Noriega to resign, or else.

But for Noriega the hits kept coming. In February, Noriega was indicted by two U.S. federal grand juries in Miami and Tampa. The Miami indictment included 12 counts of racketeering, drug trafficking, and money laundering, allowing the Medellin cartel to build a cocaine-processing plant in Panama and providing shelter for drug traffickers. The Tampa grand jury charged Noriega with three counts of assisting American-based operatives to smuggle 1.4 million pounds of marijuana into the United States in return for a payment of more than $1 million. The drug indictments and Barletta's dismissal signaled a significant cooling in relations between the United States and Noriega.

Peaceful protests and marches now began to be brutally dispersed by Noriega's army and a paramilitary force known as Dignity Battalions. Thugs began to single out and attack Noriega's opponents. Many Panamanians were incarcerated, some were dragged from their cars at blocked intersections in Panama City and severely beaten, and several were killed during Noriega's brief reign of terror.

The presidential election of 1989 was dogged by predictions of fraud. Fearing Noriega planned to rig elections, opponents, with the help of the Catholic Church, used an antiquated law to count the votes at election precincts and report the results immediately, before the results were sent to election's district centers, where they would disappear. Dignity Battalion members swapped phony vote tally sheets for the real ones and took those to the district centers. However, by that time the opposition's more accurate count had already been made public and showed the opposition candidate, Guillermo Endara, winning in a landslide even more massive than in 1984. Endara was beating Noriega's candidate, Carlos Duque, publisher of the country's oldest newspaper *La Estrella de Panamá,* by a 3-to-1 margin. Noricga had every intention of declaring Duque the winner and installing him as president, regardless of the election outcome. However, Duque's conscience got the best of him. Knowing he had been badly defeated, he refused to go along with Noriega's plan.

Rather than display the results, Noriega voided the election, claiming "foreign interference" made it impossible to assure that the results were valid. Former U.S. President Jimmy Carter was invited to Panama as a neutral election observer, along with Bishop Marcos Magrath. Carter, seeing his worst nightmare coming true, according to his canal treaty critics, received Noriega's promise to respect the election outcome. Carter sent Noriega a message through an aide asking him to set an example for history and step aside. The aide returned with Noriega's answer: The ex-President needed to leave the country within 24 hours or his safety could not be guaranteed. Carter and Magrath both denounced Noriega, saying the election had been stolen. Carter left. The next day President-elect Endara and his two vice presidents, Arias Calderón and Guillermo Ford, drove through Casco Viejo in a triumphant motorcade. They were intercepted in the narrow streets by a Dignity Battalion detachment. Both men were attacked and badly beaten. Images of Ford trying to flee Noriega's club-wielding thugs with his shirt soaked in blood were broadcast around the world. Noriega then named a longtime associate, Francisco Rodríguez, acting president. Most nations including the United States, however, recognized Endara as the new president.

OPERATION JUST CAUSE

The first Bush administration had no love for Manuel Noriega and little use for Jimmy Carter, either. But when President George H. W. Bush learned that the Panamanian dictator had threatened Carter, he was incensed. Bush imposed strict economic sanctions against Panama. In October 1989, an unsuccessful military coup attempt produced bloody reprisals. Deserted by most of his inner circle and distrustful of his cowed and demoralized army, Noriega increasingly relied on his Dignity Battalions. In the months that followed, a tense standoff occurred between the U.S. military in Panama, known as Southern Command, and Noriega's patchwork of regular and paramilitary troops.

Noriega continued to provoke the United States by condoning his supporters' daily rock-throwing at the U.S. Embassy and harassment of American soldiers in Panama. On December 15, 1989, the PRD-led Panamanian National assembly appointed Noriega chief of the government and declared him "maximum leader of national liberation." Further, Panama was now in a state of war with the United States. In the days that followed, Marine Lieutenant Robert Paz was killed by Dignity Battalion thugs while returning from a restaurant. A Navy lieutenant and his wife who witnessed the shooting were arrested and beaten; the lieutenant's wife was sexually assaulted. With this chain of events, the indicted dictator's fate was finally sealed.

On December 17, 1989, President Bush directed the Chairman of the Joint Chiefs, General Colin Powell, to execute PLAN 90-2 on December 20: the Invasion of Panama. Some 20,000 troops were alerted, marshaled, and launched on a fleet of 148 aircrafts. The elite 75th Ranger Regiment was sent ahead and dropped into Omar Torrijos International Airport (today Tocumen) to clear the way for the aircraft and troops that followed. Parachuting from only 580 feet, they achieved complete surprise. Dignity Battalions guarding the airport were cornered and after brief battles were overcome. Noriega's private jet was located and destroyed.

After the seizure of the airport, the 82nd conducted combat air assault missions in and around Panama City. Zonies phoned anxious relatives to report skies full of attack helicopters and explosions throughout the early morning. The attack on Panamanian military headquarters touched off several fires, which destroyed most of the adjoining and heavily populated El Chorrillo neighborhood. With his military surrendering or throwing away their weapons and going home, Noriega fled, and a manhunt ensued. With few places to run, he threatened a call for guerilla warfare if the Apostolic Nuncio in Paitilla did not give him refuge. Discovered to be hiding in the Holy See's embassy, U.S. troops set up a perimeter outside the building while the Nuncio and his staff attempted to compel Noriega to leave.

During the resulting standoff, U.S. forces bombarded the embassy with 24 hours of flood lights and loud rock-and-roll music. Following a massive demonstration a few days later by hundreds of thousands of Panamanians demanding he stand trial for human rights violations, Noriega believed his best chances for survival lay in the hands of the United States government, rather than vengeful Panamanians. He surrendered on January 3, 1990.

The operation cost the lives of 24 U.S. soldiers, with 325 wounded. The U.S. Southern Command estimated the number of Panamanian military dead at 205. Considerable controversy exists over the number of Panamanian civilian casualties resulting from the invasion. How many were killed by shop owners protecting their stores from the widespread looting that followed the collapse of the Dignity Battalions and police, who usually kept the streets under control, is unknown. According to official Pentagon figures, 516 Panamanians were killed during the invasion. The Organization of American States (OAS) claims more than 5,000 were killed. The United States gave each of the 2,700 families displaced by the Chorrillo fires $6,500 to build a new house or apartment in or near the city.

After the operation, a CBS news poll reported that 92 percent of Panamanian adults supported the invasion, and 76 percent wished U.S. forces had invaded earlier in October after the failed PDF coup. That percentage remains roughly, though quietly, the same today.

On December 27, 1989, Panama's Electoral Tribunal invalidated Noriega's annulment of the May 1989 election and confirmed the victory of the opposition candidates. President Guillermo Endara and Vice Presidents Guillermo Ford and Ricardo Arias Calderon took office as the head of a four-party minority government, pledging economic recovery, transformation of the Panamanian military into a police force under civilian control, and a strengthening of democratic institutions. The bankrupt country's treasury was depleted by years of military dictatorship. With a nonexistent economic framework, Endara's administration had little to work with. However, since his death on September 29, 2009, Panama has been mourning the former president as a symbol of new democracy after a wretched dictatorship. Endara's government favored the right to free speech, something other governments were infamous for repressing, and during his presidency Panama's citizens saw their country's annual economic growth rate rise to eight percent. Perhaps his most enduring contribution was the 1994 constitutional amendment permanently abolishing a standing military in Panama. Above all, Panamanians felt safe under Endara's presidency, and the world recognized Panama as a stable Latin American nation.

Democracy became a fact in Panama in 1994, when the most transparent elections in the nation's history were held. Ernesto Balladares, of a remade PRD, promoted the iconic memory of Torrijos over that of Noriega and became president. Balladares steered the country toward globalization by privatizing a number of government entities. Scandal plagued his administration when his brother-in-law, the Panamanian consul general in New York, displayed and sold pre-Colombian artifacts from the Panamanian consular offices and fled to Panama just as FBI agents entered the consulate with an arrest warrant.

The PRD lost the 1999 election and Arnulfista Party candidate Mireya Moscoso, widow of Arias, became the first woman elected as president. Four months later, on December 31, on the steps of the Panama Canal Administration Building in Balboa, she presided over the transfer of the Panama Canal from U.S. to Panamanian hands. Moscoso, meanwhile, proved a disaster. After her election in 1999, before a critical vote on the proposed budget, all 72 members of the Legislative Assembly received a "gift" of expensive Cartier watches and earrings worth an estimated $146,000. Money for these Christmas gifts, she claimed, came from her own funds and not public expense. Every month the Panamanian press uncovered new scandals. The most famous was the "Durodollar" (frozen dollar) scandal, in which Moscoso's secretary accused her gardener of stealing thousands of dollars from, of all places, her freezer. The gardener was jailed, but the police never revealed why a secretary had thousands of dollars inside her freezer. She claimed she didn't trust banks. Predictably, the Moscoso administration ended with an approval rating of only 15 percent.

The PRD, reeling from the election loss of 1999, looked to 2004. A new and undefeatable candidate was to be found in Martín Torrijos, the son of Omar Torrijos. The younger Torrijos was educated exclusively in the United States where he studied political science and economics at Texas A&M. During the Balladares administration he served as deputy minister for the interior and justice. As minister he drafted into law the privatization of Panama's water utilities. The utility later reverted to government control and the government water agency, IDAAN was created. IDAAN has since been criticized by its customers for being inept and unresponsive to its customers. Panamanians, who have often gone without clean water from a few days to a few weeks, whether in new high-rise Panama City condos or in poor villages in the interior, have come to regret the change.

A revitalized PRD with Martín Torrijos campaigned in 2004 with three major promises: zero corruption, more employment, and improvement of personal security. Once elected, his administration was always more popular than successful. Torrijos oversaw fiscal and social security reforms while corruption at all levels of government plagued the country. Bribery, commonplace despite efforts to eradicate it from the culture, existed throughout his administration, from the policeman in the street to immigration and customs officials to the courts. While colorful corruption scandals dogged the previous governments, the practice never seriously hurt Torrijos because he presided over a booming Panamanian economy. In 2006, when more than 300 Panamanians died from ingesting antifreeze-tainted Chinese cough syrup obtained from Social Security system health clinics, the government did little to indict those responsible. Martín's most significant accomplishment was the Panama Canal expansion project, approved by a national referendum in April 2006. The ceremony marking the start of the project was attended by surviving signer of the Panama Canal Treaty Jimmy Carter.

Martín was less successful fighting a meteoric rise in crime and drug trafficking that accompanied the Panamanian economic boom. Though he took extraordinary measures by granting himself "special legislative powers" that allowed him to rule by decree in certain crime-infested areas and militarizing the National Police, the rate of violent—mostly drug-related—crime steadily increased.

Government

Panama is a constitutional democracy. The country gained independence from Colombia on November 3, 1903. From 1903 to 1968 democracy functioned under a oligarchy, and the military began to challenge the government in the 1950s. In 1968, President Arnulfo Arias was ousted from office by a military coup, and a dictatorship was formed under General Omar Torrijos. Upon Torrijos death in 1983, control was taken over by General Manuel Antonio Noriega. Although a constitution was created on October 11, 1972, and amended in 1983, Noriega ran the country as a firm military dictatorship until 1989, when the U.S. government intervened with Operation Just Cause. The U.S. military entered Panama City to arrest Noriega and drive his people out

WELCOME TO PANAMA

© SKY GILBAR

The Presidential Palace is still the working administration building for the government today.

of Panama, restoring democracy to the Panamanian people. The constitution was amended once again in 1994 and reformed in 2004.

Today Panama exists under the organization of an Executive Chief of State, who serves one term of five years. Traditionally there have been two vice presidents, but due to reforms in the constitution in 2004, the 2009 election maintains only one vice president. There is a legislative national assembly that holds 74 seats, and a judicial supreme court of nine members who serve 10-year terms. An electoral tribune supervises voter registration, the election process, and political party activities.

POLITICAL PARTIES

Panama has five main political parties. They are the Panamenista (previously known as the Arnulfista party), The Party for Democratic Change, The National Liberal Republican Movement (MOLIRENA), the Democratic Revolutionary Party (PRD), and the Patriotic Union. Martin Torrijos, the son of General Omar Torrijos, who served as president from 2004 through 2009, belonged to the PRD, which is also known as Torrijista party. After seeing crime rates rise and corruption filling the pockets of government administrators, Panamanians were looking for a change from the Torrijista government. In 2009 they elected Ricardo Martinelli, a wealthy businessman and owner of one of the largest supermarket chains in the country, Super 99, from the Party for Democratic Change. Martinelli and his party promise to control corruption and crime by raising wages for public defense. He also faces a huge challenge left over from the Torrijos Administration, which is the modification and implementation of a public transportation system. Martinelli defeated Balbina Herrera, a former Noriega ally and member of the PRD.

Economy

Despite a visible tear in the social fabric, the Panamanian economy has always been a source of good news. While the rest of the world was affected by a serious global recession, Panama's economy continued to expand in 2008 and 2009. Newly constructed multi-million-dollar high-rise projects dot a skyline reminiscent of Miami. Panama in 2009 boasts a solid financial system, government fuel and transportation subsidies, and low interest rates for the agricultural industry that help maintain growth. Panama City, the nation's capital, is the focus of several major infrastructure improvement projects, but problems persist.

To alleviate almost daily gridlock, the city of 800,000 desperately needs more than the extant 150 traffic lights and a highway bypass. Today the multi-million-dollar Cinta Costera (Coastal Highway) is being constructed around the bayside of the city. For years the Panama Bay was so polluted from raw sewage that if Balboa waded into it to today his sword would have fallen in the water as he held his nose. With foreign investment, an ambitious project is under way to clean the bay enough so that marinelife might return. High-rise occupancy in turnkey projects slowed to a crawl; some are being cancelled and others threatened as the worldwide economic slowdown convinces many that moving to Panama for investment and to live the lifestyle of the rich and elite may prove too risky for their retirement dollars and Euros.

However, the dichotomy continues; with an economy that has expanded for 23 consecutive quarters, including an 11 percent growth rate in 2007, Panama is a regional phenomenon. In 2008, the jobless rate fell to 6.4 percent from 14 percent in 2001; Panama's poverty rate dropped to 29 percent of the population.

Despite economic progress, desperate poverty remains an ongoing problem throughout the country. A visible paradox exists just a few blocks from Panama's most upscale shopping mall, where upscale development ends in slum squalor and shoeless children beg at car windows in the choking traffic. This is the life of a developing country without a strong middle class, one that is hurriedly trying to fix its place with honest work and efforts for education.

INDUSTRY

In 2007 it was estimated that Panama's work force was about 1.4 million, out of a population of 3.1 million, with the highest amount of labor in commerce (17.9 percent) and manufacturing (16.1 percent). Construction is the third highest labor industry with 9.8 percent of the workforce. This number is growing and dependent on the real estate and development boom that has been growing since 2005. Tourism employs only 5.4 percent of the population, and real estate is roughly 5 percent.

locks at the Panama Canal

The per capita gross domestic product (GDP) in Panama is $11,900. The service industry is produces 78 percent of the GDP, with finance, insurance, health, medical, transportation, telecommunications, Canal Maritime Services, tourism, the Colón Free Zone, public administration, and general commerce. The Panama Canal has been able to produce and maintain business for the country and keep the economy growing. The last noted increase was 8 percent in 2008. Economists are predicting less growth in 2009 but anticipating only two to three percent less than the previous year. Agriculture produces the next largest income, with 6.2 percent coming from bananas, corn, sugar, rice, coffee, shrimp, timber, and vegetables.

Industry and manufacturing account for 16.1 percent of trade and export of about $10.37 billion. Panama imports $15.18 billion in capital goods, roughly $4.9 billion or 32 percent of which comes from the United States.

PEOPLE AND CULTURE

Panamanians, *istmeños,* are the heart of this country. Whether standing to the left or right in their values about politics and society, they are steadfast about being close with family and don't stray far from the values they've been raised with. In many ways the traditional Latin culture thrives here: Women often dress to the nines, Sunday is family day, and gossip is a national pastime. But in other ways, the medley of cultures forming bridges in Panama is creating open-mindedness, especially in the younger generation, one interested in promoting their nation's arts and customs.

As Panama's economy grows and foreign interest remains strong, the inevitable forces of cultural growth have also arrived. The interactions between foreign and Panamanian artists are showcased in events such as the Panama Biannual, completing its eighth cycle since 1992 and evolving into a contemporary art exhibition for regional and international artists. Likewise, foreign businesses and embassies as patrons to the fine arts have opened avenues to Italian opera, Mexican dance, and North American theater companies to run

productions and workshops in Panama. The hope from this private funding is that the government will catch on to the importance of including the arts in the regular budget. In some cases, such as the celebration of an annual Jazz Festival and the International Day of Music, it has proven to work, and the government does participate to promote their national artists. These events also increase arts audiences—residents who seem to come out of the wood-work, and then meet to discuss their interests, beliefs, and values in organized groups. You will be pleasantly surprised to see the creativity and innate talent in so many young Panamanians, but many lack the motivation or support to remain productive. Many of the best national artists get frustrated and end up working and living abroad, where they feel they can make a living from the arts. However, the community holds faith they will return to support arts education, at risk of being taken out of the public schools.

Established a little more than 100 years ago, Panama is still a very young society and remains impressionable. Reforming beliefs in the arts, women's rights, outdoor education, or religious tolerance is constantly in progress and is the key factor in building a strong road to cultural prosperity.

Ethnicity and Class

MULTICULTURALISM

If you've followed the historical timeline of Panama up until now, you will no doubt understand that determining the nature of what is Panamanian is as challenging as determining the nature of what is American, a term used by North Americans to describe their nation-ality. As a matter of fact, Panamanians are also Americans and will also describe their culture as one big melting pot.

The Panama waterways served as the Ellis Island to this young continent way before the first immigrant stepped on Lady Liberty's toes. Traces of Chinese, coming to

© SKY GILBAR

Chinese culture has a place in Panama.

© SKY GILBAR

The Festival de Diablo is a major event each year in Portobelo, Cólon, rain or shine.

work on the Canal; Africans, who escaped Spanish slave-traders en route to North America; Northern Europeans, looking for either religious freedom or tax-free settlement; Afro-Antilleans coming for the Banana boom in the Caribbean; Middle-Eastern settlers of the 19th century, arriving to seek business opportunities. French canal-probers; and then a second layer of mixed cultures arriving with the North Americas who came to manage the construction and production of the Panama Canal…all these are present in the face of the average Panamanian. These foreigners and new immigrants (you readers included), coming from the north and west with their investments and social experiences, are paving the way for a more outspoken sense of multiculturalism.

Although there is much ethnic diversity, the class structure stays somewhat divided. As noted by Marta Sanchez, a Panamanian-born poet, artist, and activist, "although Panama is known for its diversity and is often referred to as a "melting pot" of ethnicity and culture, you wouldn't know it by looking at our billboards, ads, and commercials." Sanchez refers to the idea that whiter skin is preferable in a class hierarchy. While the community is proud of its mixed cultures, the structure of order is still very guided by what is (or is not) old European last names and white skin. The *rabi blanca* or "white tail" is another way of referring to the upper class of Panama. The middle class is the working class, at times more absent than others, depending on the state of the economy. The lower class, Panamanians at or below poverty level, is the largest class represented in Panama and is made up of urban dwellers, *campesenios* or farmers in the interior, and the indigenous groups.

AFRO-CARIBBEAN CULTURE

Given where Panama is located, there is confusion about whether it actually belongs to Central America, South America, or the Caribbean. Whether Panamanians affiliate themselves more with their once-Colombian nationality or with the independent nation within Central America, one character trait is absolute—the Caribbean lives on profoundly here. So much points to a very defined Pana-Caribbean culture—the joy for warm winds and beachside barbecues, the history of African roots, shrimp sauces and hot, hot pepper in everything, the influence of drums in music, Santeria, and a leisurely approach to life. The Festival of Congos, a dynamic re-enactment of the rebellious African slaves who escaped Spanish control in 16th-century Panama, is performed yearly in March, in the small town of Portobelo on the Atlantic coast, highlighting its magical history as one of the important, founding ports of the Americas.

INDIGENOUS GROUPS

The indigenous communities are mostly settled within their *comarcas,* a partially autonomous political district, across Panama's provinces. Because urban life can be so daunting for their survival as a group, the struggle to keep their customs and historical land ownership has become a lifestyle for many of them, uniting groups and alleviating historical tensions between them. Still using their traditional dress to identify their heritage, albeit at times only for the tourists, the Guaymi, Embera-Wounan, and Kuna are the three surviving communities that can be seen throughout Panama. Expression of their cultures varies within their sociopolitical, family, and economic organizations.

© SKY GILBAR

Embera-Wounan baskets are handmade, each one with a unique detail.

Guaymi

The majority of the Guaymi population, now known as Ngöbe-Buglé, is situated throughout the northern and western parts of Panama, in

Veracruz, Chiriqui, and Bocas del Toro, all mountainous areas. Their culture and survival relies on a detailed knowledge of the forest flora. Communities are made up of large plots of land, or hamlets, where one extended family will reside. Living by the land means rainfall seasons are months where food may be scarce, forcing many Ngöbe-Buglé men to become migrant laborers. Traditionally, men are expected to provide for their families and women are not allowed to work in the fields. However, when the men are gone, women are forced to go out and find solutions to feed their families. Land rights are built into marriage agreements. Many couples pay off their dues to their in-laws by working on their land. Polygamy is not standard but it is practiced by some men, especially if there has not been a male born into a family. The religion has changed over the years, since missionaries have found their way into Ngöbe-Buglé communities, and small houses of worship adorned with crucifixes are common. There is no strict political organization, as the Ngöbe-Buglé consider the most skilled arbitrator capable of settling disputes. However, since the 1980s, land rights have been threatened by government authorities, and the Ngöbe-Buglé have created positions of government officials to represent their needs in the interior, assuring that new projects such as hydroelectric dams, pipelines, and highway construction won't affect their means of living—fishing, farming, and sufficient water supply. Today many Ngöbe-Buglé who have migrated into cities and become educated, speaking both their traditional language and Spanish, contribute to the workforce in the cities. The women can be identified by their colorful dresses, often red, purple, orange, or green, with patchwork necklines of other vibrant colors. Men dress in common clothes. As a people they are strong, quiet, and excellent workers, known to work long hours in the heat or rain.

Kuna

The best-known indigenous group in Panama is the Kuna. Traditionally from the Darien Province and along the Atlantic coast of Colón, they eventually migrated northeast to the area of San Blas, traditionally known as Kuna Yala, an archipelago where close to 50 villages of Kuna now reside. Since the late 1920s they have succeeded in establishing their *comarca* as a sovereign entity from the national government. The Kuna are a strongly autonomous indigenous group. They have established their own governing bodies and worked to gain their independence from Panamanian legislation. They believe their status as a self-autonomous community relies on their success of maintaining a purely homogeneous group—in their physical communities, governing laws, and customs. The Kuna are known to be so independent they are said to be strongly opposed to outsiders. However, the Kuna have learned to make money from the tourism in the San Blas Islands, remarkable islands in far-off waters of the Atlantic between Panama and Colombia. Yet, they are not willing to let go of their heritage, and therefore are very particular in their hosting philosophy. Taking their pictures will cost you money or obligate you to buy their craftwork. They have unique craftsmanship and make beautiful *chakiras* (beads) and *molas* (intricate woven fabrics), which the women wear on their blouses. There is a small community of Kunas living in Panama City, approximately 5,000, and they stay close knit, working together, establishing co-operatives

© SKY GILBAR

The Kuna women often wear traditional dress.

to promote their artwork. Many Kunas who have been identified as potential leaders of their communities are sent to the capital city to become educated. The Kuna are said to have the highest incidence of albinism of all indigenous people. They consider their fair-skinned kin to be the "chosen" ones, and usually these men and women are given positions of power in their villages, often becoming village chiefs or lobbyists for Kuna rights.

Embera-Wounan

The Embera and Wounan are perhaps the youngest of the indigenous cultures to enter Panama. The Embera can be traced back to the early 20th century, and the Wounan were said to settle in the 1940s. Embera-Wounan settlements can be found throughout Ecuador and Colombia up through the Panama Canal territory. Anthropologists speculate they have Amazon roots. In Panama the majority live within the Darien Province. Their growth in this region influenced the Kuna to move farther up the coast toward the San Blas Islands to maintain their independence from other indigenous groups as well as the Panamanian government. Since the 1960s the Embera-Wounan have established independent communities helping them to receive semi-sovereign status in the 1980s. The Embera *comarca* now contains more than 50 villages.

They are skilled tradesman in welding and carpentry and rely on the export of machetes, rifles, bullets, pots, pans, and ax heads, as well as fabrics. They have beautiful basket-weaving techniques and their *chakiras* and metal jewelry add intricate detail to their daily dress.

Many Spanish-speaking blacks live scattered throughout Embera-Wounan communities, some of whom are Colombians seeking refugee status.

Customs and Etiquette

FAMILY TIME

At 18–21 years old, most North Americans are renting our first apartments and sealing our childhood bedrooms as a trophy room to our youth. At this point, many Panamanians are nestling in even further, enjoying the comforts of a rent-free situation. Coming home to Mom and Dad is not rare, and moving out depends on opportunities such as marriage or career development. In many cases, you will find homes built or renovated to include generations of growing families. One street block might be developed to include homes for the in-laws, siblings, and later grandchildren. Some beach homes are built as three- to four-level high-rises, where each floor is an apartment for adult members of the same family. All of this is quite traditional in the Latin culture in general, but as Panama continues to flirt with the inclusion of newer cultures the divide of norms remains wide. Younger Panamanians who have spent their college years abroad often come back with a clenched jaw, but they return to their family homes just the same.

Whether living with your immediate family or not, Sunday is a day of family meals, outings, or beach gatherings. Birthday parties fill up with cousins and *"tios,"* a term that encompasses friends of the family, not just blood-related aunts and uncles. These relationships are key in Panamanian family life. Nepotism is not considered taboo here. Companies are developed based on family history and heritage. Every little branch of the family tree is valued.

Latin family dynamics also include nannies and live-in help. A child's nanny, the mother's helper, is ideally an additional adult fixture in the household until a child is well into his or her teens; in fact, many chauffeurs, housekeepers, and cooks become trusted members of the family. Of course, a domestic employee's responsibilities depend on the hiring family's personal lifestyle, but many parents who use domestic employees have more freedom to keep up with their social lives and further their careers. The nanny culture is very common, and even middle-class and lower-class families may have them. In fact, nannies even put their own children with nannies in order to work. At best, some families allow domestic employees to bring their own young children with them to work.

BOCHINCHE (GOSSIP)

Whether you live in Bocas del Toro, a Pacific side beach community, or the highlands, Panama City is a centripetal force that is impossible to avoid for matters of business, civic responsibilities, or resourceful shopping. Eventually, you create social contacts and networks and next thing you know you have entered into a world of *bochinche* or gossip. You would think Panama City's population of one million should make you feel quite lost in the muddle, especially if you are accustomed to quaint mountain or oceanfront living most of the year, but it's not the case. You will find anonymity remains close to impossible in Panama. The ambience of the country, regardless of land size and population, is in fact one of a small town or village. Panama plays the game of four degrees of separation—not even six. Be discreet with your personal stories and activities, especially when it involves naming other local people, as you never know whose cousin, business associate, or childhood friend is in your conversation circle. People don't gossip to be malicious; it's just a hobby, born out of boredom and the need for small-town excitement. Communities are small, and in some circles a family name is sacred. It may not be your style to partake, but before you know it, after a week's absence from your new Panama social circle you will look forward to gathering together your *compinches* (buddies) to catch up on the latest gossip.

JUEGA VIVO

No other known country or culture seems to have this trait Panama cannot seem to rid itself of: *juega vivo,* a "me first" attitude criticized by many including Panamanians themselves. *Juega vivo* literally translates as Live Game, a kind of risky game-playing seen in politics and business and among friends and even family members. The problem with the *juega vivo* attitude is that a person who displays it is willing to win no matter the consequences, no matter who or what is affected. It tends to work in a subtle manner, but it can burn bad. It is an attitude that has cost government administrations their popularity, severed business relationships, and caused old friends and family to part ways. Strangely, no one can really trace the roots of *juega vivo,* and no one knows why it persists. Of course, this is not true for all Panamanians. There is a call to change, and you will find commentaries by writers, journalists, and politicians calling for this collective personality trait to fade out, particularly if they want their country to develop to its still-unseen potential.

GREETINGS AND SALUTATIONS

Latin culture in general is warm and familial. Despite the undercurrents of *"juega vivo"* or a tell-all gossip atmosphere within groups, first impressions are extremely cordial, amiable, and will leave you with the glow of belonging. *Mucho gusto* and *un placer* are expected courtesies upon meeting someone for the first time. Don't be afraid when someone approaches you closely to give you a kiss on your cheek (in Panama it is a one-cheek kiss, as opposed to the European kiss of one per cheek), when perhaps you feel you barely know this person. Save the shaking hands for business reunions. Kisses, albeit "air kisses," are common salutations in Panama, and while you may see it as fake, they also send out positive vibes, with the energy of hopeful relationships and new beginnings. Most phone calls end with the spoken salutation *un beso*—"a kiss"—or *un abrazo* (a hug). The same goes for closing written correspondence between friends and family.

TROPICAL TIME

At first you might complain about slow service and lack of customer care, but later it will begin to seem normal. For example, you will get in the habit of sitting down at a restaurant when you are not hungry, so as not to fuss over slow service with a growling stomach. You should also expect long lines and all-too-brief explanations at a public office, so you may enjoy the pleasant surprise of quick and efficient service when it does occur. These are the ways of the tropics. In the interior, you will find people with soft voices, slow speech, and all the time in the world. You might envy their inability to lose their patience, and the first time you lose your car keys in the wave of a Pacific swell and you have to tell your friends to drive three hours and meet you under the northernmost coconut tree, you will further understand why waiting is seriously okay.

In the capital city, people tend to give you a relatively more rushed feeling, but it's not a real rush—nothing compared to what you know from home. In fact, upon your first outings meeting up with friends, be sure to ask if the evening starts at *la hora panameña,* usually about 30 minutes to an hour after the given meeting time, or *la hora gringa,* generally punctual. If you don't, you may find yourself sitting alone in a huff for 30 minutes to an hour, and upon your friends' arrival you will only be further aggravated by their lack of an apology for their tardiness.

Another thing to note is that the word *ahora,* traditionally meaning "now," is used to mean "later," provoking a general lack of attention to time. The word *ahorita,* something you would think means "right now!" really means "much later." If you hear someone say *"nos vemos ahora,"* don't get dressed in a fury and await their arrival. You will wait all day. It means "See you later." While dinner is not much later than the global hour of 7:30 or 8:00 P.M., a night out for drinks may start after 11 P.M.

Gender Issues

Panama remains loyal to the traditional Latin culture of machismo. You will find machismo ranges from soft and unintentional to misogynistic and down-right offensive. Women should be themselves and not settle for less respect than they would anywhere else. Most Panamanians are able to see the value in respecting both sexes, and even expect more from foreigners, knowing that in Europe and North America, women have more rights.

COUPLES AND MARRIAGE

Traditionally, women marry young in Panama. Developing a career is accept-able as a Panamanian woman, but it is no priority over starting a family. Once a woman has hit 30, it is better to be divorced than never married. At ages 23 to 25, many young women are already married. Men, of course, are allowed a different standard; marrying after completing their studies and are well into their careers is fine. This is also OK because marrying a much younger woman is often their choice.

Given the traditional aspects of partnership, it's ironic that there is also a tendency to overlook ceremonial rituals and focus on the domestic lifestyle of a couple; that is, the union is valued rather than the wedding. A couple who has never been married but lives together might as well skip to the public status of *marido* and *mujer* (husband and wife). Better to use that term from the start than talk in public of living in sin. Among the lower and middle classes, civil weddings are extremely common. Religious weddings are enormous events saved for the upper class, where most of the invitees, except immedi-ate family, skip the ceremony and head straight to the party. With so many ethnic communities present in Panama, it is in fact a very interesting study to attend the different rituals.

Don't be surprised to see some men with mistresses, men you might know to have a long-term partner or wife. This is a cultural norm that unfortunately has taken a long time to reform. Traditionally speaking, partners have had to accept the bad behavior of their spouses and turn the other way in order to honor the family name and avoid gossip.

IN THE WORKPLACE

According to local newspapers in 2009, more women than men were graduating from Panamanian universities with professional diplomas. That said, the International Labor Organization reports that Panama pays a woman 78 percent of what a man would earn in the same position. This statistic puts Panama on par with many nations regarding the wage gap. Longevity, loyalty, and nepotism are more vital requirements for getting a job than gender. And where family businesses are concerned, a son is usually expected to take over the reins.

WOMEN IN SOCIETY

In Panama, publicity has never quite advanced from the old-school philosophy that women in tiny bikinis, sweaty skin, and tight outfits sell. You will find young women dressed up in suggestive outfits selling all kinds of products on posters and billboards and in the flesh in supermarkets, bars, public relations events, and even political campaigns. Taxi drivers honk, as a catcall to every woman walking alone on the street. Some even install a whistling-type horn sound in their cars. To many Panamanians it's laughable and rarely offensive. Construction workers and men on the street will use a hissing catcall. How do you deal with it? Just don't. Say what you want, try to teach them a cultural lesson, but it is unlikely to change. The best you can hope for is that you learn to ignore the remarks and avoid intimidating eye contact. If you are a single woman, it is a good idea to travel with a group of friends. In the interior, women who are alone are considered available. But if a woman appears to have a *pareja* (partner), men who would be likely to approach or catcall won't make advances toward another man's woman.

GAY AND LESBIAN CULTURE

In Panama City, like any major world city, gay and lesbian clubs and events are more public than elsewhere in Panama, but it takes a long time for homosexuality to be spoken about openly. In Panama, the annual gay pride parade has gathered fewer than one hundred people, rather than hundreds or thousands. A machismo culture, and especially religion, impose limits on public

CLOTHING

The tropical lifestyle is colorful and vibrant, and standard dress includes bright summer colors – yellows, oranges, blues, and greens. Flip-flops and tank tops are common, except in government buildings, and so you will find many people suffering through the heat in long pants and sleeves on their way to fill out paperwork. The insides of many buildings are overcooled with central air-conditioning, and therefore winterizing your wardrobe is not a bad idea. Sweaters, layers, and closed-toed shoes or boots are more common in the workplace than they were in Panama 50 years ago, when businessmen went to work in *guyabera* shirts and loose pants. But layer warily, because as soon as you step out of the office you are hit with sticky, stammering heat compared to the air conditioning, and you will want to strip down immediately to more practical clothing.

Because Panamanians are very stylish, always dressed with detail, contemporary styles take priority over practicality when it comes to dress codes for social events. For women, "no pain, no gain" is a standard fashion code of conduct. Women go all out in stiletto heels, tight pants, and sometimes highly unsuitable fabrics for the unbearable temperatures. Like the feature film *The Tailor of Panama* depicts, fabric and dressmaking is still very reasonable and popularly done in Panama. Most young women get dresses made for their *quinceaneras,* the 15th birthday celebration of a woman as a young adult. Men can get away with most any kind of dress. The upside is that beach clothes are a common denominator between all Panamanians. When in doubt, a pair of shorts, a T-shirt, and some sandals will hold you through most of the day. Having your own style and sense of fashion here, anything more or less than standard or conservative, will probably get you labeled an "artist."

behavior, and in Panama religious communities have very strong influences on their members. Thus, those members of the gay and lesbian community who do rise above this intolerance tend to be confident, proud, and therefore successful in Panama. Many are artists, designers, and leaders in cultural organizations. Interestingly, the Kuna indigenous culture is one of the communities most accepting of homosexuality. Transgender Kuna are equally accepted in Kuna culture.

Religion and the Arts

RELIGIOUS GROUPS

Panama is traditionally a Catholic country, but other religious communities have managed to build strong roots in this country, with religious leaders based out of Panama City. There are many Evangelical, Episcopal, and Presbyterian churches and other sects of Christianity, started by members of the Zonian community. The Jewish community is said to be one of the strongest in Latin America, mostly Sephardic (from the Middle East), but a few synagogues represent the European or Ashkenazi side. The community tends to be very tight and is a little resistant to outsiders. There is a beautiful Hindu temple; this community opens its festivals to the public, displaying a peaceful tradition of dance and meditation. Recently a Mormon temple opened in the reverted Canal Zone, closed to the public and one of only a handful in the world with a very special gold interior decor. The Bahai religion has a beautiful temple on an elevated hilltop, also one of seven in the world. The Greek Orthodox church has an established community of approximately 3,000, according to one member.

Inter-marrying between many of the tighter religious communities is rare; hence so many have their own schools and places of worship. Because staying in the community is so important to many, families work hard to be able to send their children outside of Panama to meet people of the same religion, expanding their social network to their religious counterparts in other countries.

THE ARTS

Even with Panama's reputation as a cosmopolitan city, the arts are a topic of confusion. With a country so gifted in musical talent, so full of colorful textiles, and with a plethora of modern resources and inspirational landscapes, there is only still a small, budding community of local artists who feed off one another to move forward. The movers and the shakers in the arts community are those with foreign connections or experience, who have been bold enough to relocate to this country and share their knowledge, perhaps sacrificing a career in a more popular market. Panama moves well within the Latin American art scene, but a lack of public awareness, education from primary school onward, and public funding inhibits the serious potential within this country as a cultural crossroads of fine art media. Fortunately, in the Internet and mobile age, a large population of young Panamanian artists is working toward that today.

Music

The best-known sounds to come from Panama are salsa and a touch of merengue borrowed from the Caribbean islands of the Dominican Republic. With Ruben Blades leading the way in Latin American salsa sounds, Panama is ready-made for old school salsa at parties, on the radio, and fluttering in the streets. The combination of jazz, calypso, salsa, and típico thrives in the sounds of today's contemporary Panamanian music. The marching band, traditional during Panama's November *fiestas patrias* (national holidays), has spawned generations

The accordion is a very common instrument in Panama's *típica* music.

© MIRIAM BUTTERMAN

of drum-rolling, horn-tooting talent. Danilo Perez, a modern Panama jazz pianist and composer, inaugurated the annual Panama Jazz Fest in 2004 to recognize the famous Panamanian jazz legends such as Luis Russell, Victor Boa, Barbara Wilson, and John McKindo, who played in the jazz bands of Colón City's 1940s heyday. The congo, a drum with African roots, is played throughout the Caribbean coasts. The indigenous contribute to Panamanian sounds with a folk dance called *tamborito,* including a clapping chorus and drums. Panamanian music stemming from the interior provinces is called *típica.* The vocals are mostly sung by men and are combined with the accordion and other classic instruments.

The rich African culture that has manifested itself on the isthmus has swept its way into many of the original sounds still evolving today in Panama. The great *combos nacionales* of the 1960s, musical groups with Latin jazz sounds mixed with soul, funk, and calypso, paved the way for an incredible infusion of musical talent still standing in modern times. Panamanian rock groups from the 1980s and 1990s such as Los Rabanes and Os Almirantes are still popular today. Younger pop fans still listen to them but tend to lean toward the more integrated and evolved sounds of music by Señor Loop, Collectiva Maleza, el Papo Vecino, and the famous Canal Zone group Shorty and Slim, as well as independent artists like Carlos Mendez and Alfredo Hidrovo, who are keeping young talent on its toes and playing to fans throughout Central and South America. These artists play in venues such as La Casona, Teatro

Anita Villalaz, or outdoors along the Causeway and in the Casco Viejo's (the Old City) plazas. Several theaters that would be perfect for live music, such as in Parque Omar, are unused as of today.

Although reggaeton was mostly made popular by Puerto Rican artists, this aggressive version of reggae mixed with salsa, calypso, and characterized specifically for its Spanish rap lyrics was born in Panama. Many say the well-known Panamanian artist, El General, is the father of reggaeton.

Live international music makes its way to Panama, but rarely are concerts planned outside of Panama City. Keep your eyes pegged to the newspaper announcements, because publicity tends to be slim and not far in advance. The main venues for big concerts are Atlapa and the Figale Convention Center in Panama City. Most big Panamanian producers have contacts in Miami, Bogotá, or other international cities of the region and are good about bringing pop artists such as Shakira, Paula Rubio, and others of Latin Rock and Pop this way, even if only for one night. The Panamanian symphony, a 60-person orchestra, has not reached its potential as a regional highlight, but the summer series of concerts hosted by the Panama Canal Administration is a wonderful way to listen to them free in outdoor parks.

© SKY GILBAR

Many cultural buildings, like the Balboa Teatro, were left by the Americans from the Canal Zone and are still functioning today.

Theater and Dance

In October 2008, The National Theater in Casco Antiguo, celebrated its 100 year anniversary as a monumental structure in Panama's culture and arts history. The year featured Italian opera, ballet, international symphonies, and the International Festival of Theater and Dance, of which Panama has been a host since 2003. It was a year of high hopes for those who had been missing theater culture in Panama. Talent in the theater arts is generally overlooked here, forcing many interested artists who want to develop their talents to leave the country to do so. Fernando Bustos, an up-and-coming opera singer who studied his musical training at the Opera house of Buenos Aires, came back to Panama to promote more culture in the classical theater and since 2006 has worked on several mainstream classical productions. Director Bruce Quinn, a popular Zone-born Panamanian, puts on plays and musicals popular with the English language community. The Ancon Theater Guild is a small, antique-looking theater house in the reverted Canal Zone, one of few community theater troupes still in production.

Children's theater is becoming more popular as an extra-curricular activity for young ones. In the upper class, most young girls start off in ballet and continue with modern dance or ballet. Those who seek more arts education leave the country, some coming back to start dance studios and helping to evolve the foundation of modern dance with improvisation, yoga, and modern acrobatics—giving back and instilling a greater love for the fine arts in the coming generations.

Visual Arts

Visual arts in Panama are rather controversially discussed as either present or not present in the Panamanian culture. Of course there are a plethora of talented Panamanian painters, sculptures, photographers, video artists, and illustrators, but the support system is very small and one must work very hard to investigate who's who in this intimate world of fine arts. La Escuela de Bellas Artes (The School of Fine Arts) has closed, and the University of Panama has not had the resources to implement a strong arts program, either. Ganexa, the private arts university in Panama City, is an option for aspiring artists, but most successful artists are self-taught or have had the advantage of studying outside the country and being exposed to a wider array of styles. Perhaps the most famous contemporary Panamanian artist is Brooke Alfaro, most famous for his paintings, utilizing "magic realism" in the everyday portraits of Panamanians, depicting both the grotesque and the beautiful. He transitioned to video work in the last decade but has returned to painting. Alfredo Sinclair and his daughter Olga Sinclair are exalted names in Panama's fine arts community. Other well-known Panamanian artists are Guillermo Trujillo, Juan Manuel Cedeño, and sculptor Isabel de Obalida. The expat community has launched a few important names as well, such as Donna Conlon, sculptor and video artist and Emily Zukov who have both rooted themselves in Panama— stimulated by the many global matters that manifest themselves here, issues such as vanity and the environment.

Gustavo Araujo was perhaps the most famous photographer in contemporary Panamanian art. Later he turned to painting, showing his unstoppable talent for finding beauty, whether through film or his mind's eye. He had been

GALLERY LIFE

The following Panama City galleries are exhibition venues to some of the finest visual artists that reach the isthmenian community. Art openings are seldom closed to the public, though many gallery affairs are still intimate ones. The MAC, Museo de Arte Contemporaneo, is home to the permanent collections of many well-known artists, and its opening events are social galas. Exhibitions are lively and a wonderful space to see the true essence of how Panama perceives contemporary art. It is also a fun place to see and be seen.

GALLERIES AND EXHIBITION SPACES

- Allegro
- The Arlene Lachman Gallery
- ArteConsult
- Biblioteca Nacional
- Casa Gongora
- Diablo Rosso
- Galeria Alianza Francesa
- Galeria Casco Viejo
- Hombre de la Mancha
- Huelgas Galleria
- Mateo Sariel
- Weil Art

MUSEUMS

- Museo Afro Antillano
- Museo de Arte Contemporaneo
- Museo de Biodiversidad
- Museo del Canal Interoceano
- Museo Explora
- Museo Reyna Torrez de Arauz

the marker of influence on a new generation of Panamanian artists, leading the way for Jonathon Harker, conceptual artist, videographer, and illustrator; Miky Fabrega, painter; Abner Benaim, filmmaker, photographer, and painter; Cisco Merel, painter and sculptor; and photographers Miguel Lombardo, Francisco Barsallo, and Rachel Mozman. These artists, give or take a few, are usually the ones representing Panama in the National Biennial and at similar events outside the country.

Literature

Reading for pleasure is not a heavily practiced pastime in Panamanian culture; in fact, finding a good bookstore is a difficult task throughout the country. Cultural advocates and thirsty readers throughout the nation will not let you forget how disappointing this is. The culture of sitting down in a café-style bookshop and thumbing through endless books atop your tableside is rarely seen here. There are a few cafés that will allow you to bring your books and computer, but a bookstore open to the public for ongoing loafing would not be feasible or profitable here. There are people who talk about the need for a meeting ground for the small circle of bookworms in Panama, but few are

PANAMA'S LITERARY ELITE

Panama is not known for its literary greatness. The authors most read are, unfortunately, limited to a national appreciation. Perhaps the lack of enthusiasm for reading has stifled the authors' drive to promote themselves outside of the country, or perhaps because this country's history and present day is so rich in nepotism, corruption, and small-town gossip, the newspapers tend to take the stage with respect to entertaining readings. Either way, if art imitates life, and Panama is where you will call home for a period of time, here are some well-known authors you should read.

- Justo Arroyo
- Rosa María Britton
- Amelia Denis De Icaza
- Ernesto Endara
- Enrique Jaramillo Levi
- Ricardo Miró
- José María Sánchez
- Tristán Solarte
- Rose María Tapia
- Maria Guadelupe Tejada
- Jorge Thomas

willing to take the risk and do it. Hombre de la Mancha, a bookstore with about nine locations around the country, has started to break those barriers in the last eight years, but its selection of books in other languages is limited. Excedra Books, in Panama City, has a section in English that is good enough to go and pick up a book or two you might not yet have read. Excedra is a little more inviting in terms of "browse-ability" but nothing to cozy up in your favorite old T-shirt and kick off your shoes for. Argosy Books has the best selection of books for readers in Spanish and English. There are stacks of great fiction, poetry, and humor. Prices are high, but you can haggle a bit with the sellers. A few literary circles have managed to form through the bookstores themselves or word-of-mouth.

Entertainment

Panama is a young country, and not only in history. According to the *Encyclopedia of Nations,* in 2000 the majority of the Panamanian population fell between the ages of 9 and 14; by 2025, the majority of the population will be 30–39. This means the first few decades of Panama's booming real estate industry and economic growth is also focusing on youthful demographics. In less than five years, three gigantic shopping malls have converted the country into a regional shopping destination. Bars and restaurants are opening and closing weekly, trying to keep up with the fads of the young and restless. Every two weeks, when *quincena* (payday) hits, the streets, movie theaters, bars, and restaurants are jam-packed. A popular way to celebrate is with *ron abuelo* (Panamanian rum) or *seco,* a national drink made from fermented sugarcane. In good times or bad, *la rumba* is always popular when *quincena* comes around. It's come one, come all, so when you do, bring a bag of ice and you'll be the hero of the party.

SHOPPING

Unless you are looking for something very culture-specific, Panama City is now equipped to provide for not only all kinds of budgets, but also all kinds of styles and tastes. A variety of stores offer high-end price tags to discount savings that will simply drop your jaw. Remember, Panama is home to the free zone, and there is a ton of merchandise available that is en route to market in other nations. Stores have made killings getting what comes their way and selling it in bulk. Brand names fly by and might never land here again, so get the merchandise while you can, especially since the prices are good.

One of the most interesting and adventurous places to enjoy shopping in this intricate and lively country is Avenida Central, or the Peatonal (pedestrian boardwalk). It is a lively street still standing from colonial days, leading into the heart of San Felipé and Casco Viejo. Staying on the main Central Avenue, you will find an array of street vendors, ice cream parlors, and *almacenes* (department stores) with discount prices, gadgets, and brightly colored supplies for all occasions. Farther up the boardwalk is a hidden side street called Salsípuedes, literally meaning "Get out if you can." It's a smelly alleyway of vendors selling used magazines, books, handmade leather sandals, and really a bit of everything. The best is visiting the Santeria and fortunetellers, who sell magic potions as well as giving you an unsolicited but tempting window into your destiny.

Lots of people have stopped visiting the Avenida Central since the Albrook Mall has opened, offering almost all the same *almacenes* as found on the Central, without the hassle of security and parking. The Albrook Mall is a huge project attached to the Bus Terminal and is packed at all hours of the day. It's become the most affordable national mall for everyone who passes through Panama City by bus.

Outside of Panama City, there is the Free Zone in Colón City, which allows shoppers to find specific products duty free. Some products, such as electronics, are not much cheaper in Panama than in the United States or Europe; in fact, in some cases they are more expensive. But if you go to the Free Zone

PANAMA CITY'S FLEA MARKET: BRINGING URBANITES TOGETHER

They say that in Panama's colonial period, when aristocracy and bourgeois resided side by side in Casco Viejo, locals and street vendors filed through the Old City, not just pushing merchandise but pushing life. Due to obvious decay since that period, and especially since the Invasion, *el Casco Viejo* has not attracted bustling crowds of *paseadores,* not even street musicians, and not even more than a few street vendors hustling the same plazas daily selling *chichas, empanadas, paletas,* and *churros.* Sparse groups of tourists seem to be the only enthusiastic public *el Casco* has seen treading its brick-laid streets.

And still every year since the Jazz Festival began in 2004, and whenever Panamanians gather for an annual soirée of old town culture, there are whispers in the air, "This is how the Casco should be every weekend!"

After a long wait for busy outdoor activity to revive the community's open-air ambience, a group calling themselves *las pulgas de acción* (fleas in action), together with the Casco Antiguo Office, has gifted the monthly flea market to us. *El Mercado de Pulgas* has been successful since its start in the March 2007, held at the Plaza Cathedral in Casco Viejo the first Sunday of each month.

The flea market concept is part of a vision to witness the gathering of mixed cultures and interests rather than segregated events sponsored by embassies and other cultural organizations. The original organizers, Coca Morazo of Spain and Ana Cecilia Gomez of France, first began in April 2006 in Clayton's City of Knowledge as a neighborhood event. But they were motivated to create more than a one-time effort. They wanted to see a ritual launch.

The team of "pulgas" contacted the Municipal Old Town office and proposed to bring the flea market to a central and public domain, a destination to unify real-life urban activity and not structure the city as a constant route or passageway to other parts of the city. It was agreed that Casco Viejo was the right place. The event is now a collaboration between the municipality, INAC, the national department of Arts and Culture, and the president's office.

Now a thriving monthly event, the Mercado continues to create a Sunday harmony in a city sometimes negatively affected by the stress of new development and constant change. The plaza changes to a white canopy of tents, with hundreds of vendors offering used and hard-to-find books, antiques, handcrafted furniture, jewelry, art, food and beverages, and a rare variety of other peoples' "nostalgia for sale." Musicians chill out and play a few riffs, and sometimes a local theater group will perform a small sampling of their recent work. Neighborhood children skate on the sidewalk, snow-cone vendors are heroes of the heat, and people of all ages sit in the shade, on the park benches. If nothing more, the day brings back the old rituals of people watching and slow but vibrant urban life, in a city that has been rushed to compete with the developed world. The stifling heat is only a small price to pay for this gathering of urban reality.

for Prada or Swarovski crystal, for example, you will probably find just the deals you have dreamed of.

NIGHTLIFE

In Panama, partying and especially payday-weekend outings are a major ritual—even the way you go out at night and how you plan your evening has a particular custom. One notable part of the ritual is how many plans Panamanians make during a one-night outing. Stopping in and out of parties is a tendency that simply doesn't change regardless of age. It's part of the energetic personality and the spark of small town desire to be everywhere at once. Parties or nightclubs don't fill up until after 11 P.M. and only leaving the house

© SKY GILBAR

Casco Viejo is an elegant spot for nightlife, such as here in Plaza Bolivar.

to go out at midnight is not unheard of. There are more and more options for nightclubs these days, but generally speaking, the country still lacks the old-fashioned bar culture where people sit around and talk over a few beers and a jukebox favorite. That is saved for house parties, or Bocas Town. In the interior, nightlife revolves around the local cantina. Women are advised not to go to these cantinas alone. The men are not dangerous, but their machismo attitudes can be. For a Panamanian male, there is no logical reason that a woman would be visiting a cantina unless she is looking to "hook up." Always go escorted. In the interior, more respect is given to married women than to those who are single.

EATING OUT

Eating out in Panama City is one of the best aspects of the social life, in this expat's opinion. The display of international fare sustains excellent standards. It used to be that only one street, Calle Uruguay, offered the best epicurean options, with token international fare on each block, but now the city is replete with various and authentic choices for Italian, Asian, American-bistro, Middle-Eastern, and Latin American food. The most wonderful part about eating out in Panama is that restaurants have a literal cornucopia of ingredients fresh from local suppliers. This allows for creative fusion that is an obvious benefit to their menus. Unlike other Latin American countries, Panama's outdoor eateries and cafés are still safe, especially along the Causeway and Casco Viejo.

Next to Panama City, Bocas del Toro and Boquete have the best international fare. With the large number of international "castaways" who have settled there, the food is one of the most exciting parts of the islands.

OUTDOOR RECREATION

Panama is well equipped with natural landforms and resources for all kinds of sports such as hiking, scuba-diving, fishing, riding all-terrain vehicles (ATVs), biking, kayaking, and white-water rafting. Understanding the seasons and the protected areas is key to truly enjoying yourself. For example, fishing in Coiba is illegal for certain protected fish. The national parks and hills are not as filled with hikers as one might hope, but the trails are newly protected and marked, and more and more Panamanians are learning to enjoy the incredible nature and outdoor activity gifted by the topography. Since the 1950s, Panama has hosted a national rowing event called the Cayuco Race, initiated by U.S. Canal Zonians. The Cayuco is a traditional canoe made out of tree and used throughout Panama as a means of transportation by indigenous peoples living near rivers and oceans. In this race, teams of three or four racers paddle for three days from Atlantic to Pacific, across the Canal. It is a popular race, especially with 14–18 year olds but also with adults, and the encouragement, months-long training process and spirit behind it is a true celebration of the Panama Canal waterways.

For daily conditioning, you will see runners and bikers up and down neighborhood blocks and parks, and swimmers flooding neighborhood swimming pools after school and work. In the past decade, triathlons have grown into a very popular activity, with groups for adults and children training for the swim

© ALEJANDRO CHICHERI

The Cayuco Race is a popular tradition.

© SKY GILBAR

Wherever there is green space, there is *fútbol*.

portion in and around community Olympic-size pools. The Causeway in Panama City is the perfect area for in-line skaters, runners, walkers, and bikers. As a newcomer, you will probably be surprised at how many people fail to take advantage of the outdoor boardwalk along the water, but every January (just after New Year's resolutions are made) you will be sorry you complained how empty it once was.

Surfing and skateboarding are popular sports that take place throughout the year. One feeds into the other, as those surfers who are not at the beach practicing their paddle and stand-up are usually near the ACP building in Panama City, skateboarding down the flowing hill.

PLANNING YOUR FACT-FINDING TRIP

After I decided I was going to move to Panama, I was waitressing in a swanky New York City hotel bar by night and teaching high school by day. One evening I overheard a table of couples speaking Spanish. Practicing my rough Spanish for my future trip, I asked them where they were from. When they said Panama, I was so surprised I dropped my tray of drinks, which fortunately did not hit the customers (who turned out to be parents at the school where I taught). I was so excited about the Panama connection that it didn't occur to me to feel embarrassed that their sons' future 10th-grade teacher was serving them cosmopolitans. I still have the order ticket on which I wrote down their names and numbers and the neighborhoods they recommended I look into when I moved there. There are many guidebooks and nonfiction and editorial texts about Panama, and you will most likely get your hands on as many as possible to appreciate the many perspectives circulating about Panama. But, in

the end, going through the motions yourself, meeting people, and letting go of expectations is what makes it feel like home when you actually get there.

A fact-finding trip to Panama will allow you to look around the country without making a commitment to moving here. If, after returning home and thinking it over, you are still interested, that's great. Rushing into a move like this is never a good idea. Take time to get to know Panama before you decide whether it's the right place for you.

Preparing to Leave

When traveling to Panama, always keep in mind that you are traveling in the tropics. Everything you bring and wear should be as lightweight as possible. Plan ahead to rent a car or hire a driver so you can avoid waiting for public transportation under the hot sun or getting caught in sudden tropical storms. Don't underestimate the climate. Don't walk long distances carrying heavy baggage or wearing some stylish get-up. It is easy to find a recommended driver, and an easy way to start your Panama tour. If you speak Spanish well enough or manage to find an English-speaking escort, this will be a great chance to gather a wealth of useful information.

Another useful thing you can do in preparation for your visit is to read as much about the country as possible, in books and on the Internet. Getting a basic understanding of the country and its politics, history, and geography is time well spent. Study maps of the country, so when you hear people talking about places once you are in Panama, you will already have an idea of where these places are.

LEARNING BASIC SPANISH

One of the first things you will read about Panama is that almost everyone speaks English. One of the first things you will find out about Panama when you get here is that this is not true. While English is widely spoken here, it is more common among the higher echelons of society and among middle- and upper-management. So, the people you come face-to-face with in the service industry, like taxi drivers, shop assistants, bank tellers, food servers, and bartenders, are likely to speak little to no English. Learning a little basic Spanish will help you out more than you can begin to imagine—learning a lot is even better. Speaking the language is not only a survival skill; knowing Spanish will enable you to interact more with Panamanians in every situation and thus heighten your enjoyment and understanding of this country. There are many Spanish schools in Panama, but if you can get a head start before you arrive, that's even better. Learn at your own pace with audio language courses like Rosetta Stone and Pimsleur, or enroll in a local class—with Hispanic communities in nearly all parts of the United States, it's easy to find native Spanish speakers willing to give private or group lessons.

WHAT TO BRING

Packing advice is simple: go light—in quantity, color, and fabric of your clothes. In addition to clothing and your airline ticket and passport, you should also bring insect repellent (Panama's forests and beaches are home to a variety of mosquitoes and sand flies), sunscreen (being just a few degrees above the equator, the sun rays in Panama are incredibly strong and will burn you fast), and your camera (Panama is full of photo opportunities, and you will also want to take shots of interesting real estate).

© SKY GILBAR

Panama is meant to be explored, and camping facilities are available.

Clothing

Panamanians dress more formally than you might expect for such a sweltering country. Forget shorts and Hawaiian shirts—these folk rarely show off their legs, especially men. Away from the beach, you will rarely see a man in flip-flops. Instead, they wear long trousers every day, with slacks being the norm during the working week, and jeans for the weekend and evenings. Women also wear trousers; knee-length pants (capris) or long skirts are also commonplace. Take into consideration that most buildings are air-conditioned to the max here—some people jokingly refer to Panama as Latin America's coldest city. With that in mind, it's easier to understand the wintry attire.

Despite the way the locals dress, it's normal to see tourists and foreign residents here dressed as if they were going to the beach, and while Panamanians are not about to follow suit, they are not offended by Western fashions.

Whatever style of dress you adopt in Panama, make sure you also pack comfortable walking shoes and simple rain gear; even in the dry season, rain is possible.

Visas and Passports

Whether you need a visa to enter Panama depends on your country of origin. Citizens of the United States and Canada do not need a visa, but upon entry into Panama, they need to purchase a US$5 tourist card, which works as a visa for 90 days. British citizens do not need a visa or a tourist card. Other nationalities should check the entry requirements with a Panamanian embassy. All visitors to Panama require a valid passport with at least six months validity remaining at the time of your intended departure. Technically, you must also have a valid return ticket and be able to prove that you have enough money to sustain yourself in Panama for the duration of your stay, but immigration officers in Panama are unlikely to ask to see either, unless you are Colombian, which has different implications to the Panamanian government. It has been known for airline workers in the United States to deny passengers access to a plane destined for Panama if they only hold a one-way ticket, however.

It is recommended that you bring the following items with you on your fact-finding trip:

- Passport
- A photocopy of your passport
- A second ID; usually a driver's license, but anything with your photo and signature
- A few extra ID/passport-size photos of yourself
- Tourist visa
- Photocopies of your plane tickets or itinerary

Currency

One of the easiest things about traveling to Panama is the currency. Since the U.S. dollar is legal tender here, there is no need to change money (if you are from the United States), and there is no confusion about prices. Panama doesn't have its own bills, so all the banknotes you see here will be identical to those in the United States. Panama does produce its own coins, but they are equal in size and denomination to U.S. coins.

Credit cards, mainly Visa and MasterCard, are accepted widely here, especially in Panama City. Outside of the city, it's worth making sure businesses accept credit cards before eating or shopping to avoid any inconvenience later on, but generally, you will find they do. There are ATMs, called *claves,* on almost every corner in the capital, and outside, you will find one in most large supermarkets. Banks are prevalent in each town; there is always Banco Nacional, at least. Don't bother with traveler's checks, as they are rarely used or exchanged in Panama. One issue you might run into is that many establishments don't accept US$50 or US$100 bills, and if they do, they have to take down your passport and phone numbers and it turns into quite a hassle. Try to carry bills of US$20 or less; in the interior of the country, outside of Panama City, try to bring lots of singles and fives to avoid vendors running around the corner to find change.

WHEN TO GO

While there are seasonal differences in Panama's climate, fortunately the changes are not dramatic enough to keep visitors away. Temperatures are fairly constant throughout the year, ranging from 21°C to 32°C (70°F–90°F) along the coasts and from 12°C to 21°C (55°F to 70°F) in the highland areas.

Rainy Season

The rainy season, or winter as it is known by the locals, runs about May to November. Don't be misled by the term winter, as it is not cold during this season. Instead, it is hot and more humid than the rest of the year, with a monsoon-like downpour lasting for a couple of hours most afternoons. This said, in the height of the rainy season—October in Panama City—there are occasions when it rains constantly for a few days, and there are also sunny, dry stretches lasting for a few days at a time. Weather here is generally difficult to predict, but a few hours before a downpour, the sky turns inky-black and you know the rain is coming. Thunderstorms are extremely common during the rainy season and can be excitingly dramatic. Surprisingly, for a country used to incredible rainstorms, the city comes to quite a standstill during a downpour and traffic becomes severely congested. A rainy day is not a good time to try catching a cab.

The Atlantic Coast of Panama receives far more rain than the Pacific, with rainfall at its highest in Bocas del Toro in the months of July and December. The driest months in Bocas are September, October, February, and March.

Dry Season

The dry season, or summer, lasts from December to April and is characterized by little to no rain, slightly lower temperatures and delicious breezes. Evenings

© SKY GILBAR

Life on the street is faster than you might think for the tropics.

in the dry season can actually get quite cool, even in Panama City. Rain is uncommon but not unheard of during the dry season, although it is never as intense as in the rainy season.

Holidays and Festivals

In order to get a true feel for Panama, you might think about planning your first trip here to coincide with one of the country's major celebrations. From the Christian traditions celebrated by Catholics around the country to the unique traditions of Panama's seven indigenous peoples, there is almost always a party in swing somewhere along the isthmus. The most important festival of the year is Carnival, described by some as the second best in the world after Brazil. Held each year on the three days preceding Ash Wednesday, the most important Carnival celebrations take place in small towns on the Azuero Peninsula, with the biggest celebration of all in Las Tablas. Las Tablas is a sleepy little town, where very little happens during the rest of the year and whose people essentially spend all year saving money and making preparations for the following Carnival. The result is a series of ornate processions in which the Carnival Queen is selected (one queen is selected for each town in Panama) and Carnival-goers indulge in absurd amounts of beer and liquor while they party throughout the three days and sometimes up to a week. Performances by Panamanian bands and artists are held, and tankers (the kind used for transporting milk) laden with water drive through the streets spraying the party people with refreshing doses of water. The hilarious result is similar to an enormous drunken wet T-shirt contest.

Another of Panama's important festivals is the celebration of the Black Christ of Portobelo, held each year on October 21 on the Atlantic side. The Black Christ, also known as "El Nazareño" is an imposing six-foot statue housed within the Iglesia de San Felipe in Portobelo, Colón. For many years now, pilgrims have flocked to Portobelo—estimates state that around 200,000 people embark on the pilgrimage each year from different places around Panama—to pay their respects to El Nazareño. Not all the pilgrims come for celebratory reasons—far from it, in fact. The Black Christ of Portobelo is said to have prayer-answering powers and so the pilgrims—many of whom are reformed or reforming criminals—are actually seeking forgiveness from the Black Christ. Other people visit the Black Christ simply to view the elaborate statue depicting a Black Jesus Christ, and yet others because of the mythical stories of the statue's arrival in Portobelo and becoming the town's patron saint. While there are several stories, the most widely believed seems to be that the statue washed up in Portobelo toward the end of the 17th century, when cholera was gripping and killing people in many countries in the region, especially Colombia. El Nazareño washed ashore in a crate and the locals took his arrival as a sign. They decided that if their town were spared of cholera, it must be because of the Black Christ's arrival and he would be named their patron saint. Indeed, Portobelo never became victim of the disease and to this day, El Nazareño remains the patron saint.

Arriving in Panama

TRANSPORTATION

Panama's International Airport is located in Tocumen, about a 20-minute drive from downtown Panama. Most hotels in the city have a shuttle service from the airport for guests; this is the easiest and cheapest way to get to your hotel. There is also a taxi service at the airport. The fare for a single passenger is about US$30. Sometimes you can find other people at the airport who would like to share a taxi with you, and the taxi company can organize this. Tell them you want to go *colectivo* and then wait for someone else to come along. As in any foreign country, beware of "gypsy" taxi drivers. Ask to see the driver's taxi commission license.

All the major rental car companies also have desks at the airport, so if you've reserved a car, you can collect it upon your arrival. If not, you might want to think about getting a cab into the city for the first night and then exploring by rental car the next day. Panama City is devoid of useful road signs. So, if this is your first visit, you are likely to get extremely lost, not to mention quite flustered by illogical and unpredictable driving directions. Street names are rarely used, and if they are they are "nicknames" rather than the official ones posted on the street corners. Many locals use markers such as the "old church" or the "big tree in front of the ex-president's house." As a foreigner, you will not know these landmarks and cannot be expected to find your way easily by them.

If a rental car is not for you, ask your hotel to recommend some drivers who could take you around the city. It's usually an economical and valuable tool for making the most out of your trip. There are plenty of buses operating within the city, although we don't recommend it for first-time visitors, without prior knowledge of the routes or exact indications for where you need to go. The buses are retired U.S. school buses that have been shipped down here and now roam the streets in an even crazier fashion than the regular auto drivers. They are generally noisy and cramped and none of them have air-conditioning, but they sure are cheap, at US$0.25 a journey. The safest option is to take cabs everywhere, with most city journeys costing around US$1.50–4. Your hotel can give you some taxi telephone numbers, or call one for you, to make sure you are in safe hands and a decent, air-conditioned taxi. They will be a little more expensive from the hotel, but again, worth your peace of mind.

© SKY GILBAR

In-country flights are easy and affordable.

Sample Itineraries

It's important to understand that the city is not just one big, green forest with beaches nearby and that safety, like anywhere, is not guaranteed in Panama. If you know you want to live in Panama City or within an hour of it, you will probably only need one week to scout out the fundamental aspects of your new lifestyle. However, if you are looking for something more exotic or are even ready to go deep into less-explored areas of the country, two weeks to a month is recommended for a detailed idea of your options. Furthermore, the best practice is to keep one to two days on each end open for Panama City. You may need some time to talk to relocation professionals and you want to give yourself ample opportunity to get as much advice as possible. Also, if you decide to stay in one area longer or shorter than planned, you will have some room to be flexible before making your departing flight. One note: There are many areas you can go to in Panama besides those suggested in the sample itineraries. The Kuna Yala islands of San Blas, for example, or the Pearl Islands are recreational locations; while you could decide to relocate there, it's not a common choice and you will probably need to know the country a bit better before you decide how to go about this. You will most likely prefer to visit these places on delightful weekend escapes once you are in Panama.

ONE WEEK: PANAMA CITY AND VICINITY

One week is a good amount of time for you to see Panama City, understand what is on offer in terms of shopping and recreation, and make an overnight or weekend visit to nearby beaches and a delightful two-day mountain retreat in El Valle. In a week, you won't realistically have time to visit the tourist and expat hotspots of Boquete and Bocas del Toro. To get a good feel for those places and Panama City, consider a 10-day trip or longer.

Days 1-2: Panama City

Arrive at Tocumen International Airport and take a taxi or hotel shuttle into the city center. Spend your first night relaxing at your hotel, or if you are feeling energetic, enjoy dinner in one of the city's great restaurants. The next day, rent a car or hire a taxi and driver for the day to show you around the main neighborhoods of Panama City. Downtown, you should check out the neighborhoods of El Cangrejo, Obarrio, Marbella, Paitilla, Punta Pacifica, and San Francisco. All of these are popular among expats and have all the amenities you should require. Then, after a drive down Avenida Balboa, the city's waterfront avenue complete with a brand-new oceanfront park, visit the Casco Antiguo, Panama City's old quarters.

From here, you are a short ride from the former Canal Zone, home to some of the city's most affluent suburbs. Take a drive around Albrook, Clayton, and Cardenas and then cruise down to the Amador Causeway, where you will find a whole new kind of city living. Neighborhoods comprise mainly single-family homes or duplexes with a lot of green spaces. While in the Canal Zone, you should also leave yourself an hour to visit the Miraflores Locks at the Panama Canal. If you're there in the afternoon, chances of seeing a huge ship cross the locks are pretty high.

In the evening, enjoy dinner at another of the city's fine restaurants and perhaps a few drinks. Casco Antiguo has some of the best restaurants and a great jazz club.

Days 3-4: Pacific Beaches and El Valle

On day three, make an early start for the beaches. For a simple day of relaxation at the beach, you can't beat Santa Clara, about 90 minutes from the city by car, where you will find a beachfront restaurant selling local seafood and ice-cold beer. Get there early so you can enjoy some sunshine before lunch in the shade. The midday sun here is very strong. If you want to check out some real estate at the beach, there are several developments here, most of which are still in their infancy, but a couple are at least partially complete. Coronado Golf and Beach Resort is an old residential community with some new aspects currently under construction. It is located about 50 minutes from the city by car. Coronado is the most developed of all the beach towns, with a large supermarket, banks, fast-food and sit-down restaurants, and two malls currently under construction, promising to bring even more conveniences to the area. The residential community is enormous and includes an 18-hole championship golf course, a large hotel, an equestrian sports center, several condo buildings, and hundreds of individual homes. It is the Pacific's beach "city."

Farther away from the city, you will find Vista Mar and Buenaventura, two luxurious residential communities, currently in their second phases, that are worth visiting. You will also find other communities, such as Bijao, Hacienda Pacifica, and Rio Mar, all under construction. They all have on-site sales offices so you can stop in for information.

After a relaxing lunch and some more time on the beach, you should drive up to El Valle de Anton, where you can spend the night. El Valle is a gorgeous mountain town nestled in the crater of an extinct volcano. Favored as a second-home destination with many Panamanians, El Valle boasts a cooler climate, spectacular landscapes, and quaint hotels. Heaven for nature enthusiasts, El Valle is home to an abundance of birds and a tiny spotted golden frog that lives only in El Valle. There are also many hiking opportunities, as well as a canopy tour and some thermal mud baths. If you are lucky enough to be in El Valle on a Sunday, don't miss the handicraft market, where people from the village and its surroundings come to the marketplace to sell their wares. Here you will find everything from traditional souvenirs to tropical plants. Gardening enthusiasts who decide to move to Panama will definitely come back to El Valle: The gardens are admirable here. Try to return to Panama City before nightfall. Chances of a car accident are much higher at night along the winding road returning from the valley. Many people live along the Pan-American Highway, and it is almost impossible to see them as they cross the unlit road in the dark. Also, many cars traveling on the road here don't have headlights or taillights, further increasing the risk of accident.

Days 5-7: Panama City

The last two days of your trip are going to be the best opportunity for you to meet with lawyers, bankers, and relocation professionals, if you feel you are ready for this next step. If you have been in contact with local lawyers before your visit to Panama, this is the time to meet with them. If you have yet to make contact with anyone, ask at the hotel for recommendations. If you are ready to house hunt, check the real estate magazines or contact a realtor and

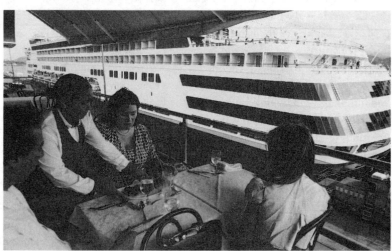

Don't forget to check out the Panama Canal on your fact-finding trip.

look at some apartments or houses to get an idea of what you can get for your money here. A visit to the bank is a good idea to start research into financial issues. Alternatively, you might choose to spend the last days shopping and eating in the city's malls and restaurants, reflecting on the days prior. There are vast differences between the city and the interior.

TEN DAYS: BOCAS DEL TORO, BOQUETE, PACIFIC AND ATLANTIC COASTS

In two weeks, you have time to explore a lot more of the country and its varied living options. Again, it's a good idea to spend a couple of days at the end of your trip in Panama City to get some solid relocation fact-finding accomplished.

Days 1-2: Panama City

Arrive at the Tocumen International Airport. There's no need to rent a car, as you will be catching a plane in a couple of days, but you should hire a taxi, ideally accompanied by an English-speaking driver, to visit the key neighborhoods in the city and do some sightseeing on the way. Take a walk around the Casco Antiguo part of town and the central neighborhoods of Marbella, Obarrio, and El Cangrejo. While you get around much faster in a car, it's important to also stroll around on foot and get a feel for the neighborhoods. Do you feel comfortable here? The central areas are safe for walking around during the day. By night, the risks are a little higher and you would be well advised to take a taxi. Also have a look at the facilities and amenities available to you. Go to the supermarket to see if it carries the products you need and if the prices fit into your budget.

At nighttime, spend some time enjoying the city nightlife. The Amador Causeway is a great place for alfresco cocktails and to enjoy the view of the city skyline while surrounded by the luxurious yachts.

Days 3-6: Bocas del Toro or David and Boquete

The next part of your trip depends very much on your preferences, and since you are limited to two weeks, it will be difficult for you to see both Boquete and Bocas del Toro, unless you skip the last part of this itinerary.

The choices here are the tropical islands of Bocas del Toro, or the highland destination of Boquete. If you see yourself enjoying island life, using a boat more often than you use a car, and wearing shorts and sandals for the foreseeable future, Bocas could definitely be the place for you. If you are more of a spring-weather person who enjoys nature hikes, bird-watching, and tending to the garden, Boquete could be your perfect choice. If you wind up choosing either of them as your new home, they are only a short one-hour flight away from each other, so you can easily visit either place for the weekend.

OPTION 1: BOCAS DEL TORO

Take the morning flight from Panama's Albrook Airport to Bocas del Toro, on either Air Panama or Aeroperlas. It takes about an hour, and you should arrive in time for breakfast at a restaurant overlooking the Caribbean. There are hotels and resorts on several of the islands, and if you decide to move here you'll be deciding which island you'd like to live on, so it's good to get a feel for the different environments in Bocas from the get-go.

You should spend the first night in Bocas Town on Isla Colón, where the airport is located. Choose a central, waterfront hotel like Hotel Bocas del Toro, and check in as soon as you arrive. If you get into town early enough in the morning you will probably have time to take a tour of the islands by water taxi. One of the most popular tourist activities in Bocas is a full-day tour of the archipelago that includes a visit to Dolphin Bay (where you can see dolphins leaping out of the water), Coral Cay (a good snorkeling spot), Cayos Zapatillos (two beautiful secluded islands that are part of a marine park), and Red Frog Beach on Bastimentos Island, one of the nicest beaches in the whole island group, now largely depleted of its natural aspects by development. This is a pretty good way to get a feel for the lay of the land in Bocas and the potential changes in its future. Returning from your day trip, take a stroll up and down Main Street and enjoy some sundowners at a waterfront bar/restaurant. When it comes to dinner, ask around for a good recommendation. There are a lot of restaurants here, many of them owned by foreigners, with service by locals, who are in no rush whatsoever. See the *Practicalities* section of this chapter for recommendations.

During your second day in Bocas, it's time for a change of scenery. For a true jungle experience, consider

© LORETO BARCELO

a house in Bocas del Toro

staying at La Loma Jungle Lodge on Bastimentos Island. This comfortable yet rustic lodge gives you a real feel for living amidst the jungle, close to an amazing variety of animals and birds. The lodge also has a close relationship with the local community, so staying here is a good way to start understanding the people of Bocas del Toro. From the lodge, you can take a trip to the gorgeous Red Frog Beach just five minutes away, or take a hike through the jungle with a local guide, who will impart his knowledge of the animals, plants, and medicinal wonders of the rainforest. All in all, a day here is a very rewarding experience. If you are more interested in staying around Isla Colón, it is recommended to rent a bicycle (weather permitting) and explore the back end of the island, on the way to Playa Bluff or Boca del Drago. It is an arduous journey along half-paved roads, but the pot of gold at the end of the rainbow is well worth it when you arrive at the beaches. There are also buses on the hour from the center of Bocas Town's main square to Boca del Drago, with the last bus back to Bocas Town at 5 P.M.

Day 5, your last complete day in Bocas, should be spent relaxing at one of the area's finest beach hotels. Which beach resort you choose depends a lot on your budget. If you can afford it, consider Popa Paradise Resort on Isla Popa, a small but full-service beachfront resort complete with swimming pool and all the conveniences. Another high-end resort is the Punta Caracol Acqua-Lodge, a string of South Pacific–style thatched cabins standing out over the ocean; however, there is no land to explore here. For a more down-to-earth but still comfortably luxurious option, consider Al Natural Resort at Punta Vieja, the southeast tip of Bastimentos Island. This resort was designed 100 percent around the natural environment, using the building techniques of the local Indians. The hotel offers a variety of tours and activities, including kayaking, snorkeling, and nature trails. With jungle trails to the back and ocean paradise to the front, as well as a nearby village of local Indians, with whom the resort owners have a very nice relationship, you are bound to understand life in the archipelago a little better. Vincent, one of the European associates of the resort and an exquisite chef, is a pleasure to talk to. He has experience, a keen perspective, and a passion for the islands that you will definitely enjoy.

The next day, having completed your taster tour of Bocas del Toro, make your way back to Panama City. After transferring back to the main island from the beach resort, you will probably have time for a quick lunch in Bocas Town before jumping on the afternoon flight back to Panama City. Spend your last few hours on the waterfront, with a cold beer, and you will leave enchanted. Check into your hotel in Panama City and spend the night relaxing or out for dinner or drinks. You deserve it.

OPTION 2: DAVID AND BOQUETE

Boquete has been touted as one of the best retirement destinations in the world. It certainly is a beautiful place, and if you're looking for a quiet and peaceful lifestyle, Boquete really cannot be beaten. Boquete is located about a 40-minute drive from David, the provincial capital of Chiriquí. When visiting Boquete or any of the other towns in the area, you have to go through David, a 6–8 hour drive or one-hour flight from Panama City. If you fly to David, pick up a rental car at the airport. Driving up here is far less intimidating than in Panama City and gives you a lot more freedom. There are plenty of places to see around the area, and in four days you'll get quite a good feel.

Take the morning flight from Panama's Albrook Airport and rent a car. Ask for directions to Boquete (don't worry, the drive is simple and well marked). Apart from grocery stores and other useful facilities, David doesn't have much to offer and is usually unbearably hot, so head straight for Boquete. On the drive up to Boquete, you will pass a multitude of billboards advertising residential developments and hotels. You should stop and have a coffee or drink at the Casa del Risco Hotel in Hacienda Los Molinos, a nice residential community about 10 minutes before you get to Boquete. Here you will get a feel for what a gated community in Panama is like, as well as a spectacular view of the scenery surrounding. Close to Los Molinos is the entrance to Caldera, a very small town where another community is being constructed. Montañas de Caldera is a large development that already has a number of homes constructed. Both of these places have sales offices on-site, so you can stop for information if you like. Continuing on into Boquete, drive up and down the Main Street. Central Boquete is not a large place, but it does have a good selection of amenities and a variety of accommodation options. The hotel at Valle Escondido, the area's first gated community, is a good option. The development is close to town, has a spa and a nine-hole golf course, and was really the starter-motor to Boquete's rise to fame. The classic accommodation option, however, is the Panamonte Inn & Spa, a delightful small hotel on the banks of the river. The Panamonte was built at the beginning of the 20th century in the style of an English country garden. The food here is, without question, the finest in the area, and the service also second to none.

With three days in the area, you don't have time to enjoy all of Boquete's attractions, but you should be able to fit in at least one activity. Good half-day activities include the ATV tour, which takes you all around the town and its outskirts, past coffee plantations and some gorgeous homes. The trip affords you some of the best views of Boquete. Another option is the zipline tour through the jungle canopy. If you do have more than half a day in Boquete, a rafting trip is a great experience that allows you to see some of the finest landscapes in the whole country. If you're a hiker, there are opportunities galore to hike up the Barú Volcano or, for the more adventurous, along the Quetzal Trail which ends (or starts) in the nearby town of Volcán.

Leave Boquete early in the morning and drive to Volcán. This drive takes just over 1.5 hours, and you need to drive back down through David and head toward the Costa Rican border. The area around Volcán and its neighbor Cerro Punta is very much the breadbasket of Pan-

© MIRIAM BUTTERMAN

The Caldera River runs through the town of Boquete.

ama—nearly all the fresh produce you consume on your trip to Panama will have been grown here. It is an area of spectacular scenery, albeit much less developed than Boquete. A number of expats have relocated to this area, but residential development is rare. Spend the night at the Los Quetzales Eco-Lodge, a beautiful rustic hotel in Cerro Punta.

The next day will entail the most traveling you have done in the area. Forty minutes past David, you will turn off the Pan-American Highway at Horconcitos and head down to Boca Chica, a gorgeous little jumping-off point for the Golfo de Chiriquí Marine Park. There are several islands here with opportunities for great scuba diving, snorkeling, and whale watching. Most accommodations in the area are located either in Boca Chica or on the island of Boca Brava. The Seagull Cove Lodge at Boca Chica is a fine boutique hotel with a great restaurant. The Gone Fishing resort—the first hotel in the area—is a nice place with great sportfishing tours. You could easily spend a couple of nights in this area before returning to David and flying back to Panama City on Day 6 of your trip.

Days 7-8: Atlantic Coast

After spending the night in Panama City, you have a couple of options for the next two days of your trip. You can visit the Pacific Beaches and El Valle, as described in the One-Week Sample Itinerary earlier in this chapter, or you can visit the Atlantic Coast of Panama.

Pick up a rental car in Panama City, and head off from the city around 9:30 A.M. If you leave any earlier, you will hit a lot of traffic, as many people commute to work in the Colón Free Zone. There is a newly completed road that takes you all the way to Colón, making the journey much faster and much less hectic than the previous highway. Along the highway just before a small town called Sabanitas, you will find a Rey Supermarket. From here, turn right and take the road to another three-way intersection and take another right, to a road that meanders along the wavy, raw coast to Portobelo. Portobelo has some interesting tourist attractions since it was the site of Pirate Henry Morgan's great battle to capture the Spanish gold. Check out the fort and Iglesia de San Felipe, the church with the Black Christ statue, and you can be on your way. Before you get to Portobelo, you will pass a couple of nice beaches, Playa Maria Chiquita (home to the Bala Beach Resort, currently under construction) and Playa Langosta. There are some delicious restaurants, such as Los Canones, just before the entrance to Portobelo. You will also find Coco Plum Hotel and Restaurant. You can take *lanchas* (water taxis) from here across to other beaches such as Puerta Frances or Playa Bonita. The fare is about US$10 per person, and the boat will drop you off and pick you up at your hotel. Going to these beaches will help you appreciate the jewel of the Caribbean you are visiting. There are no resources on these small beaches, so pack yourself a picnic and a garbage bag for ecofriendly tourism, and enjoy. You want to stay close to the lagoon side at these beaches, because if you venture too far out the tide may whisk you away into the great sea. Snorkeling is a must here. To say the beaches are nice is an understatement—words won't do them justice. Just remember, this is the area of the earth where we remember what nature truly is.

Farther along the coast from Portobelo, you will drive into a small fork that goes right along the road. Take a right up to the highest points of Costa Arriba; if you are interested in off-the-beaten-path living, Costa Arriba is somewhere you should check into. Not only are the beaches rustic, but you are moving into isolated territory and very Caribbean seashore towns that will leave you feeling that you are at the end of the earth. Nombre De Dios, a small but important town, was visited by both Christopher Colón (Colombus) and a few of our favorite pirates. The road up to it has been fixed, and a very few are beginning to build on this raw and beautiful coastline, so near to the San Blas

Islands. Your other option is to skip this area and move through the intersection from Portobelo to arrive at La Guaira, the jumping-off point for Isla Grande. Isla Grande is a crowded vacation spot on the Caribbean Coast; a night here is always good fun. If you are a seafood lover, you will be right at home here. The restaurant at Cabañas La Cholita serves excellent king crab and lobster, freshly plucked from the ocean. For an all-inclusive stay, you might consider the Bananas Resort, located on the opposite side of the island. Activities on the island are limited to snorkeling, swimming, and sunbathing, but if you are after a relaxing day, with perhaps a few cold beers on the beach, this is a great place for you. Despite being one of Panama's key points of commerce, Colón is unfortunately a run-down city, and crime here is very high. The city offers few points of interest, and care should be taken at all times here to ensure your safety. Don't bother going unless you can go with a trusted Panamanian who can guide you through the city. At the end of Day 8, return to Panama City and check into your hotel.

Days 9-10: Panama City

Having spent a fair amount of time in Panama's interior, you should have a good feel for the country. Back in Panama City, spend your last few days exploring daily city life, revisiting neighborhoods that you liked when you first arrived, and possibly meeting specialists for your move. Most of all, get out and about, eat and drink, and try to meet some expats who have already made the move. There is nothing like talking to people who know exactly what you have been through and who will be completely honest with you. After all, realtors, lawyers, and relocation experts are all going to tell you what you want to hear, which is not always the way it really is.

ONE MONTH

With a full month in Panama, you really do have the opportunity to see most everything the country has to offer and enough time to relax while you're here. If you like a place, you have the luxury of extending your stay there without having to sacrifice seeing another one.

Days 1-5: Panama City

Spend four days in Panama City and you will have a good feel for everything on offer, the neighborhoods, and the pace of life. You will no doubt get caught in a traffic jam and have some time to ask yourself, "Do I really want to live here?"

Days 6-16: Bocas del Toro and Boquete

For the next five days, you will want to combine the Bocas del Toro and Boquete options described in the 10-day itinerary. Fly to Bocas del Toro first and spend four or five days there, and then fly down to David where you can rent a car and visit the Boquete area. You'll have a few days to indulge in activities like rafting and hiking in Boquete. Also, be sure to spend a few lazy days settling into the Panama pace, watching the world go by.

Days 17-20: Central Panama

From David, take the Pan-American Highway back toward Panama City. About three hours into the journey, turn off the highway at Divisa and make your way down into the Azuero Peninsula. This is a whole different side of Panama, also very agricultural but almost with a European flavor. The locals have lighter complexions than people from the rest of Panama, and the towns and villages have a very quaint, colonial feel. Pedasi is the nicest of all the towns and is a good base for exploring nearby villages and attractions. If it is within your budget, stay at the fantastic Villa Camilla, an out-of-this-world boutique hotel and resort community designed by renowned French designer Gilles Saint-Gilles.

From Pedasi, take a day trip to Isla Iguana, a protected wildlife refuge known for its abundance of iguanas and frigate birds. You can visit the island by jumping in a water taxi at the Pedasi Port. Take a picnic, as there are no amenities on the island, and enjoy the afternoon swimming in the crystalline waters and sunbathing on the white sand.

The next day, spend time exploring the stunning coastline around the peninsula. From Pedasi, Playa Venao, one of Panama's finest surf beaches, is a just a short drive away. The area is rich in traditions and folklore. Nearby Las Tablas is home to the country's biggest Carnival celebration and is also the birthplace of the pollera, Panama's national dress.

Days 20-24: Pacific Beaches and El Valle

Leave the Azuero Peninsula toward Panama City, and stop to spend a night or two at the Pacific beaches and in El Valle de Anton. There are many accommodation options at the various beach developments along the Pacific coast here, from all-inclusive mega-resorts Playa Blanca and Decameron to the boutique Bristol Hotel at Buenaventura. If you are looking for something more low-key, there are several small hotels, including the El Palmar surf camp at San Carlos or the Las Sirenas Beach Cabins at Santa Clara. From all these places you can spend a day or two exploring, getting to know the different beaches, checking out the residential options, and soaking up the sun. From the beach, venture up to El Valle de Anton and spend a night at the elegant Hotel Los Mandarinos, with a spa and a great restaurant, Casa de Lourdes. Since you have a whole month, you will be able to enjoy nature hikes along La India Dormida, horseback riding, and possibly a rafting trip out of El Valle, as well as all the other activities mentioned in the one-week itinerary. In this area, you have the luxury of time to choose your activities and determine how long you spend in each place. Aim to head back to Panama City on Day 24.

Days 25-28: Costa Arriba and Costa Abajo

At this point, you might not feel like getting back in the car just yet, in which case you could spend an extra day relaxing in Panama City before heading off to the other side of the country. Whichever way you choose to do it, be sure to venture over to the Atlantic coast before leaving, even if it's just for the day. In the 10-day itinerary, a visit to Portobelo, with a stay at Isla Grande, was described. This area is known as the Costa Arriba (Upper Coast). Now, with a few extra days, you also have time to drive over to the Costa Abajo (Lower Coast), where you will find some gorgeous coastline and great opportunities for wildlife-watching. There are not many opportunities for living on this side of the Canal, although this is expected to change with the completion of the Colón Highway and the expansion of the Canal. In the meantime, however, it's an interesting area to explore, and bird-watching enthusiasts should not miss the Achiote Road Bird Haven, where there are good chances of spotting the rare Plumbeous Hawk and the Blue Cotinga. Another attraction of the area is the Gatun Locks of the Panama Canal, which you will actually have to drive over to get to the Costa Abajo. A good base for exploring the area is the Melia Panama Canal Hotel, located a few miles from Colón City.

Days 29-30: Panama City

You are now very close to the end of your trip. Having returned from Colón Province, you can spend the last couple of days in Panama City wrapping up loose ends with relocation specialists and maybe doing some souvenir shopping. Take brochures and magazines from your trip with you; they, along with your photos and memories, will help you remember everything you saw in Panama. No doubt your head will be buzzing once you return, trying to make what could be the decision of a lifetime. The more tools you have to make that decision, the better informed it will be.

Practicalities

This is not a comprehensive list, and things do change from year to year. These are recent and solid recommendations, but definitely ask around. There is nothing better than discovering your own local scene, which you may end up becoming part of, or a recently opened enterprise.

PANAMA CITY
Accommodations

The delightful **Canal House** (tel. 507/228-1907, www.canalhousepanama.com, rooms from US$195 per night) in Casco Antiguo is a beautifully renovated residential home, complete with wraparound balconies and a very colonial feel. Three gorgeous guest rooms share access to an impressive dining room and library. Reserve early to avoid disappointment.

Most of the international hotel chains are represented in Panama. Try one of the 300 rooms at the **Miramar Intercontinental Hotel** (Avenida Balboa, tel. 507/206-8888, www.ichotelsgroup.com, from US$200 per night), with direct access to the bayfront promenade known as the Cinta Costera.

For an intimate escape in the former U.S. Canal Zone, try the newly refurbished **Albrook Inn** (tel. 507/315-1789, www.albrookinn.com, from US$99 per night), a 30-room hotel with all the necessary amenities, including swimming pool, Internet, and restaurant.

Food

Café Beirut (tel. 507/214-3815), in the banking area just a stone's throw from the Marriott Hotel, offers great Lebanese cuisine at great prices and with the fastest service in town. The menu is extensive. If you're new to this food, try one of the taster platters that include falafel, hummus, baba ganoush, pita breads, and stuffed vine leaves. After the meal, you have the option of relaxing with some flavored tobacco from a hookah.

Boulevard Balboa (Avenida Balboa/Calle 31, tel. 507/225-0914) has long been recognized as the place to go for an authentic Panamanian breakfast or lunch. Here you will find all kinds of Panamanian specialties, including *sancocho* and ceviche. The real stars here are the sandwiches. Check out the ham, mozzarella, and tomato sandwich in *pan de la casa* and the daily set menus. Prices are very reasonable—Boulevard is an unbeatable value.

Ego y Narciso (Plaza Bolivar, Casco Viejo, tel. 507/262-2045) is the ultimate destination for alfresco dining in Panama City. Ego serves up a delightful menu of tapas, while next-door Narciso offers a full menu, combining international cuisine with a touch of Peruvian flair.

Limoncillo Pony Club (Via Porras/Calle 69, opposite Parque Omar, San Francisco, tel. 507/270-0807, www.limoncillo.com) is the second creation of co-owners Jennifer Spector and Chef Clara Icaza, recognized as one of Latin America's best chefs. The original Limoncillo was a favorite among Panamanians and tourists alike, and the new Pony Club continues with excellent food standards in a unique atmosphere. Jennifer is a native New Yorker and really understands what it means to be a hostess. Together, Jennifer and Clara have raised the bar for dining in Panama.

Market (Calle Uruguay, one block from Avenida Balboa, tel. 507/264-9401) is a classic American steakhouse and one of the city's best restaurants. The atmosphere is relaxed, with a slightly more formal dining area. Prices are reasonable, and the food and wine menus are excellent.

Market's owner has another great restaurant just a few blocks away called **La Posta** (tel. 507/269-1076, www.lapostapanama.com), serving international cuisine in a restored colonial home.

If you are looking for a good pizza in Casco Viejo, visit **Caffe Per Due** (Avenida A, Edificio Las Bovedas, tel. 507/6512-9311, caffeperdue@gmail. com) at the end of Avenida A, just before the old Club Union. Husband-and-wife duo Marco and Emanuela are expatriates from Italy and have enjoyed success here since they opened in December 2007, filling the void for an authentic pizzeria and sandwich shop with some great sweets for desert. It's an excellent stop for a midday coffee as well.

Mercado de Mariscos (tel. 507/212-3898), the seafood market located at the entrance to the Casco Antiguo, has a modest restaurant on the second floor. You will not find fresher seafood in the entire city, and the *ceviche de corvina* is truly outstanding. Best of all, the prices are low, the portions large, and the people-watching opportunities endless. You will have to manage the fish market smell, but it is worth it.

Parrillada Jimmy's (behind the ATLAPA Convention Center, San Francisco, tel. 507/226-1323, www.parrilladajimmy.com) is a perfect example of good Panamanian-style cuisine with a Greek flair. Specialties include grilled octopus, gyros, and the New York strip steak. All meals are served with a small salad, garlic bread, and your choice of fries, rice, baked potato, or *patacones* (twice-dipped fried plantain chips). The best thing is the price, with entrées starting around US$7.

Sights

The country's most important tourist attraction is the **Panama Canal,** attracting thousands of visitors each year. You can watch ships go by at any of the three sets of locks. **The Miraflores Locks,** just 15 minutes outside of Panama City, have a good viewing gallery, museum, and gift shop. Entrance to the visitors center is US$10.

Casco Antiguo, a UNESCO World Heritage Site, is worth a visit. Spend the day strolling the streets, looking at the beautiful architecture. It's a walkable part of town, but don't veer off past Calle 8 unless you know where you are going. **The Panama Canal Museum** (Cathedral Plaza, www.museodelcanal .com, US$2), which houses a complete history of the Canal, makes for an interesting visit.

At the end of Avenida A, you will find **Plaza de Francia,** home to the French Embassy, the Cultural Institute of Panama, and some interesting monuments commemorating the French efforts to construct the Panama Canal. Beyond the Plaza de Francia is the beginning of the **Paseo de las Bovedas,** an oceanfront promenade that enjoys spectacular views of the city skyline, the Amador Causeway, and the Bridge of the Americas. One of the most romantic spots in Panama City, this walkway is frequented by amorous couples, as well as Kuna Indians selling their handicrafts.

Panama Viejo (www.panamaviejo.org), on the opposite side of the city, was the first settlement on the Pacific Coast of Panama, founded in 1519 and later burned down by British pirate Henry Morgan. Today, several ruins remain and are being restored by the Panama Viejo Foundation.

The **Amador Causeway,** a long stretch of land connecting mainland Panama City with the three islands of Naos, Perico, and Flamenco, was constructed by land excavated during the construction of the Panama Canal. Part of the former U.S. Canal Zone, the Causeway is now a tourist hot spot, with a plethora of restaurants and bars and several nice marinas. Lined with palm trees, it is a popular spot for jogging, cycling and rollerblading.

THE WESTERN HIGHLANDS
Chiriquí Highlands
ACCOMMODATIONS

The Panamonte Inn & Spa (tel. 507/720-1324, www.panamonte.com) is Boquete's best hotel and also home to the finest restaurant in town. Dating back to the beginning of the 1900s, the stylish hotel exudes class while still maintaining a friendly and relaxed atmosphere.

Isla Verde (tel. 507/720-2533, www.islaverdepanama.com, from US$80 per night per cabin) is one of the town's more economical options. The hotel comprises six self-contained roundhouses that include kitchen, bathroom, and beds for up to four people. A good breakfast is served under a gazebo in the garden.

La Casa del Risco Hotel (Boquete, Chiriquí (Hacienda Los Molinos), tel. 507/6676-0653, www.lacasadelrisco.com) is located in Boquete in the Chiriqui Highlands. It is a cozy boutique hotel in the residential project of Hacienda Los Molinos. With a view of Baru Volcano's protected cloud forest and the rushing waters of the Cochea River, guests are quite pleased with this choice. There are river-rafting trips available from here as well.

The Valle Escondido hotel (tel. 507/720-2454, www.resort.valleescondido .biz, from US$157.50 per night) offers 39 rooms, all individually designed and decorated. Facilities include a spa, nine-hole golf course, and country club.

Los Quetzales Eco-Lodge and Spa (tel. 507/771-2291, www.losquetzales .com, from US$14 dorm room, US$66 private room) is a rustic yet comfortable hotel in the cloud forest of Cerro Punta. The hotel offers a variety of excursions in the area, specializing in birding tours.

Seagull Cove Lodge (tel. 507/851-0036 or toll-free from the U.S.: 786/735-1475, www.seagullcovelodge.com) is a small boutique hotel and a Boca Chica highlight located in the Chiriquí Gulf. There are five seaview cabins, a quality restaurant, and an array of activities such as deep-sea fishing, sailing, diving, and snorkeling. Relaxation is definitely a number-one priority here. The Italian hosts have essentially opened up their dream home and guest houses to you. Rates run US$145–175 per night. A full a la carte breakfast is the only meal included.

FOOD

There are a good number of restaurants in Boquete. The best dining experience of them all is dinner by the fireplace at the **Panamonte Hotel** (north on the Avenida Central, tel. 507/720-1324, www.panamonte.com).

Another good option includes **Punto de Encuentro,** a great breakfast spot serving American-style breakfasts at reasonable prices. They have no phone number, but it can be found on a small side street east of Avenida Principal and next to the ATV rental. You can ask any early bird who loves to eat big pancake, waffle or stuffed omelette breakfasts where to find it.

Bistro Boquete (tel. 507/720-2596, eat@bistroboquete.com) is located on Main Street, just past the park, is a popular lunchtime spot serving a variety of sandwiches, appetizers and daily specials.

One of the town's two Peruvian restaurants, **Delicias del Perú** (Avenida

Central just north of Juan Bastista Church, tel. 507/720-1966) enjoys a lovely terrace with views down to the river. The food, particularly the seafood soup, is worth trying.

SIGHTS

Boquete is famous for its coffee, so you shouldn't miss a tour of one of the area's many coffee plantations. **Café Ruiz** (tel. 507/720-1000, www.caferuiz-boquete.com) offers three different tours, covering every aspect from the planting to the tasting of the coffee. Café Ruiz is located just a few kilometers from the center of Boquete.

Paradise Gardens (on the road to Volcancito, tel. 507/6615-6618, www.paradisegardensboquete.com) is a nonprofit wildlife rescue center. Expats Paul and Jenny Saban have an incredible setup around their home, with living areas for a variety of animals, both ones they hope to return to the wild and ones that will have to remain in captivity. Permanent residents include margays, scarlet macaws, monkeys, and a kinkajou.

At 11,398 feet, the extinct **Volcá Barú** is Panama's highest point. On a clear day, you can see both the Pacific and Atlantic oceans from the summit. Tour companies in Boquete offer a variety of hiking trips up the volcano, with a favorite being an overnight trip, which includes camping a short distance from the summit and reaching the summit just as day breaks to enjoy the spectacular views. Contact Spanish school **Habla Ya** (tel. 507/720-1294, www.hablayapanama.com) for more information.

An all-terrain vehicle (ATV) is a good way to explore Boquete and get a feel for where everything is. **Boquete ATV Adventures** (tel. 507/6678-5666, www.boqueteatvtours.com) offers a variety of tours.

Golfo de Chiriqui Marine Park (tel. 507/208-9434, www.marviva.net) is in the northwest region of Panama, along the Pacific coastline and in proximity to Costa Rica's Osa Peninsula. Within 14,740 hectares there lies 25 islands consisting of 18 large islands seven small islands of marine coastal ecosystems including mangroves, swamps, coral reefs, and rock sea beds. Twenty-four species of coral, four of which are exclusive to Panama, have been recorded here. The marine park contains 85 percent of the fauna found in the tropical eastern Pacific, including 33 species of sharks. Whales are also quite prevalent here; humpbacks, sperm and killer whales have been spotted. **Cabanas Boca del Brava** can be found on Isla Boca Brava, a 3,000 hectare island inside the marine park. The rates are very reasonable at these efficient lodges (tel. 507/6676-3244, no reservations).

Gone Fishing Resort (tel. 507/851-0104 or toll free from the U.S. 786/393-5882, www.gonefishingpanama.com) is a world-class fishing resort located in the Pacific Chiriquí Gulf at Boca Chica. Big game fishing is available here, as well as in-shore sport fishing, snorkeling, and diving. Fishing packages require six days and six nights or longer. Rates for fishing packages range from US$800 to US$3,000. Nightly accommodation rates are US$110–130 per night, not including transportation from the David airport.

Santa Fé de Veraguas
ACCOMMODATIONS
La Qhia (tel. 507/954-0903, www.panamamountainhouse.com) is a quiet, family-run hostel, owned by a warm Belgian-Argentine couple. Guest rooms are well kept and affordable, and the house is wonderfully designed, with panoramic views of the mountains.

FOOD
Santa Fé de Veraguas has few food options. There is a small grocery store in the center of town where you can buy basic food items. The hostel **La Qhia** (tel. 507/954-0903, www.panamamountainhouse.com) will include you in its family-style dinner for an additional US$5 per person per night. Just give the hostess advance notice if you will be joining for the night. If the hostel is not busy, and you clean up after yourself, staff might let you use the kitchen facilities to prepare your own food. The breakfasts are simple but definitely hit the spot!

SIGHTS
Santa Fé is a little-known highland gem. The dramatic scenery is a hiker's paradise that includes several dramatic waterfalls. The market is the best place in Panama to purchase real Panama hats—not the ones made in Ecuador. Tourism in this area is just beginning to take off. For guided tours, contact Cesar Miranda of **Aventuras Cesamo** (tel. 507/6792-0571), who is very knowledgeable and pleasant.

CENTRAL PANAMA
El Valle de Anton
ACCOMMODATIONS
Hotel Los Mandarinos (tel. 507/983-6645, www.losmandarinos.com, from US$97.50 per night) is El Valle's finest accommodation. This family-style establishment has 31 rooms, a spa, Irish pub, and superb restaurant.

The 10-room **Anton Valley Hotel** (tel. 507/983-6097, www.antonvalley-hotel.com) is a simpler and cheaper hotel, but it is impeccably clean and has everything you should need.

FOOD

For a true gourmet meal, have lunch or dinner at **Casa De Lourdes** at Hotel Los Mandarinos. Several other restaurants dot the main street. For a relaxed lunch, try **La Bruschetta** for a good selection of bruschettas, sandwiches, and ceviches. **The Pizzeria** next door is owned by the same family and is also quite good.

SIGHTS

La India Dormida, one of El Valle's most famous attractions, refers to the shape of one of the mountains behind El Valle. The sleeping Indian makes a good hike. Ask at your hotel for directions or a guided tour.

El Macho Waterfall, just a few kilometers from the town center, is an 85-foot high cascade with a swimming hole at the bottom, perfect for taking photos and a refreshing dip.

The **thermal baths,** very close to the town center, are a group of natural hot water pools good for soaking weary muscles after a long hike. Before getting in the pool, cover your face with the "therapeutic" exfoliating mud, which the locals claim has healing and cleansing powers.

Colón Beaches: Costa Arriba and Costa Abajo

ACCOMMODATIONS

Finca Flor de Café and **Finca Don Pedro** (tel. 507/448-2291, www.florde-cafe.com, from US$50 per night) are two small hotels in Puerto Lindo, close to Portobelo. Together, they offer accommodation for 10 people and share a good restaurant called El Caballo Loco, the Crazy Horse.

Bananas Resort (tel. 507/263-9510, www.bananasresort.com, from US$139 per night) on Isla Grande is an all-inclusive, 28-suite hotel offering pool, snorkeling, kayaks, boat trips, and simple relaxation.

Cabañas La Cholita (tel. 507/232-4561, from US$40 per night) is located on the other side of Isla Grande in the town center and offers far more rustic accommodations. The hotel is home to a great seafood restaurant.

Coco Plum Hotel and Restaurant (tel. 507/448-2102 or 507/448-2309, www.cocoplum-panama.com) is one of the only hotels in the Portobelo area of Colón where you can satisfy yourself with standard comfort and friendly atmosphere. The restaurant is also a good option, if you only want to stop and dine. The fish is fresh and the wine is good. Rooms come with air-conditioning, cable TV, and a private bathroom. Rooms are not beachfront, nor are they luxurious exactly, but the location and proximity to the very special town of Portobelo here is key. The hotel site has a game room, with a pool table and darts, and a dock full of hammocks on the Bay of Portobelo, where bar and restaurant service comes to you. If you are interested in spending a day at one of the beaches, you can simply ask the hotel to hire a water taxi for you to pick you up at their dock. Room rates at Coco Plum hotel run US$45–75 per night. Driving from Sabanitas along the Portobelo route, Coco Plum is at 32.5 km, along the left side of the road. Signs are well noted.

The **Melia Panama Canal Hotel** (Antigua Escuela de las Américas, Lago Gatún, Colón, tel. 507/470-1100, www.solmelia.com/hotels/Panama/Colon .com) is located in the old Canal Zone of Colón, near to the Gatún Locks, in Fort Sherman, an old military base in the Atlantic Canal Zone. It is a 10-minute drive from the historical Fort San Lorenzo at the mouth of the Rio Chagres. The Melia is a refined resort, where you can eat well and sit by a luxurious pool while sipping a cocktail in the Caribbean jungle air. Don't expect any seaside views, but you might see some monkeys and iguanas. The Melia is recommended for a one- or two-night stay, or if you are traveling for business in the Colón area.

FOOD
Los Canones (tel. 507/448-2980) is a well-known restaurant stop along the road to Portobelo in Costa Arriba, Colón. The restaurant sits along the left side of the road, 7 kilometers before the town of Portobelo. It has an upstairs and a downstairs dining area. A path out to the waterfront opens up into a beautiful beachside garden, where customers can also dine. The food is an amazing combination of local flavors with grilled fish, fresh lobster (when in season) and ceviche. The prices are extremely affordable, at US$7–12 a full plate. This is a great pit-stop on your way back from Portobelo's beaches.

El Caballo Loco, about 15 minutes past Portobelo within the Finca Flor de Café and Finca Don Pedro hotels, is an unusual restaurant that combines a casual rustic environment with quality gourmet French cuisine, all prepared and served by French owners.

The Don Quijote Pizzeria is located about 15 minutes past Portobelo, on the road to Isla Grande. It serves a good selection of thin-crust pizzas, all made from local ingredients, most of which are sourced locally. The atmosphere is homey, with an attractive outdoor seating area at the back of the restaurant with views of the surrounding scenery. Prices are reasonable, making this a great stop on the way to Isla Grande.

SIGHTS

Portobelo is one of Panama's most interesting historical attractions. Founded in 1597, Portobelo became an important gold and silver trading center and home to many international trade fairs. The old Spanish fort at Portobelo is right in the center of the town. Nearby is the museum of the former counting house, where gold and silver was counted before being traded.

Inside the **Iglesia de San Felipe** is the statue of the Black Christ, Portobelo's patron saint. Each year thousands of pilgrims make their way to Portobelo to pay their respects to the Black Christ, also known as El Nazareño.

The Gatun Locks are the final set of locks for ships transiting the Canal from the Pacific to the Atlantic Ocean. They are the most complex of the three sets of locks, comprising six steps, unlike **Miraflores Locks,** on the Pacific side, which only has two steps. The viewing gallery at the Gatun Locks is free; these are the most interesting set of locks for viewers.

The **Colón Free Zone** (www.colonfreezone.com), or Zona Libre, as it is known, is the second-largest free trade zone in the world, after Hong Kong. Visitors to the Zona Libre can take advantage of tax-free shopping (visitors must pay tax at the time of purchase but may collect a refund from the international airport when leaving the country). Popular items here include luxury watches, clothing, and electronic items.

Pacific Beaches

ACCOMMODATIONS

The Bristol at Buenaventura (tel. 507/264-0000, www.thebristol.com/Buenaventura, from US$195 per night) is the newest hotel to open on the Pacific Coast and includes 126 luxurious rooms, three restaurants, and every amenity you could need.

Playa Blanca Resort (Pan American Highway, Km 118, Farallón, Cocle, tel. 507/993-2105 or tel. 507/399-1111 (Panama City), www.playablanca.com, from US$105 per night) is a large-scale all-inclusive holiday resort with 219 rooms. Amenities are good, but food is average.

Las Sirenas (tel. 507/993-3235, www.lasirenas.com, from US$130 per night) has several beachside cabin-cottages that include a terrace, hammock, kitchen, and one or two bedrooms. The beachfront location on Santa Clara beach is hard to beat. It's the next best thing to having your own house on the beach.

Villa Camilla at Azueros (tel. 507/995-9595, www.azueros.com, from US$225 per night) is the ultimate in boutique luxury.

Eco-Venao (tel. 507/832-0530, www.venao.com) is a highly recommended rustic and ecofriendly spot located on a reforestation project right across the road from Playa Venao. It is ideal for surfers, beachcombers, and nature enthusiasts. A yoga center is currently in the planning stages. Dorm rooms cost US$10 per night; private homes, appropriate for one or two families, cost US$125–400 per night. The managers are very warm and welcoming—helpful, but they let you do your own thing if you wish.

If you are looking for an all-inclusive no brainer vacation, the **Decameron Resort** (Avenida Principal Farallón, km 115, Carretera Interamericana, tel. 507/993-2255, www.decameron.com/eng/panama.com) might be your choice. Quantity is preferred over quality here. The rooms are quite standard, the pools are big and loud, and beach is the perhaps the most pleasurable feature of all. This chain resort is located on the Pacific coast at Farrallón Beach. Daytime activities for adults like water aerobics, volleyball, and ping-pong tournaments are arranged by activity coordinators, and tours to nearby El Valle or other beaches are available. If anything, you will escape to one of the prettiest beaches only 1.5 hours from Panama City, and perhaps take a walk-about in what's left of Antonio Manuel Noriega's vacation home in the same neighborhood. Rates run about US$150 per night for a double standard room, but specials and other all-inclusive packages such as flight and a rental car are offered over the Internet.

El Palmar is a small beach along the Pacific coast in the district of San Carlos, on the Pacific side, and only one hour from Panama City by car. There are two choices for hotels at Palmar. One is the **Bay View Beach Hotel and Resort** (end of Palmar Beach Rd., tel. 507/240-9261, room rates US$50 weekdays, US$60 weekends). Hardly a resort at all, it is a concrete structure with basic rooms, air-conditioning, cable television, and a pool. The beach is open to the public.

The other Palmar option is the **Palmar Surf Hotel** (tel. 507/240-8027 or 507/264-2272) located at the corner turn on the main road. The rooms are small but efficient, with private baths. There is a larger room that can sleep six, with kitchen facilities available. Rates run about US$33 on weekdays and US$43 on weekends. There is a small restaurant under a thatched roof that overlooks the beach on a mid-sized cliff. The bar is a great rest stop for thirsty surfers. The hotel sets up surf lessons as well for US$25 an hour.

FOOD

The restaurant at **Bay View Beach Hotel and Resort** (end of Palmar Beach Rd., tel. 507/240-9261) is an open space with a beautiful ocean view and offers delicious food, even though the cheap decor may suggest otherwise. It is highly recommended if you are looking for a nice, simple stop for lunch or early evening dinner along the beach. Prices are reasonable and the fish is fresh. It gets crowded on weekends by Panama City folks.

Las Camisones (on the Pan-American Highway, between Las Uvas and Santa Clara, tel. 507/993-3622) is a great example of Panamanian cuisine and the best restaurant in the Central Pacific area. The specialty here is seafood, but there is also a good selection of meats. Diners at this relaxed outdoor spot should try the *langostinos a la criolla* (creole prawns) and the *almejas al ajillo* (clams with garlic). The homemade sangria and desserts are also excellent. It is not cheap and accepts credit cards.

Quesos Chela (tel. 507/223-7835) is recognizable by the hordes of people here every Saturday and Sunday. Almost a compulsory stop for Panamanians en route to the beach, Quesos Chela is not quite a restaurant, but a small specialty food market selling a wide variety of homemade cheeses and great empanadas. The tutti-frutti *chicha* drink is also worth a try. Quesos Chela is located on the Pan-American Highway, just outside of Capira, on the way to the beaches. It's along the right side of the road, just after an abandoned Texaco gas station. Watch for where all the SUVs on the way to the beach are parked, especially on Saturday and Sunday mornings.

Carlito's (tel. 507/240-8526, www.carlitospizza.com) is a Panama City transplant recently opened in San Carlos. It offers a wide variety of Argentine-style pizzas and empanadas to eat in or take out.

SIGHTS

Playa Santa Clara is the one true public beach in Panama, complete with bathrooms, showers, and a nice, albeit very slow, restaurant. Try the *camarones del rio,* similar to crayfish. On the weekends, the beach is always buzzing with activity, as tourists and locals alike gather here to sunbathe, swim, eat, and drink. Entrance to the beach costs US$2 per person; if you want to rent a *ranchito* (open-sided shelter), you will pay US$5–10 depending on the season.

Another of the nicest beaches in Panama is **Playa Blanca.** While all beaches here are technically public, the positioning of resorts makes it difficult to access them. A little-known secret is the beach referred to as **Pipa's** (named for the bar located here), an access point to the beach right between the Decameron and Playa Blanca resorts. Drive past the main entrance to Decameron and continue into a small village. You will eventually come to an opening to the beach. Park here and make your way down. Pipa's serves up ice-cold beers and a decent selection of local seafood. It also has bathroom facilities for restaurant customers.

Capital of Los Santos Province, **Las Tablas** is the center of Panama folklore. Except during Carnival, Las Tablas is a sleepy town. The church in the main square, **La Iglesia de Santa Librada** is a gorgeous example of early Spanish architecture on the continent.

Playa Venao is the surf capital of Panama, home to impressive breaks and various contests throughout the year, particularly in summer (December to April). Aside from the surf, it is a beautiful beach and the area is becoming increasingly popular among real estate investors.

Santa Catalina is another key surf spot on the Pacific Coast, but it is farther away from Panama City. Get to Santa Catalina by turning off the Highway at Santiago and driving toward the coast. Santa Catalina is also the jumping-off point for **Coiba,** a protected marine reserve that is home to some amazing marine and wildlife, including a large colony of scarlet macaws. Aquatic activities in this area are excellent, from scuba diving to sportfishing. Panama's version of Alcatraz, Coiba also housed the country's high-security prison until the early 2000s. Visitors to the island can now tour this fascinating but terrifying facility.

BOCAS DEL TORO
Accommodations

Al Natural (tel. 507/757-9004, www.alnaturalresort.com) is an opportunity to live a desert island experience while enjoying at-home comforts and family-style, gourmet cuisine. The resort closes May–July each year. Bungalows start at US$220 per night, but rates may vary throughout the year. It is a great price when it includes three full and delicious meals. Be sure to call for reservations.

Hotel Bocas del Toro (tel. 507/757-9018, www.hotelbocasdeltoro.com, from US$126 per night), located on the waterfront on Isla Colón, has 11 comfortable rooms with all necessary conveniences.

La Loma Jungle Lodge (tel. 507/6619-5364, www.thejunglelodge.com,

US$110 per person per night) comprises three *ranchos,* constructed in harmony with nature.

Popa Paradise Resort (Isla Popa, tel. 507/832-1498, www.popaparadiseresort.com, from US$215 per night) has 10 cottages.

Punta Caracol Acqua-Lodge (Isla Colón, tel: 507/6612-1088 and 507/757-9718, www.puntacaracol.com) is a intimate eco-resort that charms guests with its seclusion and beauty. Built on the other side of Isla Colón away from Bocas Town, Punta Caracol can only be reached by boat. The nine cabanas are literally built over the Caribbean waters, and each lodging has its own swimming hole. Rooms are luxurious, equipped with handmade furniture, romantic designs, quality fixtures, and bedding with mosquito nets. Day trips and adventure tours can be arranged for an extra price. If you think you will enjoy being at sea most of your stay, than Punta Caracol is for you. Otherwise the lack of land available may tend to bore you. The food and lounging deck are worth the try. Prices are very high. Room rates run US$300–600. Complete breakfast and dinner are included in the rates.

Food

Om Café (Avenida E at Calle 2, above Flow Surfshop, tel. 507/6624-0898) located on the other side of the town square above the surf and skate shop, is an authentic Indian cuisine restaurant—serving the best A.M. and P.M. meals on the island, and quite possibly the best Indian food in the country. It is very often the dining spot on the main island to which visitors most want to return. The breakfasts are delicious, as big or as light as you want them to be, and traditional lassis (sweet yogurt drinks) are served in the tropical flavors native to the island. Sunanda, the Canadian-Hindi owner, uses just the right amount of spices, never betraying a true Indian-food lover's palate. She and her staff can recommend menu items if you are unfamiliar with Indian food. Service is excellent in this funky bohemian hangout. Ask about renting the red room in the back for small parties.

Casbah (Avenida Norte, between Calles 3 and 4, tel. 507/6477-4727) is another great hangout spot, owned by Christopher, a friendly "I've lived everywhere" guy. You can't go wrong in his cozy bistro spot, located just at the beginning of the road back to Saigon. He always has an inventive menu and knows how to combine a bit of traditional with a bit of local flair. There are great wine choices, and it's a fun little spot to watch people move through town for the night—the island's foodies love this restaurant.

El Ultimo Refugio (off Calle 3, Main St., on Avenida Sur, 100 yards down from the ferry dock, tel. 507/6726-9851, www.ultimorefugio.com) is an unassuming rustic restaurant operated by two young American expats. They have created what is widely known as Bocas' best restaurant. There is no menu; instead, the owners serve whatever they get fresh that day. Common treats include deviled eggs, seared tuna, and meat loaf.

Lemongrass (Calle 2 above Starfleet Scuba, tel. 507/757-9630), a Thai-fusion restaurant, is another good find. English owner Mike brings some interesting dishes to the table, including a crazy but delicious "sushi sandwich."

Nine Degrees (Calle Primera, perpendicular to Avenida E walking past Om Café, tel. 507/757-9400), located in the Tropical Market right on the oceanfront, offers up a great gourmet menu, cooked by chef TJ, a seasoned chef with experience in excellent restaurants around the world. Specialties include the filet mignon.

For a quick lunch, or if you are in self-catering accommodations in Bocas, stop by the **Super Gourmet** (on right-hand side of Main Street, walking toward the ferry dock, after the Bocas Breeze hotel). It offers a great selection of breads and hard-to-find ingredients, plus a full deli counter with excellent sandwiches.

Lili's Café (First St. at the Clearnwater Building, tel. 507/6560-8777, www .kodiakbocas.com), located next to the Tropical Suites Hotel, offers a variety of Caribbean-style meals throughout the day. Her specialty is "Killin' me man!" hot sauce, the perfect souvenir to remember your trip to Bocas. While Panama has an impressive selection of hot sauces, Lili's may just be the best for the sandwich-hungry diner who wants a good homecooked meal, with savory and delicious flavors.

Sights

Finca Los Monos (tel. 507/757-9461, www.bocasdeltorobotanicalgarden.com) is located on Isla Colón, just past the Smithsonian Institute. This impressive botanical garden is home to an array of tropical flowers, palms, and trees. It also has a nursery where you could buy plants for your new home.

Cayos Zapatillas are the quintessential uninhabited tropical islands. Visit them on a tour that also goes to **Dolphin Bay** and **Coral Cay.** Any of the water-taxi operators will be delighted to take you on this tour, for a cost of about US$20 per person.

Playa Primera on the opposite side of Bastimentos is a beautiful beach, once desolate but now more of a beach party scene. There are still spots to find solitude. To get there, take a water taxi to Bastimentos town and walk up the hill, through the woods, and back down the hill. Alternatively, a water taxi could take you around the island to the beachfront.

Starfish Beach is located in Boca del Drago on the opposite side of Isla Colón. The beach is filled with huge starfish—but also filled with lots of sand flies. To get here, take the bus from Bocas Town (US$1), leaving every hour on the hour. Or take a taxi out to the beach and ask the driver to come back for you, so you can get the best round-trip rate.

DAILY LIFE

MAKING THE MOVE

If after several visits to Panama and plenty of research, you, like thousands of expats before you, have decided that you want to live here permanently, then it's time to begin taking the necessary steps to move yourself, your family, and all your possessions overseas. One of the first things to consider will be whether you plan to live year-round in Panama or just spend a few months a year here. This will determine the immigration status you obtain, as well as what you will bring with you. Depending on where you are moving from, you will likely find that many of the items you use daily at home will not be useful in Panama.

Of all the things that you bring, probably the most important is an open mind. This is an enormous change, and it will be fun, but also challenging. You are moving to an entirely different country, with different customs, habits, and traditions. Keep in mind that you're packing up and moving abroad *because* you want a change, so try not to get frustrated by the fact that things are very different in Panama. Prepare to wait longer for things to happen and

© SKY GILBAR

try to appreciate the uniqueness of unfamiliar situations you may encounter such as chaotic traffic, waiting for utility installations, or not having your familiar Sunday morning coffee shop. Rather than get frustrated, consider these daily changes part of your adventure. Pretty soon you and your new friends will look back on any difficulties of adjusting to a life in Panama and laugh.

Immigration and Visas

Whether you are coming to Panama motivated by work, a lifestyle change, or to join a loved one, you will find that the immigration process is ever-changing. The government is known to change laws frequently, leaving you and your new visa out of date and calling for a trip to your lawyer's office. Often, the laws are discussed in the news and media prior to changes being approved, so staying on top of local news will help. There is always a way to work out immigration matters, but be vigilant about the rules and regulations at all times to avoid misunderstandings.

Some nationalities are forever at peace with Panamanian authorities, such as Italians, who have a bilateral residency agreement with Panama. But Panamanian officials can be inconsistent with other nationalities, such as immigrants from the United States. What works for one applicant may not work for another. Come prepared for all situations; bring every last paper the government says you will need, signed and notarized. Most of the time it is worth retaining a lawyer who knows the ins and outs of the immigration labyrinth. If you do decide to go it alone, take a deep breath and assume it will take time. Keep organized files and be polite to the immigration officials. There are practical ways to solicit your residency in Panama, and it is very much worth it, since the laws change recurrently. You don't want to be stuck trying to enter the country only to find that your visa is no longer valid. The most efficient way is to work through a lawyer who can advise you of your options. If you will be employed under a contract in Panama, start the process upon signing your contract and find out if your company is willing to sponsor you by signing a letter of employment and/or paying the immigration fees. In order to ensure your visa remains valid and that you won't be left with any surprises at the airport, keep an eye on your expiration dates, call your lawyers to ask what papers they need, or if you are going the process alone, go to immigration at least a week prior to see about an extension. There will always be a waiting period for the first one-year visa, but if your paperwork is in order, the immigration department will continue to give you a three-month visa card, a *cedula,* until your one-year visa is issued.

A VISIT TO THE IMMIGRATION OFFICE

Your first encounter with the immigration office, or for that matter with anyone who has ever been to the immigration office, will no doubt be an alarming one. While government agencies in Panama, and in many parts of the world, are bureaucratic, illogical, and inefficient, the Panama Department of Immigration (Departamento de Inmigración de Panamá) is probably the worst.

Unfortunately, there is no escaping a visit to immigration, unless you come on a simple tourist visa and always leave before your 90 days are up. Any time you wish to extend your tourist visa, you must apply for one of the more specific visas, such as a work visa if you are employed or the Jubilados (permanent tourist) visa if you are retired. If you overstay your welcome as a tourist and have to pay a fine, you will need to present yourself in person at this dreaded establishment and surely will regret your carelessness.

The immigration office is located on the corner of Avenida Cuba and Calle 28 in Calidonia, next to the National Lottery building. However, at the time of writing there were plans to move the offices to a new location by the end of 2009. Note also the immigration office dress code: The sign at the door states clearly that you may not enter immigration wearing shorts, T-shirts, short skirts, or flip-flops. Officials will send you out if they find your dress inappropriate. So, ladies, leave those miniskirts at home!

Using a Lawyer

If you were thinking you could get your residency in Panama without the help of a lawyer, reconsider. Hiring a lawyer will save you time and make the whole ordeal much easier. For many of the *trámites* (processes), your lawyer should be able to get things done without you having to be present. However, there are a few steps, such as taking your photo for your *carnet* (ID card), for which you really have no choice but to present yourself in person at the immigration office.

When your tourist visa is expired, or when it's time to renew your temporary residency, your lawyer will usually send an intern to stand in line at the immigration office on your behalf. He or she will take a number and wait patiently in line, well in advance of the time you have arranged to meet, so you can leisurely join the intern to participate in whichever part of the process requires your physical presence.

The best way to handle your immigration experience is to follow your lawyer or intern around like a sheep, obey his or her commands and hand signals, enjoy a US$0.25 coffee from the machine, take a good book or newspaper, and wait patiently. You will not be leaving any time soon.

TYPES OF PERMANENT RESIDENCY
Retiree Visa

Panama's *pensionado,* or retiree visa, is a well-developed residency program with an impressive list of benefits and discounts. In fact, this visa has been a huge selling point for Panama to attract baby boomers looking to retire outside of their home country. Designed to allow foreigners to live legally in Panama once they are retired or collecting a pension, this visa is also one of the most straightforward to obtain. The requirement is that the applicant's monthly, lifetime retirement income must be more than US$1,000, which can come from a private pension fund or a government pension such as Social Security. The source of the funds must be proven by authenticated documents such as a letter from the government or your pension fund manager. Once the application is approved, the retiree will receive a Permanent Residency Card (*cedula*) but will not be eligible to apply for Panamanian citizenship. Note that the age requirement to apply for this visa is only 18 years old; however, the discounts are only available to women over 55 or men over 60 years old.

To apply for this visa, you will need proof of income, your original birth certificate, and in the case that your spouse is to be included on your visa, your marriage certificate.

Reforestation Visa

Reforestation Visas (Programa de Inversion en Reforestacion) are awarded to individuals purchasing a parcel of land that is part of a government-recognized reforestation program. Trees are then planted on the land purchased. As the trees mature, usually in about 15 years, a percentage of them are harvested for timber. New trees grow, creating a sustainable forest, while at the same time providing a return on investment to the individual. For many years, teak has been the tree of choice, since it is a fast-growing species and also yields expensive and highly sought-after timber. Now, programs are favoring a mixed-species forest, both to prevent diseases from wiping out the entire forest and also because a mixed forest mimics a naturally occurring forest and thus provides a habitat for a wider range of wildlife. As the forest grows, weaker trees are felled as part of a "thinning" process. This is done every two to three years.

The Reforestation Visa in Panama has come under a great deal of scrutiny over the years and has also undergone many changes. In order to obtain the visa, the government requires an investment of US$60,000 for a

"Micro-Investor" or US$80,000 for a "Macro-Investor," with a minimum of 20 hectares (49 acres) of reforested land. According to Jeff Duda of Panama Forestry, it is impossible to plant 20 hectares for only US$80,000; he says it may require up to US$300,000. Since this is expensive and subject to frequent change, a Reforestation Visa is probably not your best option.

Work Permit Visa

Unless you are retired, probably one of the first questions you will ask is whether you can get a work permit in Panama. Panama has agreements with certain countries, such as Italy, which make it is easier for people from those countries to get a work permit. Workers from the United States and Canada are awarded work permits far less frequently, although it is not unheard of.

Panamanian companies seek to hire foreigners who possess special skills or training that employers are unable to find in a Panamanian employee. It is easier to obtain a work permit in certain professions than others, and it is typically easy for dancers, boxers, artists, and, remarkably, prostitutes to obtain a work visa in Panama. These professions tend to be more open and less competitive, and therefore, Panama is open to filling the industries' needs in these areas of culture, sports, and "recreation."

The Marrakech Treaty, or Temporary Visitor Visa, allows suitable applicants to work in Panama for a total of five years. Suitable applicants include foreigners who work for a small company of 3–10 employees and the applicant would be the only foreigner on the payroll. There is also a Panamanian Work Visa, also sometimes called the 10 Percent, whereby up to 10 percent of a company's employees can be foreign.

You can also apply for a Panamanian work permit if you are married to a Panamanian. This involves presenting your work papers to the Ministry of Labor and submitting to a matrimonial interview with a Panamanian official before your general work visa will be approved. This could take from three months to a year, at which time you will need to renew the work visa again, even if you do have a matrimonial visa.

In all of these instances, the company for which you work must sponsor you with a letter of employment and a copy of your contract throughout the process. The paperwork is substantial, and no permits are issued overnight. Permits last three months to start and then are renewed year-to-year for up to five years. You can then apply for your permanent residence visa. If contracted from abroad, a company should take control of the entire process—visa paperwork and expenses. If you are hired after you move to Panama, a company that values you and your skills will offer to support you with employment letters and give you the time off to do the necessary steps at the immigration office. However, they may not contribute to the fees, which can add up to a good US$800 per year, including lawyer's fees. A labor lawyer can provide more information about work visas.

Some companies employ foreign workers on a "Professional Services" or contract basis, not really intended for someone working full time in an organization. This is one way of getting around not having a work permit, but it is frowned upon legally, since it will impede your obligation to be taxed as a resident of this country. During customary inspections from the Social Security Department, all employees working in a company's office will be asked to present identification, and the inspectors will expect to find all workers on the payroll.

Investment Visas

SMALL BUSINESS

Those coming to Panama to invest have a variety of options when it comes to visa applications. As long as you have a significant amount of money that you can afford to invest here, this visa application is a straightforward process. The Small Business Visa, later named the Business Investor Visa, requires that you invest a minimum of US$160,000 in a new business (although the corporation can be an existing one), employ at least five Panamanians, and provide a plethora of documentation including a business plan, commercial license, and rental agreements. Investors receive a two-year temporary residency, which is renewed three times before obtaining full residency after six years. This implies an investment of a lot of time and paperwork.

SELF ECONOMIC SOLVENCY

An easier and more popular option is to apply for a Self Economic Solvency Visa. There are three possible ways to obtain this visa. You can invest a minimum of US$300,000 in titled real property (mortgage-free), deposit US$300,000 or more in a three-year fixed-term deposit in a Panamanian bank, or do a combination of both so your investments total a minimum of US$300,000 (such as purchase real property for US$200,000 and place US$100,000 in a fixed-term Panamanian bank deposit). Applicants who choose this route should gain permanent residency after just 30 months. After five years, you can apply for citizenship and obtain a passport. Another advantage of this program is that the interest accumulated on the bank deposit is transferred monthly to the account of your choice and is not subject to tax.

QUICK REFERENCE GUIDE TO RESIDENCE VISAS

Visa Requirements

RETIRED OR *PENSIONADO*

Applicant's lifetime monthly retirement or pension income must be at least $1,000. Alternatively, you can purchase real estate in Panama valued at a minimum of $100,000 and then the monthly income would need to be a minimum of $750.

- Letter from the government/foreign pension/trust/mutual fund company, stating that the funds exist.

- Proof of payment through bank statements or copies of payments.

SELF ECONOMIC SOLVENCY VISA
Option 1: Certificate of Deposit (CD)

$300,000 investment requirement in a Panamanian Bank

- Money must be deposited in a Panamanian bank in a 3-year CD.

- The CD account must be in the name of the investor, not a Panamanian corporation.

- The applicant must prove he/she has sufficient funds to cover costs of living.

SELF ECONOMIC SOLVENCY VISA
Option 2: Panama Real Estate Investment

$300,000 investment requirement

- The $300,000 must be equity invested. There can be no mortgages.

- Title deed from Panama's Public Registry showing ownership of a property worth at least $300,000.

TAX FREE

The world's second-largest distribution center, the Colón Free Zone, is one of four Tax Free Processing Zones in Panama, and a good investment option for those who are looking into a business investment visa. The country is keen to attract investment dollars here, and to look specifically for investment in the areas of export/import, manufacturing, and software development and call centers. Anyone investing in these areas within one of the Tax Free Processing Zones can apply for permanent residency. The only condition is that you rent an office or piece of land through a 10–20 year concession within one of the Tax Free Zones. There are other new options arising with development of the Panama Pacific free zone now under construction in Howard, just outside Panama City.

- The applicant must prove sufficient funds to cover costs of living.

SELF ECONOMIC SOLVENCY VISA
Option 3: Combined Real Estate and Certificate of Deposit (CD) investment

$300,000 investment requirement divided between real estate and a Panamanian bank CD.

- Same conditions as in Options 1 and 2.

BUSINESS INVESTOR VISA

$160,000 investment requirement

- Must invest in a new business
- Hire five Panamanian employees and pay at least minimum wage and all Social Security benefits.
- Obtain appropriate business licenses.
- Proof of investment and the provenance of funds.

REFORESTATION VISA (Small)

$60,000 investment requirement

- Purchase at least 10 hectares of land in government-certified reforestation project.

REFORESTATION VISA (Large)

$80,000 investment requirement

- Purchase at least 20 hectares of land in government-certified reforestation project.

Panama Offshore Legal Services, 2009

DAILY LIFE

TYPES OF TEMPORARY RESIDENCY

While in Panama on any temporary visa, you should carry your visa or temporary *carnet* (ID card) with you at all times, along with your driver's license or passport. The police do regular, random checks at certain road stops as well as in the street and ask for ID. They have been known to detain tourists who cannot prove they are within the limits of their entry and exit dates.

Tourist and Student Visas

If you have already visited Panama on vacation or for a fact-finding trip, you know that the tourist visa is issued upon arrival to the country. The United States and Canada are two of the countries whose citizens must purchase a

US$5 tourist card upon arrival, whereas visitors from the United Kingdom are allowed to enter for free. The tourist visa is valid for 90 days and can be extended for 30 days by visiting the immigration office. Once a tourist leaves Panama, he or she can reenter the country after three days and will be granted another 90-day visa. Many foreigners living in Panama take advantage of this law and are known as "perpetual tourists." They cross the border into Costa Rica or take a short break back home every 90 days. This can be fun and avoids the need to ever get a real visa. The drawback is that the law could change and leave you stranded outside of Panama. If you overstay your 90 days in Panama, you will need to go to the immigration office and pay a fine before leaving. The fine varies depending on how long you overstay, but it must be paid at the office downtown in Panama City or at the immigration office in David, Chiriquí. It cannot be paid at the airport upon exiting the country, and you are likely to miss your flight if you go there thinking you can just pay and leave.

If you're coming into Panama to study, perhaps on an internship program, chances are you're staying for less than three months, in which case the tourist visa is for you. Any longer and you will probably want to acquire a Student Visa, valid for one year but extendable for up to six. Under this visa, you can study but are forbidden to work. Proof of curriculum is required to obtain the visa.

THE APPLICATION PROCESS

While every visa application is a little different, the majority will request the same initial paperwork. All the applications begin with the registration of your passport at immigration. Once you have gathered and handed in all of the necessary documents, and the initial approval has been given, you will be issued a temporary *carnet* (ID card). This will likely need renewal several times before you get any kind of permanent documentation. Once you have your *carnet,* be aware that you now need a visa to leave the country. This is called the Multiple Exit Visa and is applied for once your application has been initially approved. This is a separate application through the Immigration Department and is important to have if your visa is only good for three months to a year. Once your temporary visa is granted, you will need to give up your passport for a few days, so officials can register the number and create a page in your personal travel document for the Multiple Entry and Exit seal, which the airport officials will look for. The stamp will contain the same expiration date as your temporary visa; you should present this along with your *carnet* to the airport customs agent upon leaving and entering the country. Basically, the seal on your passport informs customs officers that your application process is under way, but you are legal to enter and exit Panama as you wish. Your lawyer can take care of this for you. Once you are granted your permanent visa, you will no longer need to present the Multiple Exit and Entry seal at the airport; your new *cedula extranjera,* or foreigner's ID card, will be sufficient.

Don't be surprised if your application documents go missing in Panama's immigration offices. In fact, this is quite likely to happen at immigration, the bank, even your lawyer's office, and it will be up to you to submit the document again. Keep a copy of everything you have submitted, and perhaps even have the officials sign it "received" so as to prove you have submitted it. Once you submit the papers, you will need an official letter from your lawyer or the immigration department stating that your visa is in process, which you can present to the police or any official who may question your legal status in the country. Keep a copy of the original in your wallet with your personal identification. The process can take from three months to a year. All kinds of excuses can be made for the delay. If you are lucky enough to never experience a delay, such as your paperwork being misplaced or the lamination machine at the immigration office being broken, you may only wait up to 30 days.

Application Requirements

The paperwork required will vary depending on which visa you are applying for. Some of the requirements, however, are the same across the board. You must have a valid passport, with at least one year of validity remaining, and four to eight original passport-sized photos. To avoid any problems with the size of the photos, it is advisable to have them taken at Arrocha Pharmacy; this is the most popular chain of pharmacies in Panama City, with outlets at the Los Pueblos Albrook Mall, in Paitilla, on Calle 50, and in El Dorado, among others.

It is also a good idea to bring an authenticated police record less than five years old, or a letter of good conduct from your home country; this is required for work visas, especially for teachers, and sometimes it is requested for other visas, or sometimes not, without any rhyme or reason as to why. Not all countries issue police records for their citizens, such as the United Kingdom, in which case you would request a letter of good conduct from the British Embassy. The United States, however, does provide police records. It's a good idea to get a copy from your local police department before leaving home, if you know you are planning to start a visa application process. You should also bring your birth certificate and your university transcripts and diplomas, or a notarized copy of all of the above.

DAILY LIFE

In the case of the retiree visa, you would need to obtain a letter from the government or your pension fund manager proving that your monthly retirement income is greater than US$1,000, your original birth certificate, and in the case that your spouse is to be included on your visa, you should also bring your marriage certificate. All of these documents need to be authenticated or "apostilled" before they leave their country of origin. An apostille is a stamp that legalizes a document for international use. Documents first need to be notarized by a notary public, and then certified with an apostille stamp. They are then recognized as legal documents in all member states of the Hague Convention. These include Panama, the United Kingdom, the United States, and Canada, among many others. You will also most likely need to undergo a medical examination and provide a certificate of good health, including results from a HIV test. This can be done in Panama.

Unlike many other countries, the application for a Panama visa nearly always begins in Panama, although you can start the process from abroad by contacting a Panama law firm, either by telephone or online. Quite early on in the process, however, you will need to come to Panama to register your passport at immigration.

Hiring a Lawyer

Choosing your lawyer will probably be the single most important thing you do when moving to Panama, especially if you are planning on doing business here. Your lawyer will become your go-to person to answer your queries and ease any confusion and doubts you have about how things work in this country. A good lawyer in Panama means a connected one who knows how to get things done. Ask around for recommendations and take your time in selecting a lawyer you feel you can trust.

Unless you are fluent in Spanish, with a decent knowledge of legal terminology, you want to find a lawyer who can communicate with you in English. You will find that many of the country's lawyers have done at least part of their training in an English-speaking country and thus speak English well, if not perfectly.

English contracts are not valid in Panama; contracts must always be made in Spanish. The translation of legal documents is recommended in order for you to understand them, and a Certified Public Translator who stamps and certifies that the translation is accurate and true must do this. Translators charge US$8–15 per page or US$15–25 per hour. Your lawyer will be able to recommend translators.

The law regulates legal fees, but these are minimums, so you will find lawyers charging anything from US$50 an hour to well over US$500, depending on their experience and specialty.

Immigration Processing Fees

The costs of "getting legal" in Panama vary dramatically according to your lawyer's fees. The actual fees of the government are standard and also vary according to visa application. It is advised to contract with a lawyer to facilitate all of the processes for you, or else it might never happen. For example, the work visa costs US$800 per application in government fees. This does not include legal fees, which will run US$500–800 per year. The entire process of the Self Economic Solvency Visa costs more—just under US$3,000 from initial registration to citizenship, but you can add to that US$7,000–10,000 in legal fees. These fees do not need to be paid up front; there are several stages to the process, spanning the several years it will take to become a citizen. The retiree visa, on the other hand, costs around US$400 in government fees and a further US$500–1,000 in legal fees.

Moving with Children

Panama is a very child-friendly country. Educational facilities for children, from pre-Kindergarten through high school, are plentiful and have high standards. Since Panama attracts people from all over the world to live here, your child will probably not feel out of place and will most likely have the opportunity to mix with children from varied ethnic and social backgrounds at school, the local playground, and your building's social area.

CHILDREN'S DOCUMENTATION
Non-Panamanian Children

All children, by law, require a passport from their home country in order to enter Panama; these can be issued as soon as the child is born. When applying for a visa or residency in Panama, your children must be included on your application as dependents, for which there is a cost. Costs for applying for children's visas (dependents under 18 years old) run US$800 in government fees.

Panamanian Children

When a child is born in Panama, he or she is automatically considered a Panamanian citizen. If your children are born here and you wish to take them back to the United States, they will need a Panamanian passport and must travel with at least one parent or a legal guardian (they will need documentation of the guardianship to leave the country). If the child is born to a Panamanian father, and the mother wants to take the child out of the country, she needs to have documentation of the father's permission. In actuality, any one parent traveling alone with their Panamanian child(ren) must have consent from the other parent, divorced or married. In general, it is a good idea to travel with your child's birth certificate and a notarized letter from both parents giving permission for the child to travel outside the country.

Moving with Pets

To many of us, our pets are a very important part of our family. Bringing Buster to Panama and caring for him once you arrive is actually quite straightforward, although Panama has strict animal import regulations that you'll need to navigate. If bringing your pets into Panama by airplane, confirm details with the airlines, as they all have different restrictions and these vary according to seasonal changes. For example, U.S. airlines will usually not take an animal between June and August, because the weather is too hot and can present health risks to the animal.

Depending on the animal you wish to import to Panama, there are different regulations. As you might expect, a dog is far simpler than, let's say, a scarlet macaw, although both are possible.

CATS AND DOGS

For cats and dogs, it's a fairly standard procedure to bring your pet with you to Panama. You will need to get a vaccination card and health certificate from a veterinarian in your home country no more than 10 days before your arrival in Panama. The Panamanian Consul or Embassy in your home country should stamp these certificates. Your dog will need to have a rabies vaccination at least 30 days but no more than 180 days before its arrival in Panama. You will need to complete an import form, available from the Health or Quarantine offices at the Panama International Airport.

Depending on the size of your pet, it will either travel up in the cabin with you or in a designated area below the cabin. Dogs under 15 pounds and cats are usually allowed in the cabin with passengers. Again, you need to check with your airline for its specific regulations. The animal should be carried in a traveling carrier just large enough for him to be able to turn around. He should have access to fresh water, but no food. It is advisable for the animal not to eat within 12 hours before the flight, to avoid accidents on the plane and to reduce the nausea the pet will most likely experience. Flying is a stressful experience for your pet, and as such you should fly with him as infrequently as possible. Many people leave their pet at home until they are settled in their new Panama home, and then return home to collect the pet or have someone send it down to you.

Once your pet arrives at the airport, it will be subject to a health inspection. As long as it passes the test, you can take it from the airport right away. If the pet must be quarantined (this usually occurs when your plane arrives after the health office has closed), then you would pay a daily fee of US$7 to the Health Department. Alternatively you can request a home quarantine of your pet for a fee of US$120. In this case, you must promise to keep your pet inside your home for the required period. To qualify for home quarantine, your request must be delivered to Panama's Health Department two weeks before your arrival.

EXOTIC PETS

Importing your exotic pets is significantly more complicated, and their entry into Panama is not guaranteed. Panama is a signatory to Convention on International Trade in Endangered Species of Wild Fauna & Flora (CITES), and therefore you must meet all of the requirements for the transport of a CITES-listed species. See www.cites.org and click on "How CITES Works" for more information. Even with a CITES authorization, the final decision is still with the Panamanian authorities, specifically Autoridad Nacional del Ambiente (ANAM), Panama's Environmental and Wildlife Protection Agency.

What to Bring

When you decide to move to Panama, you need to think hard about whether you want to bring all your old stuff with you or if you want a fresh start. Usually, younger expats are more likely to come with whatever is in their backpack and start a collection of possessions once they are in Panama, whereas older emigrants are more likely to ship their entire households down here. It makes sense: One of Panama's Retirement Visa benefits is a one-time, tax-exempt import of household goods to the value of US$10,000, and a tax-free import of a new car every two years. If you do not qualify for the retiree visa, then you will have to pay tax on anything that you import. The amount of tax is usually

10 to 15 percent of the value of the goods imported—a somewhat questionable subject, since most everything you bring will be used. You will be required to present an inventory list when your shipment arrives in Panama, so make a list of everything in your container or package and put a minimal, yet realistic, value on each item. You might think you will get away with valuing the new 52-inch flat-screen TV at US$25—think again. Customs agents do inspect the goods you are importing, and, unfortunately, they are rarely looking to make your life any easier. In fact, they may look at you as a mark for a bribe, so it's best to be fairly accurate when valuing your goods.

Be ready with all the necessary paperwork, your passport, and a letter of employment or authorized letter of change of residency. If you plan on being super-organized and shipping your things months before you personally make your move down to Panama, think twice. In order for you to be able to receive your items, you must be personally present with all the correct documents, identifications and signatures matching your passport. Usually you will need a list of all the items in each box, at least three photocopies of your passport, and a letter that verifies that you are the owner of the items in the packages and that you have been the one to present yourself at the customs office to pick it up. The letter should include your identification number, your nationality, and gender, as a standard format. All signatures must match your signature on your passport. You may also need receipts from the packing or shipping company from the place of embarkation.

Also don't be surprised to see that your boxes were opened and inspected. You may also be charged a storage fee per day if your shipped items do arrive before you can pick them up. If you expect that you can send someone in your place to pick up your shipments, you will want to ask your customs agent if this is possible. It is common for them to ask for a letter of authorization, and copies of both yours and your couriers' ID, if they even allow this. Customs requirements may change at any time, so always double check the Panamanian consulate or embassy web page (www.embassyofpanama.org) to find out more.

If you are not benefiting from tax-free imports, it might be worth considering holding a garage sale and selling your main items, then starting fresh in Panama and purchasing everything you need here. As far as household items, you will find all appliances can be purchased here, with the brands you know and love at very similar prices to the United States and Canada. You will also find obscure Asian brands at far lower prices. There are many furniture stores here, selling a wide variety of items from very cheap beds to high-end designer mattresses or sofas. The selection of furniture stock is constantly growing here, but currently, Panama still lacks inexpensive, fashionable furniture like that sold at IKEA.

You might also choose to hire a carpenter or ironworker to custom make furniture for you according to your design. This would be an especially good option if you will be living outside of Panama City, where shipping your belongings through a local shipping agency can be costly, time-consuming, and cumbersome with paperwork. Woodworkers and ironworkers here do an excellent job if you tell them exactly what you want and need. This last option is highly suggested, as you can get handmade original pieces, with good and long-lasting materials and loyal and well-priced labor.

The best advice is to visit furniture stores on one of your fact-finding missions to Panama and price everything out. Then you can decide for yourself if it makes sense to bring your belongings with you.

SHIPPING OPTIONS

Whether you bring a little or a lot of your possessions to Panama, you need to choose whether you will use ocean, land, or air transport.

By Freight

Since Panama is such an important shipping center, land freight doesn't make sense as a shipping method. It is simply too time-consuming and complicated. The only way this might make sense is if you are driving down to Panama from the United States, and you can load up your car. Even then, be careful: Some of the areas you will be driving through in the Americas will not be particularly safe, and having a car full of electronic appliances and other valuables might not be the wisest idea.

By Air

Assuming that you have fewer than two suitcases of goods, the cheapest way to bring your items into Panama would be by airplane. If you have just a little more, it would be worth checking into airline charges for excess baggage. However, you need to do this beforehand; agents will include a note on your reservation that you are traveling with extra bags. If you do not reserve ahead, they are not obliged to load your excess baggage; if the plane is full, you will have to leave your things behind or arrange shipping from the airport, which can be extremely expensive.

Shipping goods to Panama by air can be expensive.

You can also send packages to Panama by air, but this can be expensive, and unless you use an international courier like FedEx or DHL, it is difficult to guarantee when the package will arrive, if at all.

By Container

By far the most cost-effective way of shipping a larger amount of goods here is by ocean freight. The most common shipping route is from Miami to Manzanillo Port in Colón, on the Atlantic Coast of Panama, which takes 5–7 days. From there, your goods will be unloaded, subject to a customs inspection, and then shipped across country to Panama City, or wherever you will live.

The next decision is how much container space you need. If you are bringing your entire household and car, then you will probably require a whole container. If it's less, you can consolidate your cargo, and share a container with other people's belongings.

The easiest way to coordinate your shipment is to employ the services of a moving company, either from Panama or your home country. You will want to find a company that has experience shipping household goods to Panama; since every country's regulations are a little different, it's helpful if your mover knows what to expect. If you choose door-to-door service, the moving company will take care of everything, including customs procedures when your goods arrive in Panama. The movers first arrive at your home and take a detailed inventory of everything you are shipping with them, carefully wrap each item, and pack it in the container or the shipping crates. They take your

SHIPPING YOUR CAR TO PANAMA

Upon moving, some people may benefit from importing one car, tax-free, to Panama. These people are generally retirees who possess a *pensionado* visa or members of the diplomatic corps. In theory, this exemption sounds like a great perk to moving down here, but many of those who have done it realize in hindsight that it may not have been the best idea.

When shipping a car, there are a set of variables you must take into consideration in deciding if it is worthwhile. First, you need to know the value of your car in your home country, and in Panama. Second, you need to know if your car and its spare parts are sold in Panama. Some makes are just not sold here, like Dodge, for example. Now, you can buy a Dodge in Panama through another dealership, but there is absolutely no after-sale support here, so when the time comes for repairs, they will be expensive, not to mention the wait to receive ordered parts. Understandably, this has a very negative effect on the resale value of your car here. On the other hand, a car like the Toyota Yaris holds its value extremely well in Panama, and parts are readily available at reasonable prices. It is worth having a look at a classified ads website like www.encuentra24.com to get a feeling for the value of secondhand cars here, before making a decision to ship your car. As a rule, Japanese cars are the most popular, followed by American, and then European. Consequently, Japanese auto parts are cheapest and Japanese cars hold their value best, whereas European parts are the most expensive, and the vehicles depreciate much faster. Another consideration is the specifications of your vehicle. For example, some Japanese cars are built to American specifications and others to Japanese or European specifications. You might think, for example, that your Toyota Land Cruiser is worth importing to Panama, and then something breaks and you find the parts here are not exactly the right ones, and you have to import them anyway. Generally, Japanese cars in Panama are built with Japanese specs.

Once you have valued your vehicle, you need to know how much it will cost to ship it down here. There is little sense in spending US$5,000 to ship a car that might sell for only US$4,000. The price of the shipping will depend on your point of origin and whether you are shipping other items. If you have many items, you can put your car together with the items in a container and ship everything together (never pack any items inside the actual vehicle), and this can make it a more economical option.

If you are not one of the lucky ones who can import a car tax-free, you will have to pay an import duty on the vehicle once it arrives in Panama. The customs inspector decides this duty once he sees the car. He should charge 5 percent tax, based on the value stated on the car's original invoice, which you must have, together with the car's title and, if the car is financed, a letter from the lienholder authorizing the release of the vehicle from the United States.

If you decide to ship your car, do it through a shipping company with experience in this field. Individuals who opt to take care of the shipment themselves together with a customs broker in Panama often find themselves waiting weeks and even months to get the car out of the port compound, incurring an ever-increasing storage fee. All in all, even if you are benefiting from a tax-free import, you need to carefully weigh the pros and cons before making your decision.

© SKY GILBAR

Container shipments to Panama are very easy to arrange.

items, initiate the shipping process—from your home to Miami, on to the ship, down to Panama, off the ship, through customs, onto a truck and to your new home, where they unpack everything for you. Obviously, you pay a premium for this service, but the peace of mind is probably worth it.

Alternatively, you can split up the service into parts, and take care of each part individually. The more logistical organization you take care of yourself, the cheaper it will become. If you pack everything and drive it to the port yourself, you will save a lot of money. Then you need to find a shipping company in Miami that will load everything into a container for you and bring it to Panama. If you are not using an entire container, then you must hope that someone else is also shipping a partial container in the same time frame so you can consolidate your cargo. Once your shipment arrives in Panama, the shipping company will notify you, and you will need to find a customs broker to liquidate the items from customs and deliver them to you in your new home. This sequence will save you a lot of money but will most likely take more time and definitely a lot more hassle and stress for you.

HOUSING CONSIDERATIONS

Once you have decided to live in Panama, your actual living situation is something you want to consider wisely. Remember, not only are you looking for something that suits your style, but you must consider all the details of living in the tropics. Air quality, concrete versus wood construction, high or low ceilings, window screens, and noise pollution can greatly affect your comfort level when you are nesting. Of course, there are tricks to be learned about how to live in harmony with innocuous house insects and avoid damp closets (and moldy leather goods). It comes down to taking special care of your goods and respecting that Mother Nature usually does have the last word.

You also want to consider your needs, possessions, and lifestyle in choosing a home. The salty sea air near the ocean is not ideal for high-tech equipment, and keeping those homes air-conditioned is quite a waste of beautiful ocean breezes. You should also see what resources are available to you. Do you need

high-speed Internet in your home, or can you get by picking up your emails every few days from a local Internet café? If you enjoy eating out and frequent social events, you will want to be close to the city. There are many opportunities in Panama to create your dream home, but you have to be willing to do the legwork and manage the construction workers. If that is not your speed, you will find turnkey operations are also in abundance along the provinces east of Coclé and in Bocas del Toro.

Renting

While your long-term goal will probably be purchasing a home in Panama, you would be well advised to rent for a while, before making the final decision about where and in what kind of home you would like to live. You will need to choose among Panama's cities or a rural location. You will have to decide whether you like a hot beach setting or a cooler mountainous place. If it's Panama City you choose, then you must decide in which neighborhood and whether you want a house or apartment. You must also consider who you want your neighbors to be: Do you want to live close to many other expats, or are you happier surrounded by Panamanians?

Your financial standing will factor in to most of these decisions. By and large, you can't make these decisions until you are fairly familiar with Panama and its people, but renting for at least six months should acquaint you with your preferences. In addition, just because you are moving to a Central American country, don't expect that rents will be that much more affordable than Southern Florida, for example. The building boom has inspired many owners to renovate their properties and raise the rent.

FINDING THE RIGHT PLACE

Rental properties, both apartments and houses, are readily available all over the country, and resources on how to find them are also plentiful. Ultimately, you will probably require the help of a real estate agent to find a property, but before you contact one, it's a good idea to peruse the information available on the Internet and in the newspapers. There are three websites that you should check out as part of your initial search, and they will help you get a feel for the prices and options out there. Craigslist (www.craigslist.org), the classified ads site from the United States, has a Panama section where you will find a fair range of properties, especially those advertised by fellow Americans and Canadians. Encuentra24.com is a good source of classifieds information—not just real estate—for Panama and Central America, and Compreoalquile.com is a real estate listings site from Panama. On all of these sites, you will find properties for rent and for sale, and if you find something you like, you can contact real estate agents directly from these sites. People renting or selling their own property are likely to advertise them with slightly elevated prices, so always try to negotiate. Another good source of rental properties is the newspaper. *La Prensa* usually has the best selection, and newspaper ads often have more realistic prices than those on the Internet.

© SKY GILBAR

You might like the urban feel of Punta Pacifica, a constantly developing location.

Short-Term Rentals

Short-term rentals in Panama, like anywhere else in the world, are more expensive than long-term rentals but can be a good way to ease you into life here. Generally speaking, the rental will include all utilities and be set up with cable TV, Internet access, and telephone, thus saving you the hassle of contracting these services on your own. Short-term rentals can be anything from one night to three months. There are several companies that specialize in short-term rentals. See the *Resources* chapter for details.

Long-Term Rentals

Long-term rentals usually come with a one-year or two-year lease and require one month's deposit up front with the first month's rent. You should get this deposit back at the end of your lease, provided you leave the property in the same condition you found it. Oftentimes, the landlord will clean and paint the apartment after you vacate it, and he or she will take these costs out of your deposit. The landlord should be willing to show you the receipts for whatever work he has done, so you know he is not taking you for a ride.

© SKY GILBAR

Bella Vista, an old colonial neighborhood, is opening up to high-rise development.

PROPERTY MANAGEMENT

Buying a property with the intention of renting it out on a short- or long-term basis can be a fruitful investment. If you are living in Panama, you might be happy to manage the property yourself, collecting rent, dealing with maintenance issues, and finding tenants. Most owners, however, choose to hire a property manager to take care of the property. Property management is a growing business in Panama, and the high demand for rental properties has made it an easy business to get into in recent years. As supply increases, it will no doubt become significantly more competitive.

Property managers typically operate on a commission, charging one month's rent per year for each apartment managed. This is the standard fee for long-term rentals. Commissions for short-term rentals vary dramatically, as they are more labor-intensive.

RENTAL AGENTS AND LEASES

Most real estate agents in the country work with both rentals and sales, and there are so many licensed realtors in Panama that it won't take you long to find one. You might, however, be surprised by the lack of response you receive when inquiring about a property on the Internet. It seems that while realtors take the time to place their listings on these sites, they don't all take the time to answer their emails, so it's often more efficient to call as well as email.

Once you find an apartment or house you wish to rent, your realtor will get the contract from the owner/landlord. You should take the contract to a lawyer

ABBREVIATIONS USED IN CLASSIFIEDS

Any quick search through the classified listings will leave you asking a few questions. The following glossary of terms and abbreviations are useful when starting a search:

Term or Abbreviation	English Translation
a/a, a/acondicionado, aire acondicionado	air-conditioning
amoblado/sin amoblar	furnished/non-furnished
a/s, a/social, area social	social area, often comprises swimming pool, gym, sauna, party room in an apartment building
b, baño	bathroom
c/b/e, c/b/empleada, cuarto y baño de empleada	maid's quarters, usually a small bedroom and bathroom next to the laundry room
estac/estacionamiento (techado)	parking space (covered)
l/b, l/blanca, línea blanca	household appliances, usually oven, refrigerator, washing machine, clothes dryer
p/alto, piso alto	high floor
r/rec/recamara	bedroom
s/c, s/comedor, sala/comedor	living/dining room
v/ciudad, vista a la ciudad	city view
v/mar, vista al mar	ocean view

to check it out and, if necessary, have it translated into English to make sure you understand all the clauses. Panamanian housing contracts are generally straightforward, but it's worth double-checking. The realtor will receive one month's rent as a commission from the landlord; the tenant is not responsible for paying this. Once the contract is signed, make sure you have the landlord's contact information, so you can get in touch in case of any problems. You should not deal with the realtor again.

Some landlords will request proof of your income in the form of the last few months of bank statements, or an employment letter and a copy of your passport. They might also want to check your credit status at the Panama Credit Bureau (APC), in which case they will ask you to sign a permission form. (If you have not borrowed money from any institutions in Panama, you will not appear on the Bureau's records.) Similarly, some will want to register the rental at the Ministry of Housing, in which case there will usually be extra paperwork. These requirements depend entirely on the landlord. However, registering at the Ministry is best for the tenant, since laws are designed to protect you more than the owner.

Buying

It is always a good idea to spend time living in and traveling around the city and country to make sure you are familiar with all your options before making the commitment of purchasing your permanent home. Even if it is your second home, be sure it's in a desirable location before taking the plunge.

Many of the properties in Panama designed for foreign buyers are located in preconstruction projects that are still on the drawing board. In order to obtain financing and begin construction, the developer must sell at least 70 percent of the units in the project. Take this into account if you are the first person to purchase and it's a 200-unit development. You could be waiting a while. Background research on the developer is a good idea at this point. Has the developer built projects in Panama before? Are buyers in those developments satisfied? Does the developer follow through with his preconstruction promises?

Also think about how realistic the development plan is. In a development that hasn't broken ground yet but promises to offer multiple hotels, spas, golf courses, restaurants, health clubs, and much more is going to take a long time to build and requires a lot of money. Does the developer have that money, or

© MIRIAM BUTTERMAN

Living on the ocean allows for views like this along the Atlantic coast.

is he dependent on buyers and bank financing? You could find yourself living in a development with no facilities whatsoever, miles from anywhere, waiting for other people to move in and all the promised amenities to be installed. In 2006-2007, several 100-plus–story buildings were announced in Panama City, all promising to be the tallest building in Latin America and among the tallest buildings in the world. Three years later, none of the towers have been constructed, and two have been officially cancelled, leaving preconstruction buyers fighting to get their deposits returned. Some say the technology was never here to build such a building. Generally speaking, steer away from developments that seem too adventurous, especially by foreign developers, as they often turn out to be too good to be true.

Nevertheless, many of Panama's residential developments have been constructed successfully and buyers are generally very pleased with their purchases. Home values have steadily risen over the last few years, and such investments should remain positive as tourism infrastructure increases along the coastlines, around Panama City, and in the Western Highlands.

PURCHASING LAND

There are three types of land in Panama recognized by the government: Titled (Titulado), Rights of Possession (Derechos Posesorios), and Concessions (Concesiones). It is important to understand the details of each type.

Titled Property

Panama's constitution guarantees the right to own land for both national and foreign citizens. All titled properties are registered at the Public Registry, which verifies the title of the property in the owner's name. Since the title can be verified, purchasing titled property in Panama is nearly always a secure, straightforward transaction, and title insurance is not usually required. As part of the negotiation process, be sure to establish, in writing, all terms and conditions, including payment dates and amounts. Your lawyer should write the initial agreement between you and the seller, known as a Promise to Purchase Contract (Contrato Promesa de Compraventa).

This Promise to Purchase is signed by both the buyer and seller and a down payment is made to secure the property, giving the buyer time to conduct a title search, verify the seller's ownership, and discover any liens against the property. This search is done at the Public Registry. At this point, the buyer must arrange any necessary financing and set up a corporation to hold the title, if required. The contract is registered at the Public Registry, preventing the seller from offering the property to anyone else prior to closing the deal.

Your lawyer should handle the title search at the Public Registry and also ensure that the property has no liens or other encumbrances that would affect the transfer of the title. His or her search should also include a review of the survey maps registered with the Land Registry office (Catastro). It is advisable to carry out a professional survey on the property (especially if the house is not built yet) to verify map coordinates and land boundaries and thus avoid any future conflict. Your lawyers should also check that there are no outstanding debts to utility companies.

Once you're satisfied with your due diligence, the buyer and seller sign a formal Buy-Sell Contract (Contrato de Compraventa). This agreement protects both the buyer and seller from the other party reneging on the contract, with penalties stipulated by law. The use of an escrow service is advisable at this point to protect you and your funds and ensure smooth transfer of title. The deal is considered closed once the title is officially transferred to the buyer and this has been registered with the Public Registry.

In the case that the property is owned by a corporation, it is possible for the buyer to simply purchase the shares of the corporation, and consequently, the ownership of the property, removing the need to transfer the title. An escrow service is also recommended in this instance; alternatively, a Promissory Note can be issued from the buyer's bank in Panama, which ensures full payment will be made to the seller once the change of ownership is registered with the Public Registry.

Rights of Possession (ROP)

First and foremost, rights of possession land should be purchased with caution, and significant research on the property should be carried out. Many people have compared the rights of possession law to "squatter's rights" in other parts of the world, although it is not exactly the same. When untitled, public land is "occupied" by a Panamanian person or company for a lengthy period of time, rights of possession can be granted through a simple document issued by the local municipality or another government agency such as the Agricultural Reform Department. No property taxes can be levied on these properties, since the dweller does not own the land. However, structures on the land may incur property taxes.

There is a lot of ROP property throughout rural Panama, particularly along the coastlines. It is possible to purchase this land, and then obtain a title from the government, although it is usually not a simple process. In fact, a government campaign has been running for several years now, aiming to title much of the untitled land around the country. Not all land is eligible for

If you work in Clayton's City of Knowledge, you are eligible for housing there.

title, particularly islands and some coastlines; however, these cases may apply for concessions. At the time of writing, the law concerning obtaining a title for ROP land was changing frequently. As of April 2009, people possessing ROP land and worrying they would never have a title are finally be able to obtain one for an affordable price and without red tape. This law establishes the costs in hectares: Those titling up to 20 hectares would pay US$50, from 20 to 50 hectares would pay US$100, and for larger parcels of more than 50 hectares would pay US$150.

Concessions

Certain pieces of land are protected from ownership and development by the government. These are usually islands, coastal areas, and national parks. In special circumstances, usually for purposes of tourism, the government will issue a concession allowing a private entity to use the land for a specific purpose. The tourism developments on Amador Causeway of Panama City are a good example. While hotels and apartments have been constructed there, nothing can be sold. Instead, units there are offered on a renewable 40-year lease.

PURCHASING A HOME OR APARTMENT

For those wishing to live in Panama City, an apartment is usually the logical option, especially if you will be living here part-time. Living in an apartment or condominium (here the two words are synonymous) is much simpler than a home, because you don't have to maintain a yard and security is less of a worry. Nevertheless, the purchase process for an apartment is very similar to that of a home, except with a previously owned house, a title investigation (to check for liens and other tax burdens or outstanding payments) is recommended.

In the search for a new home in Panama, one of the first things you should know is that real estate brokers work differently than in the United States. There is no Multiple Listing Service (MLS) and no listing exclusivity, meaning the same property can be sold by every broker in town, possibly at different prices. Make sure to negotiate the purchase price with the broker and get the best deal possible. When it comes to a preconstruction or newly constructed unit, these can be purchased in three different ways. You can purchase directly from the developer with no broker, or you can purchase from the developer via a broker. This should not affect the sale price to you, but the developer will have to pay the broker's commission, usually 5 percent. The other alternative is to purchase the unit from someone who already bought it from the developer and now wants to resell the property. From 2005 to 2007, many speculators purchased preconstruction apartments in Panama City and the newly developed coastal properties with the goal of "flipping" them before they were completed and making a sizeable profit. Speculators purchase with an initial payment of only 10 percent of the sale price. The developer price increases as the project nears completion, so the investor should be able to sell the unit to another buyer beneath the current developer price but above the initial purchase price.

At the beginning of the boom in 2005, speculators managed to flip the units successfully, making fast, healthy profits. However, as seemingly endless preconstruction projects were announced, combined with the global economic downturn of 2008–2009, supply began to outweigh demand, and many speculators found themselves with units they were unable to resell.

Payment for preconstruction units is made in three installments of 10 percent each. The first 30 percent must be paid by the time the building is completed. Then, the remaining 70 percent must be paid in full. At this point, if you are not paying for the unit in cash, you need to have an approved mortgage from a local bank. The bank will provide the developer with an Irrevocable Letter of Payment (Carta de Promesa de Pago) and at this point the title can be transferred to the buyer's name. The problem some speculators have experienced is that they have not been able to sell the units and have been unable to secure financing on the unit once it has been completed, resulting in a certain number of "distressed" units on the market that must be sold below market value. If you are not in the market to speculate, it is a good idea to meet with a mortgage specialist at the bank before purchasing a preconstruction unit and make sure you will be eligible for a loan.

Purchasing such a property can be your ticket to a great deal, but you need to be sure that the property is going to be built and in a reasonable time frame. That said, nearly all properties here incur some kind of delay in the construction process, and you should be prepared for this, but there is a limit to what is acceptable. Six months to a year delay seems to be the norm, and anything over that is cause for complaint, although complaining probably won't do you much good. Check your purchase contracts for this, because there is rarely a clause

There are plenty of options for those who want to live in luxury high-rises along the water.

to protect the buyer in case of a delay; more often, there is a clause that allows the developer to increase the sale price by up to 5 percent upon completion to compensate for price increases in materials. Even if there has been no price increase, you can almost guarantee you will have to pay this extra 5 percent. Even if the price of materials doesn't increase, the developer will use the 5 percent clause to his benefit and con you out of the extra cash, saying a cost has gone up. Essentially the buyer is completely unprotected in this event. My advice is to plan on this 5 percent cost on pre-construction from the beginning, and discuss it with your lawyer and the developer to see how the contract is written.

You will want to be pre-approved for a mortgage in Panama prior to making a bid on a home. The bank bureaucracy can take up to a week or two after you fill out the application. You will be asked about your monthly income and credit history. Once you are approved for the mortgage, expect the bank to take up to four weeks to return a response to you, in the form of the bank deeds (*escritura*) and mortgage agreements. Find a good contact at your bank, a reliable bank official who will return your phone calls and emails, and keep you updated on a regular basis as to when the official papers will be ready.

REAL ESTATE BROKERS

Real estate brokers in Panama must be licensed by the Board of Realtors (ACOBIR). In order to become licensed they must take an examination including all the laws and regulations pertaining to the real estate industry. They must also pay annual dues to ACOBIR. Before purchasing any property in Panama, you should ask to see your broker's license. Real estate brokers in Panama must be Panamanian citizens, although real estate developers can be foreigners. Oftentimes, you will find foreigners selling real estate in Panama. They get around the law by having at least one licensed broker working with them in their office, who will be the official broker of the deal. When shopping for your new home, be sure to visit several real estate offices and find a broker you feel comfortable with, one who speaks English and has experience helping foreign buyers. A good real estate broker will be happy to help you with other aspects of your move to Panama, including establishing a corporation, opening a bank account, and setting up household utilities.

CONTRACTS

Purchase contracts, as well as all other contracts, must be in writing and in Spanish. Unless you are fluent in Spanish, you should request a translation of the contract, which should be provided by a Certified Public Translator. Make sure that everything you have negotiated with the seller, from price to appliances and social area amenities, is included in the written contract. Make sure your lawyer reads through the contract before you sign it. The Ministry of Housing (MIVI) keeps a record of all residential buildings, including the floor plans and the incorporation documents of the condominium. Your lawyer should get a copy of these plans for you, and you should both read them carefully to make sure there are no loopholes that would favor the developer. Spend some time to make sure you are satisfied with the contract before signing it—this step could save you a lot of grief in the future.

PURCHASE FEES AND TAXES

When a real estate transaction is completed and the title deed is transferred, the seller must pay a real estate transfer tax. The buyer does not have to pay any tax. The tax is set at 2 percent of either the current registered property value or the sales price, whichever is higher. The current registered property value is calculated from the original purchase price (or the value submitted to the Public Registry) plus 5 percent for each year of ownership. Real estate transfer tax can be deducted against any income tax due for capital gains on the sale of the property. If the property is owned by a Panamanian corporation, this tax does not need to be paid, as it is the shares of the corporation that are transferred, not the title deed of the property.

Property Tax Exemptions

In an effort to promote investments in Panamanian real estate, the government introduced a law in 1990, exempting all newly constructed properties in Panama from property taxes for 20 years. The law, which has expired several times, has been consistently renewed. The most recent renewal extended the exemption to buildings completed, and their occupancy permits issued, on or before December 31, 2009. The exemption is transferable, so if, in 2009, you purchase an apartment that was built in 2000, there are still 11 years of tax exemption remaining on the unit. The real estate boom in Panama was largely fueled by this law, since the law extends to both builders and end users.

RESTORATION

While some investors have chosen to purchase old apartments in the downtown areas and refurbish them, the most popular area for investors looking for rehab opportunities is the Casco Viejo or Casco Antiguo part of the city. Declared a UNESCO World Heritage site in 1998 because of its unique architecture and rich colonial history, the Casco Antiguo is often compared to the old towns of San Juan; Puerto Rico; Cartagena, Colombia; and Havana, Cuba. It was the foundation of Panama City after Panama Viejo was ransacked by pirates, and then, circa 1930, the city center moved to the current

© SKY GILBAR

Many people buy older homes and restore them.

downtown area. At this point, many of the buildings fell into disrepair, even more so after the invasion of the United States, Operation Just Cause, in 1989. The area became extremely neglected. Investors in the area are attracted by the opportunities to turn old, ruined buildings back into glorious residential and commercial spaces. Such opportunities can also present high returns on investments.

Law 9 of 1997 was designed to encourage investment in the area by offering fiscal benefits and also restoration guidelines to streamline the rehabilitation of the area. Monetary incentives include exemption from transfer tax on the sale of properties in the area, preferential mort-

© SKY GILBAR

Casco Viejo is a UNESCO World Heritage Site and the facades must be kept intact when restoring any buildings.

gage rates from banks, no real estate tax for 20 years on restored properties, and no income tax on profits generated from businesses operating in restored buildings in Casco Antiguo for 10 years after restoration. One condition for renovating in the Casco is that restoration activities must begin within a year of the purchase date. The government has had problems enforcing this ruling; as an unfortunate result, buildings purchased many years ago remain untouched and dilapidated.

BUILDING

Whether your goal is to build a new home from scratch or renovate an older building, there are several things you need to do before you start. Before you purchase the land or the old building, you need to seek an appraisal from a professional surveyor to make sure it is a feasible project. A licensed surveyor or topographer will physically verify the map points on the land or property to avoid any future conflicts over boundaries. It is a good idea to clearly mark and fence your property to clearly demarcate the boundaries.

You should also evaluate the cost of building a home versus the cost of purchasing an existing one, or even purchasing a prefabricated home from the United States and shipping it to Panama to be assembled. In order to calculate building costs, you should hire an architect or engineer, discuss your plans, and they will provide you with a quotation that is hopefully within your budget.

Once you decide to go ahead with the project, your main point of contact for the project should be the architect or engineer you hired. If you are not in the country, ask for regular updates on the status of the construction. You should also ask someone reliable to go to the site periodically to check that the status updates are true. You should be prepared for the construction to take longer than originally planned, and it is in your best interests to supervise the construction as often as possible to ensure it is to your liking.

Materials

One of the first things you will notice about construction in Panama is that the materials used are different than what you are used to at home. The majority of homes are built with cinder blocks and then covered with gypsum. Wood is used on the Caribbean coast of the country but is rarely found on the Pacific. Tall buildings are made from steel rebar and cement. Despite the lack of earthquakes in the capital city, all skyscrapers constructed in Panama must be built with seismic activity in mind, although some people question whether developers actually take such regulations into consideration.

Construction materials are available throughout the country, with large hardware stores in Panama City, Coronado, David, and Colón. Those accustomed to constructing in their home countries will find the variety of materials available here more limited than at home, but all the basics are here. The same applies to construction techniques: Workers here are trained in and proficient at the techniques used most frequently. If you are "thinking outside the box" when it comes to the design of your home, you may struggle to find workers able to convert your dream into a reality.

Going Green

A wise piece of advice when building or renovating is to consider green materials and techniques. You can expect the sun to shine every day for 4–8 hours in Panama. Why not consider using solar panels and large open ceilings and windows, building in a breathable garden or greenhouse balcony? Consider designing open rooms to let the cross-breeze come through, building a skylight (solar paneled of course), and creating a garden to lighten up the thick, humid air.

Why not also consider using new and updated practices to alleviate the stress on your home and on the personal environment? Jaime Carlson, a three-year resident of Panama and a Green Management professional suggests installing solar panel windows, and using salvaged wood (either scraps or from old canal zone homes), which is easy to find in Panama. You can also use Forest Stewardship Council (FSC) certified wood. The FSC is a nonprofit organization that certifies that the wood comes from responsible forest management practices. Because of the heat and sun effects in Panama, Carlson also suggests using a passive energy design. This design encourages installing west- or north-facing windows to minimize the direct sun and heat in your home. Landscaping also maximizes energy use. According to Carlson, environmental-friendly landscaping "includes using trees to mitigate the fluctuations in climate; for example, planting trees near very sunny windows to decrease heat in the house." In addition, you can use low-flush toilets, save your organic garbage for compost, and create a local produce garden. It is quite easy to set up a greenhouse balcony and to lighten up a dull city terrace. In Panama, tomatoes, papayas, pineapples, oranges, lemons, and herbs such as lemongrass, basil, and mint grow like wildflowers if you find the right combination of light and temperature. You will be surprised how much you will save on your living expenses in the long run, and how much more satisfied you will feel once you are living in an appropriately designed residence, to mesh with your natural environment.

Green roofs are also an ideal system in Panama's humid and tropical environment. These roofs are partially or totally covered by soil and vegetation. Also called "living roofs," green roofs have several benefits, such as absorbing rainwater, creating insulation, and lowering urban temperatures. They also create a habitat for wildlife. The use of green roofs has been said to combat the heat island affect, which is when metropolitan areas suffer much hotter temperatures than their neighboring rural ones. Going green in Panama is so easy, since most of the resources are grown in your backyard (quite literally).

Contractors and Labor

As in most parts of the world, Panama has its fair share of "construction cowboys"; you should ask around for recommendations before signing a construction contract. Take the time to find someone who has experience working with foreigners and who has previously built homes you like. Many people who have built homes in Panama will warn against it, saying things like "it was the worst experience of our life," or "we went through five contractors before we got the job done properly." Usually, such people are prime examples of cost-cutting. There is a frequently heard expression in Panama: *lo barato sale caro,* which means "cheap things turn out to be more expensive," and it is usually true. Don't go with the less-experienced builder just to save a few thousand dollars. In the long term, the cheaper contractor will probably increase his price, or his work will be shoddy and you will have to find a new one. That's not to say always go with the most expensive quote, but shop around, and try not to scrimp too much. According to Dirk Schwalb of Constructive Solutions, raw construction costs were around $550–650 per square meter in early 2009. You need to add on another $150–250 per square meter for interior finishings (tiles, appliances, bathroom fixtures, etc). He says prices are similar throughout Panama City, Casco Viejo, and the interior provinces where beach home developments are rising; what you save in manpower costs outside of the city, you have to add back in transport. In the case of a remodel, part of these costs would go toward demolition, but you may save money because the exterior walls are already in place.

The contractor will be responsible for every aspect of the construction process, including finding appropriate plumbers, electricians, and carpenters. Your initial contract with him will be based on a certain budget. Therefore, all of the subcontractors he hires should plan to work within the parameters of this budget, and you will only ever have to deal with the contractor, making the process a lot easier for you. If you were to arrange to build a house on your own, you would have to deal with and schedule all the workers individually, which would be extremely challenging. Construction workers here are governed by a very specific set of labor laws, and working with them can be complex if you are not up-to-date with Panamanian labor law. If you decide to build this way, you should consult with an experienced labor attorney before hiring anyone.

Moving In

Once you have purchased or rented your property, you will need to start furnishing and decorating. In recent years, the variety and price range of home furnishings on offer in Panama has increased dramatically, and now it is quite easy to find furniture and appliances that suit nearly all tastes and budgets.

"WHITE LINE" APPLIANCES

Anyone looking through the rental classifieds for the first time will undoubtedly ask, "What is *linea blanca?*" *Linea blanca* (white line) is the collective name for the following household appliances: oven, refrigerator, washing machine, and clothes dryer. Often, this will be included with a rental apartment, even an unfurnished one. If you need to purchase these appliances, you will find most of the same brands you see at home are here and at similar prices.

INTERIOR DESIGN

Interior decorating options, such as home furnishings, plumbing, lighting, audio equipment, paint, and outdoor patio furniture are plentiful, particularly in Panama City where you will find countless stores offering home furnishings and interiors. While the more expensive stores are the most prominent, there is something for everyone, although budget-conscious shoppers will have to look harder to find something to suit their taste.

Depending on the item purchased, most stores offer free delivery to your home and installation, if applicable. When an item is delivered to your home, be sure you check it thoroughly before signing for it to ensure no damage has occurred in transit. It will be difficult to return it later.

Do-It-Yourself

The two main hardware stores, Do It Center and Novey, have many branches all over Panama City and a few throughout the country, where they sell everything from blinds to tiles, ovens to air conditioners, hardware materials to cleaning supplies and everything else you will need to make your house a home. Items in these stores are reasonably priced, and there is a great selection.

Interior Designers

Those who prefer to have everything done for them by experts rather than getting their hands dirty will find several great interior designers in Panama. Reputable English-speaking designers are listed in the *Resources* chapter. While labor in Panama is cheap, be prepared to pay good money for services like this, as these are specialist skills not widely found in Panama. Nevertheless, you will definitely get more bang for your buck in Panama.

In 2007 and 2008, a unique event called Casa Cor was held in Panama, showcasing the best designers in the country and the products available. The next one is planned for 2010 and will be held in Mansión Danté (Calle 50). The event is usually held in June. For more information, visit www.casacor-panama.com.

Household Expenses

Promotional materials about Panama usually tout the decreased cost of living in Panama as one of the advantages of living here. Household expenses vary wildly according to the lifestyle you lead, but generally speaking, household expenses are not significantly cheaper here than they were back home. In some cases, like electric costs, they may be more expensive than you had expected.

RENT AND MORTGAGE

Rental prices have been somewhat inflated in recent years due to lack of inventory. Now, as more new apartment buildings are being completed, supply is catching up to demand, and rental prices are falling. While prices had increased to around $20 per square meter, they have returned to $10 per square meter. Several years ago, depending on the area, apartments were renting for as little as $5 per square meter in downtown Panama City. It remains to be seen if they will return to these prices.

A mortgage is usually issued for a term of 15–30 years. For foreign clients, banks will generally finance up to 70 percent of the value of the property, whereas Panamanian borrowers may finance up to 90 percent. Interest rates are approximately 6.5–8 percent, which can be adjusted by the bank; rarely are mortgage rates fixed. If you purchase more than one home in Panama, the second mortgage will be offered over a shorter term, usually 15 years.

UTILITIES

Household utilities in Panama include electricity, water, and gas. Most homes use all three services. If you are living in an apartment building, chances are the gas will be included in the maintenance fee or rental cost. This is because the gas comes into the building through one single pipeline that services all apartments and therefore cannot be metered. Electricity, on the other hand, is always contracted by the tenant, unless it is a short-term apartment, in which case the cost of electricity would be factored into the rental price.

Water

Rental prices will often include water, because it is very reasonably priced and it is easier for the landlord to put the utilities contract in his name than change the contract every time he has a new tenant. For those who own property, water is supplied via the public institution IDAAN (National Institute of Aqueducts and Drains). Once you have fulfilled all the requirements to

contract water with IDAAN, it will take up to four days to connect you to
the water supply.

Electricity

Panama is said to have one of the top three most expensive electricity rates
in the world. This has something to do with the long-standing monopoly of
services. Rates vary according to neighborhood. The nicer the neighborhood,
the more expensive the electricity, or *luz,* as it is known here. For example, in
San Francisco, electricity is charged at $0.181 per kWh. In a two-bedroom
apartment (110 square meters) with four air conditioners, electric washer and
dryer, refrigerator, and two televisions, the monthly consumption is around
1,345 kWh, at a monthly cost of around $245 including other fixed charges.
Air-conditioning is the culprit for high electricity bills, so if you don't mind
the heat, your bill will be lower. Electricity is supplied by two semi-private
companies, Union Fenosa and Elektra. The company you use depends on the
area you live in.

Gas

Mainline gas supplies into homes are not common, except in the case of apartments. Instead of having a gas line coming directly into the house, a large
gas tank is placed outside the house which connects to all the gas appliances
within the home, usually the oven and the water heater. The main supplier
of gas throughout the country is Tropigas, which will usually deliver the gas
to your home. Small gas tanks, such as for the outdoor grill, can be filled at
a Tropigas station. The other supplier is Panagas. Sometimes the regulator is
different, so you should check which one you are set up for.

Gas is cheaper than electricity in Panama, so any gas appliances are an
advantage. Gas water heaters should definitely be chosen over electric ones,
unless you need a large tank of hot water available all the time.

LANGUAGE AND EDUCATION

There is nothing like being able to understand the nuances of someone's humor, or why they are put off by what you have just said. Language is essential for getting to know the people in your new home. Furthermore, quotidian Panamanian Spanish is original in many ways, and you'll want to take lessons in traditional Castellan so you know the difference between Panamanian lexicon and other Spanish language norms. This chapter will explore some of the language expectations you should live up to once you move here.

Language in Panama has evolved throughout the last 100 years, responding to the founding of an independent nation, the influx of Caribbean migration, and the U.S.-constructed Canal. Each incoming community has created its own education systems. As international interest in Panama continues into the 21st century, and bilingual schools have become mainstream, including schools focusing on French, Italian, and Chinese education systems and

© SKY GILBAR

religious foundations such as Jewish schools featuring Hebrew language options or Greek Orthodox featuring Greek language.

With each passing year, the options for education in Panama are broadening; this is especially the case for privately funded schools. There are a few excellent public schools that accept students based on achievement, but most foreigners enroll their students in international schools or private Panamanian schools, which have excellent standing in the community. These schools are either in Panama City or David, the eastern and western capitals, respectively. One Panamanian mother who works as a nurse at the Hospital on Isla Colón, in Bocas del Toro, said she sends her young children away to live in David, where there are better options for education.

Learning the Language

I have only one thing to say when it comes to this topic: Learn the language! Not only is it a major part of who Panamanians are (they simply love to play with language and slang), but it shows respect to those hosting you. You will find that although Panama is a bilingual country, that doesn't necessarily mean that the majority speaks English, nor does it mean they appreciate having to speak your language. You may also find that not speaking Spanish will limit your social options, and keep you living in a bubble. In that case, you may as well just have stayed in your own country. There are many bilingual programs here and a few recommended schools, but the best way to learn a language is a total immersion program or hiring a one-on-one tutor. Practice speaking the language whenever you have the opportunity, and insist that your English-speaking Panamanian friends speak to you in Spanish.

SECOND LANGUAGES

Panama is a diverse country with a colorful history of immigration. Despite the United States's major presence during the Canal construction, this does not mean English is the only other language spoken here. The majority of Afro Latinos are the descendents of West Indian immigrants who settled and still reside throughout Colón and the islands of Bocas del Toro. They speak a mixed Creole and English as a first language, but they also speak Panamanian Spanish quite well. They can easily change back and forth depending on whom they are speaking to, but among themselves they speak Juari-Juari, pronounced wari-wari. If you listen closely you will hear Spanish words mixed in with English and then a Creole accent that throws you off completely.

PANAMENGLISH: THE NOTEWORTHY VOCABULARY OF PANAMANIAN SPANISH MIXED WITH ENGLISH

Panamanian Spanish or street talk is unique. It mixes its Spanish foundation with a Caribbean slang and then adds to it American English vocabulary that has somewhat trickled down from its gringo neighbors. There is no avoiding it, and vocabulary heard in supposedly "pure" Spanish conversations can be a surprising linguistic experience. Better to learn some of the phrases below – even then, only use them after you have heard and practiced the pronunciation.

Panamanian	Definition	English Origin
camarón	a man who does odd jobs	come around
chiliando	hanging out	chilling out
chotiar	to say hello	shot in the air for a high five
ese man/esa man	that man/that woman	man
fren'	friend	friend
guial	a girl	pronounced without the "r"
gruviar	to tease	to groove
manes	people	men
pai	a sweet girl	sweetie pie/apple pie
parquear	to hang out	parking
pinta	any beer, any size	a pint
pritty	beautiful	pretty
shortcuteando	to take a shortcut	short cut
wachiman	a security guard	watchman

There is a large Chinese population that speaks Mandarin or Cantonese. There are also a number of Panamanian nationals of European descent, such as German, French, Italian, and others, whose grandparents still speak their first languages. As Panamanian born nationals, they have had to assimilate by learning Spanish, but many have raised their descendents to be bilingual.

Due to the Canal construction and continued American presence, including the thousands of extra jobs it created, many non-English speakers benefited from the necessary acquisition of English as a second language. When the U.S. military and its Canal Administration began to wade out of the isthmus in the late 1990s, the need for the English language at many levels left with them. While high-society Panamanians continue to educate their children at the bilingual and international schools, there has also been a pull back to strong nationalism, which extends to a rejection of English, especially among the generation who were adolescents when the U.S. invasion on Panama occurred in 1989. The government didn't see it the same way, and in 2002 the national legislature proposed a law to make English the official second language, whereby all schools would be required to teach English. The motivation was clearly business-related, to promote bringing international call centers to the Panama job market. Panamanians were nonplussed, believing they should not need to learn English to be successful. Despite the resistance, in 2003 an act was passed legislating English must be taught in all of Panama's primary and secondary schools.

The influx of international businesses has opened up another great economic advantage for the country, and the need to speak English is a reality, regardless of the bitter sentiment it may create. Speaking English definitely gives a leg up on professional success here, but thanks to new Canal construction and investments, proficiency in German, Italian, French, Mandarin, and Japanese are nearly equally beneficial.

INDIGENOUS LANGUAGES

According to the International Work Group of Indigenous Affairs, in addition to Spanish and Creole, seven indigenous languages are spoken in Panama, stemming from two linguistic families, the Chibcha and the Chocó. An article in the Panamanian Constitution "guarantees the protection and popularization of aboriginal languages."

While it is reported that one in five indigenous persons does not speak Spanish, some, especially migratory workers, do speak the national tongue, and 15 percent don't speak their indigenous languages at all.

The Kuna Indians have been working with the Spanish Embassy to create an official dictionary of their language, as well as assimilate Spanish into their schools on the archipelago. The Kuna are also reported to have the highest percentage of monolingual Spanish speakers, with 29 percent who don't speak any dialect from their native tribes.

TOTAL IMMERSION LANGUAGE SCHOOLS

It can be difficult to learn to speak fluent Spanish in Panama if you are only here for a seasonal residency, but seeking out the opportunity will add so much pleasure to your Panama experience. In this section we'll discuss a few of the best-known language schools and the benefits of one-on-one tutoring.

Berlitz Language Schools

Berlitz language schools are an international language agency with 500 locations in 70 countries worldwide. Its experience in over 100 years of linguistic education is mostly geared toward businesses and individuals needing immediate language acquisition. It also offers language courses for children, teens, and families. They are located in Marbella, on Calle 47 in Panama City. Prices vary according to the program and how many lessons you will take; don't expect this to be one of the cheaper options, due to Berlitz's brand identity.

Spanish Panama

In the heart of Panama City, in the well-populated neighborhood of El Cangrejo, lies a small, friendly, trustworthy Spanish language school, offering a down-to-earth experience for those wishing to learn Spanish. Spanish Panama (www.spanishpanama.com) has been around since 2000 and is celebrated by its clientele for its flexibility in designing courses that fit your learning style or lifestyle needs. The teachers are native Spanish-speaking professionals who specialize in one-to-one classes or small groups, but both offer total immersion experience. The director is a Canadian-born national who understands that expats need to immerse both culturally and socially. He has established a network of resources for his clients who might be moving to Panama, including real estate contacts and travel information around Panama. The school also hosts social outings to great city restaurants, salsa classes, and other leisure activities. The program offers homestay options and customized experiences catering to your exact Spanish-language needs. Spanish Panama is a wonderful meeting center for expats or transit students.

Habla Ya Panama

If you are moving to Panama's western towns in Chiriquí, you might want to consider a relatively new but raved about school called Habla Ya Panama (www.hablayapanama.com). The co-owners and directors are two young, innovative Panamanian guys who started the travel, language, and cultural center in the popular expat town of Boquete. Only a few years old, the school has acquired a hip crowd of clientele, who consider the classes and activities professionally handled, affordable, and fun. According to co-founder Carlos Rojas, Habla Ya Panama has established a large list of tour and travel contacts, including adventure trips in and around the provinces. The owners pride themselves on their hands-on teaching methodology, giving their clientele a total immersion experience, including travel and adventure with either private lessons or group lessons of up to four students. The courses are diverse and highly specialized, with courses designed for medical Spanish, children, DELE exam prep (a Spanish proficiency exam for higher education), and part-time courses for new residents.

Habla Ya has reached out to the community, by offering volunteer programs for students interested in working with and acclimating to the communities in and around Boquete. The Habla Ya school can also help you find housing on a weekly or monthly basis or can put you with a host family during your stay if you are serious about total immersion. There has been talk of adding a Panama City school, but at the time of writing this book it is not yet in the works.

Bocas del Toro Spanish Programs

Spanish by the Sea, located in Bocas del Toro on Isla Colón, was one of Panama's first tourist-oriented Spanish programs. Its founder, Ines, was a volunteer from Holland who came to Costa Rica, fell in love, and set up her first school over the border in Bocas. The school's program focuses on learning a second language while enjoying surfing, diving, sailing, and other outdoor fun. Since then, she has opened a Spanish by the River in Costa Rica and another school in Boquete, Panama—both focusing on river fun, white-water rafting, and horseback riding. The school now has 15 years of experience and is family run. They also arrange housing, including private cabanas or homestays with local residents. Volunteering, excursions, and cooking classes are available for interested students.

While the coursework and accommodations are comparable to other language schools, the location of Bocas del Toro Spanish by the Sea is a weak point—Bocas is probably the one place you can get along the entire day speaking only English. However, this school is a good option for those who want to be near the beach, with something constructive to do.

PRIVATE TUTORS

Getting a private tutor is a good idea when your Panama schedule is sporadic or limited. Many teachers from the school system enjoy supplementing their salaries with *clases particulares* (private classes). If you are moving to Panama with children and they need to learn Spanish or acclimate to the Panamanian school system, whether private or public, a private tutor outside a classroom environment can be helpful. Adjusting to a new school is hard enough without having to learn a second language! Ask about Spanish tutors through the schools, or check the classifieds in local newspapers.

Education

The quality of the education system varies in Panama, with more and more private schools opening throughout Panama City and David. There are at least four or five all-English-speaking private schools, with about a dozen more bilingual schools where subjects are taught in both Spanish and English (and in some cases a third language). The expat population includes many professors who come to Panama specifically to teach the cultures and languages of their home countries in the private-school atmosphere.

Because of an influx of international professionals with higher education and bilingual abilities, the desire to move on to higher education is also growing. Panama is at a pivotal point for improvements in its education system. New industries are laying ground here, such as telecommunications and regional advertising companies; opportunities for management-level positions are rolling in with them. This clearly affects both private and public education, as demand rises for post-graduate studies in these areas. Following the creation of the City of Knowledge—Panama's version of a "Socratic Square" campus dedicated to housing national and international organizations and their employees who work in the areas of research, technology, academia, and human aid programs—many overseas universities have started small local programs in Panama City, with credit course offerings.

COLLEGES AND UNIVERSITIES

The national university, Universidad de Panama, has free tuition. The majority of its graduates hold degrees in business and administration; however, in the last decade many students have begun to obtain degrees in creative fields like graphic design or video production. More and more young people study these careers due to international companies increasingly using Panama as an exotic and affordable home base, providing more opportunities in these fields. As with all public universities, the quality and quantity of educational options and course offerings at the national university can be affected by politics and shrinking government budgets.

Private universities can be expensive by Latin American standards. The most expensive tuition and enrollment costs range US$7,500–10,000 at universities such as ULATINA (Universidad Latina de Panama), USMA (Santa Maria La Antigua Catholic University), University of Louisville, and Florida State University Panama City Branch (FSU). Ganexa University, the only all-arts university, is an option for *artes plasticas* (fine arts). University of Louisville and FSU are among the first American-accredited universities to have programs in

Panama City, accepting international students and teaching bilingual classes toward associate, baccalaureate, and masters degrees. It is possible to audit classes in many of these universities where space is available.

If continuing education is something you are interested in, another option is distance learning or online courses. Internet connections are reliable and flights are accessible for when you need to make an appearance at the institution.

INTERNATIONAL SCHOOLS

Panama offers excellent college preparatory schools for students interested in studying outside of Panama at the university level. The two most popular and competitive schools among expat families with school-aged children are the International School of Panama, which offers the International Baccalaureate (IB) program, and Balboa Academy, which offers the AP (Advanced Placement) program; the curriculum is geared toward college readiness from preschool onward. Both schools teach students from pre-Kindergarten to grade 12 and are accredited by SACS (Southern Association of Colleges and Schools), a U.S. educational organization that ensures schools in Latin America conform to academic standards in 11 southern U.S. states.

Magen David Academy and Crossroads Christian Academy are also considered international schools, both of which are religiously oriented. The Lyceé François School is another option for parents who seek a European-accredited education, specifically aligned with the French Ministry of Education, offering the IB program and teaching English and Spanish as second languages. The international schools must have a certain percentage of international educators to maintain international accreditation, either in SACS or aligned with their

---

STUDYING ABROAD IN PANAMA

From a cross-cultural perspective, Panama offers a world of knowledge to a student studying abroad. Not only are you exposed to the Spanish language, but also to a rich account of American history and global economics and hands-on training in careers such as engineering and science. Panama-based universities such as Florida State University, Panama Canal branch, and University of Louisville all offer study abroad programs. Furthermore, some North American universities have established a relationship with the Smithsonian Institute of Tropical Research to host undergraduate and research graduates, which is an elite opportunity for those interested in biodiversity. High school groups travel throughout the country for summer programs, volunteering in the interior, learning about the indigenous people, and experiencing the glory and hardships of a tropical lifestyle firsthand.

© MIRIAM BUTTERMAN

Panama City and David offer the best options for education.

home country's national education standards, thus exposing students to a culturally diverse faculty.

On Bocas del Toro's Isla Colón there are one or two small private schools where international children are a majority. However, even those schools are not fully supported by foreigners with high educational standards. The pre-Kindergarten and early education classes are good enough, but many island expats move to bigger cities for secondary schools or home-school their children.

One important tip on choosing a school is to review the academic calendars and consider which works best with your lifestyle. Panamanian schools follow the southern hemisphere academic year, starting in March and graduating students in December. The international and SACS-accredited schools follow North American calendars, starting in August and ending in July, and incorporate both Panamanian and other international holidays throughout the year, as well as a long 5–6 week holiday over Christmas and New Years. The French school follows the academic calendar of France's national schools, a trimester program.

BILINGUAL SCHOOLS

Many bilingual schools, accredited by Panama's Ministry of Education, have good reputations among the Panamanian community. These schools, although supporting a mostly Spanish-speaking community, have strong English programs. St. Mary's, Academia Interamericana, Colegio Issac Rabin, and the Oxford International School have affordable tuition and Panamanian teaching staff who have credentials to teach in English as well.

The options for all-around culturally inclusive education are excellent in Panama. If you are an expat who has school-aged children or is planning to enroll in a continuing education program for yourself, the only complaint you may have is the ridiculous number of national holidays during the academic school year.

HEALTH

Panama is a developing country and full of modern amenities, but the climate and the general environment, even the urban ones, are undoubtedly different from your home country. Health issues are no exception: Expect your bug bites to swell more, expect to have more reactions to food, and expect to get more colds and flu viruses during the rainy season. I know many people who were diagnosed with allergies for the first time in Panama, because dust and mites are more common due to wind, rain, and the humid weather. The humorous diagnosis is, "You are allergic to Panama." Staying healthy is a matter of good habits: cleaning out your air-conditioning systems frequently (or learning to depend less on them), eating healthy fruits and vegetables, and using the natural products such as aloe, papaya, avocado, or coconut oil, which are so accessible to you in a land so rich in plantlife. Luckily, there are many alternatives from which to choose in private and public healthcare and affordable medications. The doctors are well trained, and many study abroad in Europe or North America. Health insurance is also extremely affordable,

and you will be pleased with the services provided once you find an agency you are comfortable with. Many procedures are even cheaper and more commonly performed here, for example plastic surgery or corrective eye surgery. And if you are really particular about your healthcare, a flight to Miami or Bogotá, Colombia, to receive care there is a simple solution.

Panama has been one of the safest countries in Latin American since the 1990s, after Noriega was ousted and Panamanians started to trust their government again. There are precautions to take, like in any big city, but you will greatly enjoy the freedom of wandering on warm nights and effortless, friendly smiles from the public.

Hospitals and Clinics

Fortunately, private hospitals and clinics in Panama offer excellent care and experienced doctors who have studied internationally and therefore are multilingual. Best of all, the prices are cheaper than in most foreign countries, so you need not fly home if an important procedure needs to be done—save the trip and a few bucks besides. Public healthcare works well enough for Panamanians; as a foreigner, you are not entitled to socialized medicine unless you have been on a local *planilla* (payroll) for several years, and even then you must endure long lines at the public hospitals and waiting lists for surgical procedures. Because private care is so relatively inexpensive, you are well advised to stick to private hospitals and clinics, which tend to have more cutting-edge procedures and research practices.

Because prices for most procedures are less than half what they would cost in the United States, and because Panama's location is convenient for many along the American continents, medical tourism has become a big industry, mostly centralized in Panama City. Plastic surgery procedures such as face or neck lifts, rhinoplasty, and liposuction run US$1,700–2,500 here; in the United States they can cost four times more. Further, plastic surgery has been practiced for a very long time down here (we are in the land of beauty pageant mania) and is a common choice for many in the Latin culture. So you can be sure experienced technicians and doctors are available. MRIs in Panama run just US$550–900, again a fraction of what you'd pay in the United States or Europe. Many doctors have privileges at more than one hospital or can recommend other doctors, which allows you to choose the most convenient location and the most comfortable healthcare facility for you and your loved ones.

Panama's best-known hospitals are located in the capital city. The Punta

© SKY GILBAR

With new facilities like the Johns Hopkins Hospital, medical attention is first-class.

Paitilla Hospital, San Fernando Hospital, and the Hospital Nacional are acclaimed, respectable, and central to three major areas of Panama City. Each of these hospitals also has a large community of *consultorias* (doctor's offices), where you can see doctors in their private practices and still be close to the hospital in case any important tests are needed on the spot.

By far one of the most impressive additions to Panama's medical offerings was the Punta Pacifica Hospital in 2006, a Johns Hopkins International affiliate, rich in progressive medical practices, high-end technology, and an internationally trained staff. Relative to the other hospitals it is the "upper class hospital," catering mostly to foreigners and wealthy Panamanians. However, many of the services, such as maternity stays, cost the same as other local hospitals. The excitement over this new hospital is that it has brought state-of-the-art medicine to Latin America, which means not having to fly to Miami (the usual destination for Central and South Americans wanting more progressive care). It also offers incredible solutions to Panamanians in need of certain types of medical attention, such as reconstructive tissue surgery, that were simply not available in Panama's other facilities.

Serving the other side of the country is Hospital Chiriquí, Mae Lewis Hospital, Hospital Cooperativo, and Hospital Cataan. The largest of the four is Hospital Chiriquí, which finished construction of a new addition in 2005 and increased its staff size from 60 doctors to 100. David and the surrounding Boquete and Volcán Barú communities draw thousands of expats, so it is in the doctors' best interest to study English and train outside of Panama. Despite the facilities available locally, many expats still head to Panama City to seek medical treatment, mostly an issue of health insurance coverage (for those who keep international plans with companies originating outside of Panama) or wanting to be close to the hub of medical treatment.

Health Insurance

LOCAL PLANS AND SOCIAL SECURITY

Once you commit to receiving the majority of your healthcare in Latin America, you can choose from several domestic health plans. It is not common for a Panamanian company to provide its workers with health insurance; Social Security is really the only option for employer-sponsored health benefits and it isn't a great option. Instead, you should look for insurance that offers decent and responsible coverage on catastrophic illnesses or accidents. Fortunately, an outpatient doctor's office visit is quite reasonable, and unless you have a chronic medical condition, it's easier to pay for these visits out-of-pocket.

Local plans are affordable. The costs will seem phenomenally low; if you are in good health, a monthly fee of perhaps US$45–60 to insure yourself against a major accident or illness will seem like you are finally getting a good deal on healthcare. But dreamers, beware! Take time to review and re-review the plan, which usually includes inconvenient clauses like a pre-approved out-of-network doctor fee, or a policy year that begins midway thought the calendar year, making it difficult to ever meet your annual deductible. The biggest disappointment is often that coverage is very conservative. Preventative medicine is, for instance, not covered. Dental insurance is very rare. Mental health insurance is also a rarity, or only covered minimally or after several years of membership. In-network providers are quite limited as well. My best advice is once you've found a general practitioner you like, ask what insurance company he or she contracts with and buy your policy there.

Customer service from health insurance companies can be very disappointing. Sometimes the best plans are the low-cost, simple ones, because they own their own clinic of recommended doctors and the client service is much more efficient than some larger regional facilities. It is rare for larger companies to cover your costs up front, and therefore you must pay the bill, deliver the form to your provider, and await the check. Most companies will tell you it takes only 15 business days to process your claim and issue the check, but it always takes longer. In following up, the customer service agents can be frustrating to speak with as they learn to respond to your needs. The best way to manage these problems is to work with an insurance broker. They have a vested interest in staying on your side and make sure that you are satisfied.

Some of the larger healthcare companies are ASSA, Pan-American Life, British American, and HSBC Seguros, which used to be called CONASE. All of these companies are located in the banking district just off Avenida Balboa. They are all so complicated when it comes to procedures and paperwork—another reason to consider an insurance broker to make the communication process more tolerable for you.

MediSalud (www.medisalud.com.pa) is one of the smaller healthcare coverage services. It has two clinics in Panama City, one in La Cresta with 24-hour emergency service and another in El Dorado, which is more for outpatient appointments. Your co-pay is always US$5, with a monthly fee of US$30–45. MediSalud clinics are clean, the service is attentive, and emergencies and major injury and illness are covered, with more services, such as maternity and oral surgery also covered once you have owned the policy for some time. It also provides emergency numbers to call if you are traveling outside of Panama and need assistance. The customer service is some of the best I have personally experienced in the healthcare industry in Panama.

INTERNATIONAL INSURANCE PLANS

Most foreigners who move to Panama with an established income and a second home in their native country will stick to their international insurance plans, which is the most practical idea. There are two kinds of international plans: One covers you in Panama for basic healthcare and emergency services but will also cover you for emergency services while outside of Panama. The other kind of international plan is more expensive, with the option to have a major surgery or health procedure in your home country, depending on your deductible. Both plans offer a network of providers established in your home country but depend on the insurance company as to whether the network expands beyond Panama or is limited to only one region or country. The cost for international insurance plans from locally based international companies is higher than the average plan, up to several thousand dollars a year, with or without a deductible.

Pharmacies and Prescriptions

Many medications that are only distributed with a prescription in the United States or Europe can be purchased here without a *receta* (prescription), including a variety of birth control pills, anti-anxiety or antidepressant medications, and mild antibiotics. However, pharmacies simply run out of some medications, which tend to lack reliable distribution. These things really disturb

Natural sources of vitamin C are plentiful in Panama.

foreigners used to total efficiency in medicine and should be a consideration if you rely on meds taken daily—perhaps get into the habit of buying two packs at a time when available. Medications, too, cost a fraction of what you might spend in the United States or abroad. If you want them to be covered by insurance you will have to get a doctor's prescription, whether they are normally sold over the counter or not. Doctors visits and medication are tax deductible in Panama.

ALTERNATIVE HEALTH

Because of the large Chinese population in Panama and incredible access to nature's ingredients, a strong Eastern medicine practice exists in Panama. Many doctors who generally practice Western medicine tend to support these options if it gives you peace of mind. Many people in Panama are believers in alternative health and homeopathic options; acupuncture, iridology, naturopathic doctors, and herbal apothecaries are only some of the branches of alternative medicine you may want to seek out in Panama. Sometimes it's easy to fall into the misconception that a developing country is less sophisticated about medicine and healthcare, but in reality the plethora of vegetation and unique plantlife offers nature's pharmacy right in your backyard. Scientists can tell you that the cures for many diseases that stumped Western doctors have been here for years.

DAILY LIFE

NONI: THE MIRACLE FRUIT

Living in the jungles is a natural supermarket of wondrous plants and fruits. One fruit, noni, has been used by indigenous cultures throughout Polynesia, Central America, China, and India for over 2,000 years for its natural health benefits. Noni was first discovered by Dr. Ralph Heinicke, who researched its effects for 45 years. It was presented to the commercial market in 1996.

Noni *(Morinda Citrifolia)* is not a medicine, but a natural plant. The essential curing agent found in many parts of the plant and fruit is called Proxeronine, which later forms into Xeronine when introduced in the body. Xeronine acts to repair damaged cells and can fortify general health, contributing to the improvement of health problems such as gastric ulcers, high blood pressure, depression, indigestion, skin abrasions, drug addiction, and arthritis, just to name a few. According to studies done at the University of Hawaii, noni may act as anti-cancerous agent. These same studies report that 90 percent of people who use noni daily have felt results within the first three days. Furthermore, noni can be used by pregnant women and children.

Brave naturalists have been sipping fermented noni juice, with its bitter flavor and offensive smell, for years to gain its positive benefits of general well being and anti-aging properties. However, for the past decade, botanists have been trying to make it easier to swallow, combining it with other natural juices, diluting the noni flavor but not reducing its effects. Panama is a central location for marketers and distributors, due to the prevalence of noni fruit throughout the country and access to shipping facilities from the Canal. You can find national noni products in supermarkets and pharmacies throughout Panama.

Melissa Arauz, Director of Marketing for V-Noni in Panama, says that drinking noni helps the body inside as well as outside – it is great for the skin too. Noni can be found in Panama and other tropical climates, but, like the aloe vera plant 20 years ago, it will be everywhere soon enough.

Preventive Measures

VACCINATIONS

There is no absolute requirement to get vaccinations prior to coming to Panama. There are however, recommended vaccinations. According to the World Health Organization, vaccination against yellow fever is suggested if you plan to travel to Eastern Panama, the Darien, or Kuna Yala for long periods of time. In Panama City, the Canal Zone, and the rest of the country, you are safe from exposure.

Most often heard from travelers and new residents alike is whether they need to worry about malaria or take anti-malaria pills. In reality, what once wiped out the French workforce while building the Canal is no longer such a great threat in Panama. If you are traveling into very rural areas, such as Darien, Kuna Yala, Ngöbe-Buglé for long periods of time, the World Health Organization recommends that you take anti-malarial pills as a precautionary measure.

TRAVELER'S DIARRHEA

You aren't made of steel, so put away your ego and watch what you eat. Panamanians are used to heavy foods like rice and beans, plantains and *patacones* (plantain chips double dipped and fried). They eat *marañones* (the cashew fruit) off the trees and dried beef from the side of the road. It may seem like fun to do what the locals do, but don't push it. Incorporate local foods little by little and find your own way through the delectable discovery of tropical ingredients.

Here's a common scenario: You find the restaurants in Panama to be sophisticated and clean. The food is simple, mild, *no tan picante* (not so spicy). The water tastes refreshing. The taco you bought on the street was delicious. Later, it strikes, and you won't ever forget it. Call it what you will, but traveler's diarrhea will hit at the worst moments, regardless of how strong you think your stomach is. You may ask, if Panama is so alert to the health standards, where does it come from? The heat produces all kinds of bacteria that find their way to the fruit and vegetables, and no matter how strong your stomach is, it is not accustomed to the local flora and your body will not tolerate it right away. Washing your hands before and after every meal, washing fruits and vegetables thoroughly before consuming, and staying away from heavy wheat and milk products when your stomach feels upset is the easiest way to prevent bacteria build-up and gastrointestinal sickness.

DENGUE FEVER

The most common disease carried by mosquitoes in Panama is Dengue fever. There are two types. The first affects many Panama residents and is the flu-like virus whose symptoms include mild to high fevers, muscle and joint pain, and rash. The fever shows up an average of 10 days after you are bitten and symptoms can last for a week or more. The Dengue hemorrhagic fever can be a potentially fatal version of the virus with high fever, diarrhea, and vomiting. It mostly affects children and the elderly, and while there is no cure, there is a good chance of survival if you seek proper medical treatment and possibly hospitalization. Staying hydrated is vital. Precautionary measures for either of the fevers include using insect repellent and staying away from very dirty or wet areas. The mosquitoes carrying Dengue are usually identifiable by their large size and long, white-capped legs.

TYPHOID

Typhoid fever is rare but can be caught if you are working in infected areas, perhaps where sewage or rainwater has built up. If you are working in old construction sites or doing a community beach cleanup, wear a medical mask and gloves to avoid being exposed to the bacteria. Also beware of street food vendors since eating at the side of the road is really only for the strong-willed. Panama's Ministry of Health has been excellent in recent years about holding street vendors to high standards during Carnival time, when hundreds of thousands of Panamanians are gathered in small spots, near rivers and parks of the interior, and contagions from diseases such as typhoid can be high. The Ministry of Health also uses its public workers and waste management service by assigning them to clean street blocks and community areas. If you insist on eating street food, eat it in small quantities to see how you feel before you decide on ingesting large quantities of fried meat from a street-side barbeque.

AIDS

In Panama, the first AIDS case was reported in 1984. By 2007, the World Health Organization reports an estimate of 20,000 persons living with HIV in the country. That is less than 1 percent of the population. The highest form of transmission is unprotected homosexual sex between men. However, many of the 33 percent of men having sex with men in Panama are also having heterosexual sex. Approximately 2 percent of female sex workers are infected with HIV. Because prostitution is legal in Panama, the government mandates weekly tests for sexually transmitted diseases, but this does not account for street prostitutes who don't report their health conditions.

LIVING WITH INSECTS

According to the many rainforest biologists who study our creepy crawly friends and their ecosystems, there are over 30 million different species of insects in the world. In an ecosystem as diverse and fruitful as Panama, the rainforest is home to loads of them. Most new residents to Panama behold in wonder and amazement the colors, shapes, sizes, and sounds of the insects found in the nooks and crannies of our world. I have seen moths the size of bats, nests

FUNGUS IN YOUR CLOSET

Besides frizzy hair, some of the hassles of living in a tropical country with an average 95 percent humidity are the constant accumulation of fungus and the quick decay of perishable goods. Any type of food, besides canned, should always be refrigerated or frozen. Closed dark places, such as closets or storage boxes, are fertile ground for the development of small fungi and spores; some clothing items kept unused for a long time in closets can develop a white film on their surface, a clear sign that fungus is on the move. The very efficient mothball is an excellent preventative measure; spreading a few in closets and drawers should help avoid fungus on your clothes. Another key thing to know is that this fungus develops in part because of the sweat that remains on fabric, so wash your bed sheets and towels regularly, don't wear the same pieces of clothing over and over without washing them, and keep shoes, dresses, and suits in proper boxes and storage bags.

Using a dehumidifier in certain rooms also aids in preventing fungus proliferation. If you are a book lover, definitely consider a small dehumidifier in your personal library. The best solution, although the costliest and most energy-consuming one, is to have central air-conditioning on in your home or room all day. Panama is hot and humid, but your belongings don't have to pay the price.

Contributed by Raul Altamar

of black flies rendezvous on the corners of my balcony, and ants the size of cockroaches; I have heard some kind of wing-rubbing insect that sounds like a National Guard siren. They are not just in the wilderness and jungle settings, either. There might not be quite as many as in more rural areas, but living cityside will not protect you from the *hormigitas* (microscopic ants) that nestle in the cracks of the kitchen counters. Insects are a daily reminder that you are living in the jungle, concrete or otherwise…If provoked by even the tiniest morsel of food, wood, or pool of liquid sugar, great masses of insects will appear within 15 to 20 minutes. Most are harmless, and if you are curious enough to live in a tropical climate you must be tolerant enough to remember this is their home, too. Embrace them, admire their beauty, and shoo them on out the door where they belong, in underbrush and grassy patches. Many people who can afford it simply keep the air conditioner running, making the interior climate uncomfortable for our many-legged neighbors.

The biggest challenge living alongside these pesky little creatures is preventing bites. Aside from the many vitamin B12 or garlic supplements that some people swear by, there are two simple solutions: repellent and a mosquito net. That first time you come back with itchy red dots from under the surface of your skin, you will never forget to pack either of them again.

Applying repellent just prior to the sunset hour can make all the difference. Better yet if you are living in a mosquito-infested area, skip the perfumed moisturizer in the morning and move straight to repellent. Aside from the common mosquito, there are tiny, microscopic sand flies, called *chitras* (also known as no-see-ums as they are invisible to the human eye), whose bites clutter your skin with tragically itchy red spots. If you give in and scratch the bites, they can evolve into open wounds and infections. Find yourself an easy, effective topical remedy as well as a good repellent. Alcohol dabs work to dry out the bites; aloe vera may relieve the itch. In Panama City, it is not necessary to use a mosquito net.

SNAKES

While you may expect to have to watch out for snakes in the wild areas, remember that the whole country is kind of a jungle. It may surprise you to hear that in Panama, there are stories of snakes coming up through the plumbing and finding their way into showers and sinks in urban areas. Unused storage rooms and rooftops are also comfortable lodging for snakes and their young. And these aren't just your garden-variety snakes. According to Dr. Norman Elton, former chief of staff at Gorgas hospital, venomous snakes in Panama fall into three families: pit vipers—the most poisonous and dangerous snake in the world—corals, and sea snakes. Elton says it is rare for snakes to attack humans since the tropics are such a rich feeding environment. The only times they are really hazardous to humans are at night when they are out hunting for food, or after eating, when they are less mobile and thus likely to strike if bothered during their three-week digestion period. Don't go hiking alone in the bush. Snakes will be more likely to flee if they feel the vibrations of many feet tromping through the forests. It's also important to have someone who could attend to your wounds if you are bitten.

Boa constrictors are also common, both the kind that live in the high grasses as well as tree boas, who tend to camouflage with their verdant surroundings. Not poisonous, friendly boas are often spotted around urban, but green, areas. Many people shrug them off, appreciating that they eat any rodents in the vicinity, as if this is any consolation. I'd rather call in the fumigator.

SCORPIONS

Scorpions are endemic to Panama. Most sightings and stinging incidents occur in the interior, although gardeners working in the green areas of the city will claim differently. If you live in the mountains or deep bush, you should take precautions like the locals do. Shake out all your clothes before putting them on; some people even hang their clothes inside out after washing, so they are forced to give them a good jiggle before wearing. Many Panamanians who live in the interior also keep their top sheet folded at the foot of the bed until they are ready to sleep. It's sound, practical advice for those of us who don't want to be sleeping with a scorpion.

Environmental Factors

While you will find many modern conveniences in Panama, it is a developing country. Combating pollution, having access to clean water, and upholding defined sanitary standards are processes constantly in progress. Like any country, Panama has its challenges, but it is getting more and more environmentally friendly, learning to save its wondrous resources and beginning to encourage recycling and ecology at all levels.

AIR QUALITY

Even though traffic in Panama City's metropolitan area has increased dramatically over the years, Panama's air is very clean compared to other Latin American capitals like Buenos Aires or Mexico City. One factor related to this is its size; Panama City is considerably smaller and less populated. The other beneficial factor is the ocean breeze, ever constant and felt throughout the city, a natural way to clear out pollution. Also, Panama City is literally surrounded by a tropical rainforest, with verdant foliage forcing its way through concrete holes and helping reduce air contaminants. The recent real estate boom takes away from this natural process, with numerous skyscrapers built around

© SKY GILBAR

Given the hot weather, many people like to exercise at night in open areas in Panama City.

SAVING THE PANAMA BAY

The Panama Bay is a beautiful sight that enriches the overall ambience of the city. Lined by the Avenida Balboa and located at the border of the Bella Vista neighborhood, this Pacific Ocean coast was once a decent, swimmable beach, until the shortsighted solution of spilling all the city's sewage into its waters began in the late 1950s. Over the years, locals – mostly the residents of Paitilla – have actually gotten used to the awful smells that accompany such a nice view. Complaining of the smell became small talk, and Panamanians accepted this for a long time until it got out of hand.

In the 1980s and 1990s, Panamanians started to develop a consciousness of ecology and general environmental health issues, which began to push the governments into action. Later environmental groups also began raising awareness of the dangers and health issues that a dirty bay brought to the city's populace, but still nothing was done. With the new millennium came a fresh interest in solving this problem, and the international community chipped in to help: The Japanese Agency for International Cooperation (JICA) produced a multimillion dollar study almost three years in the making, which shed some light on how to change Panama City's sewage system so that the bay started to clean up. The recommendation of the study was that new drainage water canals should be built throughout the city, so the water reaches treatment plants to clean it before it reaches the bay. This multi-million-dollar effort will reach its final stage no earlier than 2010, mainly because it involves drastic changes in piping and sewers throughout the city.

President Martín Torrijos's administration (2004-2009) also had other plans. Aesthetically, the Panama Bay is receiving a dramatic face-lift in the form of the Cinta Costera (Coastal Strip) project, a seaside park and recreational area that will cover most of the Avenida Balboa bay area. This mammoth city project has been rushed by the Torrijos Government for two reasons: Firstly, the President wants to leave this landmark as a legacy before he leaves office in 2009, and secondly, he wants to impress all the foreigners who bought million-dollar condos along the bay (one of the city's most expensive real estate areas) and assure them that their investment is well worth the cost. This Cinta Costera will push all current sewage spills further into the ocean, so bad smells will surely decrease in the short term, and with the long-term plan already in action to clean Panama City's entrails, the future smells quite fresh.

Contributed by Raul Altamar

the bay and coastlines blocking passage of fresh air to areas ironically named for their views and proximity to the breezes, such as Brisas del Mar (Ocean Breeze) and Bella Vista (Beautiful View).

Local statistics show that the two most polluted areas in Panama City are El Puente de la Cervecería, the bridge on Transístmica Avenue next to the Cervecería Nacional (National Brewery), and El Puente de San Miguelito, another bridge that borders the San Miguelito and Panama municipalities. These two toxic hot spots are at their worst around peak traffic hours, 6–9 A.M. and 4–7 P.M. Avoiding these bridges during these times is a simple way of limiting exposure to pollution. Most drivers are forced to roll up their windows and use the air conditioner to avoid the unregulated exhaust fumes from cars in high-traffic areas. In Panama's interior provinces, things are quite different: Air is fresh all over, especially in the Chiriquí highlands.

SMOKING

First San Francisco, then New York, then London, and now the rest of the world's main cities are catching up with smoking regulations for public areas. Panama is no exception. Law 13, established in January 2008, strictly prohibits smoking in public areas, with fines of US$10–100. The Ministry of Health does nighttime inspections in nightclubs and other public spots to monitor the compliance, and there's even a hotline for citizens to report irresponsible smokers (tel. 507/512-9444 or 507/800-5500). Signs and banners indicating smoke-free areas are visible throughout the main cities.

Smoking is also banned in public parks, casinos, buses, taxis, hotels, and hallways in office buildings. So, if you are a smoker living in Panama, your habit must be kept under control in public areas, or else a fine or an uncomfortable slap on the wrist may come your way. Some bars and restaurants do allow smoking, at smokers' own risk (it's still illegal). You may smoke in open spaces with few people around, or in your own home.

WATER QUALITY

By international standards, Panamanian water is very clean. In most African countries, and even in Central America and Mexico, drinking tap water is a terrible idea, courting illness that could land you in an emergency room. The National Water and Sewage Institute, or IDAAN, annually spends around US$10 million monitoring the country's water quality; almost 90 percent of the population gets its water through IDAAN-controlled water ducts, while the rest, mostly in the rural country, uses wells and cisterns. So, pouring a glass of water right out of the kitchen faucet is OK in the city, but in the interior it's still suggested to use water filters at home and to buy bottled water in public. This is because some small impurities may get through the well water, the water may taste of chlorine, or some restaurants, depending on their quality, may serve water with oily residues.

You may read that the Panama Bay is polluted but notice that some locals from Casco Viejo surf and bathe in these waters without any repercussions.

They can do this because they are accustomed to the local "germs"; in a way, they inherited the antibodies from their parents, whose bodies acclimated to these same waters years ago. Foreigners would be at risk swimming in the city waters. The moral of this story is that even though the tap water in Panama is basically safe, it is still good to take some precautions in the beginning and use filtered or bottled drinking water when you first arrive. Over time, getting used to tap water is fine. You can find bottled water everywhere and Panamanian bottled water is quite good; there is no need to buy the international brands, though they are available.

SANITATION

Panama possesses up-to-date standards of sanitation in public places and in most commercial outlets. Bathrooms in shopping malls, restaurants, bars, and discos are cleaned daily and follow Ministry of Health regulations; those that don't are fined or closed down. In the food industry, routine checks allow inspectors to spot unhealthy working environments or bad practices like selling products past their expiration date. Restaurants, shops, and markets have been fined and publicly exposed for not meeting sanitation standards. In rural areas or smaller towns, these regulations and practices are more flexible, so be wary.

Government advises new local entrepreneurs who launch business ventures like small restaurants or food manufacturing to follow international standards of sanitation and production, not just because it's the correct thing to do, but also because it is an added value to their customer. Official sanitation licenses should always be visible in public establishments, either at the front door or by the cashier.

ASEO-The Garbage System

Panama City's mayor and municipal offices are in charge of the garbage system, or *aseo,* through the Direction of Metropolitan Urban and Home Cleaning (La Dirección Municipal De Aseo Urbano y Domiciliario, or DIMAUD for short), which picks up domestic trash. The institution retrieves almost 500,000 tons of trash a year in 113 collection routes worked around the clock; waste is then taken to the Cerro Patacón landfill in the eastern part of the city. Employees also sweep the city constantly on foot and are identifiable by their yellow jumpsuits. In 2008, DIMAUD bought 54 new dump trucks to update its fleet and improve its services.

DIMAUD's performance isn't always tip-top, though. The collection service can be spotty in some areas of the city. There is also the small problem of where to put all the waste. The Cerro Patacón landfill is reaching its limits and the Bay of Panama is already at dangerous levels of sewage contamination. Still, no major health or social crises have come out of this, and the service is as efficient as one might expect. In 2009, the mayor's office promised to invest $16.7 million in waste-management offices and equipment.

Each municipality is in charge of its own public waste system. In the interior, many locals burn their trash or have a spot for community waste, which they later burn, as the city might be unreliable when it comes to garbage collection. The Spanish Cooperation, a human-aid division of the Spanish Embassy, helped to create a garbage system in Portobelo, a small town on the Caribbean coastline in Colón. If it weren't for the Spanish Cooperation's support and implementing the system's administration, this historical sea town would be drowning in garbage.

There are private contractors that can be hired for waste management, but usually only businesses use these. There are more than 20 agencies that recycle materials such as metals, plastics, paper, and glass, but they do not promote their services; if you want to recycle in Panama, you have to find the services in your town and manage the process on your own. Fortunately government and private organizations promoting green living are beginning major awareness campaigns and more green, blue, or gray recycling bins (for paper, plastic, or aluminum) can be seen around public parks and some gas stations. Some neighborhoods have been able to collaborate and organize weekly pick ups by a recycling agency, but generally it is up to you to create your own sorting system at home or in the neighborhood, and bring recyclables to the appropriate locations. There is hope the government will take on this service one day soon.

Safety

PERSONS WITH DISABILITIES

Laws in Panama do exist to support persons with disabilities. Children with special needs are required by law to be integrated into classrooms, and since the 1990s the Ministry of Education has been responsible for training minors with disabilities. However, there are private services to help with training and education for minors with special needs.

Access for persons with disabilities is available in public places such as parking lots, public parks, most schools, museums, movie theaters, and shopping centers. As of 2008, the government has raised public awareness and fines for parking in handicapped spaces without a license. New buildings under construction are required to have general access for wheelchair users, and fines for failing to provide adequate access are generally enforced. Unfortunately, bathrooms and sidewalks generally are not made to accommodate people with wheelchairs.

STREET CRIME

For the past decade, street crime had been relatively low, with most unfortunate incidents happening to those who forget that using common sense and street smarts applies just as much, if not more, outside of your home country. Learning your way around before exploring on your own is always wise. There is always a possibility of getting mugged, especially if you look or act out of place. If you are a victim of a mugging, just give up your wallet and don't play around with someone who claims to be armed.

At the time of writing, street crime in Panama has noticeably changed for the worse. The changes are a result of the global economy hitting one of its all-time lows and the Torrijos government's lack of attention to bettering the police force, which is expected to improve with the change of administration in 2009. In Panama City, reported crimes are much more common than in other areas and are mostly gang related. More violence is occurring in neighborhoods that were once safe for walking and driving around with open windows. Carjacking is historically rare, but as of late stories are circulating about drivers with luxurious cars being held up at stoplights.

Scam artists frequent hot spots visited by middle- and upper-class residents. While a friendly looking vagabond is asking you for some extra change to fill a prescription for his sick baby, you may not notice that he is also swiping your wallet or cell phone. These petty thieves will not hurt you, except for the inconvenience of losing your personal documents, cash, or friends' contact information. The crimes are happening to Panamanians and foreigners alike. Beware, keep your valuables out of sight, and don't roam around the streets or remote beaches drawing attention to yourself. It all comes down to street smarts: Use them, and you will be fine!

ILLEGAL DRUGS

Panama borders Colombia, both by ocean and land. The stories you've heard about it being a major throughway to Europe and North America for illicit drugs is not an exaggeration. Border police have much more of a presence since Martín Torrijos assumed the presidency, and bands of foreign drug traffickers have been caught throughout the country. The U.S. Drug Enforcement Agency (DEA) always has been and continues to be heavily stationed here, both in the eastern and western provinces, though you are unlikely to notice them.

Marijuana and cocaine are the most common street drugs, and many night-clubs and bars have been raided and closed down by local authorities for distributing them. Both are illegal in Panama. A foreigner caught with drugs in his or her possession can be thrown out of the country. If your personal pleasures include drugs, don't push your luck or talk up your habits. Your property can be confiscated if you are caught growing marijuana, even for medical use. Punishment for drug trafficking is severe, and if you are caught doing so the Panamanian government will pay your room and board at La Joya, Panama's most infamous correctional facility and a place you definitely do not need to personally visit. Panama City street sellers of *pegon,* a type of cheap, local marijuana that is made with ammonia so it sticks together like a brick are not very discreet. Often police officers are not far behind them.

POLICE

Panama's National Police look quite military, in fashion, but in the end they have the same jurisdiction as the police you will see in their khaki uniforms. The policemen in khaki uniforms are seen at traffic stops but also patrol regularly. The National Police, more oriented toward tourists, also patrol and are available for checking out crime scenes and call situations.

As in other countries in Latin America, some police officers will stop you for minor traffic infractions—or they may even make up an infraction just to pull you over if they think you have money. If the officer asks you if you want to pay the ticket on the spot, this is probably not a legitimate citation but rather a subtle request for a bribe. A police officer does not earn much in Panama, and soliciting bribes is a way to supplement their salaries. If you are at fault and you choose to go along and pay the bribe to get out of the ticket, be aware that you are contributing to corruption. It is better to insist upon receiving the citation, which you can pay through proper legal channels if it is legitimate; if the officer made up your alleged traffic violation, you will probably be sent on your way. Not all police practice this kind of "law enforcement," so don't automatically assume that an officer is corrupt. Oftentimes, they are helpful and do their best to uphold the integrity of their country.

If you are victim of a crime, or witness to one, the process for reporting it to the police can be quite frustrating. The law enforcement agency is divided into four seemingly unrelated departments: the sheriff's department,

RETEN: POLICE ROAD CHECKS

Just about every 15 days, conveniently falling on payday weekends, called the *quincena,* major city avenues will be backed up late at night due to a *reten* (police check). At a glance, what you see is a police check slowing down cars or waving some through; what you get is authorities keeping the roads safe for you by checking for driver's licenses and proper identification, or people driving under the influence. Passengers in the car are also responsible for showing ID, and foreigners are asked to show immigration papers or passports and up-to-date visas.

Payday calendar dates are the most popular time for a *reten* because that is when the majority of the Panamanian population is on the road spending its wages, and also when the majority of public events occur. Main city throughways, often difficult to avoid if you live in certain areas, are the converging points for these *retenes,* proving effective for local police to nab those who don't follow driving regulations. Each time a new immigration law is approved, or a few bad eggs are reported loose around town, you are also likely to find police checks throughout a province. Holiday weekends are very popular for *retenes* on the Pan-American highway.

In the past, *retenes* have also been done in the form of *manodura,* where the government issues police authorities the right to stop anyone walking on the street and ask to see identification. Sometimes they will even check your purse or backpack. Supposedly the Torrijos government (2004-2009) has disallowed that practice, but it's not uncommon for police to stop you and do it anyway.

National Police, Personera, and Judicial Investigation Department (DIJ). In each area of Panama, the process for reporting a crime is different; in the islands of Bocas del Toro you might have to go to the sheriff's office for small crimes, while in Panama City the DIJ's office is supposed to take care of all police reports, big or small. However, midway through the investigation (and depending on how far the investigation is actually taken) your case might be transferred to another department altogether. Now your case might fall in the hands of the National Police (if are lucky enough to have them work with you, as a foreigner). They simply are not used to having to work as hard as the authorities in your own country, and they tend to offer you ambiguous and difficult options for resolving your problem. Always talk calmly to the police and try to understand their process. The system works quite differently from what you were used to, so the best advice is to go to the local Departamento de Investigaciones Judicial (DIJ) in your district and tell them you have been victim to a crime. Next, simply follow the steps they outline, and don't question them too much, as you really want them on your side so they will help you as much as possible.

The tourist police are quite positive and really do work to protect people from hazardous encounters. In the Panama City's Casco Viejo, there are many police patrolling the San Felipe area, and while some restored houses are mixed into older sometimes risqué neighborhoods, the Tourist Police will follow you closely and warn you if they don't think it's a good idea for you to venture down there. If you are a resident of these areas, you will appreciate their guardianship equally as much as someone who might not have known better. Any crime that happens to you in Casco Viejo should be reported to them.

THEFT

It can be frustrating to watch the police do nothing for you when you have been the victim of any kind of crime. If you have been robbed of something of value, such as a computer, MP3 player, or car stereo, don't expect to see it again. In most cases, the police will know exactly who has committed the crime, as criminals are local and tend to "own" certain streets. Some longtime residents prefer to ask around to see if other locals might know where to find their items, for a small reward. This is not recommended, as the repercussions can be dangerous, but when it does work it is far more effective than waiting for the local authorities to return your valuables.

Fill out the police report and ask what are the chances of getting your items back. Don't expect it, but retrieving minor items like a wallet has happened. In the States and perhaps in Europe, pickpockets or thieves who rob you of your wallet will usually take advantage of the credit cards and bank cards within it. In Panama, thieves are usually only interested in your cash and your cell phone or other electronic equipment that can be sold on the black market. When thieves are caught, most documentation, identification, credit cards, and bank debit cards, as well as the other personal contents of your bag, are returned to you untouched. Some advice: do not put all your credit cards and documents together in one wallet, and do carry copies of your passport rather than the real thing.

EMERGENCIES

Because Panama is not affected by natural disasters such as hurricanes, earthquakes, and tornadoes, national emergency services other than Red Cross are not very common. There are floods, which can and do affect populations living near the coastlines or riverbeds; international services do work together to get many of these people back on their feet.

In or near major cities with hospitals, such as Panama City, David, and

Santiago, emergencies are responded to quickly and with care. Air service is almost always called in for any kind of major accident, whether in a plane, car, or boat. Private ambulance services are available for a small monthly fee. Consider where you live and what kind of resources you have available for emergency situations when deciding whether to buy an ambulance plan.

In 2008, Panama implemented a 911 emergency line paid for by the phone company. It is still not certain if this is a long-term program or not. Therefore, keep a list by the phone of all direct emergency lines, including police, fire departments, and ambulance services.

EMPLOYMENT

Panama is indeed a paradise. It intrigues and invites retirees, young and old, and people looking for a change in lifestyle, a break from the mundane, and a move toward simplicity. Yet it is also a new nation, growing in resources, products, and business relationships with the rest of the world, and for this reason, many of the country's residents choose to live in and around the cities. Even if you wish to live on the beach and hide in the outskirts of civilization, Panama is an opportune location to work in various industries, ranging from executive to creative and with high-tech telecommunications access.

In 2009, a falling dollar and crashing markets affected the economy in Panama as it did in other parts of the world. The difference on the isthmus, however, is that hiring has not slowed. In fact, foreign interest is higher than ever with the Canal expansion handing out concessions left and right for the 2007-approved $5 billion project, whose budget was still growing in 2009. There is also a long list of nongovernmental organizations and multinational companies showing interest in Panama's biodiversity and regional convenience.

If you are in the right place at the right time, you may hear about a new endeavor, and if you are willing to speak up about your skills, you may just land a job. Most companies look to fill positions with Panamanian talent first, as they should. But foreigners often look attractive in the job market, offering bilingual skills and international experience. As industries from abroad enter the isthmian market for the first time, universities are adding these careers to their study programs, looking for professionals to teach Panamanians the ropes, and hoping to raise the bar on skills such as design, management, and film production.

Among all of your considerations about working abroad don't neglect an investigation of the Panamanian work attitude; you may be surprised when you see your work ethics are not always compatible with theirs. For example, you may find that many Panamanians are not willing to go above and beyond their job description if it means staying at work for longer hours, and this is generally accepted. Most companies operate similar to an assembly line, where each person is assigned a specific duty, and multi-tasking is generally not encouraged or recognized. To avoid becoming frustrated at your job, research the work culture and environment of your potential employer to see if it's a good fit. If you will be employing others, don't be surprised by the difference in work attitudes. Most Panamanians work to live, rather than the other way around.

Self-Employment

If you are looking for a job in Panama but aren't sure where your skills will fit in, think about self-employment until you can find a truly satisfying position. Self-employment and freelance work are a wise way to begin scouting the job market, as well as understanding the value put on professional services and the general work attitude in Panama.

Similarly, if you are planning to open your own business, you will find Panama has a lot of room for innovative entrepreneurs, who are fortunate to work without much competition and for lower start-up costs. Good business ideas go far here. Many expats come to Panama with a relatively new business trend that has fared well in their home country, filling a market void no one has yet on the isthmus. Understanding the market, business laws, and local practices is the prime factor in starting a business and making it succeed.

FREELANCE

If you are planning to keep a freelance identity with ties to clients around the world, you are at a pivotal location for telecommuting. Panama's low costs on Internet and telephone are a great asset to the work-at-home expat. Still, you will need to take a long look at the best hours of the day to work at home. Living in perpetual spring and summer weather can be quite challenging to your self-discipline for work. Likewise, the city traffic can be utter madness at certain times, so a few quick morning errands before you start your day may turn into an all-day detour, keeping you from your well-intentioned work routine.

Working freelance in Panama is a great way to learn about the market. If you are serious about your work and establish a small but loyal clientele, you will ride the wave of successful freelancing easily, especially if you live within your budget until that next big something comes along. Depending on your lifestyle choices, your expenses will dictate how hard you have to hustle for your next gig. Translators, tutors, photographers, graphic designers, interior designers, and film or television producers or editors are only a small sampling of the careers that can work on a freelance basis in this community. You may even be able to command excellent rates if you work to be one of the best in your field. Lawyers and accountants with international business experience can consult only on a freelance basis, and this can be a lucrative way to do business. You cannot work full time in law or accounting without the credentials required by Panamanian law.

Always declare your earnings when you freelance in Panama. Contact a local accountant to find out the exact procedure for invoicing and how to acquire your personal Registro Unico de Contribuyente (R.U.C.), a registered identification number issued by the Ministry of Finance that is required to pay taxes on income earned in Panama, for services provided or property owned. If you do not declare your income, you risk having to defend any income produced while in Panama prior to getting residence.

STARTING A BUSINESS

Whatever type of business you want to start in Panama, whether full time or part time, it will require a lot of legwork. If you are involved in the process hands on, you will literally feel the blood, sweat, tears, and perhaps dizzy spells from running in circles from government office to government office. After your culture shock wears off, the hard work of setting up your business will perhaps motivate you to succeed even more when the company is finally

EXPAT PROFILE: JON HURST: PANAMA CITY'S "BAGEL GUY"

The New York Bagel Café, located in Panama City, was opened by an Arkansas-born, longtime Northern California resident who learned to make bagels in Fort Worth, Texas. So where does the New York name come from? It just goes with the bagels!

Jon Hurst arrived in Panama in 1997 as a U.S. Peace Corps volunteer in Colón. It was the beginning of a 10-year career in Central America with various social outreach programs. In 2005, his employer mentioned plans to move the organization back to Maine; Jon decided the cold was no longer for him. He considered Miami and California, places he had previously lived and worked, but he was accustomed to Central America and not quite convinced he wanted to move back to the United States. He asked himself, "How can I support myself here permanently?"

Jon took a leap. At 37 he decided he would open his own business. He had experience opening and operating state-funded social programs, but this was his first independently owned business venture, and it was in a foreign country. His next step was identifying what was missing in Panama: bagels. Prior to 2000, there was a bagel shop in Panama, but its American owner had left with the U.S. military in 2000. As Jon continued to investigate, he decided to move forward with his idea (he learned his competition was the frozen bagel industry!).

After learning to make bagels in Fort Worth, Texas, Jon came back to Panama in May 2006 and went to work opening New York Bagel Café. Three years later, Jon is running a successful neighborhood food and beverage business. He has a regular clientele, maintains an outstanding rapport with his employees, and, after six months of sunup-to-sundown work schedules, now feels comfortable leaving the business at 5 P.M. in the hands of his employees.

Some of the major factors that helped Jon to facilitate his business venture:

- Sticking with a real estate broker who was easy to work with, he was able to accelerate his hunt for the appropriate commercial space.

- Looking for a viable idea and understanding the market he was working in.

- Enjoying his host country and its people: Jon believes Panamanians are the friendliest people of all the cultures he has lived among in Central America.

- Having 10 years of experience prior to starting his business

up and running. However, if you sit comfortably behind the computer while legal representatives push the workflow for you, set your timing expectations a little lower. Even if your legal team is out there doing everything possible to get your business up and running, there are a lot of brick walls that can be hit and very little they can control.

average Panamanians were simply not the ones coming into buy or sit in the café. The majority of my clientele is international, and so I adjusted my prices. They can afford $5–6 sandwiches. No one complains: people enjoy the food, the free coffee refills, and the free Internet," says Jon.

- Being patient but proactive in the face of Panamanian red tape. John's biggest frustration in opening his business in Panama was getting electricity. Despite doing everything correctly – his deposit was paid, he presented the engineering design to the Regulatory Services (twice!) – he was rejected. Soon, he realized officials were playing a game with him. "It was the end of my innocence," Jon recalls. "I refused to give in, and eventually I made a few phone calls and the job was done."

© RUEBEN

Jon Hurst and his bagels

here, he understands how the system and the Latin American culture works.

- Being a realist: Panama is not the United States. Although on the surface real estate and media may sell to foreigners as if it is in southern Florida, it's imperative to understand that from a long-term investment perspective, it simply is not the same culture.

- Adjusting his business to the reality. "When I opened up my business, I was selling a bagel and cream cheese sandwich for $1.50. But soon after, I noticed that the

- Learning that there are certain things you simply can't train someone to do when working between cultures. Know your employees' strengths and weaknesses and work with them.

- Knowing he would have to do a lot of the work himself for a long time. Once he trusted his employees, he showed it with increased responsibility. This makes the difference in the level of teamwork.

Incorporating your Business

First, you will have to decide whether you want to open your business as a partnership or a corporation, both of which will need the assistance of a Panamanian lawyer to create valid contracts between the parties, or as a sole proprietor, which works best when you go it alone or keep it within the family. In the case of opening a corporation *(sociedad anonima)* you will have to file Articles of Incorporation and have at least three board directors, one of whom must be Panamanian. Panama is replete with trust companies that can help you to do this for a fee. In a partnership, you will have to decide how many shares each partner is getting, define it as a general or limited partnership, and register all the partners and their corresponding capital with the Public Registry.

Next, you must apply for an income tax ID number, acquire a commercial license, register with the local municipality, and obtain your R.U.C., essentially a Social Security number for your business. You will also have to apply for the health permit and fumigation permit for your locale. If all of these documents are in order, you are fully recognized by the government and authorized to begin operations.

Offshore Structures

Panama has a long-standing history as a principal jurisdiction for offshore companies for European and other Latin American business investors. Its geographic convenience, use of the U.S. dollar as currency, central banking location, and the Colón Free Zone, used for storage and shipment of goods, are only a few of the factors that make it a popular choice for international investors. Panama is also a tax haven, meaning it is tax-free for investors who establish a corporate identity here but keep their business services and products outside of the isthmus. The law pertaining to offshore structures offers confidentiality to the original shareholders, through the issue of bearer shares. Many Panama law firms and trust companies will provide nominee directors for you for a fee, thereby establishing complete confidentiality and never having to put the owner's name on paper. Tax-exemption regulations change frequently, with certain nuances added or removed depending upon the nature of the organization of the offshore entity. It is advisable to look for a legal consultant who can guide you through the incorporation and tax laws correctly. The *Resources* chapter of this book offers recommendations.

The Job Hunt

With the recession of 2009, jobs have become less available worldwide, but in Panama, companies haven't stopped hiring. In fact, the local market has job opportunities created by project investors, developers, and the Canal expansion. Schools are growing to support the families coming to Panama to work, and teachers are needed. According to the President of ACOBIR, the Panama

Association of Real Estate Brokers and Developers, the construction of the Panama Pacific Residential and Commercial Center, which opened in 2009, will create up to 40,000 jobs, countering any fear of economic instability for the isthmus community. However, expat job hunting can be different, especially when companies are encouraged to hire locally. To be considered for Panamanian employment, your skills will have to be outstanding, and highlighted loud and clear on paper and later in the interview. Employers are looking for someone who can do a job that cannot be filled by Panamanians.

WHERE TO LOOK

If you are interested in making a living in Panama, all you have to do is open up the classified section of any of the three major newspapers, and you will find a plethora of ads in Spanish and English.

When you become a resident of Panama you are in a good position to get hired by any company looking for bilingual talent, such as call centers, shipping companies, schools, multinational companies, hotels, real estate sales and development companies, and relocation services. However, you may need to work on a freelance basis until you can obtain a work visa with the employer.

Aside from searching in the classifieds of *La Prensa, La Estrella de Panamá, and El Panamá América,* Panama's three largest daily papers, you can check online at Craigslist Panama, which offers an interesting array of part-time and flexible opportunities for those willing to telecommute.

The City of Knowledge offers extensive benefits for those who start initiatives in research and technology.

CITY OF KNOWLEDGE: A BUSINESS MODEL OF INTELLECT AND PRODUCTIVITY

In 1999, as the U.S military world phased out of the Canal Zone, one abandoned United States Army Southern command post was slowly transforming itself into a different kind of international identity: from Fort Clayton to the City of Knowledge, or Ciudad del Saber.

The process started five years earlier, when a few interested Panamanians including then-president Ernesto Perez Ballardes, presented the idea of a "Socratic Square" in 296 acres of Fort Clayton. With approval ratings high and the Summit of the Americas backing its foundation, the cornerstone was laid. Using the same barracks structures and adding innovative designs for sustainability, the City of Knowledge Foundation was officially born in July of 1999 as a interdisciplinary campus environment set up to host international organizations, academia, a technology park, research sciences and investigations, and business management.

Today, the City of Knowledge is not only an incorporated foundation, but also a smoothly running community, with over 150 affiliated agencies working within an evolved office park and campus setting. Since its inception in 1999, the campus has come alive with United Nations programs, USAID teams, corporate training centers, university and human development programs such as the Red Cross, environmental research, cultural and recreational spaces, restaurants, cafés, and other essential facilities.

A work group must petition to become an affiliate of the City of Knowledge and fit into its categories of information technology, bioscience, environmental management, human development, business management and entrepreneurial services, or academia. Tax incentives and government benefits are available for foreign employees who work within the City of Knowledge campus. The City has become an amazing proposition – some say a bubble for the intellectual elite in Panama. Residences are maintained and offered at reasonable rents to those who work within the campus, thus allowing for sustainability and convenient infrastructure. The dynamic parks and pool offer leisure and activity, and the center of the campus comes alive with cricket games, ultimate Frisbee, soccer, bicycling, and jogging.

The best parts about the City of Knowledge are the ability to go by foot and the obvious synergy of healthy, satisfied, productive community members who scurry along the green flats of the old Fort Clayton, from UN office to coffee shop and from American schools to Olympic-size pools. The general public is invited to share in the culture, the cafés, the parks, the swimming pool, public roads, and the land that is part of Panama and open to all. Clayton's City of Knowledge is really a Panamanian Pleasantville that is impossible to hate.

For more information, see www.ciudaddelsaber.org.

INTERVIEWS

Interview protocols in Panama are not very different from U.S. or European standards, although waiting periods to learn if you were accepted for the job can be much shorter. If you are talented and available, companies will sweep you up. The only factor that could delay a company's decision to take on a foreign hire is whether there is money in the budget for you (foreign workers tend to make a higher wage). Interviews are generally less formal; a suit is not necessary. Someone who likes you on paper will decide if you are right for the job prior to meeting you, especially if you are an expat. The interview is really the clincher—getting to know if your personalities will mesh and if you are as good of a catch as you seem on your resume or curriculum vitae and photo. Note that Panamanians expect there to be a photo on your resume, and most employers will not even consider interviewing you if you don't provide one.

DAILY LIFE

Volunteering

Many international organizations come to Panama to establish headquarters and identity throughout the region. According to the Directory of Development Organizations, there are at least 25 international developmental organizations working in Panama. The United Nations hosts approximately 13 regional offices in the capital, at the City of Knowledge campus. The Smithsonian Institute has well-established research facilities along the country's Pacific and Atlantic coasts. International scientists, anthropologists, historians, and human rights activists routinely seek out Panama for their programs and studies.

NONGOVERNMENTAL AND ENVIRONMENTAL ORGANIZATIONS

Panama is a hub for more than just airlines. It is a core location for regional information, environmental feedback, and analyses. Human rights activists and those working to help the environment have a good chance of finding a nongovernmental organization with which to collaborate. According to an Earth Trends country survey, Panama listed over 1,000 nongovernmental organizations in 2003, with the number growing throughout the decade as a result of new communication lines opening between the Americas.

Almost any major issue regarding the earth's tropical and subtropical aspects, including indigenous communities, is being actively worked on or studied in Panama. Environmental organizations such as the Peregrine Fund, which works to breed them and protect the habitats of raptor birds, or Mar Viva, a regional foundation to protect marine waters, as well as countless numbers of organizations working to preserve the rainforests, see Panama as a prime location to promote their causes. While countries in Africa and Southeast Asia share many of the same wondrous characteristics and essential resources for advancing environmental issues, Panama's central location and access to modern technology satisfies those who want to work in these fields.

VOLUNTEER WORK

Once here, you will see how Panama and its people will engage you. If you want to get involved in helping people—children, the poor, or the sick—there are numerous local organizations that will welcome your helping hand. Your contribution can be as simple and significant as visiting a local orphanage to hold a newborn baby or as defined as offering your technical services in translations or public relations. Either way, your organization and especially your enthusiasm will be highly appreciated. Before you get involved in the volunteer experience, however, get to know the foundation you are interested in. Many organizations requiring volunteers might already have a program in collaboration with a local goodwill group, and going through the group is the safer option in a new country. You don't want to hang around some of the neighborhoods or churchyards by yourself, even though you have the best intention in mind. Culture clashes are common, and it would be best to involve yourself without creating misunderstandings.

Be clear about what your expectations are for the hours and the services you are offering. While it can be extremely fulfilling to be part of a significant event or program that might genuinely help people, you want your involvement to be a positive experience for both you and the organization. Low salaries and violation of minimum-wage laws is a problem in Panama, and sometimes this can lead to an abuse of volunteer labor as well. On the other hand, you don't want to leave an organization feeling resentful if they think you are volunteering while you were expecting compensation. Be patient and keep your good intentions in place.

Paid-to-volunteer groups, such as the U.S. Peace Corps or U.S. Agency for International Development (USAID), can train you in the transition between cultural expectations when working with local communities. If you work with a spirit of empathy and respect at all levels of volunteer services, you will enjoy the experience that much more.

Labor Laws

Despite the enthusiasm about Panama's growing economy and opportunities, the problem of low wages and much-needed labor reforms is still present. When in an interview or preparing to accept a work contract in Panama, call attention to the differences in benefits and wages compared to your home country and speak up with your expectations. For example, don't expect private health insurance to be included in your work contract. While healthcare is socialized, you will not receive this public benefit if you have a professional services contract. Even if you are part of the *planilla* (payroll) and receive Social Security, you should still consider an independent healthcare plan.

Consider your options for obtaining your work visa, whether it will be paid for by your employer or you will receive compensation in your salary for your legal and administrative costs in obtaining the visa. You will have to renew this visa yearly in coordination with your work contract, and the costs can add up. Still, this hassle is worth it if you are interested in long-term residency, as you are eligible for a long-term residence visa once you have contributed to Panamanian Social Security for five years or more. You will need to work with your lawyer, the Ministry of Labor, and the Immigration Bureau for the visa.

WORKERS' RIGHTS

Panama law protects the employee and inhibits the employer from taking advantage of the workforce. Panamanians are well aware of their basic work

DAILY LIFE

© SKY GILBAR

Fishermen are up at the break of day to be able to catch the freshest produce and sell it the same day.

rights and will expect fair treatment. Panamanian law guarantees a full-time employee a 45- to 48-hour workweek and 30 days of mandatory vacation. Women are granted 14 weeks' maternity leave, and overtime is paid at 150 percent of the normal rate. In some industries this overtime rate varies, so check the labor laws.

If you start your own company, work with a lawyer as you hire people; the majority of lawsuits brought against an employer will favor the employee. The benefits outlined below are designed to help the employee advance in a country defined by Third World infrastructure but with the potential of a First World economy. As a foreign employer you should contribute fairly to your employees' development.

If you believe you can fill your company with only foreign hires, you will have to reevaluate. Not only should you invest in local labor as an ethical matter, but the government's many incentives to foreign investors require you to contribute to the Panamanian workforce with in-house training and help alleviate the 12–14 percent (in 2009) unemployment rate. Ninety percent of any Panamanian corporation's labor force must be Panamanian by nationality, married to a Panamanian, or have been a resident for 10 years at the time of hire. The other 10 percent can be foreign hires. Companies with fewer than 10 employees can have one foreign worker. Companies can petition the Ministry of Labor for higher percentages, but it must be justified by requiring technical labor or special skills that cannot be fulfilled by Panamanian talent.

Thirteenth Month

Any employee on a Panamanian payroll is automatically paid a bonus called the *decimotercero,* or the thirteenth month. It is paid as one month's salary for every 11 months that you have worked by contract. The bonus is paid in thirds, in April, August and December. Social security taxes are also paid on this bonus, but at a lower rate than the regular monthly salary.

Contracts

There are three different types of work contracts in the Panama labor structure: the fixed-term contract, the indefinite-term contract, and the defined work labor contract, determined by the job performed. In order to enter into any of these contracts, a foreign employee must maintain a work visa and pay into and receive Social Security benefits. Fixed-term contracts cannot be extended. Indefinite-term contracts are extended automatically unless the employer decides to terminate the contract, pursuant to documented justified causes. In the latter case, you will need to understand your indemnification

DAILY LIFE

© SKY GILBAR

The real-estate boom has helped create employment opportunities for Panamanians.

and severance rights, detailed in this section. A three-month probationary period is written into these contracts, whereby either party can terminate the contract for any reason. A labor contract should include the employee's job description. This protects both sides if a termination is contested or one or both sides feel the job duties have not been fulfilled.

You will have to sign three copies of these contracts, all of which should be stamped by the Panamanian Ministry of Labor. One will go to the employer, one to the Ministry of Labor, and the other is your personal copy. Always ask for your copy of the contract if you do not receive it within your first three months of work.

Professional contract services are usually paid in the form of *honorarios* (service fees). This agreement should also be in writing in order to be enforceable. The professional contract worker is simply a consultant and does not receive Social Security, indemnification, vacation pay, or thirteenth month pay.

Indemnification and Severance

Panama law requires that if an employer terminates your fixed or indefinite contract after the three-month probationary period, the employee has the right to receive an indemnification fee, which amounts to a percentage of the salary, vacation, and thirteenth month rights paid according to the duration of employment and the type of contract signed. If an employer is the one terminating the contract, a 30-day notice must be given, with the option to pay the employee for the 30 days and terminate him or her immediately.

The government favors employee rights and makes it relatively expensive to lay off an employee.

Social Security, Education, and Income Taxes

Similar to taxes withheld in your home country, your wages in Panama will come to you with a slice already gone. Foreign employers should know what seems like a low cost for wages will add up to a much higher expense when paying Social Security taxes.

Social Security is paid monthly by both the employer and the employee. The company must make a payment directly to the Social Security office, which at the time of writing amounts to 11.5 percent of the total salary. The employee pays 8 percent of his or her salary, which is directly deducted from the paycheck. These percentages are changing under a Social Security reform begun in 2007, which will bring higher Social Security payments, implemented in phases through 2013, and higher monthly pensions.

If wages are under US$800 per month, Social Security payments and education taxes are the only deductions withheld from an employee's paycheck. Any salary above this amount is subject to income tax, at progressive rates up to 30 percent, based on salary. Thirteenth-month salaries are also taxed for Social Security, but at a lower rate. Other employee or manager's bonuses do not have taxes withheld but are still taxable on your personal tax returns.

WAGES

Salaries are negotiated monthly in Panama, so unless you are negotiating a contract from abroad, stay away from yearly figures. While Panamanians will assure you that you are worth your weight in gold, you must be aware of the reality of the salary scale in Panama. A prospective employer might not be able to comply with your demands, no matter how badly they want you.

Here's a peek into what you might expect in particular careers: Bankers and business employees are paid modestly, while most sales employees who earn monthly wages plus commissions will do very well. Architects' salaries start very low, despite rising costs in construction. University professors are underpaid. Teaching positions at public schools pay depressingly little; private schools may pay US$650–800 per month, and some private international schools go above the $1,500 mark for U.S certified teachers, with administrative positions in education paying well above that.

Most reception and personal assistant jobs will pay US$300–600 per month. A mid-level position such as supervisor or executive will earn up to US$1,000 per month, considered a solid salary in Panama. A group manager or small business general manager may make US$2,000–2,500. A small business owner may earn US$3,000 monthly. Multinational corporations will pay their VPs and CEOs anywhere from US$4,000 to US$15,000—a wide range, but given the medley of global industries based in Panama the average can be hard to pinpoint. If hired to work here with a contract from abroad, make sure the company is paying for your work visa, your relocation fees, and possibly even a housing fee. Moving is extremely expensive and can take a big chunk of your salary.

As employer you can use the above figures as a basic range, but definitely ask a consultant or Panamanian colleague of confidence to review your salary allotments. The worst thing you can do is underpay your staff. On the other hand, if you pay too much, you might tip the scale and contribute to the rise of expenses, which the majority of the population simply cannot afford.

DAILY LIFE

FINANCE

Undoubtedly, one of the major reasons you are considering a move to Panama is its reduced cost of living. The real estate industry has hyped this benefit considerably in attempting to entice people to move here. Other reasons include the excellent shopping, cosmopolitan lifestyle, and superb medical care. Yes, all these things exist in Panama, but if you want to be out shopping at the malls, eating out every day in the finest restaurants in the city, and have an insurance policy that covers treatment at the best medical facilities, then life here really isn't that cheap.

Perhaps you plan to get a job once you get to Panama, and earn a little extra pocket money. Even if you do find ample job opportunities, you will also find that salaries are low and your buck doesn't have much bang! The middle class is pretty squeezed here, and the government has not recognized the need to raise minimum wage or control rents. Due to rapid development in New Babylon, the average professional salaries (around US$500–800 per month) are not enough to cover the rising costs in food or housing expenses. If you have

© SKY GILBAR

a nice bundle of money to invest here, you will get more for your money than you would in your home country, and you will probably be pleased with the outcome. But if you are coming here to live a simple life and get away from the "Keeping up with the Joneses" game, you should carefully research how your budget will play out.

Cost of Living

Panama's cost of living is largely dependent on where and how you choose to live. Generally speaking, the areas where most expats live, such as Boquete, Bocas del Toro, and the higher-end parts of Panama City, are the most expensive. Ten years ago, they were not that much more expensive than the rest of the country, but the influx of foreign residents to an area nearly always hikes up the prices. PriceSmart (a membership warehouse store) and retail stores such as Nine West shoes, Zara clothing (from Spain), Puma, and MAC cosmetics make it possible to keep living the middle-class competition in Panama City. In Bocas and Boquete, the arrival of small grocery stores that specialize in imported food brands and vegetables are also adding on more to the cost of living for those who find this selection hard to resist. Even with the 2009 recession under way, you will find even basic goods in the principal cities of David and Panama City significantly more expensive than they used to be.

There are a lot of factors to consider in how much it will cost to live in Panama, not just the neighborhood you desire and the type of housing you prefer. If you are relocating alone, you can live in a nice neighborhood and treat yourself to luxuries more freely than if you are moving with your family. If you are bringing the family and you expect to maintain a luxurious lifestyle, a decent healthcare plan, and a good bilingual education for the children, then you need to budget about US$6,000 for a family of four per month. And, if you want to enjoy the same vacations you used to and visits to your home country, add those to the budget as well. Oh, and don't forget the beach house!

The key to living well in Panama is first establishing the budget by which you would like to live, then finding appropriate housing—the rest should fall into place. If you have come to Panama in search of the simple life, and you don't need to be surrounded by the conveniences of downtown Panama City, then you can definitely reduce your cost of living by making the move. To give you an idea of the life you would be leading, you would be living in a modest house with a garden, in an area inhabited mainly by lower-middle class Panamanians and possibly a few foreigners, such as Cerro Viento or Las Cumbres on the outskirts of Panama City. You might have a used car, or travel by bus or taxi, and you will eat out in typical Panamanian restaurants. Be honest about whether you are going to enjoy living frugally before you embark on it as a permanent lifestyle. Perhaps rent for a short while in some of the areas where you are considering buying to get a real feel for life there. Life in a modest neighborhood in Panama City will no doubt be very different from where you came from, so don't rush in too quickly.

HOUSING EXPENSES

During the high-construction real estate boom years of 2005–2009, housing prices increased dramatically, particularly in Panama City, as a response to the influx of expats from the United States, Canada, Venezuela, and Colombia and the lack of available housing—everything was still under construction. Rental prices in downtown Panama City skyrocketed to the point where you could hardly rent anything for less than US$1,200 per month, and that would get you a small or old apartment in an average location. A large, three-bedroom apartment in Punta Pacifica or Costa del Este, Panama City's most desirable neighborhoods, would run you about US$3,000 per month. If you bought the apartment, it would have cost around US$350,000, plus the maintenance fee on the condo (usually charged at US$1–2 per square meter). As more properties become available, a surplus is developing, which is slowly starting to bring the prices down, although some realtors and owners are still in denial of this fact at present.

Housing expenses will vary depending on whether you require a short-term or a long-term residence. If you will only be here for three to six months, you will want to live near your job or project. Your housing expenses will be higher—US$1,700–2,000 a month (or US$750–800 per week)—since short-term rentals include the cost of all furnishings and utilities, and you will pay for those conveniences. However, if you are looking for something long-term, budget US$800–2,000 for a simpler lifestyle, or US$2,500–5,500 for more luxurious living—central air-conditioning, electric water heater, premium cable TV service, and rents that start at US$1,500 a month.

If you purchase a home in Panama City or David, it will probably cost somewhere between US$80,000 and US$175,000, and then your monthly cost of living would be around US$700 for one person or US$1,200 for two. In the interior provinces, Bocas del Toro, the Highlands, and the Pacific Central, you can expect to pay less for electricity and water. Oceanfront living, however, requires a lot of maintenance and can add another US$500 a month, on average, to your monthly housing costs. You will also need a caretaker to live on the property while you are away.

Furnishings cost as much as or as little as you want. If you want to live simply, you can do it for almost nothing. You can find furnishings at secondhand or discount furniture stores, or scour flea markets for wonderful pieces. There are wonderful carpenters who can create wood furnishings and ironworkers who make cast-iron objects for very affordable prices (a few hundred dollars for a medium-sized piece); these craftspeople can help you design an original piece or copy something out of a catalog you like. This doesn't mean it will be done at rapid speeds. Expect to wait a long time for delivery on these services. Conversely, you can shop at fancy European furniture distributors and pay a lot of money (perhaps US$3,000 per room) to get settled into your three-bedroom apartment, but at least you will know exactly what you are getting. There are occasional bargains to be found, especially during April, August, and December when salary bonuses are paid.

Domestic Help

Domestic help is a very common expenditure in Latin America. Most everyone from the middle and upper class has someone in the house to help, perhaps one or two days a week for just one or two people, and often every workday for a family of four or more. If you are hiring a nanny to take care of your children and do some extra housecleaning, you might budget US$150–200 per month, if the nanny doesn't live with you. If you hire a live-in nanny, then you might pay US$250 a month plus room and board. This may seem like a steal to foreigners who pay an arm and a leg for daycare, but you will find that it is all part of the new standards and costs of living you are now adjusting to. Nannies and housekeepers work very hard, and they deserve to be paid well. If you can put them on Social Security, pay them the 13th month bonus the government obliges, and give them vacation time, you will feel good about your investment.

Housecleaning costs depend on the size of your apartment, but this cost tends to run about US$12–15 per day for an apartment of 120 square meters (1,290 square feet), if the maid does not live with you.

FOOD EXPENSES

Wherever you live in Panama, you have to see what is available in the way of food shopping in order to understand how much you will spend on a monthly basis. For instance, if you decide to move to El Valle de Anton, a popular Central Highlands destination, you will notice that it has one supermarket called

WHERE TO BUY
THE FRESHEST PRODUCE

If you enjoy natural living in a land blessed with agricultural variety and potential, you should take advantage of *"el chino,"* small Chinese-owned grocery stores specializing in the freshest selection of fruits and vegetables. In Panama City, examples are the Mini Max in the Bal Harbour commercial center in Paitilla, and la China de Corozal in the Canal Zone. They not only offer more exotic fare, imported and at a lower cost than the supermarkets, but they carefully select and handle their produce – you can taste the difference. Not all *chinos* around the country are vegetable markets, though, so scout it carefully.

Farmers markets are few in Panama. The two largest are in El Valle on Thursday and Sunday, and the Mercado de Abastos located on Avenida Nacional in Panama City, which is open every day from early morning till 5 P.M. Their offerings are not as selective, as farmers from all over will bring their entire selling stock. But the prices are much lower than supermarket produce, and you have more to choose from. The charm in buying from the markets, aside from the savings, is that you are directly supporting local farmers and you learn about the incredible variety of foods from all over the country. The sellers are noble, learning that customers will return to their kiosk if they offer a selection that fits the bill, so carefully choose the vendors with the freshest produce. Some stocks stay on for days at a time, but generally the new stocks come in on Tuesday and Saturday. Fine restaurants will only get their daily stock from the Mercado in Panama City. Learn to identify and enjoy the *marañon* (cashew apple), star fruit, *maracuya* (passion fruit), and noni fruit. The variety and prices will blow you away. Imagine the temptation to experiment with fruits and vegetables in your menu when you can buy four pineapples for a dollar or a branch of bananas still hanging as if from the tree or a sack of 100 mangoes or oranges for US$3 each.

You can buy hydroponics and organic greens and fruits, usually more pricey but locally grown and imported, in some supermarkets. A curious (and delicious) quality about the country is its abundance of mango trees; in season (around March to May) they literally explode with fruits, and a clever mango fan can often find trees in public areas and harvest free mangoes.

El Mini Super Hong Kong that offers very basic food options. In Bocas del Toro's Isla Colón, and in areas south of David or in the middle of the Azuero Peninsula, you will have small grocery stores called Mini Supers, of the same caliber. When you shop at these local markets or grocery stores, your food prices will be very affordable. You can expect to fill your cabinets for a few weeks for US$35–45 per person, but you will have to adapt your diet a little, since most of the brands you are used to in the United States will not be available. You can supplement these simple grocery items with greens and fruits from local vegetable markets and you will certainly have fulfilled your goal of living well and cheaply for a fraction of what you might spend in your home country.

If you require some food items beyond the basics, these are available in the major supermarkets around the country, like El Rey, Super 99, Extra, El Machetazo, or Riba Smith (this one only available in Panama City). If you are outside of Panama City, you will probably make a weekly or biweekly trip to one of these stores. In the Chiriquí Highlands this might be Romero Supermarkets or PriceSmart. These stores have selections priced economically by foreign standards, but they also have plenty more options that can easily hike up your bill, moving that decimal point over just a notch. You might get carried away with nostalgic selections from back home; if so, you will want to budget for a weekly food cost of US$50 per person.

CLOTHING AND OTHER GOODS

It's interesting to live in a country that serves as a way station for commercial items crossing waters to and from countries all over the world. Items come and go, and stock changes rapidly. Prices of goods such as clothing, electronics, and even cosmetics and personal hygiene products are much lower than what you paid in the States. You can buy nice products for less at the *almacenes* (department stores) on the Avenida Central in Panama City, or in the main avenues of the closest major city in your area. These stores sell anything and everything for extremely affordable prices.

Imitation designer clothes or even authentic-label goods at outlet sales will sell for US$2–11. Most of the time clothing items marked under US$3 may not be tried on, but at those prices it seems justifiable. For women who like to dress up and knock each other out with style, every once in a while you will find a one-of-a-kind opportunity, if you have the patience to rummage through the racks of the discount clothing warehouses. Most of these can be found along the Avenida Central and Caledonia, busy streets in the center of Panama City. Throughout the interior, in larger cities such as David, Santiago, and especially the border towns like Almirante, you will also find discount warehouses. There are big stores too, such as Feria Americana and American Warehouse, that sell second-hand clothes. Vintage shoppers will be all too happy to find old vinyl records, funky leather trench coats, and styles that keep coming back from days you once thought were long gone.

The other end of the spectrum is difficult to define since there are almost limitless opportunities to spend money here. At the high-end mall, Multiplaza, new items of reasonably priced clothing will easily cost US$35–100 each, and you can spend far more than that at really high-end stores like the glitzy Louis Vuitton and Carolina Herrera boutiques.

One major myth about living in the same country as the Panama Canal and its Free Zone is that electronics are cheaper here. This is false. In fact, electronics tend to be 10–20 percent more expensive. Some cheaper, less familiar Asian brands, which are actually quite decent in quality, are available which help to alleviate the costs, but the Mac store, for instance, is more expensive than buying online or in the United States. Photography equipment and video supplies are also more expensive. However, maintenance and repairs on these items tend to be more affordable, since they use secondhand replacement parts, which may be a perfectly good option. Make sure you know what you're buying.

FUEL AND AUTO EXPENSES

Although subject to fluctuation, fuel prices in Panama are very similar to those of the United States. In 2009, the prices fluctuated around US$2.30 for 91 Octane, slightly higher for 95 Octane (the highest-octane fuel sold here); diesel was slightly lower, around US$1.95 per gallon. Most gas stations offer either full- or self-service options. Full service costs a few cents more per gallon, but the attendant fills up for you and will give you a complimentary oil and water check—and will appreciate a small tip.

When the price of fuel was at its highest in 2008, the prices in Panama hit US$5 per gallon for unleaded fuel, and even diesel had gone up. Since Panama relies heavily on automobile transportation and suffers from serious traffic jams daily, gas tanks were insatiable and many SUVs were going through US$60–80 in fuel weekly. Now the market has returned to reasonable, and unleaded fuel prices have not strayed far from US$2.20–2.50 per gallon.

Autos are cheaper in Panama, by about 15–25 percent. However, this is relative to the general cost of living, so if you are on a Panamanian salary you will not be able to enjoy the difference. Car repairs are very affordable. Dents can be fixed for US$50–150, and this might include the labor. Tires are expensive, roughly US$80–100 per tire, depending on your car size. Cars depreciate quickly in Panama, since the roads and driving skills are so poor, so you can always assume a car you buying secondhand has endured a harder life than you might otherwise expect.

The national lottery is a longtime tradition.

ENTERTAINMENT EXPENSES

A big part of the Panama social scene is parties at friend's houses. They can be sit-down dinner parties where the host pays for everything, or they can be informal soirées where friends gather and each bring a bottle or a dish. The good thing about these parties, apart from being fun, is that they are the cheapest way to socialize. Now, when you choose to go out, the price of entertainment depends largely on your tastes. For example, a night at a "grill," an open-air bar-restaurant serving typical Panamanian food and cold local beer or liquor, will be a very affordable evening. A beer will cost US$1–2 and a plate of food around US$6–10. Take your date to one of the more fashionable nightspots in the city, and expect to pay around US$3 for the very same beer and anywhere from US$10 to US$25 for an entrée. Bear in mind, however, that many of the restaurants here are serving good gourmet cuisine for these prices—a similar restaurant in the US would charge a lot more—so if you have the money, you will appreciate the good value.

When it comes to other forms of entertainment, most options in Panama are very reasonably priced. Take the movie theater as an example. A regular seat in the theater (most movies are shown in English or their original language with subtitles) costs US$4 and VIP seating, which gives you a ridiculously comfortable recliner and waitress service to your seat throughout the film, costs US$6–9 depending on the theater. An hour's bowling costs around US$25. Events like concerts offer a range of ticket prices from US$15 up to US$150 or more, depending on your seat choice and the artist performing.

TIPPING

While tipping is neither obligatory nor prevalent in Panama, it is definitely appreciated, considering the server's low wages. In some restaurants, a 10 percent gratuity will be included in the check; if not, you should tip 10–20 percent, depending on how satisfied you are with the service.

Banking

Panama City is an international banking sector with 80 worldwide banks. Also present are all kinds of commerce organizations and offshore trust companies. Of these banks, about 40 have a full general banking license and offer the traditional banking service you would expect from your personal bank. The others are licensed as offshore banks and are authorized to do business with clients from all over the world, but not Panama.

CURRENCY

Panama's official currency is the Balboa, although this has been tied to the U.S. dollar at a rate of 1:1 since 1903. While there are Panamanian coins, there are no Panamanian notes; the U.S. bills are legal tender, as are the coins (they have the same denominations and sizes as the Panamanian coins). Other currencies are hard to find here, and unlike most other countries in the world, you will not see a moneychanger *(bureau de change)* here, not even in the airport. So, if you are coming from the European Union, or another country in Latin America, be sure to bring dollars or withdraw money from an ATM here. Travelers checks are not widely accepted or changed here, either.

OPENING A BANK ACCOUNT

To open a bank account, you must have several things from your home country: the last three months' bank statements from your personal account at home, a copy of your passport (every page), and references. There will also be a minimum deposit required to open the account and a minimum balance that must be maintained. Be sure to know this amount, as it will help you avoid paying fees in the future. Requirements vary from bank to bank, and some banks are unwilling to open accounts for foreigners, so shop around. You will also find that the banks here ask more questions than banks at home, such as how many withdrawals and deposits you will make each month and how many wire transfers and where to, and other similar questions. Don't worry—it is

© SKY GILBAR

Panama City is home to approximately 80 of the world's banking institutions.

nothing personal. The bank protects itself from money laundering by finding out as much as it can about its customers. Even if you are savvy enough to turn in all the required paperwork rapidly and efficiently, don't expect that you will have the account open in a day, as in the United States. It can take weeks to get off the ground, as processes change and revisions take a long time. It is highly frustrating, but better to know ahead of time so you can keep some living money handy while you get your account up and running. The same is true for opening a business account. Word on the street is that Banco General has the best service when it comes to opening accounts efficiently. There are other banks with happy clientele, so get curious and ask fellow expats or Panamanian acquaintances what banks they recommend.

CREDIT CARDS

Credit cards are widely accepted throughout Panama, with Visa and MasterCard being the most common. American Express is also widely accepted, but not everywhere, so ask before you eat. If you are looking to obtain a credit card from a Panamanian institution, you will usually need to either have a residency visa, or be working here. The bank will ask to see your income tax declaration or proof of your Social Security payments to verify your income. Be sure to understand the interest rates and the payment due date for your card. Try to get a credit card from a bank with online banking to avoid the long lines every month to pay your bill.

THE BALBOA: PANAMA'S CURRENCY

The Balboa, named for Vasco Núñez de Balboa, the first European to cross Panama and set sights on the Pacific Ocean in 1513, was created as Panama's currency in 1904, upon the country's independence from Colombia. Ever since its inception, the Balboa has been pegged at a 1:1 ratio to the U.S. dollar, and the dollar is accepted as legal tender throughout the country. Initially, Balboa coins were made of silver and were offered in denominations of 2.5, 5, 10, 25, and 50 *céntesimos*. The smallest weighed just less than half an ounce, earning it the nickname the "Panama Pearl." Denominations varied and changed throughout time, with a 1-Balboa coin coming into circulation in 1931, minted to exactly the same size as the US$1 coin.

Coins are no longer made of silver, but rather a copper-nickel composition, and they are today available in the exact same denominations as U.S. coins: $0.01, $0.05, $0.10, $0.25, and $0.50. They are also the exact same size and weight as U.S. coins and are used interchangeably in Panama, but don't try using your Panamanian coins in the United States – they won't be as welcome there.

As far as banknotes go, the U.S. dollar bill has been legal tender ever since 1904, although one Panamanian President, Arnulfo Arias, did release some Balboa bills into circulation in 1941. They didn't last long; only seven days later they were all recalled and it was back to the U.S. dollar. Numismatists on the isthmus usually have a one-Balboa bill in their collection, but that's about the only place you will find one now.

Taxes

Though Panama is known to many as a tax haven, this in no way means that there are no taxes to pay here. Although few of the taxes affect the average expat, anyone working here or starting a business will pay several taxes. Every resident pays the 5 percent ITBMS sales tax, levied on all goods and services at the time of purchase.

SOCIAL SECURITY AND EDUCATION TAX

Employees in Panama are paid on the 15th and 30th of every month. In the case that these dates fall on a weekend, they are paid on the Friday before. With each payday come Social Security or *seguro social* contributions of 8 percent from the employee and 11.5 percent from the employer. Other contributions include the Educational Tax or *seguro educativo* (1.25 percent from the employee and 1.5 percent from the employer) and the Occupational Risk Tax or *riesgo profesional* (varying amount, around 2 percent from the employer only).

INCOME TAX

Panamanian income tax on personal gains, such as salary, bonuses, and company shares, varies from a 2 percent minimum to a 30 percent maximum, depending on the Panama-sourced income earned by the individual. Only Panamanian sources of income are taxable; the Panamanian government cannot tax money earned outside of Panama. Taxation on Panamanian income applies to both citizens and temporary residents. The fiscal year runs from January to December, and taxes must be filed by the end of March of the following year. In the case of a salaried employee, the employer must withhold the appropriate tax and pay it to the government, so the employee is not required to pay any additional taxes at the end of the year.

Note that you don't need to declare the income for the tax department or Dirección General de Ingresos to know you earned it. If you receive payment for something you have done in Panama by check, the person paying will usually ask for your passport number. When the company or person who paid you that money declares their annual income and expenses, their statement will include your fee. And, yes, the tax department is connected to immigration, so not declaring monies that you received in Panama could result in immigration problems.

REAL ESTATE TAXES

Real estate investors in Panama in recent years have been able to take advantage of the 20-year tax exemption on new properties; this law was recently extended to include properties built until 2009, so anyone purchasing a new property in 2009 will not pay any property taxes on it until 2029. The exemption is transferable, so should you sell your property, you pass the exemption on to the new owner.

The other principal real estate tax is the property transfer tax, which is paid by the seller when the title is transferred. It is currently set at 2 percent of the registered property value or the sale price, whichever is higher.

TAXES IN YOUR HOME COUNTRY

In your time in Panama, you will most likely encounter individuals who haven't sent a dime to the U.S. government since they moved here, but that doesn't mean it's OK. Rules vary by country, but if you're a U.S. citizen and you are earning money outside of the United States, you must file taxes each year. Even if you are not earning any income from work, you will still have investment income, and it is a good idea to file to keep your tax record in good standing and avoid a nasty airport pickup upon your return home. Section 911 of the U.S.

DAILY LIFE

tax code permits taxpayers living and earning outside of the United States to earn up to US$80,000 per year of tax-free income. However, in order to qualify, the taxpayer must be outside of the United States for at least 330 days of a year or must become a permanent resident of Panama. If you earn more than US$80,000 , and you have paid taxes on the amount in Panama, you will not receive any foreign tax credit from the U.S. government. In order to qualify for the foreign income exclusion, taxpayers must file Form 2555. Rules about tax declaration are different in each country and subject to change, so you should always consult with a professional before making decisions about filing.

Investing

It seems over the last few years that investing in little-known nations around the world is the thing to do. Panama is no exception. As people tire of the traditional investment avenues of domestic stocks, bonds, mutual funds, and property investments, investing abroad can be an attractive option, and if you play your cards right, it can be very lucrative. However, it is important not to go into an investment in a country you know little about with your eyes closed. Panama, for many reasons, is an extremely advantageous place to invest, especially compared to other nations in the region. This does not mean that it is without its scams. If someone tells you that you will receive 20 percent interest each month from an investment you don't really understand—all you have to do is send your money—beware. Recent news has uncovered several huge international pyramid schemes operating either part or all of their operations from Panama, and investors from around the world have been stung. This does not mean, however, that it is not safe to invest here. Be sure to find a competent lawyer, get all the documents you need translated into English, ask as many questions as you want, and do as much research as you possibly can until you feel 100 percent comfortable with the investment. Then, and only then, should you part with any of your money.

PROPERTY INVESTMENT

Since the early 2000s, Panama has been one of the go-to countries for property investments in Central America. At the beginning of the boom, there were some great deals to be had, from beachfront land at pennies-per-meter and preconstruction condos in downtown Panama City for US$700 per square meter to remote Highland hideaways for peanuts. Many foreign investors found themselves some superb bargains and have since "flipped" (resold) these properties and continue to live on the profits today. Now, things are a little different. Toward the end of 2008, more or less coinciding with the beginning of the global credit crunch, the increase in prices here leveled off and the number of speculators dropped to pre-boom numbers. At the same time, completed buildings helped to push supply up to somewhere closer or equal to demand, naturally bringing the exorbitant prices down. Thanks to interest in Panama from South American neighbors Colombia and Venezuela, there are still people shopping for homes in Panama, just not as many.

As far as the deals go, there are still some good property investments out there, you just need to look a little harder than before. The fact that supply now outweighs demand is great news for a would-be investor; it is a buyer's market. This means you don't have to rush into anything, and you can shop around and bargain with sellers until you find a great deal.

Real estate on offer varies greatly, from an oceanfront penthouse apartment in a 60-story building in Panama City to a beachfront lot on the Pacific Coast, from a private laguna waterfront property in the Caribbean to a golf course estate home on an 18-hole course in the Highlands. You will find the best deals in more removed areas of the country, where not much foreign investment has arrived, or in areas where there is little infrastructure. Until recently, for example, land on the Caribbean coast of Panama was very reasonably priced because the road was in such terrible condition; although it is only 60 kilometers from Panama City, it could take several hours to get there. Now, a new highway has been completed, reducing the journey time to just one hour, and land has instantly increased in value as a result.

REFORESTATION INVESTMENT

Reforestation investments have been the subject of controversy in Panama, but they also have several benefits. The idea behind making a reforestation investment is that you purchase a piece of land, usually 10 or 20 hectares, through a specialist organization, which plants trees on the land. In return, the investor gets a residency visa in Panama, and eventually (after about 15 years), a fair return on his investment. Communities in the area where the trees are being planted also benefit from the investment, since it brings jobs to that (usually remote) area, and Panama benefits from the added forest and thus an improved environment.

By year 15, the trees are large enough to be sold. According to Jeff Duda of Panama Forestry, if global teak prices increase at a modest 2 percent each year, the return at the end of year 15 would be around US$10,000 on an US$80,000 plot (about 2.5 hectares). His company, Panama Forestry, currently

DAILY LIFE

offers 2.4-hectare parcels of land near Penenome for $3–4 per square meter, although land prices vary around the country. The 18-year return would be around US$15,000, and the 22-year, final harvest return would yield about US$130,000. The reality is that timber prices are actually increasing faster than that. Once the final harvest is done, the investor retains ownership of the land and can let trees grow naturally on it, re-enter the parcel into the reforestation program, or sell the land.

There is, however, quite a bit of doubt over the ecological benefits of teak farming. While Panama is home to one of the largest tracts of primary rainforest in the world, deforestation is a serious problem. Farmers have grown accustomed to slash-and-burn practices, and government incentives to farm cattle have prompted them to cut down trees in order to farm more cattle, instead of animals that require less land. Supporters, on the other hand, believe that the program is a win-win option, since the investor gets his or her residency and a potentially high return on investment, while Panama benefits from increased forested areas and social development in the areas being reforested. The process of reforestation also creates jobs in remote, deforested areas where there is no work and many people live either at or below the poverty line. Increased forest also adds to the biodiversity of the area, helps to prevent flooding, and reduces the amount of carbon dioxide in the air.

Reforestation investments can be lucrative for individuals who have a certain amount of money that they can afford to tie up in a long-term investment and are looking to benefit from the residency. If it's a quick buck you're after, real estate is probably a better bet due to the ambiguity and impracticality of the reforestation investment laws. You won't be guaranteed a visa through reforestation until the government can straighten out their incentives.

There are several organizations in Panama that manage reforestation investment programs, including Futuro Forestal and United Nature; you can find out more by consulting a lawyer.

TOURISM INVESTMENT

Tourism investment in Panama can come in many forms, from starting a small sidewalk café in the Casco Antiguo to a multi-million dollar investment in an international hotel chain on the beach and everything in between. All tourism investment here is done privately. Lately most investors here have been more interested in real estate since it tends to deliver faster returns, so investments in tourism have suffered a little. Those coming to Panama from Costa Rica will notice a sharp difference: Panama has far fewer tourist attractions and hotels than its northern neighbor. Nevertheless, basic infrastructure—roads, water, and electricity—is superior here, so tourism investments should be more straightforward. Would-be investors need only take a trip to Costa Rica to see what kind of tourism businesses succeed there to have a good idea of what will succeed here. After all, Panama has very similar landscapes to Costa Rica.

This said, there have been significant increases in tourist offerings in the last 10 years, mainly in the form of boutique hotels and adventure attractions like canopy tours and rafting operators. The existence of such businesses is due in part to the investment incentives offered by the Panamanian government.

Panama Law 8

Law No. 8 of 1994 is one of the most comprehensive laws for tourism development in Latin America, regulating all aspects of the tourism industry, from hotels to marinas. This law jump-started tourism investment, and some of the world's largest hospitality companies now have a presence in Panama, including Marriott, InterContinental, Sheraton, and Radisson. The law is also applicable to smaller companies.

Companies or individuals investing a minimum of US$50,000 (not including the purchase of the land) in a tourism-related venture in the interior of the country attain a series of attractive benefits, as long as they have the approval of the ATP, Autoridad Turismo de Panama (Panamanian Tourism Authority), including various tax exemptions and increased depreciation. For projects within Panama City, the minimum investment required is US$300,000.

OFFSHORE LAWS

As one of the world's tax havens, Panama offers a variety of benefits to individuals and corporations moving their assets here. Generally speaking, a corporation or an individual operating from Panama does not have to pay taxes to Panama on any income earned outside of the country. However, individuals should declare this income to their own country. Note that at the time of writing, U.S. President Barack Obama and British Prime Minister Gordon Brown are developing tax reforms aimed at further regulating tax havens around the world and thus, Panama's position as a haven could be in jeopardy.

Anonymity

The real benefits of offshore banking and operating, both to the individual and the corporation, lie in the anonymity. Corporations here are known as *sociedades anónimas* (anonymous societies) and they aid the individual in maintaining secrecy throughout his business transactions. When you open a *sociedad anónima* (S.A.) in Panama, your lawyer creates the corporation just as you would create one in your home country. The shareholders and respective percentages are defined, share certificates are issued, the company is registered at the public registry and you are good to go. You can even establish your company online at *Panama Emprende* and remove the need for the lawyer. Once the company is created, just one look at the Public Registry, which can also be done online, will tell you who the company directors are (president, secretary, and treasurer). There is no way of telling who the actual shareholders are. Under normal circumstances, the owners of the company would appear as the directors. Individuals seeking secrecy, however, will usually "hire" some Panamanians to appear as directors of their corporations and thus avoid being discovered as owners. There is nothing wrong with owning a Panamanian corporation as long as you declare the assets within that company.

To increase the secrecy of ownership, some individuals choose to start a corporation to handle all their personal business and then use this corporation to own shares in another one. For example, John Smith opens the company Smith, S.A. He then wishes to open another business, Panama, S.A with some partners. His share of that company will be owned by Smith, S.A., instead of John Smith.

The same situation will usually take place when purchasing real estate. It is advisable to purchase real estate here with a Panamanian corporation, rather than under your personal name (unless you are buying property to gain residency, then you have to purchase in your own name), since it makes transferring the property later much simpler. Also, if you were going through a divorce back home, for example, the property cannot be considered one of your personal assets.

Offshore tax laws are complicated and you should consult with a professional to ensure you fully understand them.

MULTINATIONAL COMPANIES IN PANAMA

A large number of multinationals have their regional headquarters in Panama, mainly for reasons pertaining to the country's geographic location, the logistical advantages of the Panama Canal and the U.S. dollar, the economical and political stability of the country, and the availability of bilingual labor at affordable prices. For companies operating from Panama but not serving any clients within Panama, there are tax benefits, the most notable of which is not paying tax on the income earned from outside. The most common examples of such businesses are call centers; Panama's bilingual agents remotely serve many of the U.S. Fortune 500 companies.

The technological sector and pharmaceutical sector are also turning their attention to Panama. Recently, Hewlett Packard and Procter & Gamble moved their regional operations to Panama. These multinational corporations are able to import skilled labor to Panama to work for them here, as well as employ Panamanians once they arrive. These skilled employees make up a significant part of the expat community living in Panama City.

Special Economic Zones

The creation of several "Special Economic Zones" in the country, including Panama Pacifica in Howard, just west of Panama City and the Colón Free Zone, provides international corporations with plenty of tempting incentives to move their operations to Panama.

Panama Pacifica is currently being developed on the grounds of a former U.S. Army base, on the western side of the Panama Canal. In an area covering the exact same acreage as Panama City (not including San Miguelito), Panama Pacifica will include residential areas, hotels, schools, leisure facilities, and an array of commercial areas, from assembly plants to call centers. Companies establishing their operations within the perimeter of Panama Pacifica will benefit from a long list of incentives as defined in Tax Law 41, including exemptions from real estate property tax, license tax, dividend tax, and stamp tax, among others. Other benefits include flexible labor laws allowing employers to negotiate working hours and vacation benefits with their employees outside the restrictions of typical Panamanian labor law. Employment of foreign workers is also a possibility.

Companies already benefiting from Panama Pacifica include Dell, Cabo Drilling Corp., and Panama Aerospace Engineering. Caterpillar and 3M will be opening operations here in the near future.

CORRUPTION AND BRIBERY

According to the 2009 Index of Economic Freedom, an index compiled annually by The Heritage Foundation and The Wall Street Journal, Panama has the 55th freest economy of the 179 countries included in the index and of the 29 countries in Latin America, Panama ranks 10th (the U.S. and Canada rank 6th and 7th, respectively). The index measures a variety of elements, including trade freedom, fiscal freedom, investment freedom, property freedom, and freedom from corruption. The main reason Panama's ranking is not higher is the widespread corruption, which unfortunately prevails throughout government entities, the police force, and politics in general. Campaign promises from newly elected president Ricardo Martinelli set out to reduce corruption, although success seems unlikely: Panama's border with Colombia has made it a drug transit zone for as long as the DEA can remember, and it will be difficult to change that.

Money laundering is a natural side effect of passing drugs through a country. Every now and then, you will notice a business in Panama that doesn't seem to be doing much business and wonder how on earth it hasn't closed down, or perhaps the large number of vacant apartment buildings (some call this "the darkest skyline in the world"). Truth be told, these businesses are probably reporting significant revenues even though no money comes in through the door, and then they are cleared to deposit drug money in the bank, and no questions will be asked.

Transparency International, an NGO (nongovernmental organization) that strives for a corruption-free world, ranks Panama 94th out of 179 countries in its 2007 Corruption Perceptions Index. Its organizational goal is to improve this ranking and at the same time reduce the disparity between rich and poor. There is a long way to go; corruption is, alas, ingrained in many of the Panamanians' mindsets. If you discover some kind of corruption, on the smallest level to "pay out" of a traffic ticket or on a grander level to obtain a government permit, you should walk away and refuse to contribute to the corruption. Reporting it is tough, as you never know who is involved or what repercussions it might have. As a foreigner, do your part by knowing correct legal procedures and insisting on using them, to avoid any misunderstandings.

COMMUNICATIONS

Panama has been a simple country with regards to communications. Until recently there was only one telephone company, one cable company, two cell phone companies, and a familiar group of media big shots who own the industry. Now however, competition is starting to flirt with former monopolies. For this reason, you will find that "customer service" is a new idea here, and while Panamanians will always treat you kindly, they might not get your sense of urgency or expectation for instant setup. You'll learn to deal with it; in Panama the customer is *not* always right.

Once you figure out the tricks to getting the best out of the services available, you'll find Panama really does have acceptable communications access. In fact, it is often mind-blowing to find a cell phone signal in the middle of the jungle or on remote islands. Telephone rates, both within Panama and internationally, are extremely reasonable. Because all fiber optic lines going from North to South America must pass through the isthmus, Panama has a leading position on the information highway of the 21st century.

Telephone Service

According to the CIA World Factbook, in 2007, 90 percent of Panamanians had access to either a fixed line or mobile telephone. Today, that statistic would undoubtedly be higher; within the larger cities, the figure could easily be close to 100 percent. However, in the more removed areas of the country, such as the Darien, some villages share one public pay phone, and it is often out of order.

LANDLINES

Thanks to the partial privatization of the telephone sector, there are now several options when it comes to contracting a fixed telephone line. The British company Cable & Wireless was the original provider here, and it continues to be the market leader, although it now face competition from Cable Onda and Telecarrier, with other providers slowly appearing on the scene.

Cable & Wireless, Cable Onda, and Telecarrier

In Panama's residential fixed line or landline service, Cable & Wireless is the leader, offering a traditional telephone line. In the majority of existing homes around the country, these lines will already be present, making installation fairly straightforward, and most new buildings will have been constructed with telephone lines in mind. Since Cable & Wireless was the government-chosen telephone operator in the country, its operations are unfortunately still reminiscent of a state-run system. In fact, it is often dubbed Cable & Worthless by its less-than-satisfied clients, thanks to long installation waits and the fact that, when moving house or office, you can only take your number with you if you are staying within the same neighborhood area.

The competitor Cable Onda offers the service from a cable, rather than a traditional telephone line, and is able to install new service much faster. Prices are similar and customers usually choose this service as part of a package with their Internet and cable television (Cable Onda is the only provider of cable TV in Panama). Service is generally better than Cable & Wireless, but the telephone will only work when the Internet is working. If the Internet goes down, so does the telephone.

VoIP Calls

International calls here are surprisingly affordable. From almost all Internet cafés, you can call the United States or Canada and other countries in Central

America for around US$0.05 per minute and calls farther afield, to, say, the United Kingdom, are priced from around US$0.10 per minute. These calls are all being made over the Internet and, as such, are very cost-effective. You can also make Internet calls from your home, through modern marvels such as Skype, which serves expats abroad wonderfully to keep in touch with family or maintain business contacts without feeling far from the action.

The VoIP (Voice over Internet Protocol) industry has done very well in Panama. VoIP services calls via the Internet, but it is installed just like a regular phone system, so you can have a switchboard with various lines, except that all the calls dial directly over the Internet. This is the ideal solution for a call center or any other business receiving 800-number calls or making a lot of international calls.

International Calling Codes

When making outbound long-distance or international calls from a fixed line in Panama, you can significantly reduce the price by dialing a three-digit code before the number. This function routes your phone call through another provider, but your regular provider will include this in your monthly bill. There are several different codes you can choose, and rates change often. You can check current rates on each provider's website. Principal providers of this service and their respective codes are Clarocom 055/, Telecarrier 088/, and Advanced 099/. At the time of writing, Advanced Communication Network was offering calls to the United States and Canada through its 099 code at US$0.07 per minute.

CELLULAR PHONES

Until recently, Cable & Wireless (Más Móvil) and Telefónica (Movistar), were the only two cell phone providers in Panama. At the beginning of 2009, two new providers opened operations here, generating greater competition among the providers and consequently better deals for the consumers. Of the newcomers, the first to arrive was Digicel, an Irish-backed corporation specializing in cellular communications in Latin America and the Caribbean. The company is now present in 26 countries in the region. A few months after Digicel's arrival, Claro, the largest provider in the Americas, owned by Mexican communications mogul Carlos Slim, arrived on the scene. All four providers offer prepaid or contract phones, as well as BlackBerry data plans and a wide range of cellular phones, albeit a few months behind those offered in the United States and Europe.

DAILY LIFE

Contract vs. Prepaid Cell Phones

When acquiring a mobile phone here, you need to decide whether you will opt for a contract *(contrato)* or a prepaid plan *(prepago)*. In deciding which is most appropriate for your calling habits, note that cell phone calls are paid by the caller, per minute. Unlike in the United States, if you are receiving a phone call, you don't use minutes or pay a penny.

Depending on your needs and wants, contract and prepaid both have their benefits. The contract option is ideal for those spending all their time in Panama. You pay a monthly fee, which includes a certain number of minutes, and, if you use a BlackBerry or other PDA, a certain amount of data. Contracts usually last for 18 months. Once you commit to a certain plan, you must maintain that plan for the duration of the contract, unless you choose to upgrade. Downgrading or terminating during the contract is not possible.

Increasing competition in the sector means plan prices are constantly getting lower, and signing a new contract usually entitles you to a free or discounted cell phone. The more expensive the plan, the better the phone.

Prepaid, on the other hand, means that you purchase the cell phone of your choice, and it comes with a certain number of minutes included. There is no contract. Once you run out of minutes, you can purchase a new card at a large variety of stores and even on the streets from authorized vendors—you will see them at busy intersections around the city. While calls are more expensive with prepaid phones, the cell phone companies run frequent promotions doubling, tripling, and even quadrupling the value of the top-up card you purchase, e.g. if you purchase a $20 card while the company is tripling, you will receive $60 of call value. Be warned, however, that the extra promotional dollars have an expiration date, so it might not be as good a deal as it seems!

Internet and Postal Service

ASYMMETRIC DIGITAL SUBSCRIBER LOOP (ADSL)

Panama's high-speed Internet access is offered through ADSL, which transfers information faster in one direction than traditional DSL. Internet cafés are common, offering extremely affordable rates (usually US$0.50 per hour), and contracting your own Internet service at home or in your office is simple and affordable. The two main providers are Cable Onda and Cable & Wireless. As with the telephone system, Cable Onda is a little more user-friendly than Cable & Wireless, and installation is usually faster. Prices are very similar. You will find that the bandwidths offered here are less than you would find

© SKY GILBAR

DAILY LIFE

Telecommunications is a first-class industry in Panama.

at home. This is not because the technology is not here, but rather the competition is not yet sufficient to force the providers to offer high-speed Internet. So, you might be used to getting 10 MBPS of Internet back home in the States for a few bucks every month. Here, the highest speed generally offered is 2 MBPS, and that costs around US$75 per month. Most people contract 512 KBPS or 1MB, and while it is sufficient for most people's needs, you will definitely notice a difference in your service at home. Telecarrier offers 10 MBPS to commercial clients, so the technology is certainly here, but until more providers start operating here it is unlikely that the average household will be contracting more than 1 or 2 MBPS.

One alternative to Cable Onda and Cable & Wireless is WIPET. WIPET is the marketing name for the gadget that contains WIMAX (Worldwide Inoperability for Microwave Access), the standard transmission format for wireless data, such as Wi-Fi, but in a larger scheme of metropolitan area coverage. WIPET is the first gadget of its kind, introduced in Panama at the beginning of 2008. Basically it is a wireless cable box that you purchase at any electronics store and hook up at home to pick up an Internet signal from anywhere within the Panama City metropolitan area, including out in Coronado, part of the Coclé Province. WIPET is now expanding to more areas around the country, which can be found on its website (www.wipet.com). You can purchase the WIPET box in several stores in Panama, including Multimax and Audiofoto; simply take the box home and start surfing. With WIPET you can have an annual contract and pay a monthly fee, which varies depending on the speed you wish to contract, or you can pay as you go on a weekly basis, which may be ideal for those who are not in the country full-time.

SNAIL MAIL AND MAIL-FORWARDING SERVICES

One of the most difficult aspects of life in Panama is the almost nonexistent postal service. The national mail service, or *correo nacional,* has branches all over the country where you can acquire a P.O. Box at a very reasonable price (about US$25 per year for personal or US$35 for corporate use). This P.O. Box is useful for receiving bank statements and bills from utility providers within Panama, but that's really the extent of it. The postal service does not deliver mail to your home or office. The post office in Panama is, however, adequate for sending international mail. Service takes about five days to the United States and about 10 days to Europe. Receiving mail in Panama from any other country can take between two weeks and an eternity, and often mail does not arrive.

Thankfully, there is an ingenious service that solves the problem of receiving mail from your home country. In recent years, various companies, including Mailboxes, Etc., Airbox Express, and Miami Express, have begun to offer post office boxes in Miami, to which you can have all your mail sent and then forwarded to Panama on a weekly or twice-weekly basis. They can either deliver it to your home or office or keep it at their office for you to collect. The service works well and is a fast and reliable way of receiving important correspondence, subscriptions, and items you purchase over the Internet. Each company offers a variety of plans. Some have no monthly fee, and you only pay when you receive something (in which case it is about US$2 for a letter), while others charge a monthly fee, which includes a certain number of received items each month or a monthly weight limit. When receiving a package, you need to provide the company with a copy of the invoice so you can pay the appropriate import fee, depending on the value and type of the item. This import charge will be added to the company's charge for shipping it, which is based on the weight and dimensions of the item. As an example, to receive a book that you purchased on Amazon.com, you can expect to pay about US$8 total for shipping and customs. This service works well for letters and light packages, but if you are buying large, heavy, or expensive items, have the company give you an approximate quote before you order the item or you could face a hefty bill once the item arrives in Panama. As these services are targeting mainly North Americans, you will usually find English-speaking staff at all their facilities.

MESSENGER AND COURIER SERVICES

When it comes to sending or receiving mail within Panama, there is no efficient solution. Since the mail system barely exists, most companies hire a messenger or a courier service to deliver their correspondence within the major cities here. Tasks that you took for granted as being very simple back home, such as paying your electricity bill, will now become a nuisance as you find you now have to go to the electricity company and wait in line to make the payment personally. This is undoubtedly one of the most frustrating aspects of living in Panama. However, online payments for services are available through many Panamanian banks, which will save you from the misery of going to the utility company.

If you need to send something to another town in Panama, two excellent services—Fletes Chavales and Uno Express—deliver mail and packages from Panama to Chiriquií and everywhere in between at very reasonable prices. A package sent rom Panama City to Boquete costs around US$2 and will arrive the next day. Another alternative is using the *encomiendas* (package) service of the two national airlines, Air Panama or Aeroperlas. You can deliver the package to the airline desk at the domestic terminal in Albrook, and it takes the package on its next flight to any of the Panama airports. From there recipients can pick up the packages or envelopes at their local, national airport. This is also a very cost-effective and efficient way of moving documents around the country.

INTERNATIONAL SHIPPING

When it comes to shipping something outside of Panama, you will find the major couriers are present in Panama: DHL, UPS, and FedEx. All have their main offices in the banking district of the Panama City. Most packages sent to the United States will take two days, as they have to go through customs, but FedEx can do next-day delivery to the States if you drop off your package by 3:30 p.m. DHL can do next-day delivery for simple documents, but as soon as you put something else in the package, it will take an extra day because of the customs check. Prices, as you might expect, are high. A simple letter to the United States costs around US$30.

A slightly more economical alternative is to send items with Copa Courier, the package service of Copa Airlines. It can take packages to any of its destination cities throughout the Americas and has far more economical prices than the main international couriers, although it may take a few days longer to deliver the package.

Media

NEWSPAPERS AND MAGAZINES

Newspapers in Panama have had a rather turbulent history. Due mainly to political unrest and the general lack of freedom of speech, each of the three principal newspapers has been closed down at least once. To a certain extent, the newspapers throughout Pamama's history have had to be careful with what they publish, not wishing to offend any political or otherwise powerful entities, unless they chose to align themselves with a particular party.

In 1968, after Omar Torrijos's coup d'état overthrew Arnulfo Arias's government, all media in Panama were closed down. After three days, all were given the green light to reopen, except for EPASA, publishers of *El Panamá América,* which had to wait 18 days. At this point, all media were subject to government censorship. It wasn't until the launch of *La Prensa* in 1980 that the country enjoyed a truly free newspaper, albeit not without disruption.

In its 29 years of operation, *La Prensa* has been closed down three times by the government, the most recent instance in February 1988, when it remained closed until December 1999, after the U.S. invasion of Panama. Along with the closures came vicious attacks on the newspaper's property and even assassination plots against the paper's founder, Roberto Eisenmann Jr.

Today, the same three newspapers—*El Panamá América, La Prensa,* and *La Estrella de Panamá*—continue to be the leading news sources in the country. All of these newspapers offer annual subscriptions so you can receive them at your door every morning at a very reasonable price.

La Prensa

Founded in 1980 by Roberto Eisenmann Jr., *La Prensa* is Panama's youngest newspaper; in terms of credibility, it is without a doubt the leading daily. Born after 13 years of hostility and government censorship, the goal of *La Prensa* was to provide citizens with information free of political influence. This was to become the truest sign of a real democracy.

Today, *La Prensa* continues to be directed by Roberto Eisenmann Jr., but the newspaper employs a rather unique ownership system. Every single one of the employees is a shareholder in the business, leading to a more motivated workforce and one truly interested in providing the public with accurate and truthful news.

La Prensa is printed daily and available throughout the country. Each Friday, the women's fashion supplement, *Ellas,* is included in the paper, increasing the

PANAMA'S *STAR & HERALD*

The first edition of the *Panama Star* was published in 1849, at the beginning of the Gold Rush, when Panama was still a Department of Colombia. Just four pages long, it was the product of three gold-hunters who had found themselves in Panama awaiting transport to California and hoped to make a few bucks while at the same time providing their fellow travelers with news about Panama. After just 10 months of operation, the hunters continued on their way, passing the operations on to Peyton Middleton and his brother, Lewis A. Middleton. In 1851, another Middleton brother, who also worked at the *Star*, decided to change allegiances and open another paper, the *Panama Herald*, with Colonel Edmund Green.

After further reshuffling, Lewis Middleton was left as the sole owner of the *Star* until he teamed up with Archibald Boardman Boyd in 1852. They increased the frequency of the paper from thrice-weekly to every day, thus producing the *Panama Daily Star*. At this point, the paper also included a Spanish section, called "La Estrella de Panamá."

The *Star* and the *Herald* maintained a serious rivalry, and in 1853, the *Herald* beat out the *Star* to become the first to publish a map detailing the initial plan of the Panama Canal. The bitter rivalry continued for three more years, until they settled on a merger. The *Star & Herald* was born in May 1854 and continued to include "La Estrella de Panamá" as a daily insert.

An economic downturn later on in 1854 caused the paper to reduce printing to just three times per week. In March 1855, the newspaper began to publish a French section, making it the first trilingual newspaper on the continent, and most probably, in the world. However, a few months later, the Spanish section would be temporarily removed due to differences in opinion between the then-editor, Colombian Dr. Bartolomé Calvo, and the owners of the paper. This would be the first major problem that the newspaper suffered, but others would come, including a three month temporary governmental closure in 1886 for alleged meddling in the politics of the isthmus.

With the closure, a new publication, the *Evening Telegram*, was published at the *Star & Herald* printing press, as a way of getting around the imposed suspension of operations.

The Star and Herald was acquired by by José Gabriel Duque Amaro in 1893 and began to operate as a Duque family business. In 1951, the two papers, *La Estrella de Panamá* and the *Star & Herald* were separated and published as two individual periodicals. In 1987, eight years after the United States returned partial control of the Canal to Panama, and U.S. citizens stationed here began to return to the States, the *Star & Herald* closed down due to financial reasons.

After 138 years of operations, the newspaper has essentially come full-circle, from an English-language to a bilingual to a trilingual and, until 2008, to a Spanish-only publication, *La Estrella de Panamá*. In 2008, 21 years later, an English insert, the "Panama Star," was re-established in *La Estrella de Panamá*.

Source: *Editora Panamá América, S.A.*

popularity of the newspaper on this day. On Sunday, just like most newspapers around the world, the paper is a little more expensive (US$0.50 instead of the usual US$0.35) and includes various inserts, including the *Domingo* magazine, *Mosaico* arts and culture section, and a Sunday translated edition of *The New York Times'* "Week in Review." During the week, *La Prensa* includes various other supplements, including a financial insert entitled "Martes Financiero" every Tuesday. *La Prensa* is published entirely in Spanish, although there is an English edition online at www.prensa.com.

La Prensa is the best source of newspaper classified ads and comes in handy when searching for used cars, apartments, pets, and domestic help.

El Panamá América

El Panamá América began life as a spin-off of the English-language newspaper *The Panama American,* which was first printed in 1925 by Nelson Rounsevell to serve the North American community living and working in the Canal Zone. Three years later, *El Panamá América* was first published in Spanish, directed by Dr. Harmodio Arias Madrid. Ten years later, in 1938, he acquired the majority share of Rounsevell's company, The Panamerican Publishing Company. Dr. Arias remained at the head of *El Panamá América* until his death in 1962, when ownership passed on to his daughter, Rosario Arias de Galindo. The company remains an Arias family business today.

Today, Spanish-language *El Panamá América* is the second most important newspaper in the Republic. Perhaps slightly less influenced by the country's politics, *El Panamá América* prides itself on "sharing the news that others hide," but the content is basically similar to *La Prensa,* except for it's handier tabloid size. *El Panamá América* also includes a variety of supplements throughout the week, with a weekly travel insert called "Rumbos Panamá" included every Sunday, highlighting different destinations within Panama.

La Estrella de Panamá

La Estrella de Panamá (The Panama Star) is Panama's third most popular paper when it comes to reputable new sources. *La Estrella* originated as the Spanish part of English-language paper the *Star & Herald,* created by the merger of the *Panama Star* and the *Panama Herald. The Star* was first printed in 1849 as a way of documenting the news pertaining to the Gold Rush, the Panama Canal and the Railroad at the time. The Spanish aspect of the paper was introduced in 1853, and when a French section was included later on, it became the first tri-lingual newspaper in the world. Eventually, after the departure of the Americans and the French from Panama, *The Panama Star and Herald* became *La Estrella* which evolved into an all-Spanish publication until 2008, when a four-page English section was reintroduced as a daily supplement. The new English version was launched proudly as a rebirth of the first and primary source to English readers about the Isthmus back up north.

The oldest newspaper in the Republic, *La Estrella* was operated by the Duque family since José Gabriel Duque Amaro purchased it in 1893, until its sale to a business consortium in 2000.

Panama 9°80° Magazine

Panama 9°80° is a quarterly travel and lifestyle publication printed in English and Spanish. It includes interesting articles pertaining to living, investing, and traveling in Panama, highlighting cultural aspects of the country and life on the isthmus. You can pick up a free copy in places frequented by tourists and foreign residents, particularly restaurants and airports throughout the country. There is also a lot of information on its website (www.panama980.com).

DAILY LIFE

"IF IT DOESN'T BLEED, IT DOESN'T LEAD"

Chances are, the first time you see one of Panama's tabloid newspapers, there will be a dead or severely mutilated body on the cover. In fact, most people would swear they have never seen anything else on the cover. Sensationalist news in Panama relies little on the infamous rumors of the rich and famous, and even less on political disgrace. Unfortunately, daily news in Panama is a world with little concern for the dignity of the recently deceased or injured or their families. Here, there are no laws to stop close-up footage of the day's most gnarly road accident appearing on the front page of tomorrow's newspaper or on the evening news. Often, in fact, photos and videos are published even before the victim's family has been notified of their loved one's death. Worse still, occasionally the wrong name will be attributed to the dead body, much to the distress of his or her family.

When you consider that the tabloids are the bestselling newspapers in Panama, specifically *La Crítica*, the leading paper in terms of circulation, the reason for these graphic depictions becomes clear: Sensationalism sells!

Newspaper headlines in the sensationalist papers are quite creative, to say the least. Apart from the sensationalism aspect, we must also consider that not everyone is willing or able to understand the big words and complex subjects addressed in the more serious newspapers. And, some of us are just too busy for that – all we want is a quick blast of easy-to-digest news, and we don't even really mind if it's not true. When that's the case, you just can't beat *La Críitica*, *El Siglo* or *El Día a Día*.

Lobby Magazine

Lobby is an attractive Spanish-language magazine with interesting information about upcoming cultural events, exhibitions, social happenings, and other points of interest in the world of art and culture. You will find *Lobby* at most waiting rooms around the city, specifically in hospitals, medical clinics, and offices. You can also subscribe to receive *Lobby* direct to your door. Visit www.lobbylife.com for more information.

NATIONAL TELEVISION

Once you have enough knowledge of Spanish to be ready to watch TV in Panama, you will need to contract cable or satellite television. The national channels, which all target essentially the same audience, mainly broadcast *telenovelas* (soap operas), cartoons, and news. Apart from the *La Prensa* newspaper, the main TV channels are the best sources for updated or breaking news. Check out www.TVN-2.com and www.telemetro.com.

TV CHANNEL GUIDE

Channel	Website	Programming Specialty
2 – TVN	www.tvn-2.com	News, soap operas, talk shows, Miss Panama.
4 – RPC	www.rpctv.com	Principal sports channel in Panama, specializing in baseball, but also shows news, soap operas, and cartoons. Every day 6–8:30 A.M., tune in to watch *Debate Abierto*, a topical debate usually discussing politics or other key issues.
5 – FETV	www.fetv.org	Features shows from Discovery Channel, BBC, and National Geographic, dubbed in Spanish.
11 – SERTV	www.sertv.gob.pa	State-run television and radio service, featuring news shows, magazines, and lifestyle shows.
13 – Telemetro	www.telemetro.com	Principally news and soap operas. Telemetro usually has the most up-to-date news if something important happens in Panama.

CABLE AND SATELLITE TV

Depending on how much of a TV watcher you are, and how interested you are in finding out about the national programs on television, you may want the option of receiving some mainstream programs you are accustomed to in your home country. Through WB and Sony channels, cable and satellite providers offer a decent range of North American series that should keep you satisfied. Cable Onda is the only provider of cable TV in the country, providing cable television, Internet, and telephone throughout Panama City and in certain areas of Chiriquí, Coclé, Colón, Herrera, and Veraguas provinces. Service is not yet available in Bocas del Toro, nor in some parts of Clayton and Quarry Heights, reverted Canal zone areas in Panama City. Cable Onda is continually expanding, so its coverage should be greater by the time you read this. In more remote areas you only have one option, which until recently was the satellite system DirecTV, now purchased by British-owned SKY TV. SKY seems to offer far more channels than DirecTV did, including several British channels, and its prices are competitive with Cable Onda.

With a large satellite dish on your rooftop, it is possible to pick up television from around the world, giving access to major communications such as NBC, CBS, and ABC, from the States. If you drive around Panama City or other well-populated towns in the interior, you will notice some of the larger homes have gigantic satellite dishes on the roof. This is usually a sign that the residents can watch Monday Night Football or Dan Rather on CBS News. You might want to get to know them.

Television with DVR (digital video recording) is not as mainstream in Panama as it is in North America. It will eventually get here, but for now setup and costs are going to be quite frustrating. However, changes to the television world, through Internet television access, live streaming, YouTube, and DVD collections of TV series, have made television accessible many other ways.

RADIO

Radio in Panama is an extremely popular form of media—little wonder, given the time people spend in traffic. Nearly all frequencies are

Listening to Panamanian radio is a great way to learn the language.

occupied by stations, most with music, a few with talk, but they change regularly and are nearly all in Spanish. At one point, English-language radio was quite popular in Panama. However, regulations requiring all radio hosts to be Panamanians caused a setback and some shows were cancelled. At present, there are two regular shows produced in English: *Ultra Stereo* (98.9 FM), a Hollywood showbiz report on 8–8:30 A.M. and 5–5:30 P.M. Monday–Friday, and Radio Metropolis (93.5 FM), *Sunday Night at The Metropolis,* a Panama news show hosted by Sandra Snyder 6–8 P.M. Sunday. However, listening to Panamanian talk radio is by far one of the best ways to experience Panamanian lexicon and the issues most valued by the communities.

TRAVEL AND TRANSPORTATION

Travel is part of the Panama experience. Serving as the main route through the Americas has been both its blessing and its nightmare, as Panama has lived both sides of foreign occupation, the economic benefit and the colonial arrogance. In a way, this dichotomy owes to the constant mobility within it, as natural as the laws of physics for a country that is neither isolated nor characterized by difficult throughways. It is the last or the first stop on the Pan-American Highway, and, compared to the rest of the route, the roads are in remarkable condition. Perhaps this is why traveling through the isthmus by car or bus is so common. Given the Panama Canal, a corresponding railroad line and a new highway, called the Autopista Panama–Colón, were opened in June 2009. Both run parallel along the Canal. It now takes only 30 minutes to get to El Rey in Sabanitas, the main intersection for the turn off to Costa Arriba or Costa Abajo, in Colón.

© SKY GILBAR

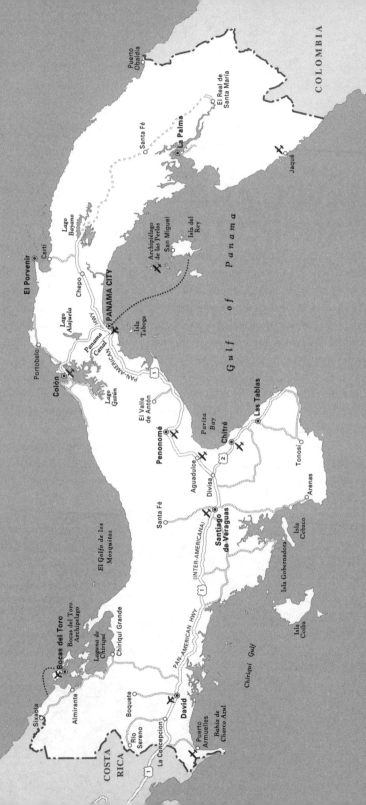

TRANSPORTATION

COLOMBIA

Puerto Obaldía

El Real de Santa María

La Palma

Santa Fé

Jaqué

Archipiélago de las Perlas

San Miguel

Isla del Rey

G u l f   o f   P a n a m a

El Porvenir

Cartí

Lago Bayano

Chepo

PANAMA CITY

Panama Canal

Isla Taboga

Portobelo

Colón

Lago Gatún

Lago Alajuela

Panama HWY

PAN-AMERICAN HWY

El Valle de Antón

Penonomé

Parita Bay

Chitré

Las Tablas

Aguadulce

Divisa

Tonosí

Arenas

Santa Fé

Santiago de Veraguas

(INTER-AMERICANA)

Isla Cébaco

Isla Gobernadora

Isla Coiba

Chiriquí Gulf

C a r i b b e a n   S e a

Bocas del Toro

Bocas del Toro Archipiélago

Chiriquí Grande

Laguna de Chiriquí

El Golfo de los Mosquitos

Almirante

Sixaola

Boquete

Río Sereno

La Concepción

David

Puerto Armuelles

Bahía de Charco Azul

PAN-AMERICAN HWY

COSTA RICA

P A C I F I C   O C E A N

0   20 mi

1

2

Getting to Panama

Upon deciding to live in Panama, you will want to consider how often you'll be visiting your home country. You may also find yourself motivated to tour cities nearer to this side of the Americas. Finding a flight from Panama to an international destination is not a problem, as it is a major hub for almost all airlines with north–south routes. However, the popularity of these routes has justified ever-higher airfares, rather than affordable ones, which tends to be a common misconception by those who move here.

BY AIR
International Air Carriers

Copa Airlines is Panama's airline, well established in Latin America and in the family of Continental. Its reach is growing yearly, adding more direct routes to popular cities such as New York, Los Angeles, Miami, Fort Lauderdale, Buenos Aires, and other major Latin American cities throughout Central and South America. They have a wonderful e-offers program, which if you sign up you will be privy to the few fare sales around holidays and on off-peak weekends. KLM, Iberia, Continental, Delta, American, and Taca offer more than just one route from Panama, other than their national capitals. Always shop for the best price, as the isthmus's location makes it a competitive market in airfares.

For those who have to slog through stopovers, keep in mind the constantly changing travel stipulations and visas needed when you are on a layover. Many Europeans choose to take a flight from Panama to South America and then onto the European continent rather than have to stop over in Miami or New York. Now that new routes are born every day, such as KLM's direct Panama–Amsterdam, added in 2008, there are other ways to get around these inconvenient layovers. Still, if cutting back on expenses is your priority, then you may have to consider the alternatives.

BY BUS

As previously mentioned, Panama's connection to the rest of Central America and up to Mexico through the Pan-American Highway makes it an affordable and secure route for large coaster buses. The National Bus Terminal, located in Albrook, of Panama City, hosts two major carriers, Panaline and Tica Bus, both of which will take you from Panama to Costa Rica daily. While Panaline only offers service from Panama to Costa Rica and back, Tica Bus is good to get you through to Tapachula, Mexico, stopping in various cities throughout the continent.

BY BOAT

Perhaps the most enjoyable mode of Panama's travel options is a boat. Navigation is easy, flowing from ocean to ocean, and even affordable if you are willing to work for your ride. If you already own a sailboat and plan to come to Panama, chances are you have a Panama flag, registered to sail the Canal and cross the seas here. But it's for more than just passing through the Canal: Panama has become a host to sailors across the world. Marinas across the Pacific and Atlantic sides of the Canal, such as the Balboa Yacht Club in Panama City, or Shelter Bay Marina in Fort Sherman, Colón, lure sailors and yachts in from across the world to careen and take respite with their friendly amenities. Many a sailor has stopped in the Panama waters for quick refueling and renovations and found that Panama is one of the most welcoming coastal communities from which to circumnavigate. Here, the time of year plays an important factor in your travel success, so if you are looking into sailing in and out of Panama, be mindful of the weather patterns and rainy season, and know that the Atlantic and Pacific will have different temperaments.

Getting Around

There is so much to see and discover in Panama, along on the main route and off the beaten path, you might find that once you move here you will regularly use your holidays to discover the country's many beach sites, mountain views, and waterfalls, rather than fly abroad. One main road, the Pan-American Highway, runs east–west through the Pacific side, and although driving it sounds easy, you will want to make wise decisions about how you travel around the country, depending on your priorities in cost, sightseeing, safety, and efficiency.

BY AIR

Panama's Marcos A. Gelabert national airport is in Albrook, Panama City, about three minutes' drive from the national bus terminal. Flights to Bocas del Toro, Las Perlas, David, Santiago, various sites in the Darien, and islands in Kuna Yala leave daily through two national air carriers, Air Panama and Aeroperlas. Both companies fly fleets of small-capacity planes, 15–45 passengers, and land in small but adequate landing fields or local airports. Most Panamanians are wary of flying within the country, and therefore tourists fill the small jet planes rather than nationals. As updated fleets of planes holding up to 50 passengers become available, there are more adventurous

Panamanians in the mix. Well-trained pilots who are familiar with the nine months of rain and unpredictable weather fly the planes. They will cancel a flight if there's even a bit of doubt about its safety. The airports in Panama City, David, Bocas del Toro, and Santiago are busy throughout the day, bustling commuters and tourists in and out of the provinces. Flights rarely fly later than 6 P.M.

Flights are affordable by U.S. and European standards. The time saved traveling by air cannot be matched if you are traveling for a week or less. You do need to travel with proper identification, a passport, or your *cedula,* the Panamanian I.D. card, even within the country. A driver's license is not considered adequate identification for air travel.

Private Charters

If you are traveling to a location in Panama that is somewhere between landing spots and you can afford it, you might consider a private charter. Air Panama or Aeroperlas can help you arrange a private charter, but the cost is exorbitant, sometimes up to US$800 per person depending on whether or not a flight is already set up to go and how many seats are available. Private charters have been known to fly into and out of Azuero Peninsula and Pacific coastline towns even farther west, but you should find out from the hosting agent at your destination before you book seats. Many hotels and real estate brokers have contacts and will be able to help you make arrangements.

BY BUS

If you decide to live in Panama without a car, taking a bus to get from point A to point B is the most popular travel choice on the mainland. Buses are privately owned, and travel costs are inexpensive. Buses run throughout the day and night, with direct routes between major cities and the National Bus Terminal in Panama City. The buses are comfortable, if overly air-conditioned. Some bus schedules even have midnight express options for routes to David or Bocas del Toro. The longer bus routes will stop midway to let the driver and passengers out to get some air and a bite to eat before moving on. The system is unique, as each bus chauffeur works hand in hand with a navigator, a sidekick who collects the fares and eyeballs the road for clear lanes and difficult turns. Bus passengers are responsible for presenting identification, so always carry your passport and visas with you when traveling. Just before David there is a big immigration checkpoint, and buses are usually stopped while an official checks travel documents. Officials may decide to loiter around your car inspecting for illegal substances, with inspection dogs.

PANAMA'S BUS ARTISTS

Stanley Heckadon Moreno noted in a 1984 article that the painters who embellish Panama City's famous buses find themselves situated within a clear hierarchy and "invisible demarcations" dividing the metropolitan area. The best of them are associated with well-defined territories, where they design the majority of the red devils and where their customers and the broader community admire their skills and look upon them as idols.

Small businessmen dominate Panama's transportation sector, and they hire the artists to help win over passengers in the fierce races around the capital and its adjacent suburban districts. The bus paintings act as a form of advertisement, a topic of conversations, and reference points for artistic appreciation, rather than museums or private galleries. Traditionally, the vehicles' hyper-masculine qualities – their loud colors, designs, mufflers, and assertive *pregones* (hawkers) have most attracted the attention of younger men, some of whom seek out the masters and train under their supervision to learn the practice.

Bus art in Panama is not an amateur activity, but rather a serious and long-term profession in which the leading figures labor for years to perfect their talents and take over the routes, where they tend to monopolize the business. Currently, Óscar Melgar controls much of the capital; however, Tino Fernández has emerged in La Chorrera and now dominates what is known as Panama West, the zone stretching out from the interoceanic waterway roughly to the town of Capira.

Tino's ascendance began in the early 1990s, when his mentor Ramón "Monchi" Enrique Hormi took a job with the Maritime Authority and devoted less time to working on the buses. Monchi himself had once apprenticed under the legendary José de Jesus Villarué. Villarué, more commonly known as "Yoyo," had been decorating vehicles in Panama City since the early 1940s, and it was he who had transferred this practice to La Chorrera with an eye-catching piece in 1960. The bus was called "the Gentleman of Paris," and it featured a scene of the Eiffel Tower and a gleaming interpretation of the town's waterfalls. Yoyo's specialty has always been water, and he reproduced the cascade with alluring colors, immediately seizing the interest of other bus owners and convincing them to seek out his services. Soon Yoyo's representations of the Bridge of the Americas, oceanscapes, and Panama's beaches became a common sight in the local terminal and eventually throughout the surrounding region.

Tino and other painters have followed these paths. They are not self-taught "primitivists," as some have suggested; they benefit from a body of collective knowledge and a long string of tutelages tying them to the past. In addition, many of them have taken formal classes. Tino is a graduate of the National School of Fine Arts, while his rival Óscar Melgar studied at Ganexa, the capital's private art academy.

As a student, Tino confronted a host of prejudices. His professors and colleagues often suggested that bus paintings lacked aesthetic merit. They were garish and imbal-

© SKY GILBAR

Bus art has its own unique style.

the popularity of an iconographic symbol and to frame it in an ingenious and compelling manner. Few people could resist "the Gentleman of Paris," just as it is difficult to ignore Tino's portrait of Jesus Christ, splashed across the hood of a more recent Red Devil.

While still at the National School of Fine Arts, Tino was also working under Monchi and was beginning to understand his luminous landscapes, which were equally capable of amazing viewers and drawing them through the vehicles' entrances. Monchi specializes in panoramas of the Interior, but he also portrays alpine villages, whose mountains and crystal streams grab attention and supposedly help to cool down passengers. Today Tino's production reflects many of these lessons, as well as his more academic preparation. He is an accomplished student of light, composition, and perspective, and he uses these skills to produce buses whose bright portraits and scenes have long fascinated Panamanians and which constitute a legitimate tradition of painting. This tradition is connected to the country's academic circles; however, it draws its true strength from its own history and standards, which Tino has mastered over the last decades to become one of the discipline's principal figures. Tino arose from the legacies of his predecessors and now extends his own legacy as the reigning "Sheriff of the West."

anced, according to these critics, and the artists relied too heavily on images taken from magazines, album covers, and the movies. Tino reacted in a pragmatic manner. He accepted the useful lessons of his mentors, but he rejected their disapproval and narrow conceptions about what constituted artistic expression. Tino's father had driven buses and had occasionally painted them in the 1950s. He had frequently taken his son around the city, introducing him to many important artists and showing him how they utilize popular culture. To beguile and capture potential customers, they "cannibalize" aspects of the mass media by imaginatively framing actors, singers, and other celebrities in spectacular designs and zigzag patterns. The goal is not to "copy" or produce an exact duplication but rather to exploit

Contributed by Peter Szok,
Associate Professor of History,
Texas Christian University,
Fort Worth, Texas

© SKY GILBAR

Buses are known to dominate the roads.

BY BOAT

Islands and aqua-fluorescent waters surround the Panama coastlines, yet the notion of utilizing *lanchas* (water taxis) in and around the capital or to interior beaches has not become a practical transportation option. The most common place for public water transportation is the ferry from Panama City to Isla Taboga and Isla Contadora, just outside Panama City in the Pearl Islands. There is also a grand passage of water taxis and one ferry from the Bocas del Toro mainland to the archipelago. However, if you are keen to travel anywhere else by boat, the best idea is to hire a private captain and venture through the delightful seas. Ask around at the marinas or with the yachters, sailboaters, and anglers who anchor in Panama, who will know who to hook you up with for any impromptu journeys across the oceans. If you are staying in Panama for any period of time longer than six months, I would not miss the opportunity to travel by sea.

PANAMA CANAL RAILROAD

The historical railway between the two oceans was given a second life in 1997 when it found a partner in Kansas City Southern Railroad Company. By 2001 renovated cars were carrying freights and passengers between Panama City and Colón on a daily basis. Today the system continues to run businesspeople to and from the Free Zone for work every day. The trip is a must for tourists who can ride through verdant landscapes, alongside Gatun Lake, and view distant cargo ships or Mother Nature's insistent creatures that still lurk between the man-made passageways. The five-car passenger train leaves at 7:15 A.M.

Don't leave Panama without going sailing.

Monday–Friday from Panama City and returns from Colón at 6:15 P.M. The last train from Colón leaves at 5:15 P.M. These are the only passenger trains that run on a daily basis. The fees are reasonable at $11–22 for children, adult, or senior citizen one-way fares. Business commuters can buy monthly passes. The Pacific train station is in front of the Albrook Residential community, and the Atlantic train station is near the Cristóbal port. When you get off in Colón, make sure you have a driver waiting for you or take a taxi immediately to your destination. Street crime is an issue in Colón.

BY BICYCLE AND ON FOOT

You'll find cyclists at a certain times of the year riding across the Pan-American Highway. This includes motorcyclists who enjoy riding for the long haul. However, it's not an easy task. For bicyclists, the days are hot and the roads have minimal shoulder space, not to mention a complete lack of sidewalks. The good part is that the roads are maintained, and these rides have been done before—you can use previously documented journeys as a reference for your preparation.

Cycling through the capital city is a challenge. Sidewalks are nonexistent and bikers are not very well respected on the roads by drivers. However, with the construction of Balboa's new Coastal Belt, there is hope that there will be a designated lane and more appropriate space for walkers and bikers. Because Panama City is compact, walking is a good alternative to dealing with traffic jams and parking congestion. Climate is the other obstacle to transport by bike and on foot. From 8:30 A.M. and until sundown, the city radiates heat. The

© SKY GILBAR

Coastal Highway belt on Avenida Balboa

concrete and constant construction are a brutal combination for city walkers. If you really do want to walk the city blocks around the center of Panama's main cities to do your errands, the best advice is to follow the elegant lead of the women who walk with an umbrella in hand and use it to block the sun as well as those sudden rainstorms.

HITCHHIKING

In the interior, hitchhiking is a very typical form of transportation. Cars are scarce in small towns and among *campesinos* (farmers). Hopping into the back of someone's pickup truck is normal neighborly conduct. Using your best instincts in towns you trust, and with people you know, you may decide that this sort of give and take works for you as well. It's also a sincere way to show you are willing to take part in the customary routines of your new community. In the cities, of course, it is wise to take precautions. Not everyone in the city has the small-town mentality of good intentions and trustworthiness, and here you're safer if you avoid accepting rides from strangers.

PUBLIC TRANSPORTATION

Public transportation is a complicated topic, with frequent disputes erupting between *transportistas* (private bus owners who compete for routes) and riders. It has turned into a government quandary of how to handle transportation demands in the capital cities of Panama City and David. Fuel is expensive, and there is an increasing desire to see the government adopt a new public

BRINGING BACK THE TRAM

Panama City has not always been weak on public transportation. When Panama was still a Colombian territory, the construction of a tramline passed from its Colombian originators into the hands of English company Siemens Brothers, which finished the track lines in Panama City in October of 1893. Six tramline cars serviced what is today Santa Ana Plaza, along Avenida Central, up along the perimeter of Ancon Canal Zone, and up to Via Espana and Bella Vista. The cars carried 25 passengers each and were designed for left-hand operation. It was one of the first trams in all of Latin America.

Unfortunately, the tram did not last long; in 1902 when the French abandoned the Canal project and the Thousand Days War ended in Panama's succession from Colombia, the tram service was suspended. In 1912, with the Americans now building the Canal, a concession was granted to United Fruit Company and later contracted to the engineers of New York's R. W. Hebard Company to restructure and incorporate new tramlines. By 1913 the new lines were up and running. (The Canal opened in 1914.) Operations expanded by 15 cars, and the service route was extended to 11.2 miles. The new cars were ordered from the United States and operated by electric service. Later, Panama Trailway purchased seven more cars from another Philadelphia company, upping the number of carriages to 22. Although bought from the United States, they maintained the left-hand service originally designed by Siemens Brothers.

Both tramlines, the English and the American, took electric power from overhead cables.

The cars ran throughout the city center for the next 35 years, but competition from the Chiva buses and auto industry of the 1920s took its toll along the isthmus. The Panama tramline slowly petered out until, in May 1941, the last tram car ran through the Central.

Today the tramlines still exist, and the pedestrian walkway of Avenida Central may seem barren to those who remember its lively transport system. As of 2008, the office Casco Antiguo, which is the municipal office that manages all issues and services related to the restoration, history, and cultural events for the neighborhood of Casco Antiguo, started working on a proposal to redevelop 4.3 kilometers of the original tram route, with the junction at Plaza 5 de Mayo along Avenida Central, extending its two-way route onto Avenida Balboa, alongside the new Cinta Costera, and in the opposite direction to the Amador Causeway. The historical restoration is intended to serve both aesthetic and practical purposes and relieve traffic and parking congestion throughout the city. In keeping with the international origins of the original tramway, a Spanish consulting firm, Soluciona, had begun a project proposal in 2008. The goal was to have the line finished, along with the Coastal Belt highway, along Avenida Balboa by 2010.

Contributions by Allen Morrison,
The Trams of Panama City
(www.tramz.com)

DAILY LIFE

transportation system to support its people. Without a solid resolution in sight, the options remain basic and antiquated. Cities are made for cars, but those who don't or can't drive ride the Diablos Rojos (Red Devils), a privatized bus service nicknamed for its malicious road driving and fierce appearance. Taxi service is available, and talk of a monorail or tram service is popular on paper, but after years of discussion, the go-ahead has yet to be authorized.

Taxi Service

Taxis are relatively cheap in Panama. In all the major cities there are taxis that run the streets. Picking up a taxi at a hotel can be much more expensive than hailing one on the street. As long as the taxi has a registered number on the outside of the car, you can be sure it is a legal taxi, especially if it is painted yellow, a new requirement by the transportation system for commissioned taxi service. Routes within the cities are priced from zone to zone rather than using meters. In Panama City, you can ask how much it will cost to get from one location to the other before you get in the taxi and there should be a fixed price. For example, taxi routes may cost anywhere from US$1.25 from one zone to a neighboring zone but could go up to US$4.50–5 if you have to move across town. The cost will go up for multiple passengers and at night. Conversely, the cost of a cab ride may go down if you can hail a taxi that is already en route to another destination with other passengers. While this is not legal, many drivers do this and many passengers quietly accept the ride. You could report the driver to the Transport Authority, using his or her license operation number, located on the ID at the car's control panel, but chances are they will think you are the one who should be locked up. It is such a common occurrence that it is a respected way of making a living for taxi drivers who get paid so little. It's a rough time at rush hour and difficult to hail a ride, so you may appreciate it when a car full of three other passengers stops to offer you a ride during a rainstorm.

© SKY GILBAR

Avenida Balboa is an important thruway for Panama City commuters.

One of the drawbacks about taxis is the quality of driving. Feel free to complain or ask the driver to slow down or drive with caution. Taxi drivers tend to take their careers a bit too seriously and end up thinking they own the roads, which causes unnecessarily risky weaving in and out of lanes and pushing through intersections. Also according to the law, if a taxi stops for you, it must take you to your requested destination. However, it is common practice for taxis to ask you where you are going and then reject you because they aren't going that way or simply won't go to that part of the city. You can't force them to take you, but know that law does not support this practice.

By finding a reliable taxi driver and using him regularly, you can call when needed and know you have a trusted means of transportation. Calling any of the taxi services in the yellow pages is also an option, but it will cost you double the price for the advance call.

Bus Service

The Diablos Rojos are old school buses from the United States painted like a Panamanian party on wheels. The colorful artwork and dynamic character of the buses are impressive, while the inside of the bus is less impressive and more worrisome. Most buses are overcrowded and fail to follow safety guidelines. Pickpocketing and random quarrels that may end in violence are not unusual, but Panamanians who don't own cars are desperate for other transportation.

Taking a bus in the city is an at-your-own-risk activity. The routes are clearly laid out and the prices run US$0.15–25 per route. For short routes in the city, they are a satisfactory means of transportation. The majority of the city's one million residents rely on them.

As of late, the government has tacitly approved these private concessions— mistakenly called "public transportation" because the government does not pay for them—by gifting the city with new and improved bus stops set up in and around the city at major junction points. Strangely, these don't dictate where the buses will stop. You will find that buses stop almost every 25 to 50 meters along a main route to pick up and drop off passengers. Since the routes are privatized, you will get two to three buses competing for passengers at the same stop. This is where driving hazards become apparent. Buses will race along main roads, stop short, and aggressively pass other vehicles to be able to attend a fare. The Diablo Rojo is therefore the main cause for *choques* (car accidents). Worse is that the bus owners rarely have insurance, whether required by law or not. In the case of an accident, drivers will pay off the police, who will later tell you it was your fault a mammoth, madly painted school bus, lacking a properly adjusted side view mirror and blaring Reggaeton music, rammed into the side of your car.

Investigate well the route you need to take and remember that from Plaza 5 de Mayo, along the Avenida Central in Panama City, you will find almost any bus route you need coming from Panama Oeste (the western side of the city and its peripherals) to the outskirts along Tocumen, near the international airport.

DRIVING

With the congestion of cars on Panamanian streets, it's obvious that many Panamanians believe driving their own vehicle is the best means of transport. Although people complain of variable gas prices and constant road detours or accidents, they enjoy the status and convenience of having a car in a developing country. The streets are made for driving, not walking or bicycling, so if you drive be aware of those few walkers and bicyclists.

Hertz car rental agency and some of the country guides like *Focus Panama* or *El Explorador de Panama* publish road maps that make driving more comprehensible in and around the provinces. With a constant state of construction and road development, there are always changes from the published maps, though. A good number of the peripherals of Avenida Balboa in Panama City have been closed down for almost all of 2009, and traffic is detouring around the back roads, causing random delays and confusing traffic rules. This means using your instincts and being alert are extremely important driving tools, and you should not take unnecessary risks. The newspapers usually print details of proposed construction changes.

Don't worry about getting lost in Panama. It's close to impossible. Just keep going till you hit a landmark you recognize. (Yes, it's that small.) Also try not to get frustrated when receiving directions. Panamanians don't use the terms left or right to explain directions. Instead they might say *por ahi* (over there) or *tomar la vuelta* (take a turn). While there are street names, most people have nicknames or use landmarks like the "by the old yellow house" to describe a route. Best is to ask them to draw a map for you.

As for the driving laws in Panama, you are on your own. There are laws, but finding a Panamanian driver who follows them is rare. Traffic cops are common throughout the main cities, but it doesn't seem to scare people into following driving regulations. People drive in the left lanes on the highway, pass on the right, and often go straight in a turn lane. It's easy to get used to but can become a negative influence on your good driving skills. As long as you drive defensively, you will be fine. A little aggression is necessary when

© SKY GILBAR

Each year there are more cars on Pamama's streets.

trying to get through an intersection without a traffic light. Do it slowly and wisely, and don't expect that another driver will yield to you. Once you learn the routes, you will know exactly what kind of driving conduct is needed.

Renting or Buying a Car

If you will be living in Panama for four months or longer, you will probably want to own a car. The bus system is unreliable, privatized, and at times unsafe. Walking is very rare in any of the major cities, since sidewalks are badly planned and cars don't respect the pedestrian's right of way. In Bocas Town, Bocas del Toro Islands, or small towns like Boquete, however, walking is acceptable if you live in the center of town.

Where you choose to reside is a significant factor in determining what kind of vehicle you will need. In Bocas del Toro, most people move around with bicycles and motorbikes. In the interior, a four-wheel drive vehicle is usually necessary. If you are located in Panama City, consider your family's needs in commuting to work, school, shopping, and social visits; Panama City traffic will probably steer you away from a gas-guzzler. Considering that every Panama resident needs to go regularly to Panama City, make sure you buy a car sufficient for that kind of journey. If you don't go to the city that much, then a plane and taxi ride might be enough.

Cars are affordable, much less than the list price of a car in the United States or Europe, and they resell fast, especially any sedan used by taxis. Leasing is not yet an option from dealerships, and renting is quite costly if you are staying in town for longer than a few months. When buying a used car, definitely

EL BIEN CUIDADO: THE PARKING SECURITY INDUSTRY

Since long before the current boom in Panama's building and construction industry, adequate parking has always been an oversight by city planners. This holds true in Panama City more than any other region of the country, but you can find some of the same problems along the main streets in Boquete, David, and some of the more populated beach towns along the Pacific coast, in central Panama. Complaints about the lack of parking stay under control mostly due to *bien cuidados,* the independently employed parking security guys and gals who work street blocks and corners, earning anywhere from US$0.25 to a few dollars per car keeping an eye on the vehicles, providing security, creating parking spots at tight corners, and their specialty – navigating you into and out of your parking destination.

Bien cuidados deserve respect. They stay outside all day long in the hot sun or late into the night, running back and forth as vehicles come and go and generally making the city run more smoothly. Take pleasure in meeting and helping employ someone so helpful at such a small cost. They know the nooks and crannies of the side streets, which will save you much time and extra kilometers trying to find a convenient parking spot. Beware, however, as competition can be fierce. You shouldn't be surprised to see two attendants running toward your car or running alongside your vehicle from the beginning of the block and bickering in front of you for the rights to the business. Depending on the popularity of the street corner, you are at least a US$0.50 commodity; at 50 cars a day, seven days a week, that's a good US$700 a month career – about twice as much as a public school teacher makes in Panama.

The more you wear "foreigner" on your forehead, the more your local *bien cuidados* will up the ante for your time at the spot. Disregard their attempts to inflate prices. Perhaps paying US$2-5 for a free parking space seems unnecessary, but *bien cuidados* are the best form of Panamanian insurance to date, locally developed and still running strong without a monopoly or government restriction, so you should certainly contribute to the *bien cuidados* industry. It's one small beauty of free enterprise in the Panamanian community.

bargain on the price. Work with the salesperson directly, as there can be lots of middlemen who expect a cut on the deal—you don't want to pay an extra few thousand just in various people's commissions. A good idea is to check out the rental car agencies to see if they are selling any of their last year's cars. The better agencies such as Hertz, National, Avis, and Budget always rent the newest models and sell the older ones, still well maintained, with very little mileage, and at good prices.

Driver's Licenses

If you have a license to drive in your home country, getting a driver's license in Panama still takes legwork but is much easier than most other processes. Depending on the time limits of your visa, your Panamanian driver's license will be valid for the same amount of time and will expire on the same date as your visa. Renewing it will depend upon the renewed visa.

In order to get a driver's license you will need to bring your original driver's license from your home country, passport, Panamanian residential visa, proof of your blood type, and results from a valid glucose test, taken within two weeks, to La Autoridad del Transito y Transporte Terreste (ATTT, or Transit Authority) office. Depending on how long your residential visa is valid, the cost will be around US$5–10 for 3–6 months, and up to US$20 if you are a legal resident for up to 10 years. Expect to wait 1–2 hours for your license, but you will leave with it in hand.

If you aren't going to bother with a driver's license, then be sure to carry your passport, with the date of your entrance to Panama, and your driver's license from your home country. Police will ask for both, so if you feel safer carrying around a copy of your passport, carry a copy of the entry stamp as well. This will only work within three months of your entry date.

If you don't have a valid driver's license in your home country, you should prepare to take two tests: one in the practice and theory of driver's education, and another for audio and visual capacity. You will also have to prove you have taken the driver's education course dictated by the ATTT or an authorized agent. The cost is US$40. Contact the ATTT to pick up the required texts you will have to study and confirm the cost for the test. Fees may change at any given time.

PRIME LIVING LOCATIONS

© SKY GILBAR

PRIME LIVING
LOCATIONS IN PANAMA

COSTA RICA

Puerto Limón

Caribbean Sea

Bocas del Toro Archipelago
Isla Colón
Bocas del Toro
Laguna de Chiriquí
Chiriquí Grande

BOCAS DEL TORO

THE WESTERN HIGHLANDS

David

Bahía de Charco Azul

Chiriquí Gulf

El Golfo de los Mosquitos

Colón

Lago Gatún
Lago Alajuela

PANAMA CITY

Panama Canal
⊗ PANAMA CITY

Chepo

Lago Bayano

El Porvenir

K u n a   Y a l a

Santa Fé

La Palma

Río Tuira

El Real de Santa María

Puerto Obaldía

COLOMBIA

Juradó

Cupica

Jaqué

Archipiélago de las Perlas

Isla del Rey

G u l f   o f   P a n a m a

Penonomé

Parita Bay

Chitré

Las Tablas

A z u e r o s   P e n i n s u l a

Isla Iguana

Santiago

Isla Gobernadora

Isla Cebaco

Isla Coiba

CENTRAL PANAMA

P A C I F I C   O C E A N

25 mi
25 km

OVERVIEW

One of Panama's beautiful qualities is its ability to accommodate diverse life-styles. You can experience the tropical summer all year long, or you can spend time in the crisp autumnlike climate of the Highlands, or you can stay in the city and experience both with minimal travel. Those moving to Panama to work will not have a very difficult decision process, as your employment will dictate your new territory, but if you have an open mind and open options, you can start with the areas described here, the most common residential areas around the country. Don't feel you have to make a firm decision right away. Know what is out there and explore the options available for your future. If staying off the beaten path is your goal, you're actually in good company. It is not uncommon to stumble across expats who have nestled themselves into a small corner of the interior.

© SKY GILBAR

Panama City

Panama City is the centerpiece in this small country, and not only because it is the capital. The only major international airport is located in Panama City; there is talk of international flights into the national airport at the western capital of David, but at the time of writing, no airlines have yet to land a plane anywhere other than Panama Tocumen airport, a.k.a. PTY. Living in Panama City is for urbanites, city lovers, and those who are ready for drama at any given time; politics, pop culture, fashion, business, and the arts move at a rapid pace here compared to the rest of the country, and sometimes the rest of the Central American and Caribbean region. Panama City is more expen-

© SKY GILBAR

It is not uncommon to see the old and new sitting side by side in Panama City.

sive than the other areas, but it also offers better salaries. Unlike most of Central America's capital cities, Panama City is at a relatively low elevation, and therefore the heat really affects daily life. It is easy to love the vibe of bright sunny days and to find a residence with a green landscape, but Panama's traffic gridlock, limited transportation routes, and 32°C (90°F) temperatures and tropical rainstorms can make life chaotic and frustrating. Panama City is sprawling and has been for the past 10 years, with the restructuring of highways and renovation of the U.S Canal Zone pushing out city limits and creating a metropolitan area that allows for new "suburbs" and more expensive residential options. Relocating to Panama City means you won't have to live completely outside of your element if you are coming from a big city, used to mixed cultures, exciting nightlife, and educated communities.

Central Panama

Just west of Panama City over the Bridge of the Americas and the Centennial Bridge is the route to the interior of Panama, or the Central Provinces. Nesting one after the other along the Pacific coast, these cities have been inhabited for most of Panama's history. Beginning in the mid-20th century, well-to-do Panamanians from the capital started to build their beach homes in Gorgona, Chame, Santa Clara, and San Carlos—districts hosting a string of beach towns one might call the Hamptons of Panama. Growing speculation about the future of Panama as a hot spot for real estate tourism has created more modern development along the open black- and white-sand beaches of these towns, with foreign buyers and project planners moving into high-rises towering alongside small fishing villages. Central Panama has an interesting mix of highlands that pop up sporadically along the northern side of the Pan-American Highway (known in Spanish as the Inter-Americana) such as El Valle and Altos de Maria, attractive to retirees who want to stay within 30 minutes of the beaches and two hours of Panama City but live in more temperate climates. Investing half a million dollars won't go as far as it used to in these areas of the interior, but it will get you started on a beachfront property or a view to both the Atlantic and Pacific oceans from above a mountain peak. Farther west along the Pan-American Highway are the provinces of Coclé, Los Santos, and the southern peninsula of Veraguas where the heart of Panama lies, with soft-spoken, easygoing *campesinos* (countryfolk) who will offer a humble nod and a sincere helping hand. Life in these parts of the country can be slow, but the beauty of open spaces and quiet echoes of rolling waves hitting against cliffside beaches have captured the hearts of many foreigners, who are ready to slip into the backdrops of these peaceful settings. You won't find expat communities as much as occasional homes tucked into a dynamic beachfront slice of land. You won't find a thrilling nightlife nor more than a few restaurants open after 9 P.M. in the towns of Pedasi or Aguadulce, unless you visit during Carnival season in Penonomé or Las Tablas, a time when most foreign residents leave the area to let the Panamanians do their thing. You will find some top-notch surf, however, and hence a few passionate and harmless youth camping out on the beaches, sleeping on their surfboards, waiting for dawn to ride a new riptide. Environmental sustainability takes more of a priority the farther west you go from the provinces of Panama and Chitré. The few developments here that cater to elite clientele have found a way to blend in with the original infrastructure of the region—most of the land and seaside remains beautifully untouched.

PRIME LIVING LOCATIONS

The Western Highlands

When the media talks of Panama's popularity among expat retirees, there is always a mention of the Western Highlands, in the Chiriquí province. These mountain towns, sitting at the base of Volcán Barú, have been named recently among the top 10 international places to retire (at number four, according to *International Living* magazine). When Sam Taliaferro came upon the small town of Boquete in 1998 and started to build a modern residential development there, he contributed to the mainstream popularity of Panama among North American retirees. He has since built an upscale development in the heart of Boquete and attracted nearly 150 families from abroad to live inside his "safe haven," never feeling the roots of Panamanian lifestyle. Just 40 kilometers north of the western region's capital, David, these Highlands provide better than average facilities, with stores and services equal to that of Panama City. Though the gated community lifestyle is not for everyone, Taliaferro's project, called Valle Escondido, is successful, supported by a growing number of English-language newspapers, restaurants, cafés, bookstores, and a large pool of English-speaking real estate businesses.

Taliaferro wasn't the first to find the location an enticing option for adventurous nomads, however. The Highlands' cool temperatures and fertile landscapes have invited foreigners from similar mountainous environs since construction of the Panama Canal and railroad more than 100 years ago; the proof remains in the Swiss chalet homes built along the undulating landscapes,

© DAVID DELL

the north side of Volcán Barú in the Western Highlands

in the midst of award-winning coffee plantations. Today, many northern Europeans still live here, adding to the impressive group of expats who occupy the region and contribute to the community in both employment and agricultural development. Just east of the Chiriquí Highlands is a much less populated but equally exotic mountain town called Santa Fe, in the province of Veraguas. Its isolated and antiquated setting is a romantic alternative to the very international flavor of Chiriquí.

Bocas del Toro

Unlike the verdant agriculture of the mainland, Caribbean island life and the sea are the main attractions in Bocas, which is why so many backpacking foreigners have traded their busy executive lives in their home country for a cute island home painted with bright tropical colors and a slow life spiced with a shot of rum. The day-to-day lifestyle in Bocas is one of relaxation and good times. It is an alluring location, and it is rare to hear of someone who does not truly enjoy it, riding around on a small motor scooter or a vintage bicycle with a basket and stopping to say hello to your favorite neighbors, driving in and out of Bocas Town. The remnants of a Antillean banana plantation town survives in the architecture of the colonial-style homes now converted into hostels, cute restaurants, internet cafés, and gourmet grocery stores, all of which are frequented by the many European, North American, and Middle Eastern expats who live on the island flaunting their new lifestyles in bohemian beach wardrobes.

Despite all this appeal, Bocas is a prime example of careless development practices. Much of the change in the last 10 years is irreversible—and don't expect change to necessarily mean progress here. Local residents don't appreciate the torn-up mangroves and bulldozed primary habitats of endangered species, environmental damage usually inflicted by real estate investors who plan from abroad and have never lived in Bocas del Toro. The small set of islands also suffers from limited access to freshwater in the dry seasons. That said, there are many sensible and enjoyable ways to live in these islands, creating an ecofriendly life away from the tourist trap.

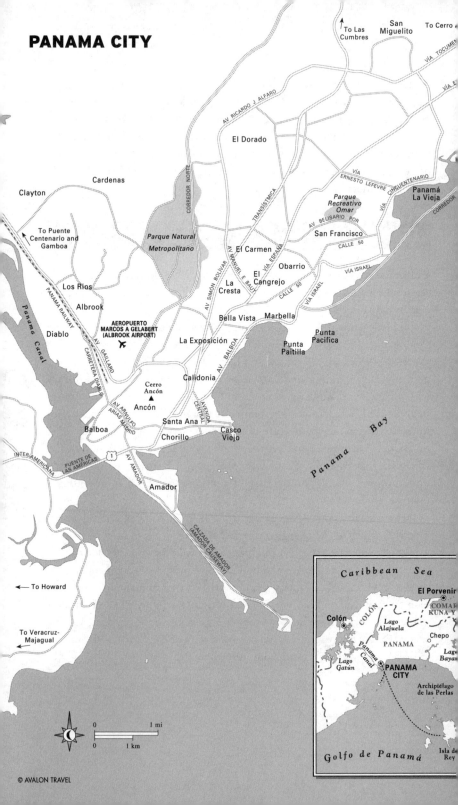

PANAMA CITY

Panama City is not even close to the largest city in Central America, but it is considered the most cosmopolitan. Newly expanding its borders into the former Canal Zone area, previously occupied by U.S. military and now occupied by civil engineers working on the Canal expansion, the city is sprawling. The constant state of development makes this an interesting time to be living in Panama City (or PTY, as many like to abbreviate it). It has some qualities of a new city built during the highs and lows of the real estate boom, but it is defended by a steadily increasing Latin American economy, which is creating confidence for businesses and the local real estate industry alike.

In this chapter, we will be looking at Panama City's prime living locations, its central districts and the reverted Canal Zone area, which act like suburbs (although only minutes from the downtown areas). You should also be familiar with residential options on the outskirts of the city, or *las afueras,* as Panamanians refer to it, which may lie a half hour's drive away but on the other hand maintain a sense of serenity after a hectic city day.

© SKY GILBAR

Green and colonial are the saving factors prevalent in this tropical city since the discovery of "progress" has rebuilt it like another Miami, loaded down with strip malls and high-rises. Therefore, bringing back metropolitan parks and restoring the Old Town are priorities for many urban architects who have their hearts in the right place. The old Canal Zone and outskirts maintain their original green and tropical feeling and therefore attract those who prefer to live next to their choice mango tree.

Practically speaking, Panama's metropolitan area is one of the easiest places to live in the isthmus, but quite possibly one of the most frustrating. With a sprawling city that redefines itself every decade, congested traffic routes guide residents to a constant stream of resources and amenities, which, despite all-day taxi horns blaring outside, can make it very tempting to carve out your ideal nesting grounds here. City malls, a vast banking district, safe urban life, and a secure and a deep job pool make the city the focal point for the rest of the country.

One-third of the nation's population of three million lives in the Panama City metropolitan area. While this number seems large to many, there is never a day that passes when you aren't reminded of the newness of the city, just over 100 years old, as the capital of the independent republic. Therefore, a small-town feel emanates through the city streets despite the international direction the city is taking.

You can find a more suburban feel, not more than 10 minutes from a central city route, with the new Ciudad Jardín (Garden City) of the former Canal Zone. However, if you are interested in living even farther out into the natural environs, rural mountains such as Cerro Azul have lured Panamanians and foreigners to settle gracefully within a 40-kilometer reach of Panama City. If you, too, decide that commuting and getting away from the foreground of urban white noise suits you better, you will find the suburbs a nice option. Unlike other capital cities of Latin America, Panama City is a tropical barrage of nature, squeezing its way through the concrete and between layers of brick. Therefore, the outskirts of Panama City are a beautiful escape into the Eden you are now residing in. Some suburban areas rest along Lake Gatún, and others are hilltops studded with residences that overhear the echoes of city life below. Still others are flat and green and border the Parque Metropolitano, a national reserve in the center of the city, which allows for nature walks and monkey and sloth sightings on your way home from that corporate meeting! Given the seemingly perfect opportunity to be alongside nature on a daily basis and yet so close to the urban resources of a capital city, it's important to take into consideration the cost of maintaining a home so vulnerable to humidity, wild animals, mosquitoes, and other tiny, pesky creatures that are easier to avoid when living in the concrete jungle!

Lay of the Land

Panama City is located along the Pacific Coast of the country and just east of the Panama Canal. The district of Panama City is 2,561 square kilometers (989 square miles), lying at sea level. The downtown area, financial district, and majority of commercial centers exist in the south side of the city toward the coastal line and along the Panama Bay. In the colonial old city, Casco Viejo was built on the opposite side of the bay, lying west along the city limits. Farther west of Casco Viejo is a long strip of land jutting out into the Pacific Ocean, a convenient landmark for ships embarking on the Pacific entrance of the Canal. This strip is an oceanside boardwalk, now referred to as the Causeway.

The former U.S. Canal Zone lies north of the Causeway and Casco Viejo, beginning with the most visible hill that stands over the city, Cerro Ancón. Going north from Cerro Ancón, runs an expanse of flat and vast land filled with tropical fauna and dotted with American, military-style homes, and, of course, the Pacific side of the Canal locks.

Along the north side of the city, connecting the Canal Zone to the downtown area, is the Parque Natural Metropolitano (Metropolitan Natural Park). It is part of the metropolitan area's biological corridor, including Camino de Cruces and Soberania National Parks and is the only wildlife reserve park that that lies entirely within the city limits.

Northwest of the Parque Metropolitano, rolling hills create diverse landscapes while moving along the Corridor Norte, an evolving highway that will eventually lead all the way to Colón on the Atlantic side, by way of Lake Gatún. One of Panama City's main transit ways, called Transistmica or El Camino al Colón (The Way to Colón), was the only route to Colón by car from the center of the capital until the Autopista was finished in 2009. En route you pass several communities such as Los Andes and Las Cumbres, where the outskirts really do start to feel outside of the city hype. Cerro Azul is a rural area located along the Chagres River and can be reached by driving east toward Tocumen. Finally, more outskirts are being populated going west over the Bridge of the Americas, as cheap land becomes available in Veracruz

© SKY GILBAR

Panama City residents seek respite from the tropical heat.

and Arrijan. The former is more interesting to expats, and the latter remains an option for Panamanians who wish to relocate from central Panama City to buy their own home and begin anew.

CLIMATE

Panama City is at the heart of the intertropical zone and average temperatures run about 35°C (95°F) during the day, with nighttime lows running in the low 20s C (70s F). Humidity can be excessive, and urban landscapes like the crowded roads, concrete layout, and narrow spaces between building lots tend to exaggerate the sensation of heat. Sweating is unavoidable. Panamanians manage the heat by overusing their air conditioners, so many people dress in northern autumn fashions but suffer for it once they are outside.

Rain showers exist for at least 20 minutes daily during the country's rainy season. Cooler dry season winds and elevated hillside climates offer a respite that Panamanians truly take advantage of. Panamanians describe these winds and breathable temperatures in the parks as *"fresco,"* which to them means cold, but to foreigners would be considered a wonderful summer breeze.

In the hills of Ancón, which can be seen from most points in the center of Panama City as the hill sporting the large Panamanian Flag, temperatures might be a few degrees lower in the day, and by night are deliciously cooler. The same is true for Cerro Azul, which is significantly higher in altitude and therefore a much cooler temperature can be expected, perhaps 18–30°C (65–85°F). Clayton and Albrook in the Canal Zone tend to be heat magnets, as the more forests being cut for new residential landscapes, the less the air breathes from its foliage. Gamboa is green, wet, and very humid, but desirable for the relative cool that comes from nature's shading.

Perhaps the most amazing factor of this tropical city is the microclimate that exists from one street to the other. I cannot tell you how many times I have driven into a downpour and, within 20 yards, driven right out of it into a dry, sunny road. It's to be expected: Constantly changing wind patterns and humid zones are the key elements of tropical climates. Don't bother looking up a local meteorology report for Panama City: Every day you can count on sunny, hot, and humid with a buildup of rain showers or thunderstorms to cool it down.

Daily Life

Panama City offers the most active, cultural, and resource-filled daily life of all the Prime Living locations, but that doesn't mean you have to live in it or near it to benefit from it. From the interior, all buses stop at the national bus terminal in Albrook, entering Panama City. The terminal is now connected to the country's largest shopping mall, Los Pueblos.

SHOPPING

The commercial shopping giant, which is the second in the city by the same name and the same real estate group (also called Los Pueblos), is filled with *almacenes* (discount department stores), small boutiques offering both economy and high-end shopping, beauty salons, and a two-level food court. There is also indoor entertainment including a movie theater and an ice-skating rink, not to mention the occasional circus or amusement park set up in tents outside the mall. Los Pueblos Albrook mall is one of the busiest shopping centers in the country and is not biased to any one kind of shopper, with a wide variety of price and quality. The mall also hosts a number of hardware stores, furniture stores, banks, and service providers like cell phone stores, electricity company, and service counters for cable and satellite TV providers. You could relocate to Panama City and have your house set up completely in a few days at Los Pueblos mall. Multiplaza is the mall on the opposite end of the city's center, in Punta Pacifica. It is less likely to have economical department store options. Rather, it has recently added a luxury wing for stores such as Oscar de La Rente, Hermès, Luis Vuitton, and Ralph Lauren, designers and retailers from abroad that are interested in having a presence in a central location the Latin American community. It is a beautiful mall, with high-quality retail options, as long as high price tags don't make you choke.

FOOD

Grocery stores in Panama have gotten so much better over the last decade. At first, options declined sharply after 1999, when many Americans closed their businesses to head on back up north, after the U.S. government passed the duty of Canal protection back to Panama. But that left a market open to new gourmet food shops, liquor stores, and even video and DVD rental stores such as Blockbuster video. The Riba Smith supermarket chain, located in Bella Vista, Punta Pacifica, and Transistmica near El Dorado, is one of the more expensive food stores, because it gears its prices to the expat community. However, it is

Punta Pacifica is constantly developing.

careful to offer excellent import choices for wines, cheeses, chocolates, sauces, and spreads. It also has a bakery that sells fresh baguettes and both French- and Italian-style flatbreads. The Deli Gourmet stores, another option for well-chosen food and beverage imports from European, Mediterranean, and North American distributors, are forever popping up around the city. There are stores in San Francisco, El Dorado, and Obarrio, all in Panama City center and mostly catering to business lunchers and shoppers making something special for dinner. The other chains are the Super 99, owned by President Ricardo Martinelli, and Supermercado El Rey, which are located all throughout Panama City and the interior. For expats living in the Canal Zone area, Supermercado El Rey's Albrook location is the quick-stop supermarket choice, although this location is not as fully stocked as the San Francisco (Calle 50) or El Cangrejo/La Cresta/El Carmen (Via España) locations. Price Costco has opened two locations in Panama City. After the driver's license, the Price Costco membership card is the second most popular ID for a foreigner to have in Panama City.

Unfortunately, the city is not made for walkers, but those who want to enjoy a long morning walk and window-shopping can enjoy the eccentric area of Avenida Central, sticking to Calle Peatonal, the pedestrian boardwalk, along Caledonia and Casco Viejo. Shopping is cheap here, and the gadgets, kitschy souvenirs, and creative materials for crafty buyers are hard to resist.

One wonderful store called El Machetazo, on the top of Avenida Central near the Santa Ana main square and near the antique Coca-Cola Café, sells everything from bedroom furniture to groceries and produce; you can get your nails done for US$5 and your hair washed and dried for less than US$10. It's a sight just to see the action going up and down in the five-story department store. Bloomingdale's beware.

ENTERTAINMENT

For the epicurean, Panama has a local life full of everything from salsa and merengue clubs to Zen lounge bars and Middle-Eastern hookah-smoking cafés. You can grab a taste of almost any little corner of the world you are interested in. There's no Ethiopian food yet, but I wouldn't be surprised if it came about soon. Indian food has finally joined the lot of international fare, alongside excellent dining options for Chinese, sushi, Thai, and South American fusion with Chilean, Peruvian, and Argentinean steakhouse influences. Italian restaurateurs are also coming out of hiding, opening up eateries that defend their heritage with authentic flavors. Daily life in Panama is filled with these cosmopolitan options befitting life in an international city. Casco Viejo nightlife allows for elegant outdoor strolls, before or after your equally elegant outdoor dining, and complementing a night of live music, national theater, or edgy art openings. Activities of the same vein occur in Punta Pacifica, San Francisco, and especially Bella Vista.

City folk are less likely to live *quincena a quincena* (payday to payday) but there will be more crowds and longer lines on the 15th and 30th of each month. You will probably notice that most events are scheduled for these dates as well. More and more public events are being sponsored in city parks, museums, and theaters throughout the capital. Young people are the majority of the population, and cultural events are geared toward crowds under 30. Most bars and nightlife are, too, but recently there have been more social scenes opening up for the "adult contemporary" crowd, in Casco Viejo and parts of Bella Vista.

When living on the outskirts such as Cerro Azul, Gamboa, or Veracruz, you must consider that your major shopping and nightlife is probably in Panama City proper. For major concerts, the Atlapa or the Figale convention centers are entertainers' one-stop venues, and performers such as Buena Vista Social Club or a group of Chinese acrobats and contortionists will draw thousands from the metropolitan region, including some from the interior cities. For grocery and shopping, truly stocking up means making a regular trip into your choice supermarket, which will also probably involve a trip into town. Panama City might as well be named "Resource City."

Where to Live

Like many major cities and capitals around the world, Panama has a metro-politan area. (It is not often referred to as such, but it is understood.) If you are thinking of relocating to Panama City, you will want to consider how important it is to live in the city center, or if you can make the time to live on the outskirts, where your commute will take a significant amount of time, but the pleasures of space and quiet evenings away from major traffic routes and noise pollution is a redeeming benefit. There are many options in the city, with cute, tree-lined neighborhoods close to major shopping and nightlife and very much desired by the hip and young middle to upper class. New building designs around the city feature studio and loft apartments. If you don't plan to rely on your car much, you will want to consider these central options.

On the other hand, it is possible to get what you want out of suburban liv-ing very close to the city. If this is your preferred style, you can look into the reverted Canal Zone neighborhoods. You are technically living in Panama City, but the green areas, Olympic-size swimming pools, and long, flat roads with ocean breezes make you feel otherwise.

If you find that the farther away from city life, the better for you, then there are still choices within Panama's metropolitan area. Living along the perimeter of the city in areas like Veracruz, Cerro Azul, and Las Cumbres, with a half-hour commute, might allow you to develop your own lifestyle and become much less reliant on central urban life while still taking advantage of the city's resources for your major food shopping, car repairs, and urban en-tertainment. Creating such a perfect balance will make you very comfortable in your metropolitan home.

HOUSING

The choice between a living in a house or an apartment is a very personal one and will most likely depend on your length of stay in Panama and your per-sonal resources. Apartments are central to commercial areas and may offer safety with 24-hour security service included in your rent. In some areas of the city, such as Paitilla, living in an apartment is really one of the only op-tions, as high-rises are the main feature throughout, mostly situated right on top of one another. The real estate market that has driven up so many build-ings since 2005 has ensured that apartments are the most available type of residence for new buyers.

If buying a house is your goal, chances are you are also looking for a lit-tle space and something green to lay your feet on at home. In that case, a suburban-type neighborhood as in the former Canal Zone might be what you are looking for. Prices are incrementally higher in this area, but the home will probably hold its value better than an apartment in the middle of the city. There are many wonderful old homes available for restoration in Panama City, whether in the old city of Casco Viejo, out in the Gamboa Rainforest, or at Cerro Ancón. Even in Bella Vista, El Cangrejo, and a few other central urban neighborhoods, the colonial or mid-20th century architecture can be fully appreciated and restored to your personal taste. The farther you are from the center of the city, the more space can be expected.

CENTRAL PANAMA CITY

Just like any other cosmopolitan city, Panama has a downtown area that is the core of the city. It falls into the same beat as other international capitals, with lots of movement, bumper-to-bumper traffic, and city noise that are difficult to adjust to on a daily basis. However, there are districts such as San Felipe in Old Town (El Casco Viejo) and Bella Vista that are laid out nicely for walking and near cultural centers, universities, government offices, and restaurants. If you live and work in Central Panama City, in any of the one districts listed below, you will feel how small of a "town" Panama is and you will also experience first-hand the changing infrastructure. You will probably even feel compelled to opine on it, just like a true local.

San Francisco District

The three overlapping neighborhoods of Avenida Balboa, Paitilla, and San Francisco all fall into the San Francisco district according to municipal divisions, although residents and city-dwellers see them separately according to their natural divisions.

A large part of the expat population that resides in Panama City is spread throughout the district of San Francisco and tend to be young professionals, single or with young families. Other expats are businessmen and women who want to be in the center of the happening events. The resources available within a three-mile circumference of this district make it a convenient location, and public transportation and taxis are available at all times due to the heavy traffic that runs through the main vein. Upscale malls and other commercial centers can be found up and down the main route of San Francisco. Just behind Avenida Balboa are some of the city's most popular restaurants and nightlife venues. Embassies, government buildings, banking and office buildings, health clinics, and hospitals are only a few city blocks away from any given location in the San Francisco district.

It is a premier living location for renters, especially those who might live in Panama for only a few months at a time and are looking for a turnkey operation. The prices and attributes of each neighborhood are similar.

Beginning with Avenida Balboa, but seen throughout all three neighborhoods, there is a major face-lift going on that resonates from this main throughway, where high-rise, luxury apartments have sprouted along the coastal city way. With the help of city planners, developers are luring prospective buyers with spacious, state-of-the-art apartments, Pacific views, and a restructured Cinta Costera (coastal highway), which will form a 1.6-mile beltway, 61 acres of green area, and four lanes in each direction. An estimated 15,000 new apartments are available along this route. These apartments are some of the most upscale in the city, together with those in the Costa del Este neighborhood. Home asking prices and rents are not bargains here anymore; rent for an apartment can run up to US$1,000 per week.

Running east along Avenida Balboa lies the neighborhood of Paitilla. This neighborhood has been expanding since the 1990s when Punta Paitilla was built, and in 2000 a new project called Punta Pacifica began. Since Punta Paitilla is on the Panama Bay, and the neighborhood is already a crowded concrete jungle of high rises, one might wonder where they are getting the land space to keep building? Landfills are the key source of this expansion, allowing for upscale apartments towering over the city to lavishly decorate the coastal way. The constant development in this area causes it to resemble a construction site; however, if living large is your style, living on the very top of a 40-story structure might help alleviate the chaos of sand trucks and power tools down below. Avenida Italia is a primary residential location.

Paitilla is traffic chaos during the workweek, but living there is easy for walkers, who can find shopping centers that host the most essential of home goods conveniences, supermarkets, eateries, small offices, churches, and synagogues.

Perhaps the most noticeable drawback to the San Francisco area is the smell of the Panama Bay at low tide. The views are spectacular at any other moment, but once low tide hits, those who enjoy the touch of natural breeze in their living quarters may suddenly opt for a quick turn of the air conditioner and sealed windows, staying as far away from the oceanside as possible.

San Francisco neighborhood (not to be confused with the district) is more intelligently designed with grid-style streets. The proximity to banks, upscale shopping malls, hotels, and businesses is a pleasant mix for city life. Development, going up at the same pace as Paitilla and Avenida Balboa, contributes to the changing skylines from the coastal waters for longtime residents. Many private homes have been demolished or renovated for office or storefront real estate, but for those who have stuck it out, there is a tight-knit culture and a neighborly feel. There are several public and private schools scattered along the main and side streets of San Francisco, where residents from all over the city send their children. Nestled into San Francisco is the urban Parque Omar, which hosts the National Library, tennis courts, a large track, and a sporadic array of food vendors. This park is extremely well maintained and sits on the borders of the San Francisco neighborhood of Altos de Golf, a very upscale neighborhood boasting mansions and high-walled homes. To the back it borders Parque La Fevre, a working-class neighborhood. Recently high-rise developers have waved their magic wands over this area as well, and for many first-time homebuyers, starting prices are more reasonable. San Francisco is a popular option for expats who want to reside in Panama City's newest apartment buildings, with chic design and high security. The prices are affordable and the central location makes it easy to catch a taxi, enjoy recreation in the park, and maintain a private life away from the banking and commercial districts. Many new buildings are going up between Calle 50 (actually a four-lane main streen) and Villa Porras Avenue, near Parque Omar. The streets run east, and between Calles 68 and 79, you will find plenty of local development offices to visit and inquire about new real estate options.

The oldest homes in the San Francisco district are distinguishable by the small backyard plots and terraces, open living areas to bring in the cross-ventilation, and a tropical urban feel. Today, these homes are the minority, squashed between concrete structures towering up to 40 stories high.

With regards to security, the busy workday traffic and equally crowded nightlife help to alleviate sketchy behavior. Regardless, this district is still in the center of a major city, and it is therefore advisable that you behave as you would in any major U.S. city. Don't act flashy or assume that a midnight stroll along the pedestrian walkway or in the city park is a safe bet.

Marbella and Obarrio

Just north of Avenida Balboa is a neighborhood called Marbella, which runs between two main traffic throughways, Avenida Balboa and Calle 50. The interesting aspect of Marbella is that it equally combines commercial space and residential, frantically assembled alongside one another, resembling a stacked Lego city. One-way roads funnel you in and out of the labyrinthine neighborhood or onto one of the two main avenues. One popular street, the "restaurant row" of Panama City, is bordered by homes and small apartment buildings. Apart from restaurants there are surf shops, clothing boutiques, bars, art galleries, beauty salons, and a number of small to midsize hotels. The benefits of this area are obvious. No car is needed, the amenities are central, and if you like social life it is your next-door neighbor, literally. It is also probably the only neighborhood within the central part of the city to have sidewalks that make it feasible (not easy) to walk. Most of the residents are either old-timers, whose homes were located in this district before the nightlife moved in, or very new and very temporary residents located there for the convenient factors mentioned above.

While it is a very busy area, the homes are not shabby. The older homes are solid structures, with 1950s to 1970s designs, and apartments can be spacious with large balconies and sliding glass doors to let the breeze through. This is pure city life, so noise from construction and taxis coming from Avenida Balboa is to be expected. Both home prices and rental prices are expensive. They run up to US$2,000 per month for long-term rentals or US$800–1,000 per week for short-term leases. One- to two-bedroom apartments may sell for US$200,000 in the 2009 real estate market.

Farther north and east begins the neighborhood of Obarrio, once all one property belonging to a wealthy landowner name Nicanor Obarrio. He decided to divide and sell plots of land when the city started to grow at the turn of the 20th century. The neighborhood now serves as a mix of commercial and residential properties, but it tends to be less energetic than Marbella and more structured on the main avenue, decorated with high-end jewelers, luxury car dealers, and expensive furniture stores—I like to call it the Rodeo Drive of Panama City. Obarrio's residents live in elegant homes, one might say mansions, along the south side of the neighborhood, while the north side hosts apartment buildings, well equipped with 2–5 bedrooms, maid's quarters, and 24-hour security. Some new developments are going up in this area, but perhaps built within better zoning limits than the mad rush of skyscrapers sprouting up in other key locations. Apartments are more likely bought as relocation homes and cost up to US$350,000 for one to two bedrooms with spacious layouts, or upwards of US$2,500 in monthly rentals.

El Cangrejo and El Carmen

North of Marbella and Obarrio lies the small neighborhood of El Cangrejo, which lives off the vein of Via Argentina, a youthful street about six city blocks long and only one to two wide. Although it is smack-dab in the middle of Panama City and much of the traffic going and coming from other parts of the city must pass through it, El Cangrejo really feels like a small village. There are old-school bars and restaurants that haven't changed for years, and quite a few hostels to stay in while testing out the area. A neighborhood park sits in a central location, along the street, where pick-up basketball or soccer games and daily exercisers can be found.

Today, walking down Via Argentina, there is a very international feel, stemming from the French Bakery, the Argentine coffee shop, the New York Bagel Café, the Canadian Cheese shop, and the few Spanish restaurants along the way. That's not to say you will find yourself in the midst of four or five different languages at any given street corner, but there does seem to be a trend of expats starting businesses here. Most of the employees of their shops are students and hard-working local kids who are interested in keeping their jobs and learning English from the expat clientele. Mostly travelers and short-term residents stay in El Cangrejo and El Carmen, until they find a permanent spot that feels like "home."

El Carmen sits only a block up from El Cangrejo. A sweeping turn from Via Argentina and you are there. It is set back from the main street just a little bit, so the city noise level varies but the architecture stays modest and elegant. El Carmen has more of a family feel, and older homes give the neighborhood a sense of history, standing strong and steady behind bulldozed remnants of smaller condominiums now being renovated along Via Argentina.

The University of Panama borders Via Argentina, and today there are numerous colleges, Internet cafés, and college students running around the neighborhood.

Once among the most affordable places to live in central Panama City and home to bohemian artists and young Panamanian entrepreneurs, El Carmen and El Cangrejo are now dominated by middle- to upper-class families, the former perhaps hosting more families than single residents. According to real estate experts, both neighborhoods are popular choices among expats, thus raising prices on properties and rents and stimulating renovations and the building over of older structures. Spaces here are traditionally some of the largest in square footage, but as old buildings are coming down and new ones are going up, they are resizing to sell more properties rather than offer more space. The average prices, as of July 2009, are about US$850 per square foot. Luxurious penthouses along Via Argentina are still quite affordable, running about US$220,000 for a three-bedroom apartment, 24-hour security, a social area, and 360-degree views of Panama City. If renting, this is also a very affordable area to consider at about US$800 per month for 1,000 square feet.

Bella Vista

Just to the north of Avenida Balboa and the Panama Bay is a small triangular neighborhood bordering the cusps of Calidonia, La Cresta, and Marbella. It was born in the 20th century to support a growing population from inside the walled city of Casco Viejo, then abutted by the expanding Canal Zone. The result was the neocolonial and neoclassical neighborhood of Bella Vista, a source of aesthetic and cultural pride for Panamanians. Although still close to the whiff of changing tides, large homes with impressive views of the ocean (*bella vista* means "beautiful view") sit upon a small piece of land, approximately three blocks wide by three blocks long.

Elite European families once dwelled within these massive Spanish- and French-style structures, but in the latter half of the 1900s many of these private mansions evolved into multiple-family residences and apartment buildings. Today the neighborhood is home to a middle-class working community, which fights with the municipality to save their historical homes every time a new building project comes in. They are professionals and families who were once so lucky as to live smack in the center of the bustling city. Today they still enjoy being close enough to walk to bus stops, restaurants, and large supermarkets. The Alianza Francesa is located in this neighborhood, offering weekly cultural events such as movies and art lectures. There is an international school, banks, and a few boutiques, as well as a few synagogues and one nearby and decadently displayed church, La Iglesia del Carmen. Bella Vista is located halfway between Via Espana and Villa Brazil, and many government offices, the Ministry of Finance, the Spanish Embassy, and the municipal courts are sprinkled throughout the avenues that run between them. Constantly re-routed traffic has caused havoc in the way of noise pollution here; therefore many new residents see the benefit living on the top floor of a high-rise in this neighborhood.

The influx of development has greatly affected Bella Vista, with many developers buying up lots, demolishing historic buildings, and creating space for bigger ones. Rents in Bella Vista have now doubled. Prices to buy a 900-square-foot apartment might be US$200,000 new and US$115,000 if it is a fixer-upper. Buying in this neighborhood usually requires buying a whole building or a lot for development, unless you are interested in a turnkey project, which would involve starting at the developer's office.

Residents are trying to fight this development, asking the city to pass zoning laws for new construction and look to restoring rather than replacing historic buildings. Fortunately, residents can rest assured that at least the buildings along Parque Urraca, the small, green city square, will continue to represent

The city keeps the parks maintained for outdoor living.

the neighborhood's historic aesthetics. These beautiful edifices house national libraries and have been declared historic (and thus protected) by the city.

Lone walkers should be wary in Bella Vista, particularly in the darker, more residential areas at night, as it borders tougher neighborhoods like Calidonia.

Casco Viejo

In 1998, UNESCO declared the Casco Viejo, the entire old city from Santa Ana to San Felipe, a World Heritage Site, saving a falling antique quarter of the colonial city. Since then, slow but profound steps toward restoring the Casco have been taken over by a few sustainability-minded developers, such as Arco Properties.

With the help of a few key personalities in the restoration of Casco Viejo and their rehabilitation programs for bad businesses and business practices, the Old Town revitalization is picking up the pace, and the mix of decadent and restored is the allure for many happy new residents. Restoration possibilities have attracted visionary foreigners, looking for panache in an exotic environment. Such wealthy and risk-taking expats have come to the Casco with the means and willingness to fully restore 18th- and 19th-century properties.

San Felipe is the end of the Casco, the point where the Panama Bay meets the three main plazas of the old town, elegant old ruins, and contemporary alfresco cafés; many investor expats are restoring properties here. Going north from San Felipe, the UNESCO limits end and the neighborhood extends to Santa Ana, whose local residents are fighting gentrification. It is a colorful area, where the Central Avenue begins its pedestrian boardwalk and can be enjoyed if you use your street smarts. Stay along the main Avenida Central and you will enjoy large residences, cheap shopping, and eccentrics who are the essence of this downtown area. You will also find more run-down but still elegant colonial structures. This is where the visionaries get lost. The neighborhood evokes images of the romantic colonial city. A feel for the real working class starts to slip into fantastical imaginings of a colonial city filled with men in top hats and women in white gloves walking hand-in-hand across the narrow, winding streets. Times have changed, but the decadent structures still stand, now with *Se Vende* (For Sale) signs affixed on cast-iron balconies and rooftop views of the Pacific Ocean and the newer half of Panama City.

Today the rustic feeling of the old town has lured bohemians and the artistic social scene to the brick-laid streets of Casco Viejo, mostly in San Felipe. These new residents are the ones who can tolerate the mix of old and new in Panama City. They love the jazz bars, Spanish restaurants, art galleries, and small eateries offering elegant fare, mixed with cantinas, street vendors, and local personalities who enjoy an honest conversation and sincere greeting by new residents. City-organized music festivals and art exhibitions are a more frequent experience than in the last few years. Tourism police work on foot and bicycle here, as they are interested in keeping this part of the city an attraction for both investors and historians. Still, take precautions and avoid walking north past Calle 8.

Renting can run from US$600 monthly for an artist loft of 850 square feet

a typical facade in San Felipe, Casco Viejo

© SKY GILBAR

and up to US$2,000–3,000 for an elegant apartment of up to 1,000–1,200 square feet with rooftop amenities. When buying, it is possible to find buildings for US$100,000 that measure about 2,500 square feet; however, these buildings are basic structures that will involve much restoration, ranging from electricity and plumbing to exteriors. Finished or developed apartments are currently selling for US$350,000–1 million based on the area, amenities, and square footage.

THE CANAL ZONE AND OTHER SUBURBS

The U.S. Canal Zone was returned to Panamanian jurisdiction in 1999. Many U.S. military personnel and civilians left the highly contained community they had learned to love and depend upon, leaving behind roughly 1,425 square kilometers (550 sq. miles) of land between Panama City and Colón filled with military and civilian residences and large empty structures that the Panamanian government would slowly sell off to private investors. These desirable green lots and magnificently tropical, palm-filled yards caressed the eastern and western sides of the Canal, offering a removed existence from fumy intersections and crowded commercial space.

Since 2000, the Panama City Canal Zone, now referred to as the Area Revertida (Former Canal Zone), is still in many ways a city paradise, with roughly 15 to 20 "town jurisdictions," not all of which will be written about here. The Panamanian government has revived them, attempting to maintain the same self-containment that worked well in the U.S. occupation years. As the humidity tends to have its way with anything left outside, homes that have not been lived in for even a few years will call for extensive restoration. However, slowly but surely the Panamanian government's bureaucratic department, ARI (Inter-oceanic Regional Authority), has sold off its concessions, and a new City Garden is coming to life.

Albrook and Diablo

Once the former Air Force grounds for the U.S. Military, Albrook has experienced the fastest turnover from strictly U.S. occupants to a mix of foreign and Panamanian residents. Bordering El Parque Metropolitano to the east and the Balboa Locks and Panama Railroad to its west, Albrook now holds a responsibility as the center of retail life in the Pacific Canal Zone. With a major supermarket, the largest and most economic shopping mall in the capital city, restaurants, gas stations, and a number of other convenient retail amenities, as well as a labyrinth of residences, Albrook has done a wonderful job of

PANAMA'S OLD TOWN: LIFE IN THE COLONIAL CITY

A visit to Panama City's Casco Antiguo evokes a mixture of feelings, from awe at the sight of the striking Metropolitan Cathedral and the three story-homes restored to their original wonder, to a sense of pity at all the dilapidated buildings still awaiting restoration. To some people, the fact that many buildings remain in disrepair with underprivileged families still living within is a reason never to return to "the Casco." For others, it incites a feeling of a colorful, enriched community, and to all the would-be developers among us, a sense of challenge and opportunity.

Indeed, it is the many facets of Casco Antiguo's community that have truly enchanted its foreign residents. Foreign residents in the Casco are largely involved in restoration projects and businesses related to tourism or entertainment, and they have therefore contributed enormously to enhancing the community and creating employment for locals. This is essentially the charm of the Casco: To move from your home country to a place where you can quickly make a difference and become an important part of a constantly evolving community is not an everyday opportunity. The real beauty of the foreigners who have made the Casco their home lies in their variety. A quick stroll around the neighborhood will bring you into contact with North American, Bolivian, German, Polish, Panamanian, British, French, Italian, and Spanish expats – a true United Nations. They come from different backgrounds, and most have lived previously in other countries – some in other old towns and UNESCO World Heritage sites that share the Casco's beauty and long history. All the residents have the same goal: to observe and be a part of the remarkable transformation happening in Casco Antiguo – a change from a forgotten neighborhood to one of the city's most desirable addresses.

The Casco Antiguo lifestyle is not for everyone, however. While safety has improved dramatically in recent years, gangs are still present in the peripheral areas and occasional violence is seen here, although very rarely does it affect foreign visitors or residents. Nevertheless, families with young children are not keen to live in the area, nor are elderly people. This neighborhood is more apt for the eligible bachelor or young couple, looking for an original and stylish place to live, an alternative to the generic downtown apartment buildings, and an energy to share with the locals.

shuttling city traffic from one end to the other. Albrook is also the location of the national airport and bus terminal.

Homes in Albrook are no longer available at an honest market price. The central location and self-sustained "small-town" feel have raised the value. Few homes have been maintained in their original structures. Whether they are built up, out, or around, homes in various phases of construction are a common view in Albrook. Perhaps it is finally ready to settle into a calmer phase, as one wonders how much more space is available to develop. Interspersed with

© SKY GILBAR

old and new in Casco Antiguo

Other disadvantages to life here include a lack of amenities. There is no large supermarket, no bank, no fancy hair salon, and no mall. But remember, while you may feel miles away from Panama City, the reality is Casco Antiguo is only a short drive from downtown, and even closer to amenities in Albrook Mall in the former U.S. Canal Zone.

What the Casco lacks in modern conveniences, it makes up for in cultural activities. As well as being home to the National Theater and several museums, Casco is the center of blossoming underground cultural activities, from rock music to sculpture and everything in between. Each year, people from around the city flock to Casco's array of open-air concerts. And let's not forget that several of the country's finest restaurants are located here.

Like any neighborhood you are considering for your new home, the Casco has its pros and cons. Generally speaking, young-at-heart people with a bohemian streak in their hearts should definitely check it out. One thing you can be sure of: In Casco Antiguo, life is never boring.

playgrounds and tennis courts, quieter neighborhoods located off the main road are the true picture of U.S. suburban life. Rental prices run US$1,000–2,000 a month for two- to three-bedroom homes and are part of a two-family structure (duplex). There is the occasional find at US$500–600 per month, but they are basement, studio apartments of a family residence. Purchasing a single-family home of two stories and 5–7 rooms in Albrook costs US$350,000–600,000 easily.

Directly across the Panama Railroad line from Albrook lays Diablo, a very interesting neighborhood once filled with civilian Canal employees. Meandering around the short side streets, one can almost sense the old images of cul-de-sac kickball games or hopscotch, neighborhood block parties, and beer-drinking Sundays. Diablo is a rare mix of cool breezes coming off the Canal and swampy mosquito air due to flat lots and natural swamplands. Many homes, closer to the Canal side, are rickety, wooden, camp-style lofts with a somewhat endearing feel. Diablo is less developed than other places, and therefore prices, even if only across the way from Albrook, can be easier to negotiate. Many have already bought, developed, and resold properties here, staking the values significantly higher now at US$300,000–350,000 for three- or four-bedroom homes measuring roughly 1,500–2,000 square feet.

The secret behind Diablo lies in the boatyard at the end of the main street. Still functioning today, this boatyard is busy daily, with small fishermen, private boat owners, and residents who have converted some of the boat hangars into seaside lofts. The mechanics of doing so are not easy, but with a lot of love and patience it can be done if there are any further lots available. The problem with buying in Diablo is that the Balboa Locks, the Panama Canal's first set along the Pacific, has the right to take over the land at any time, and your investment will be reversed at once. This has not happened yet, and many residents are nothing but pleased with their living arrangements.

Cardenas and Los Rios

Cardenas and Los Rios are two neighboring canal townships that lie north of Albrook. They are an equal mix of the Diablo and Albrook designs, with some homes outstanding and exuberant in their neo-suburban renovations and others staying humble and beautifully arranged with gardens and long patios. The communities are off the main road and away from urban traffic. These homes are better for full-time residents and families with school-aged children who want to live within the reverted Canal Zone, where schools and shopping are nearby. Prices may run US$200,000–500,000 for three- to four-bedroom homes with large backyards, something that really does feel like a metropolitan suburban neighborhood of the New York or Washington DC areas in the United States.

Clayton

Fort Clayton was once the largest U.S. military base in Latin America. According to U.S. Army records, 20,000 military and civilian personnel and their families resided in the 862 hectares (2,130 acres) of natural rainforest, lying on the Pacific opening of the Panama Canal, the Miraflores Locks.

Today Clayton, minus the fort, is just as expansive and significant within the Panamanian community. When the land was handed over in 1999, progress began for the City of Knowledge, a foundation that has successfully integrated technology, education, and culture into a solid community that works and lives on 121 hectares (300 acres) of the original Fort Clayton area, flat land surrounded by natural foliage. The wetland features of Clayton create higher temperatures than that of hillside locations in the Canal Zone.

Marked by the many scientific, research-related, and international organizations that have established offices in the City of Knowledge, the nonprofit foundation also maintains hundreds of residential properties, which are rented to personnel and students who work within the community for a reasonable price of US$650 per month. The community, mostly occupied by foreigners, has a personality of intellectual and international interest. Panamanians have found that by working with connections and long waiting lists, they too can benefit from the ideal living in this well-maintained neighborhood. The feel is one of an inoffensive college campus, with less loud fraternity parties and more corporate sponsorship. Miller's Field centers the City of Knowledge installations and office buildings, hosting soccer leagues, tennis courts, and a wonderful open track. At another field behind the United Nations offices, the official Panama Ultimate Frisbee club meets on Sunday and Wednesday evenings. An ever-changing group of international and Panamanian professionals have become obsessed with this weekly athletic catharsis. Local coffee shops, bakeries, luncheonettes, and a small

© SKY GILBAR

Many homes in the Canal Zone offer a suburban lifestyle at the perimeter of the city.

supermarket are adequate resources for those who work in Clayton and don't have cars. Most of these businesses were opened by foreigners and are doing quite well. Expats who work for the City of Knowledge may live in this part of the old Fort Clayton, but every now and again, a rare opportunity arises where they will give a contract to a non-employee. For more information, look on www.ciudaddelsaber.org.

The remaining land in the old Fort Clayton is free of City of Knowledge administration. Driving east toward the city, the road reaches the border of Parque Metropolitano, and the labyrinth of two-, three-, and four-bedroom homes reaches out long and wide. Homes and apartments are available for sale or for rent, but rental prices here are not as reasonable the City of Knowledge's rent-controlled housing. A few untouched structures are still available for a decent rate, perhaps US$800–900 a month for a 1,345-square-foot apartment with three bedrooms. A few turnkey projects are going up, offering views of the Canal. One development company is now offering up to 300 units in this area, with prices ranging from US$300,000–1 million, the selling point being the green surroundings and Canal views. The U.S. embassy finished its installations here in 2006. The immense building stands atop a hill and is impossible to miss from the back entrance of Clayton.

Costa del Este

Costa del Este claims to be the most ambitious development project surrounding Panama City. Only five minutes from Panama Centro, and 10 minutes from the international airport, the development provides American-style luxury living, with ocean views, gated communities, and high-rise apartments with every possible need on the inside except a hospital, which could very well be in the planning.

Once the garbage dump for Panama City, the area was energetically worked on by the original group of investors, who bought 300 hectares (741 acres) along the eastern side of the city and Pacific bay. The location is easily reached by the Southern Corridor, and easily seen from the San Francisco district, where tall buildings tower at the oceanside and irritate Paitilla's wealthy residents who no longer have ocean views.

There are also several office parks, housing corporate companies, retail warehouses, and private schools. This is a privileged and fairly self-contained environment; it has been said that small children of families who live, work, and are schooled in Costa Del Este can be heard asking one another, "which Este do you live in?" implying they are not aware that any other part of their home city exists. An upscale mall with movie theaters is located in nearby

© SKY GILBAR

Costa del Este is an upper-class neighborhood.

Paitilla, and getting on and off the Southern Corridor is the only dynamic change they may experience.

The area is very isolated and remains equal to downtown Miami or Key Biscayne living. Prices are comparable to this category of Miami real estate as well. In 2005, friends of mine bought a top-floor apartment in a luxury building for close to US$600,000. These prices are only starting to jiggle a little now, with the fall of the market in 2008. However, Panama's bubble is not yet bursting, so these same prices for a two-bedroom home still exist, and beyond for penthouse or gated homes.

AROUND PANAMA CITY
Veracruz

Fifteen to twenty minutes from the center of Panama City, just a few minutes west over the Bridge of the Americas, lies the beachside village of Veracruz. The budding tourism industry, vacation residences, and the Hotel InterContinental Playa Bonita Resort & Spa are transforming this humble fishing village into luxurious oceanfront living.

Despite the minor annoyance of unwelcome *chitras* (no-see-ums) and the rancid smell of low tide, Veracruz is taking shape as an option for foreign investors. There is a lot of land on offer, and realtors are getting in there fast. California-style one-level homes above a hilltop range US$200,000–350,000 and consist of three to four bedrooms with views to the ocean, on 2,000–7,000 square feet of land.

Not many Panamanians live out here, yet, but there are a few retired families

EXPAT PROFILE: AN INTERVIEW WITH REBECCA LOVE, EDITOR OF *PANAMA 9°80°*

How long have you lived outside of your home country? And when did you arrive in Panama?

I was born and raised in England, in a town called Solihull, just outside of Birmingham. I left the U.K. just after finishing my studies in Sheffield. I originally planned to travel for a brief time and then come back home and work. While traveling I volunteered in Bolivia for a few months, then to Peru, and up to Central America and Mexico. I did some more volunteer work in Honduras, then settled in Granada, Nicaragua for about 18 months. This was when I realized that I didn't really want to go back to the U.K., but I also realized there was not exactly opportunity for me there, and that was when I came to Panama – March 2005, to be precise.

What was your lifestyle before you lived here?

I was still in my university years. I had completed a dual honors degree in Business Studies and Hispanic Studies in 2002, and as many people do in England, had various office jobs and waitressing jobs to save enough money for my travels. I kept busy, working a lot, mixing with friends from school and work, partying, traveling around Europe whenever I had some free time and money, and basically saving up to go to Latin America. After having studied Spanish for so many years, I really wanted to put it into practice.

Where do you live now in Panama City, and do you rent or own?

I rent a new apartment in San Francisco but have previously lived in Marbella, Obarrio, El Cangrejo, and Campo Alegre, in the banking area.

What is your favorite neighborhood in Panama City? Why?

I love Bella Vista. I think the houses are gorgeous, there are trees everywhere, streets are wide and planned, there are several parks, and it is close to everything. Unfortunately, people seem intent on destroying it, and many of the homes have been torn down. Still, it's a cool place. After that, I would have to say Marbella – again, for the trees.

What was the turning point when you knew you wanted to move to/stay in Panama?

When I came here in 2005, Panama was just getting going in this whole real estate boom. I came with the intention of starting *Panama 9°80°*, an idea born from the magazine *Between the Waves* that I worked on in Nicaragua. At the time, there were not so many magazines here in Panama. Now, there are hundreds and competition is fierce. I think by the second edition of 9°80°, I knew that the business was going to be successful, and then I had to stay. Once I was here for a while, the initial "honeymoon" period finished, and suddenly this was my life. It's a good sign when you lose count of how many months/years you have been somewhere. At one point, when I was coming back to Tocumen airport in Panama City, I felt I was arriving *home*, and that was when it happened for me.

What is the most difficult aspect about living here for you?

I find life here to be very easy. It is getting harder, mainly because things are getting more expensive. But it is not a difficult place to live.

Is there anything you really miss from your home country?

I miss good English sausages,

English tea, and most of all the British radio and TV programs – especially the comedy shows. But what I miss the most is the culture of early evening social culture. I love to go out straight after work, have some drinks and something to eat, then be home at midnight, allowing for a productive following day. Here, people go out till 3 or 4 A.M., so you really can't get a good day's work in after that!

What is the most enjoyable aspect of living here?

I like Panama because it is quirky and it is certainly not boring. Here, every day, on the way to work or out at a restaurant or walking along the street, something so bizarre happens that I know I am in Panama. These are not always the nicest things, but they make life interesting. Driving to work you can see people make a living selling random items like birdcages and used blender parts. I also love the variety of food available, and that it is affordable enough to go out to eat here regularly.

How would you explain Panama City to someone who knows nothing about the country?

In the city, it's apparent how Panama is always pretending to be "First World," but it is not. Still, I find Panama the most exciting country in Central America. Pretty much everything you could want is here, but at the same time, it is very small, so if you are a big city person who is hungry for activity all the time, Panama is not for you. Doing nothing is a great activity in Panama. Do not expect to be entertained 24/7.

Also, if you like things to be accomplished quickly, you will hate Panama. The smallest thing can take the longest time, and words like *mañana* (tomorrow) and *ahora* (now) have no meaning whatsoever!

Why did you choose to live in Panama City as opposed to another region of the country?

Work. I don't think I could have started this business from anywhere else; the economy is very centralized in Panama City.

As a business owner and full-time professional in Panama, what kinds of opportunities have been available to you here that might have been harder to achieve somewhere else?

There is a lot of opportunity here that really does not exist everywhere. A lot of people in Panama have money, and they are willing to invest in businesses. A really great thing about Panama is that many things don't exist here yet. To get a good business model, all you have to do is go to a more developed country, perhaps to a tradeshow, find a product or idea that doesn't exist in Panama, and bring it here or make a version yourself. That way you have a proven track record.

That's good advice, but do you have any warnings to those who may be interested in working in Panama?

Oh yes. On a final note, people often think that they can start a business, hire employees, and go off to the beach while the employees take care of the shop. No, sir: A really successful business in Panama requires that the owner be actively involved, working hard alongside the employees. What's more, you may find that you have to work harder at your business here than you did in your home country, perhaps defying the original reason you considered Panama as your next home.

PRIME LIVING LOCATIONS

who are happy to be living outside of Panama City but still close enough to commute into the center of things when necessary. Veracruz offers very little in the way of local amenities. There are some wonderful seafood restaurants located along the shores, but they are a novelty, best visited once in a while to enjoy eating outside along the water. The closest shopping, gas stations, coffee shops, and banks are located across the Bridge of the Americas in the Canal Zone area. Renting or buying a car or a four-wheel-drive vehicle might be the best bet for residents, as taxis can be very expensive to and from this side of the bridge. Public transportation is limited to the Diablos Rojos, Panama's privatized and not very secure bus system.

There have been some reported crimes in the area toward foreigners, and as locals adjust to the changing face of their quiet fishing village, this can be expected. Developments usually offer security service, either in the form of a 24-hour controlled-access gate or monitored burglar alarms.

Howard

Howard Air Force base lies just in front of Veracruz, on the west side of the Bridge of the Americas. Back in 2002, Howard started selling off large residences for US$25,000, and a few risk-taking go-getters cashed in on the opportunity. Putting just as much into the renovations, these homes now sell for US$150,000–200,000 and have become one of the only affordable options left to buy green living spaces near but not quite inside Panama City. Like Clayton, Howard's land is flat and expansive and easily adaptable to new construction, albeit at the cost of sacrificing natural foliage and potentially useful and affordable apartments.

Currently there are a few streets filling up with tenants who can still rent two- or three-bedroom duplexes for up to US$750–800 monthly. These tenants are finding themselves threatened by Howard's transformation to the Panama Pacific community, but the one- and two-story homes that measure about 900–1,000 square meters (10,000 square feet) of living and green space.

In 2007, London Regional won the contract to develop Howard, and plans for a mini-city are under way. Now a very empty area, Howard maintains the remnants of now-defunct structures such as an equestrian center, an Olympic-size pool, schools, churches, and office spaces that once were part of a bustling Air Force base. London Regional has been contracted to help build Panama Pacific, the Pacific side's new Free Zone (like that of the Colón Free Zone). Therefore new plans call for knocking down most of these old structures and putting up shopping centers, newer residences, and office parks.

Residents who were used to the Canal Zone but felt pushed out by its overbearing development had moved to Howard in higher numbers as of 2004 and 2005. Some were Panamanians willing to live 15 minutes over the Bridge of the Americas, rather than paying high prices. Now that it has started to feel more populated, these residents aren't sure what will become of it, and while talk is of a very big project, only time will tell. No one is being asked to leave yet.

With large green pastures and lush rainforest land, as well as some magnificent mountain views looking toward the Panama province, Howard looks like it will become a prime location for suburban living. However, I recommend investigating exactly where the concessionary plans extend before doing so, as renting or buying now could result in getting kicked out or bought out later for a long-term project beyond your control.

Las Cumbres

Ten miles from Panama City, going north on "the old highway to Colón," an extension of the city avenue of Transistmica, is Las Cumbres. This district is a vibrantly forested lakeside community. Giving the feel of a real suburb, far off from the bustle of Panama City, Las Cumbres is a neighborhood of elegant homes and well-off families who enjoy living their lives apart from their daily work in the capital city.

Free from high-rise mania, Las Cumbres is filled with homes averaging 3,000 square feet and starting at reasonable prices, ranging US$200,000–300,000. These well-maintained houses have a history and presence of family life out in the country. They are tucked away along winding roads, along the riverbeds of Lake Gatún. Living is easy because Las Cumbres has a full array of shopping centers, grocery stores, and hardware distributors. And if Panama City is really what you need, it shouldn't feel all that bothersome to hop in your car and drive 25 minutes into city-mania.

Gamboa

A Canal Zone township lying along an intersection of Lake Gatún and the Chagres River, Gamboa takes a good 20 minutes to reach from the more urbanized Canal Zone areas like Albrook or Clayton; one must cross an antiquated, one-lane bridge to get there. This isolation has served as its fatal flaw or major attraction for so many. With no commercial properties in sight, except the Gamboa Rainforest Resort, it is a quintessential euphoria of jungle green surrounding homes with gigantic porches away from the echoes of distant trucks and honking taxis. The grandiose homes are not on top of one another, but they do rest row-by-row, street-by-street in this intimate community.

Well-meaning architects who have successfully taught the city to have tolerance for its historical architecture and jungle preserves have saved Gamboa from reconstruction and overdevelopment. However, this has not alleviated demand from outsiders who want to live there. Even though many homes seem uninhabited in Gamboa, acquiring a home is actually a competitive feat. Prices have crept up due to makeovers and the popularity of the town. In addition, many old-time Zonian residents tend to keep the buying within the family. Rather than sell off their property, they are passing it onto descendents who will be sure to keep it in the family, rather than sell it off and risk reconstruction in the area. Panamanians tend to have a different perspective about residential properties in the former Canal Zone areas, valuing the old architecture and history of the area the way many former Zone residents do. As of 2009, there is talk that the Panama Canal administration will be auctioning off properties again, as they had in 1999. This area is so desirable for Do-It-Yourself bidders that there will be a storm front arising when they do. Prices are completely unpredictable, since the last time any homes were auctioned off they were selling for US$25,000–50,000—a fantastic cost for wooden, antique homes measuring an average of 3,000 square feet.

Cerro Azul

North and just a tad east of Panama City, roughly 40 kilometers (25 miles) from the big city life, is Cerro Azul. Named so for the blue tint that is reflected over houses and rich mountain flora by the low rising clouds, the cool and often wet landscape attracts those who prefer a rural, peaceful lifestyle. Cerro Azul is actually in the midst of the Chagres National Park, and peaks give way to views of the Darien Gap, as well as views to both the Pacific and Atlantic Oceans. Temperatures are a temperate 21–26°C (70–80°F) during the day, with cool nights. Easy access to Panama City is a leisurely option rather than an obligation.

Local residents are more likely to live at the base of the mountain, and there are more commercial options there in terms of medical clinics, supermarkets, and other shopping. But riding up to the top, reaching for 950-meter to 2,000-meter peaks, the retreat to fresh air begins. Homes are situated sparsely between the mountainous foliage, with nature's song playing all day long, chanted by exotic birds, whistling breezes, and even the subtle sounds of silence. Most homes feature some kind of porch or terrace design with panoramic views into the valley below.

For a long time, Cerro Azul was a popular vacation spot for Panamanians with second homes. Today it is still a weekend getaway for many families but has become less popular due to new competition from beach communities. At the top of the mountain, there is a gated community, now directed more toward foreign retirees. It offers clubhouse amenities and less cookie-cutter housing, usually on 1.2 hectares (a half acre) of land. Construction costs within the gated community start at US$200,000. Buying an existing home costs up to three times that and can be worth the investment if you are interested in spectacular views and a home with a history.

Getting Around

BY CAR

Panama City is best done by car. With the exception of Avenida Central, a pedestrian walkway, city sidewalks for walking or biking have never been adopted here as an alternative to driving. The 2010 unveiling of the city may include sidewalks, but as a culture Panamanians prefer to drive one block and park again rather than walk in the heavy heat and possible rains. Most of the people seen along the few sidewalks are foreigners.

Driving in Panama City and the surrounding suburbs is not hard, but it can be a challenge and a danger. Driving skills are simply not good and often infuriating. At evening rush hour, which starts at 3:30 P.M. during most of the year, cars tend to stop on green and go on red. No matter how many new traffic signals are installed to relieve congestion, nobody seems to pay mind to them once the rat race begins. Bad weather and new construction can make traffic conditions even worse. In terms of finding your way, this much is true: Keep driving and you will eventually hit a landmark you are familiar with. This is how one realizes how small Panama City really is.

In truth, driving to and from Panama City from a suburb 10–40 minutes away is one of the only transportation options. Deciding to live in Panama without a car is an extremely difficult and dependent lifestyle, and unless you live in the center of the city, such as San Francisco District to Casco Viejo, you will find it frustrating to rely on public transportation or moody taxi drivers.

The only other option besides owning a car is to have a dependable chauffeur. If you have a steady job, and you know you will need a driver at set hours of the day, you will be able to get away with this option and negotiate a monthly price that may be equal to what you would spend in gas costs, with a fair service fee for your driver. However, car expenses are quite affordable in Panama City, and often it is just worth buying one and going it alone.

© SKY GILBAR

the Diablo Rojos

BY TAXI

Taxis around Central Panama are easy to catch. They will cost S$1.50–7 depending on the zones crossed. Taxis have a set fare between any two zones, so you can ask to see "the card" if you feel they might be trying to pull a fast one on you. If you have the patience and don't mind traveling with strangers, you might tolerate that your *taxista,* or driver, stops along the route to pick up other clients. That practice drops the trip cost to about US$1–2 per person.

PUBLIC TRANSPORTATION

City buses, the Diablo Rojos, are the only option for public transportation. To ride one, you just have to find a bus with the name of the bus route you are taking, "Panama Centro to Pedregal," for example. These are names of districts and neighborhoods. These buses will also drive to and from the suburbs, but you have to connect at several points. For instance, a bus passes by Clayton, coming from Gamboa, but you would have to change at Albrook and again at Plaza Cinco de Mayo (Caledonia), to continue into your job in the banking district, for example.

AIRPORT

If you work in Colón or have to take business trips around the country, you can take a commuter flight from the National Airport in Albrook. There are commercial flights that fly in the afternoon and evenings between Panama City and Colón through Aeroperlas airlines, one of the two national flight carriers. There are also private charters from the same airport base.

CENTRAL PANAMA

Pacific beaches from Panama to Coclé provinces have a well-defined personality different from that of the Caribbean. First, many Pacific beaches in the Central provinces are black-sand beaches, most likely caused by a nearby extinct volcano, which creates a distinct aesthetic feel. The Pacific side also relies more heavily on Panama's main cities as their focal point, living with greater access to electricity, landlines, and shopping. There is more movement along the Pan-American Highway on a daily basis, consisting of commuter, construction, and small business traffic. Essentially, you add an ocean breeze and take away a little stress from a suburban town feeling and you've got the average Pacific town feel. A number of turnkey developments typifying this feel have sprung up since 2005.

Those who want to do something more in the way of "country" life tend to move themselves toward the Central Highlands, that is El Valle de Anton, the mountains of Sora, and outside of Anton in Penonomé. While these towns are still very convenient locations, they offer a more rustic and natural lifestyle,

© MIRIAM BUTTERMAN

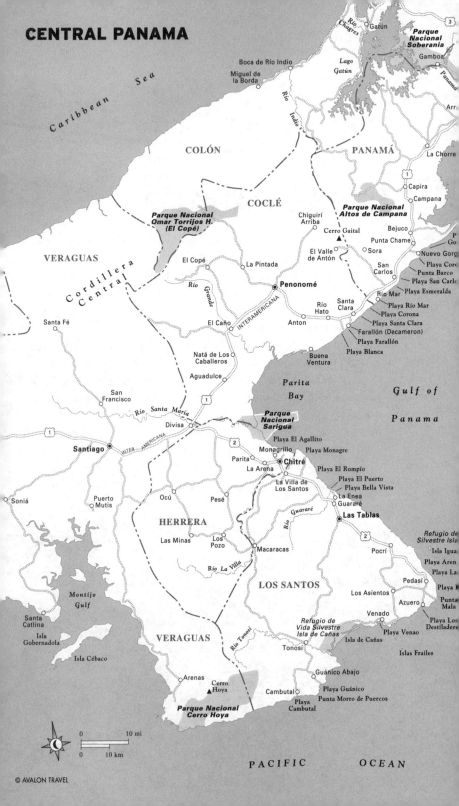

CENTRAL PANAMA

Caribbean Sea

Río Chagres
Gatún
Parque Nacional Soberania
Gamboa
Boca de Río Indio
Lago Gatún
Miguel de la Borda
Arr

Río Indio

COLÓN
PANAMÁ
La Chorre

1
Capira
Campana

COCLÉ
Chiguirí Arriba
Parque Nacional Altos de Campana
Bejuco

Parque Nacional Omar Torrijos H. (El Copé)
Cerro Gaital ▲
Punta Chame
P
Go

VERAGUAS
El Copé
La Pintada
El Valle de Antón
Sora
Nuevo Gorg

Cordillera Central
Río Grande
Penonomé
San Carlos
Playa Core
Punta Barco
Playa San Carlo
Playa Esmeralda

Santa Fé
El Caño
Río Hato
Santa Clara
Río Mar
Playa Río Mar
Playa Corona

Santa Fé
INTERAMERICANA
Anton
Playa Santa Clara
Farallón (Decameron)
Playa Farallón
Playa Blanca

Natá de Los Caballeros
Buena Ventura

Aguadulce
Parita Bay
Gulf of Panama

San Francisco
Río Santa María
Divisa
Parque Nacional Sarigua

1
Santiago
INTER AMERICANA
2
Playa El Agallito
Monagrillo
Playa Monagre

Soniá
Puerto Mutis
Ocú
Pesé
Parita
La Arena
Chitré
Playa El Rompío
Playa El Puerto
Playa Bella Vista
La Villa de Los Santos
La Enea
Guararé

1
HERRERA
Las Minas
Los Pozo
Macaracas
Río Guararé
Las Tablas

Montijo Gulf
Río La Villa
LOS SANTOS
Los Asientos
Pocrí
2
Refugio de Silvestre Isla
Isla Igua
Playa Aren
Playa La

Santa Catlina
Isla Gobernadola
VERAGUAS
Río Tonosí
Refugio de Vida Silvestre Isla de Cañas
Isla de Cañas
Venado
Pedasí
Playa
Punta Mala
Playa Los Destiladere

Isla Cébaco
Arenas
Cerro Hoya ▲
Tonosí
Playa Venao
Islas Frailes

Parque Nacional Cerro Hoya
Cambutal
Guánico Abajo
Playa Guánico
Punta Morro de Puercos
Playa Cambutal

N
0   10 mi
0   10 km

© AVALON TRAVEL

PACIFIC OCEAN

3
Panamá
Azuero

fertile land, and perfect locations for new sustainability projects such as refor-estation. The popularity of the Highland towns, only two hours from Panama City, have upped the prices, further creating a market for luxurious niches such as gourmet supermarkets, high-end bed-and-breakfasts, art galleries, and spas. The Central Highlands offer adventure activities, mountain climbing, and cool climates that are a nice change from, but close by, the Pacific beaches.

If you want to find something more original, something special, you will have to explore farther west along the Pacific Coast. After Penonomé, you will find that the beaches are much less populated by city-weekenders. Many vacation homes owned by Panamanians in this area are passed down from generation to generation, perhaps from the family roots that originated in that area. In the province of Los Santos, the beach towns are discreet and humble and development projects are much more tasteful than some of the eyesores found nearer to Panama Province beaches. Homes are built on cliffsides, set-tling into the natural landscape. There is a respect between locals of the Azu-ero Peninsula and the newer residents, and new development is minimal and thoughtful, such as well-planned building projects that maintain good use of the land around them, whether for reforestation or maintaining ocean views. There is still quite a lot of the area to explore, and it must be enjoyed firsthand. If you come across something wonderful, don't tell too many people about it or your diamond in the rough will soon fade to a less-inspiring vision.

The Central Highlands

Deciding to live in the mountains means adjustment to altitude, cool evenings, and dewy mornings. In the temperate tropics, it also means a chance to live alongside aromatic agriculture, the first picks at some of the best produce, and hands-on harvesting. The Sunday market in El Valle gathers independent farmers and interested buyers from all over the Anton Valley, talking up their fresh produce and herbs in addition to dynamic craftsmanship of practical designs made from volcanic clay, fruit seeds, and reforested wood. You will feel like you are living on nature's easel.

In the mountains, residents live humbly among themselves, with fenced-in land, watchdogs, and horses grazing in distant pastures. Every day feels like a pristine vignette of Robert Frost's poem "Mending Walls," where "good fences make good neighbors." Locals enjoy the quiet and less dramatic life of the Highlands, and expats comment on the warmth and sincerity they maintain in their relationships with locals. The cottage-type charm and rural lifestyle resonates with residents who enjoy chimneys and pleasant fireside evenings, which accent the cool weather experience. Leisure activities include hiking, mountain biking, horseback riding and bird-watching, as well as river walking to discover the many thousands of orchid species growing naturally in the altitude. Waterfalls within the sparse openings of rising hillsides give way to beautiful but cold swimming holes. The mountains of the region do not suffer from dour isolation since the provinces of Panama and Coclé beaches are within 20 miles and driving conditions are excellent.

The rain in the Highlands is not as hard and sudden as in the lowland tropics where rains are needed to break the waves of uncomfortable heat, although riverbanks might rise when the rain does fall hard. Highland dwellers find the temperatures fantastic and tend to live healthy, active lifestyles in the absence of debilitating heat. Mud baths, natural hot springs, inspirational views, and deep hikes into narrow trails contribute to Zenlike concentration levels. Perhaps this is why yoga retreats, outdoor music festivals, and artists have come to join those who have already discovered the peace and convenience of the Central Highlands, such as author Yann Martel, who spent a season writing in El Valle de Anton, finishing his award-winning novel, *Life of Pi*.

THE LAY OF THE LAND

Despite the notion that the first 90 miles west over the Panama bridges to Central Panama will take you only to the beaches, there are also the nearby Highlands, accessed by turning north from the Pan-American highway, part of the central mountain region that divides the Caribbean Ocean from the Pacific. Omar Torrijos National Park, 25,275 hectares (62,456 acres) of natural splendor, sits at the base of the mountain range, benefiting from riverbeds, vegetation, and protected wildlife. The valley and peaks of the Central Panama district offer softer climates, less humidity, and varied foliage of exotic orchids, seasonal mango, and reforested teak trees. The temperatures average 15–21°C (60–70°F), as the *bajareque* (mists) keep the air crisp. Don't be fooled by the cooler weather, however; the sun is still very strong and can burn through an overcast day. With peaks ranging 600–2,200 meters high, tropical wildlife and bright garden hues still occupy the landscape of the central mountain chain and act as the tranquil alter ego of the Pacific coastline below it.

DAILY LIVING

One of the best parts about living in the Central Highlands is that you will never feel you are too far away from the basic necessities. Perhaps once a week you can make it to the El Rey supermarket in Coronado, a 40-minute ride from either El Valle or Sora mountains, but much simpler than a trip to the capital. Coronado is the closest and most well equipped location for all supplies, food, building materials, healthcare, and hooking up or paying for phone, cellular, or electric service. Every Sunday and Thursday, El Valle holds the farmers market, with some of the freshest fruits and vegetables in the area, further proving that weekly shopping for dry goods in Coronado is more than sufficient since your local markets are well stocked with produce. El Valle de Anton has wonderful options for restaurants—Italian, German, and gourmet bistro style—that cater to tourists, so you will feel especially rewarded during those moments where you would like to forget you are actually 40 minutes away from "civilization." When it comes to medical facilities, your closest full-service clinic is the San Fernando facility in Coronado, and if you need serious attention or long-term care you are still only 1.5 hours from Panama City's best hospitals. However, now that the Central Highlands have become so popular with foreign residents, a few basic medical services are available locally, such as dentists and general practitioners.

Education, however, is the one aspect of daily life in the interior that has not yet developed to fit the needs of more competitive residents, looking for schools that will satisfy the international standards. Not even Coronado has an option for children of wealthy families there, further justifying its development as more of a vacation town than a primary residence. Perhaps the best option, if you are planning to raise a family with young children in these areas, is to look into home schooling.

Furniture stores are opening up in Coronado, which also serve the Highlands community well, and there are contractors and carpenters who have beautiful handiwork and can design furniture or decor especially for your style. If you are looking for something more modern, furniture stores from Panama City will deliver to the Central Highland towns for an extra fee. Likewise, service providers like plumbers or electricians who work with foreigners may live in Panama City because it is more central for them, but they head out to Central Highlands towns regularly to service clients during the week. If you find a good plumber in Panama City, you may have to pay a little extra, but it is worth it to have him come out to work with you on your special mountainside home.

WHERE TO LIVE
El Valle de Anton

The most popular Highland destination in the Panama province is El Valle. As its name suggests, it lies in a valley, and the mountain and hillside views are breathtaking, especially the area's most prominent attraction, La India

Dormida (The Sleeping Girl). From certain angles the hillside looks like a girl sleeping on her back. According to legend, an Indian princess walked up the mountain to die in shame after her lover committed suicide.

El Valle is the crater of an inactive volcano and is the second-largest inhabited dormant volcano in the world. The town of El Valle extends 600 meters above sea level and is surrounded by the northern hills of Cerro Pajita, Cerro Gaital, and Cerro Cara Coral, approximately 1,000 meters high. The southern hills, 800 meters above sea level, are Cerro Cariguana and Cerro Guacamayo. The rest of the surrounding peaks are Cerro Tagua to the east and La India Dormida to the west.

El Valle is a unique community for foreigners: it contains a tourist's facade in its markets, souvenirs, and adventure tours but also maintains originality somewhat like a hamlet in northern continents. Each house is an exclusive design, a ranch- or loft-style cottage where gardens are cultivated into a unique Eden. For years, expats moving to El Valle came partly because there were no gated communities. Such developments are said to be breaking ground in 2009, but they do not define the true character of El Valle. Becky and Larry, a Washington State couple who moved to El Valle and took over the Red Frog Bed and Breakfast, say they feel an affinity to the "1952/Beaver Cleaver" nostalgia and love it when they hear people say it reminds them of a town from their youth.

El Valle's center is the core of life, where bicycles scurry up and down the streets into and out of residential neighborhoods just off the main road. Even within the tiny 18-square-kilometer (7-square-mile) village, El Valle's neighborhoods have acquired distinct reputations—such as "Millionaire Mile," named for the impressive properties, or a more modest road where locals are known to mix with foreigners. There are residential streets with equally sized *fincas* (farmland parcels), and sprawling acreage above hilltops with views to both oceans. Prices for land in El Valle start at

© MIRIAM BUTTERMAN

El Valle de Anton has activities for everyone.

LIVING OFF THE BEATEN PATH

There is still one facet of Panamanian life that we have failed to mention, one important to the people who move to find that perfect place of peace and isolation: sustainability. Since the rise of expat investors that has swept through Panama over the past decade, many developer-opportunists speak of convenience; modern amenities and well-constructed transportation routes have lured many. But further down the Pacific Coast in Veraguas, Herrera and Chiriquí provinces, and up along the Caribbean coasts of Colón, there are a few places where foreigners have found solace in that eternal wave of self-sustainable life. Not everyone, but the majority of these searchers are members of the do-it-yourself (DIY) philosophy.

These foreigners are ready to sacrifice convenience. They are people with a keen sense of minimalism and sustainability and a Walden Pond mentality who come to Panama to find that little plot of land, off the beaten path, ready for the challenge of bushwhacking through the rustic, antiquated coastal towns to find their dreamland.

Patience and trust are essential when taking on a rustic lifestyle. Freshwater might be out for days at a time, or you may have no electricity and have to live within the limits of the sunlight. You will need to adjust your baths and dishwashing to the frequency of the rainfall and prepare for not seeing many others for weeks at a time before you are able to get out to a town or small city to restock. You need to be aware of the poisonous snakes that meander in your area and know how to care for a scorpion bite. Remember that small creatures can create some of the biggest problems, and that locals will take a slow approach to accepting your friendship and expect fair compensation for their services. It is not only an adventurous lifestyle, but also a character-building experience and one that teaches respect for nature.

Life is an activity in these small corners of Panama. Vacationing there is one thing, but consider the heavy burden of living out the day-to-day adjustments to this type of isolation before you leap. Families or individuals who succeed at living off the beaten path have a well-prepared plan, a sturdy, all-terrain vehicle and excellent knowledge of emergency response. They won't risk the good life by playing silly games with the wildlife, nor by offending the local culture. It takes adjustment, and oftentimes previous experience, but people who make this adjustment will tell you that the hammock awaiting them at early dusk or the morning swim in their private lagoon is well worth it.

Whether you live on an island, in the still woods of a protected forest, or a sandy coast along a wetland mangrove, you should investigate the environmental issues that affect the area and restrict yourself and your projects from causing any harm. Perhaps creating a recycling program for the communities or designing a proper sewage outlet will invoke a positive influence, not only with the local Panamanians but to potential foreign residents who, like you, want to live alongside nature and are willing to extend beyond their comfort zone. Protecting nesting sea turtles off the coast of Veraguas and reforestation projects along the Azuero Peninsula are a few examples of present activity by expatriates who invest in a simple lifestyle and Mother Nature's causes.

Living off the beaten path calls for an honest approach. Finding the right attitude – a mix of respect and open-mindedness – will make a big difference in the way you prosper.

US$10 per square meter and may run as high as to US$75. Homes situated on 0.2 hectares (0.5 acre) of land near the center of town may cost US$235,000, while a well-functioning bed-and-breakfast at the time of this writing was on the market for US$1.2 million. You will want to compare these prices with those of the other Highland options that offer an equally sophisticated style of living and are nearer to Panama City or near Boquete, Chiriquí. There is a big difference in price and atmosphere.

Sora

Sora is a mountainside community in the province of Panama, just off the Pan-American Highway about 100 kilometers west from Panama City. It is known for its gated community, Altos de Maria, a development started by the Melo Group of Panama. There they have created a 2,832-hectare (7,000-acre) community tucked into the Continental Divide with views of the green valley, both oceans, and mountains. The altitude runs between 450 and 1,100 meters above sea level (1,476–3,608 feet). With average temperatures of 24°C (75°F) there is little need for heating or cooling. Altos de Maria is highly independent from the rest of the district; the development has an independent power plant and manages its own water and sewage system. The gardens and community social area provided exclusively for residents, with a natural swimming pool and community greenhouse amenities. There is even a private heliport. This first-class infrastructure of Altos offers the advantage of living in premium real estate with prices to match. Lots are available from 0.1 hecare (0.25 acre) to 0.8 hectare (2 acres), and the prices vary depending on the views and the land design you desire. The average three-bedroom, three-bathroom home on 0.3 hectare (0.75 acre) will cost US$429,000, and a two-bedroom home on 0.2 hectare (0.5 acre) will be US$525,000. Lots per 0.2 hectare (.5 acre) are US$55,000, and construction costs vary depending on your choice of materials but average a few hundred dollars per square foot. Hundreds of homes have been built and are occupied in Altos. More construction is under way. However manicured the physical aspect of the community is, you still feel the benefits of fresh air and natural foliage. There is a road from Altos to El Valle, not yet fully paved but under way at the time of this writing.

Sora has a grocery store and is only 30 minutes from Coronado, for restocking necessities. Realtors can help you find land for sale outside of the gated community, where spectacular views and climate are still available.

La Pintada and Penonomé

Penonomé and La Pintada offer farmland, rolling hills, riverside lots, and back roads that sweep up and around into hills and where you feel the cool, humid air. Expats who choose to live in Penonomé are usually retirees who enjoy being within the throes of nature and away from main roads. Many probably come from rural towns in their home countries. Some of the best land is found several miles from the center of town, which also means better prices, but at the cost of unpaved roads and difficult journeys. There are a few turnkey operations starting in Penonomé, along with reforestation projects. According to a 2007 *La Prensa* article, locals are not troubled by the arrival of foreigners, hoping it will raise the value of land in the area and lead to the opening of new businesses and services catering to foreigners. Those who have settled there have done so quietly. Expats living in these areas don't get out much. Once in a blue moon you might run into a foreigner who has come to Panama City to get some "city life" in his or her blood for a few days. Restaurants in the town of Penonomé are dim and dusty. You need to drive along the Inter-Americana (a.k.a. Pan-American Highway) to find decent food. Much of the land for sale is replete with produce such as yucca, mango, papaya, and eggplant. In Penonomé, 81 hectares (200 acres) of farmland was recently going for just under US$400,000, and 11.5 hectares (29 acres) US$153,000. On the less ambitious side, a two-bedroom cottage on 0.4 hectare (1 acre) of land costs approximately US$50,000. Depending on the topography, undeveloped land at the center of La Pintada costs US$12,350–17,300 per hectare (US$5,000–7,000 per acre). Farther away from the main roads, 30 minutes past the town and toward the Caribbean coast, you can find a 5,000-square-meter (54,000-square-foot) property for US$10,000, but what you save on land and construction costs you will spend on transporting materials.

PRIME LIVING LOCATIONS

GETTING AROUND

You will find all varieties of cars in these small areas, but especially all-terrain vehicles for having to pass through mud or off-road throughways. In El Valle, these types of roads are rarely issues since residences and tourists pay the maintenance fees. Fancy four-by-fours coming from the city on a given weekend are the usual sight along the road. However, you should ask about the roads before you make the trek to see property. In La Pintada or Sora, small roads have been paved, but big trucks coming in and out have damaged them over time. Thus you are better off in a high-clearance car with strong shocks. For locals in these towns, bicycles and horseback are the norm. When rainfall is scarce, these simple forms of transportation add to the simple charm. Put a basket on your bicycle and you are set for daily market runs or visits to your nearby neighbors.

EXPAT PROFILE:
FRED AND CYNTHIA BISHOP

It wasn't too farfetched for Fred and Cynthia Bishop to move to El Valle de Anton. After nearly three years of full-time self-renovation of their 1920s craftsman home in Paonia, Colorado, they had passed their own tests for hard work, perseverance, and self-sufficiency. After a few trips to Panama to explore the possibilities of pensioned living here, they said good-bye to their "labor of love" home and comfortably followed their hearts to Panama. Fred, a carpenter by trade, and Cynthia, an artist and competitive seamstress, have since found a community and a lifestyle to which they are willing to commit.

In Colorado, you came from a small town in the mountains near nature. Why did you decide to make the change to Panama?

CYNTHIA: I've thought about living in the tropics ever since I did a research project on the Galapagos Islands when I was 10. Panama offers an adventure we were ready for. I don't want to live with consumerism or the rat race. In the U.S, no matter if you are in a small town or not, it is difficult to avoid it.

FRED: We were ready for the adventure, and we wanted to leave the United States. The carbon footprint is smaller in El Valle, and being self-sufficient is important to us. For example, we don't need air-conditioning, nor do we need heat.

In the small Colorado town where we lived, it was not a daily occurrence to be immersed in nature. Here, out in the interior in Panama, we are constantly aware of nature all around us. Here we saw hawks mating from our hammocks. Daily, we see hundreds of birds of all types, watch the fruit ripen on the trees, first hear the approaching raindrops hundreds of feet away like a freight train bearing down on us, and on and on.

How did you find El Valle?

FRED: I first came to Panama on my own. I was way out of my comfort zone. I didn't speak the language and I wasn't accustomed to traveling by myself, but we had done some investigating from the States. I generally liked what I saw and decided it was worth making a second trip with Cynthia.

CYNTHIA: We took a bus trip across Panama; we were going to see as much as we could. We had reservations to stay in a resort in Colón. When we found El Valle we blew off the reservations and spent the rest of the month here. We knew we didn't want a gated community. We enjoy living alongside nature and still making the change we were looking for.

Did it take a lot of adjusting to feel at home in El Valle?

CYNTHIA: Coming from a small town in Colorado, we were used to traveling far for supplies. We've made it a point to become active members of the community. I am involved in teaching students to make art projects with recyclables, and we recently worked in a volunteer Spay and Neuter clinic organized by expats and which has helped 120 dogs and dozens of cats and will keep thousands more off the street.

FRED: You never know how you are going to be received in a new place, but we feel needed and we enjoy helping out where we can. There is a large expat community here, and we are all one big family. But when we get to know Panamanian locals,

© MIRIAM BUTTERMAN

the Bishops with Cynthia's prize design

we don't feel a class difference. We are friends with weekenders; we are friends with locals. When I work around the house, or on the land, I work alongside my crew in my jungle boots.

You are both retired, so what do you spend your time doing?

FRED: Even though we are only renting, we spend each day working on this house, so we are sufficiently busy. However, I do carpentry and soldering and my studio is in the back shed. I'm out there every day. I play the guitar; I make furniture.

CYNTHIA: I work on competitive sewing and I make glass beads. Fred just finished making my art studio in a converted kiosk on the property we are renting. I finally got all the materials in place and have a place to escape to every day.

What makes living in El Valle, Panama, a great experience?

CYNTHIA: We like the idea of being self-sufficient. We have a commu-

nity we enjoy being part of, and this has helped to us to make our "home" here. We are fortunate to have clean air, freshwater, and we have each other. We also feel positively about the Panamanian services industry. With local health services, we have had top care at reasonable costs. Our lab tests are accurate, the doctors are knowledgeable, and they use up-to-date technology. When we bought our land, we had great service from the Realtor. We never felt we were doing something "risky." It was a clean sale and the broker was excellent with us.

Have there been difficult times in Panama?

FRED: When we first moved here in 2007, we bought one hectare of titled, farmable land on a beautiful green hill with views of both oceans. Four months later there was a landslide that halved-off part of the property. We were shocked, but we went back to work on it. We built a

(continued on next page)

EXPAT PROFILE:
FRED AND CYNTHIA BISHOP (continued)

cable car to take us up the section we couldn't drive through, even with a four-by-four. We were on our way to restoring it, but in November 2008, there was an earthquake in David, and it opened a fissure on our property. We had to abandon the property altogether. Then 2009 brought the downside for real estate values. Selling off our property has been almost impossible. It was a personal tragedy for us.

Where we were renting prior, we were robbed, but this could happen anywhere – it's not Panama's fault. We've moved on. On a daily basis, the language is very hard for us. We keep at it and make a point to speak Spanish everyday. We are determined to learn Spanish.

What have these experiences taught you?

FRED: We are committed. There are challenges here. The best trait you can bring to Panama is resilience. That way, the days and years tick by and they are meaningful. Here we are and we are going to stay here. It is our change, and even though it's a hard one, we make it the best we can.

Has it been expensive to get settled in Panama?

FRED: We bought our land at US$8 per square meter, but we know that the range is large. There are some turnkey developments that are going for US$45 per square meter. Aside from property prices, we know we have to spend money on renovations, but we are very do-it-yourself people. While it's not inexpensive in Panama, it's reasonable. We spent US$10,000 on a container to bring a lot of personal things we probably could have gotten here. We don't regret it.

Do you miss the States?

CYNTHIA: There is nothing about the States that we can't find or create from what is available to us in Panama. We haven't gone back to the U.S. in the past two years and don't have any plans to go back.

Pacific Beaches

The Pacific beaches of Panama's eastern coast are one of the easiest and most viable areas to enjoy the tropical sun and live with modern comforts, natural surroundings, and proximity to city life, if need be. There might be only a few popular beaches that ring familiar by name, but in fact going south of Divisa, towards Las Tablas, you will find some exceptional beaches set against rolling hills, green hills, and drier climates than the rest of the central beaches. Even though it is all endemic to Pacific waters, the beaches at the Azuero Peninsula are distinct from the eastern Pacific beaches, which in turn are also very distinct from the beaches on the western Pacific. Even if you do not decide to settle in the Central Pacific beaches, it is worth the trip just to understand the distinction between the Pacific landscapes, and to get a feel for the rural lifestyle here as compared to the urban-fed communities of the eastern Pacific.

THE LAY OF THE LAND

The coast of Coclé features the most visited beaches in all of Central Panama, at times overflowing with Panamanian weekenders, resort-goers, and expats who have found convenient beach living. At the beaches of Coclé, sun and sand are the principal feature guiding lifestyles, services, and operations in the area. It is a region that combines a rebirth of development while maintaining the remnants of Panama's "old country." Most of the locals live off of fishing and tourism, as new resorts like Playa Blanca, Buena Ventura, and Nikky Beach serenade the local residents with promises for greater economic opportunity. All this is located 90 miles west of Panama City, from Punta Chame to the white sands of Playa Blanca.

DAILY LIVING

The golden nugget of life on the Pacific coastline of Panama is the coast it-self. The proximity to the ocean breeze, the reflection of white sands, and the echoes of powerful waves help make the commotion of holiday and weekend crowds tolerable. These natural elements of Coclé are juxtaposed with ame-nities such as cell phone, cable, and internet services, a major supermarket, hardware stores, and even fine dining, where they support many of the upscale

© SKY GILBAR

The Central Pacific beaches are the most popular in Panama.

beach communities situated 90 miles west of Panama City. While you can feel the charm of history or a quiet fishing village dwelling in the midst, your everyday needs will never go unmet. Cities like Coronado, in the district of San Carlos, are fully developed with everything one might need to live full-time. Even a medical facility was incorporated in 2009. The only thing the area lacks is a school. Therefore the entire province benefits from the commercial development in this small area, resting midway between Panama West and Penonomé.

The development of this area is only part of the boom that began in 2005. The coast has experienced the domino effect of construction since the 1950s, when wealthy Panamanians began to sell off their lots and construct the many condominium complexes, high-rise apartments, and homes standing high above the coastal sands. During the week, life is calm, remote, and feels like an escape. However, on weekends and holidays, city dwellers arrive to entertain themselves, sometimes bringing large parties from the capital, always jovial and ready to let loose. The hammocks go up immediately, music blares from fancy audio equipment, and many domestic employees come to perform beach house duties, such as caring for the children or preparing the family meal. Now, with so many hotel resorts and high-end turnkey residences going up, spa services and on-site nightlife are equally available.

Surfing, boating, and riding Jet Skis are a few examples of the lively pastimes residents enjoy. As adventure sports such as wakeboarding and sand surfing become prevalent, adolescents make up the majority of the population seen out and about. On the beach itself, ATVs (all-terrain vehicles) jump out from the trails, quite a contradictory image alongside local cowboys on their horses. While residents and beachgoers have their differences of opinion about how much motorized equipment should be allowed on the beach, it is still a quite peaceful existence living along these coasts, as high season is short-lived and crowds are only an issue on the weekends and holidays. The beaches of Coclé stretch far, and if the rivers between are not high, long walks along them are a beautiful way to explore the greater area and its natural habitat.

WHERE TO LIVE
Punta Chame to San Carlos

Coastal land is abundant along the Pacific Central Coast. Hence, landowners started to sell off plots. The first community in this lucrative business was Coronado. Scattered throughout Punta Chame and the beaches of San Carlos, Punta Barco, Coronado, and Rio Mar are extravagant, luxury homes worth half a million dollars or more due to their beachfront proximity. Property is more expensive in these desirable areas, where Panama's elite families have had their homes for generations and where services are growing. Homes not situated on the beach, perhaps a walk down the path or a brief bicycle ride down the road, might have a much more likeable price tag. In 2009, the global economy has affected Panama's real estate sector; a three-bedroom single-family home on a lot of 600 square meters (6,458 square feet) is selling for US$195,000. High-rise developments, now commercializing these same areas, are going up and being sold at pre-construction costs of US$1,800–2,500 per square meter (US$162–232 per square foot). These are oceanview properties and don't include maintenance fees or unforeseen construction costs. Land in these same areas sells for US$50–150 per square meter (US$4.50–14 per square foot). However, you will have to add construction costs at the average of US$650 per square meter for the basic installations, according to Rogelio Romero of Romero Realty. He says if you are interested in the finest quality materials and workmanship, expect to pay US$1,000 per square meter (US$60–95 per square foot). It is easy to find builders with experience in these areas, as well as trusted locals who have worked for Panamanian families for years and are highly recommended throughout the eastern Pacific area. At the same time, crime, which previously was never an issue, has crept into the area due to the many new developments springing up and populating the area with wealthier communities, while locals still suffer the consequences of a poor economy.

Santa Clara and Playa Blanca

Sixteen kilometers up the road from Coronado is the town of Santa Clara, the beginning township in the coastal strip now referred to as Playa Blanca. Once only occupied by 20 or so families, this fishing village has grown into a low-key spot for second-home owners, boasting colonial and modern homes along the upper neck of the neighborhood. Driving in from the Pan-American, Santa Clara seems like any suburban neighborhood, but many homes, and even some mansions, have striking backyards, with long, winding staircases that lead down to the beach. In 2009, publicity for a high-rise residential development calling itself Santa Clara was launched full force and is bound to change Santa Clara, an everyman's beach, where a public parking area leads to thatched roof cabanas and fresh seafood restaurants. There is some oceanfront living, and contemporary designs sit side by side with humble fishermen's homes. Prices for land are similar to San Carlos district, where oceanfront homes sell for up to US$1 million.

© MIRIAM BUTTERMAN

a vacation home along the beach in Santa Clara

Farther up the coast, one can walk or drive up to Playa Blanca, a gated community in the tiny fishing village of Farallón, the location of ex-dictator Manuel Noriega's onetime weekend home (now demolished). In 2000, the all-inclusive beach resort the Decameron was opened and has since developed a golf course and time-share residences. The beaches of this area are calm and swimmable, and the coastline is flat; thus several other residential and resort facilities have started to appear in communities such as Playa Blanca and Buena Ventura.

Playa Blanca is a resort and a gated community about 10 kilometers from the Decameron. Three residential towers, selling like hotcakes to expatriates who want North American–style housing facilities, sit in the background of the resort, with a private pool, roughly one mile from the beach. There are also beach villas, two- or three-bedroom pre-constructed homes, sandwiched between the towers and the beachside, along paved roads. If you are looking for originality and a view of the ocean from your bedroom window, stay in Santa Clara, or a more quaint community such as Punta Barco. Playa Blanca is a turnkey development marketed toward investors who might use the property a few weeks a year for their own vacation convenience.

At the same turn-off from the Pan-American to Playa Blanca, only a few miles down the road to the right, is the entrance to a select beach community called Buena Ventura. The developer, a wealthy Panamanian whose own multimillion-dollar home is situated at the forefront of this immaculate beach, has created a breathtaking picture of cleanliness and sophistication alongside simple images of the tropics. Townhouses with pools and single-family homes situated in cul-de-sacs off the oceanfront start at US$500,000. Oceanfront lots are twice as much. With amenities such as an 18-hole golf course, a five-star hotel and spa, and soon a commercial shopping center, this community stands out as one of the most luxurious in the region.

GETTING AROUND

Other than arriving at the beach from the city or airport, transportation is somewhat of a non-issue since you stay in and around the house and beach, hopefully reachable by foot. Except for Coronado, where citylike infrastructure has been established, private transportation is needed to get on and off the main highway, perhaps to eat at a well-known restaurant in the area, or visit friends at another beach along the Pacific side. Since the roads are all quite developed, any car will suffice, but the hard tropic rains can cause uncomfortable driving conditions. In 2004–2005, the Centennial Bridge was inaugurated by the Moscoso Administration that opened up access from Panama City toward the interior by way of the Northern Corridor. Buses come from Panama City's bus terminal daily, with pit stops on the Pan-American Highway. Rarely do they enter the roads off the highway, but smaller coaster buses or taxis will bring passengers into towns, making short trips back and forth all day long at very affordable prices. The buses from the city cost very little, roughly US$3 to and from Panama City.

The Azuero Peninsula

Past the province of Coclé, resort communities along the Pacific coast are rare. After passing Farallón, the Pan-American saunters on into raw territory, where expansive farmland is a common sight. At Divisa, you take a long road toward the Azuero Peninsula, an important center of Panamanian folklore, represented through *las ferias* (festivals) and Carnival customs, such as the Pollera dresses and Panama hats. Here you find Spanish heritage in the form of 300-year-old colonial churches that sit at the squares of towns such as Chitré, Las Tablas, and Pedasi, which now contrast with small runways in the backdrops to serve charter planes and national carriers. To some, these towns are small villages, charmingly depicting modern-day cowboys, roadside vegetable stands, and small fishing wharfs. But to many others, those with cell phones and city manners, these same towns are important industrial centers and business routes. Agriculture, mainstream reforestation projects, and potential satellite bases fortify the district, alongside a developing real estate boom.

Playa de los Destiladores on the Azuero Peninsula

DAILY LIVING

Living in the Azuero Peninsula is a simple life. Perhaps a trip once every two weeks to the Los Santos capital of Las Tablas or Chitré is something you will need to incorporate into your routine in order to maintain your standard of living, as many retail chains, mechanics, auto dealers, lawyers, and medical facilities can be found there. For major medical assistance, Tonosí is the closest from Pedasi and Venao. If you live closer to Las Tablas, Santiago hospitals may be more convenient.

In Azuero, you are equidistant from David and Panama City, the western and eastern capitals. Your personal business and lifestyle circumstances will most likely determine where you will go for your shopping, medical exams or banking needs. David boasts a Price Costco, the membership retail store, as well as supermarkets with imported brands. Living in the Azuero Peninsula, however, means being OK with the idea that you won't be near a commercial shopping center and that you would rather be around the house, gardening, enjoying your personal hobbies and family time. The locals schedule regular trips to attend to their city errands, and you will soon acclimate to a similar routine, which makes it easier to enjoy your time away from the city and on the shoreline.

There are not many bustling expat communities here, but the majority of residents who come from abroad to research the options of beachfront living are gentle in their development tactics and mindful that the land is fragile and special to the communities that have lived and worked on it for hundreds of years. Archeologists claim the land is filled with geological history of settlements from 10,000 years ago. All this is masked by a dramatic ambience of Pacific serenity, emerald green waters, and red rocks, which many modern architects wisely take into account when designing new homes. Creatively crafted signs for eco-resorts and land for sale populate the one-lane roads here; hills roll up and down along the cliff, where homes are tucked away, allowing for privacy and a blending in with the natural landscape. Riding through Pedasi, you will find a *dulcería* (pastry shop) with signed photos of politicians, Hollywood memorabilia, and tokens from Panama's elite embellishing the walls. It's a quiet and happy life in the Azuero Peninsula for many of these people, who show pride in hard work. Woodworkers have made the most out of their craft, by providing local resources for modern home furnishing.

WHERE TO LIVE

Looking for a place to live in the Azuero Peninsula will call for patience, hands-on research, and consideration as to your basic necessities. There is a lot of exploration to be done in this region, and many opportunities for cutting-edge investment projects. While there are plenty of pre-constructed homes with family history on the market, you might also be interested in finding your own perfect gem of land and starting your own construction there. Spend time in the area—perhaps a week at several different seasons. Talk to locals and other speculators. One French developer, Gilles Saint Gilles, discovered the Azuero Peninsula through word of mouth; now, he has come to build pristine, sophisticated vacation properties covering 357 hectares (882 acres) of land, attracting worldwide clientele. He and his team train local carpenters to carve out his architect's dream of villas and stately homes, reminiscent of the Tuscan coast of Italy. In addition to the boutique hotel he has constructed, the development, called Azueros, flourishes next to residences along Playa de los Destiladores. He has gone about his work with the philosophy of sustainable living, using local materials and labor to accomplish his goal. Saint Giles has succeeded in furnishing wealthy clients with a patch of elegant paradise. Azueros development costs are high, with US$50 million invested in property development so far, resulting in exclusive and spacious living.

In the provinces of Los Santos, surfers have a recurring presence. Playa Venao is a common seasonal nesting spot for wave riders who camp there harmlessly to await the Pacific swell. Santa Catalina in the Veraguas province is one of the last towns along this central region—scarcely acclaimed by the Panamanian government, but a gem in the eyes of surfers as well as biologists who have taken on the ambitious task of protecting the biological corridor of marinelife that lies within this Pacific region near Coiba Island National Park. Moving on from there, the beaches to the west of Santa Catalina can be considered off the beaten path, extremely remote for many a foreigner. From Pedasi to Playa Venao and onto Santa Catalina, there are numerous options for home sites cradled alongside lagoons and green hilltops that overlook the vast Pacific Ocean with roaring waves below. Real estate professionals claim that land is still very affordable, but the popularity of the location is increasing and prices are rising steadily. At present, land is selling for US$3–15 per square meter.

GETTING AROUND

At Divisa, just before the city of Santiago, the National Highway, known as La Carretera Nacional, begins. The road veers south along the Azuero Peninsula, where the rural atmosphere gives way to well-constructed roads built for heavy driving. Cars and small coaster buses can be seen throughout the more populated towns along the Carretera, Las Tablas and Chitré; catch these buses to your final destination at Divisa or Las Tablas. Take a bus to Divisa if you are going or coming from David, or from Las Tablas if you are planning to go further into the Azuero Peninsula. Just ask a local at the town square in Las Tablas for directions and bus routes, or a police officer when you are nearby Divisa. Both will be happy to help you since Divisa and Las Tablas are common stopover points. If you proceed farther into Veraguas, en route to Santa Catalina, you will experience the rough and ragged undeveloped roads and come across local ranchers roaming through the one-lane roads with their cattle. Whether or not you can see signs to your final destination depends upon the condition of the roadside foliage, as overgrown tree branches or fallen signs may cover the road signs. In the Azuero Peninsula, a vehicle is important, as amenities are not likely to be close to your residence. Even though there is a runway in Pedasi, national flights have not flown there regularly since 2008. You can schedule a private charter to take you there, but you will need a rental car to get to the next destination.

THE WESTERN HIGHLANDS

Often described as the "other side of Panama," the Western Highlands, also known as the Chiriquí Highlands, and the city of David are the alter ego of the eastern side of Panama. The quiet countryside and picturesque mountains, green villages freckled with Swiss chalets, national parks, and busy towns bordering on Costa Rica's frontier lure foreigners into a markedly different scene from that of Panama City and its nearby beaches. Volcán Barú, Panama's largest peak, 3,475 meters (11,400 feet) above sea level, sits high above quaint rural towns and features the only ice-capped mountain in the country. The peaks and valleys that lie below are a highlight for foreigners who have fallen for the region's near-perfect climate and favorable lifestyle. The tropical heat of the region is found at the epicenter of Chiriquí, the capital city of David. Life and people move differently here; clouds hover over the green horizons, and the air feels crisp with autumn-like weather. Since 2000, the media has eaten

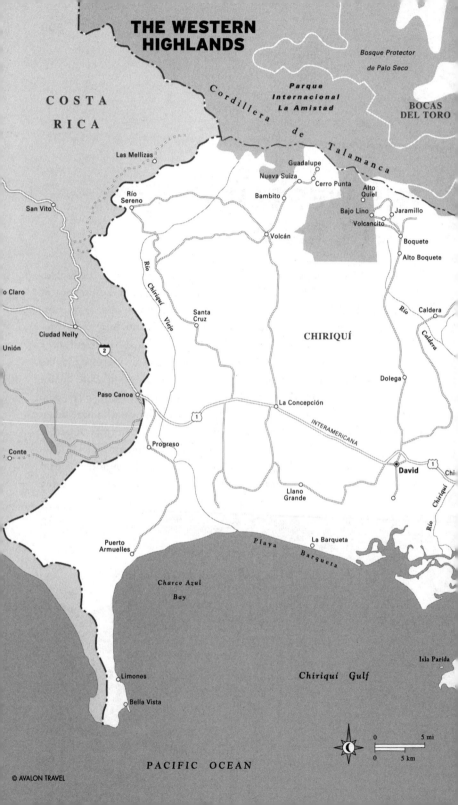

THE WESTERN HIGHLANDS

Bosque Protector
de Palo Seco

COSTA
RICA

Cordillera

Parque
Internacional
La Amistad

de

Talamanca

BOCAS
DEL TORO

Las Mellizas

Guadalupe

Nueva Suiza

Cerro Punta

Alto
Quiel

Río
Sereno

Bambito

Bajo Lino

Jaramillo

San Vito

Volcancito

Volcán

Boquete

Alto Boquete

Río

Caldera

o Claro

Río Chiriquí Viejo

Santa
Cruz

CHIRIQUÍ

Caldera

Ciudad Neily

2

Dolega

Unión

Paso Canoa

1

La Concepción

INTERAMERICANA

Río Chiriquí

Progreso

David

1

Chi

Llano
Grande

Conte

Río Chiriquí

Puerto
Armuelles

Playa

La Barqueta

Barqueta

Charco Azul
Bay

Isla Parida

Limones

Chiriquí Gulf

Bella Vista

0   5 mi

0   5 km

PACIFIC OCEAN

© AVALON TRAVEL

up the delicious towns of Boquete, Cerro Punta, and Volcán, naming the area one of the best locations for retirement. While investigating what makes the Western Highlands so rich in lifestyle, we've found that it's not only a home for international *jubilados* (retirees), but an opportunity for young Panamanians and a cooperative center for involved and active foreigners.

Lay of the Land

The Pan-American Highway meanders from the long roadways of Panama's interior provinces and empties into the city of David. As Chiriquí's capital, David is a central location for established and upcoming communities serving both the lowlands and highlands of the region and a convenient pit stop. Escape to the Highlands requires a 35-minute drive north from the Pan-American Highway, traveling the rural roadway marked with signs for Boquete's oldest hotels, quaint bed-and-breakfasts, and, as of late, real estate announcements. Once past Caldera, where Volcán Barú's rapid waters converge, you arrive at the center of Boquete. This town is a bustling tourist center and a valley of floral delight, elevated at 1,200 meters west of Volcán Barú. Panama's best-known coffee plantations are located along the slopes of the mountain in this town. To the east of Boquete, beyond the waterfalls and thermal baths of Caldera, is impressive Lake Fortuna—a hydroelectric reservoir laid out like a blanket in a bed of green, and the transit crossroad to the mainland of Bocas

PRIME LIVING LOCATIONS

© MIRIAM BUTTERMAN

An abundance of flowers grow in Boquete.

del Toro Province, which Panama's Ngöbe-Buglé Indians have occupied for generations.

Leaving Boquete going west leads to the verdant pastures of Volcán, then Bambito, and finally Cerro Punta. These towns go deeper into the cloud forests of Volcán Barú and lie alongside the La Amistad International Park, 400,000 hectares (990,000 acres) of protected land shared with Costa Rica. Trails throughout the park are home to breathtaking biodiversity, including the quetzal, Latin America's most colorful bird. During migration season, the park is home to virtually any and all species of birds traveling through the Americas. While they may seem remote, the roads traveling northwest to Bambito, Volcán, and Cerro Punta are drivable. A road through the national park planned in 2003 was cancelled as a result of protests and environmental studies that showing the potential damage by an increase of traffic through the park. Therefore, the pristine quality of the area was saved as a minimal impact territory. The hillsides offer serenity, and the cool night air offers some of the coldest weather in Panama.

Cerro Punta is seven kilometers (4.5 miles) north of Bambito. Located in the crater of an extinct volcano, Cerro Punta's dense tropical forests sit roughly 1,600 meters above sea level (5,900 feet), making it Panama's highest-elevation town. The altitude makes the communities vulnerable to landslides and erosion, so residents must prepare for infrequent tremors along the Costa Rican border. Recent floods in rainy season of 2009 left the Chiriquí River at dangerous levels with roads and hillsides in bad condition and indigenous communities with few remaining personal belongings. Despite these consequences of global climate changes, the weather is still the most acclaimed quality of the region, sporting its famous afternoon *bajareque*, or mist, and a perfect climate for growing fresh produce, such as strawberries, tomatoes, cucumbers, and lettuce, to name only a few. Up to 80 percent of the fresh produce from Panama comes from Cerro Punta's farms.

The lowland areas of the Chiriquí Province are home to miles of coastline, 25 islands, and some 19 coral reefs. Just prior to arriving at David, south off the Pan-American will take you to Las Lajas and Boca Chica, newly developed beaches attempting to attract foreigners to the Pacific white sands through For Sale signs and broker publicity. Getting to the beaches is difficult, and you should fill up on gas in David, as chances of finding any practical stopovers are slight. For a long time, these locations and their neighboring islands such as Islas Secas and Isla Boca Brava, have been home to exclusive US$400-per-day-per-person resorts. But now, a few dreamers have used their tractors to develop turnkey operations along the coast. Puerto Armuelles, lying southwest of these beaches, is the second-largest town in Chiriquí province, set along the coast of what was Chiquita Banana's Caribbean home base in the early 1900s. Foreigners have reacquainted themselves with the town believed to hold the possibility of major crude oil refineries for barges en route from Alaska.

Housing

The cost to buy a home in the Chiriquí highlands has been fluctuating, right along with the global real estate market. Since the 2009 housing crisis, Boquete, one of the leading towns for international real estate investment, has suffered a 50 percent drop in the value of its properties from seven years ago. That is, even though housing rates continue to rise, they are still at only half of what their estimated value was expected to rise to before the crisis. However, according to Rogelio Romero, a longtime professional in the market and owner of Panama's Romero Realty, the International Monetary Fund still expects a 3–5 percent increase for Panama's overall economic growth in 2009–2010, a positive sign for those who plan to invest here. Nevertheless, the housing industry is worried at present. According to a *La Prensa* article in June 2009, the Brokers Association of Chiriquí had reported a dramatic drop in construction in the Western Highlands, with up to 16 projects advancing at slower rates and three projects suspended all together. Boquete, Cerro Punta, and Volcán are three very popular areas for international investors, so much so that since

© ALEJANDRO CHICHERI

at home in Portrerillos, Boquete

2002, the price per square meter has risen from US$5 to US$35. The prices have not been cut, yet foreigners interested in the region are only disposed to spend half of what they were previously willing to invest. This has resulted in a larger rental market in the area, while homeowners await an improved real estate market, either in their home countries or in Panama.

Boquete is the firecracker of the real estate boom in Western Panama. It is virtually impervious to the market woes that affect the rest of Panama. While a global recession caused housing prices to plummet, land and construction costs have not yet fallen in the Boquete area, according to Constructive Solutions' Chiriquí Project Manager Uriah Reisman, who is also a resident of the area. Foreigners are paying US$50–100 per square foot for residential construction projects. Land is priced at US$0.50–5 per square foot. Most buyers are still foreigners, says Reisman. Around Boquete there are more choices between gated communities or independent neighborhoods, but in Volcán developments have been proposed but rarely carried out. In David, home sales are limited to Panamanian homes—block-concrete in structure, one-story with basic plumbing sans luxury fixtures or sophisticated tilework. Furthermore, the average home was built without insulation, air-conditioning, or hot water systems. Consider these renovations when purchasing a previously owned home.

Throughout the real estate rush over the past 10 years, the towns of Volcán, Cerro Punta, and their surrounding neighborhoods have managed to avoid excessive inflation. Prices are still reasonable, and environmentally conscious foreigners are more likely to settle in this area in greater numbers, compared to those interested in being in the thick of Boquete's action and North American–style construction. One can still find a good deal for US$1 per square foot in areas such as Volcán, Portrerillos, and Dolega. If you are looking for a fixer-upper, Volcán has homes available for under US$40,000, a large marginal decrease from the cost of the same house in Boquete.

Where to Live

BOQUETE

Boquete is the community most frequently noted by the media when it comes to Panama's popularity as a retirement location, but young investors, builders, and engineers have comfortably settled here over the past decade. It is a misconception that the under-50 crowd here are all early retirees; many members of the foreign community work to bring vacation-town attributes to Boquete.

Many of the coffee shops, bakeries, ice cream shops, fine dining and family restaurants, and real estate and business services are now owned or operated by foreigners. Young Panamanians from the big cities are moving there in large numbers, seeing the opportunity to cater to ecotourism and achieve some success in the process. Businesses such as these have improved the economy for the locals, who have benefited from the increase in jobs, but continued residential development still worries some locals who cannot keep up with the foreign competition or who fear their land rights might be at risk.

Despite recent investments in Boquete, there is still a small-town feel.

PRIME LIVING LOCATIONS

This past decade has hardly been the first instance of interest by foreign immigrants in Boquete. Aside from archeologists' claims that Boquete has been inhabited since A.D. 300, the California Gold Rush and 20th-century European settlers had prior claims to settlement in the Western Highlands. Remaining petroglyphs in the area, as well as modern architectural influences, are proof to these claims.

Despite the new investment and business-related reasons for staying in Boquete, the 18°C (65°F) year-round temperatures, green valleys, and activities such as white-water rafting, mountaineering, horseback riding, and gardening account for most residents' love for the region.

Boquete today is divided into six districts with approximately 20,000 inhabitants, comprising indigenous people, Panamanian locals, and expats. Caldera has a slightly lower elevation and is warmer than Bouquete. The land tends to be expansive here, likely to have more ranches and some new developments.

Alto Boquete is upscale, and home to two of Panama's ex-presidents. The views in Alto Boquete are some of the most beautiful in the area, thus making it a very expensive location. The altitude is perfect for cultivation of coffee.

At Volcancito the noise level and activity starts to fade away. The location is just far enough from Boquete to keep noise away, but you are close to its main center for shopping.

EXPAT PROFILE:
DAVID DELL IN VOLCÁN, CHIRIQUÍ

When did you move to Volcán?

We have been here four years. We Moved from Granada, Nicaragua. We used to work for *International Living* magazine and opened its first field office there.

What do you do for a living?

My wife and I are retired (or at least we are trying to). We have pensions, and I write for several newspapers and magazines. We don't have family in Panama. I have a daughter in England. We came to Panama filming for *International Living* over 10 years ago and loved the place, but at that time we were too young to retire.

What visa do you use to stay in Panama?

We have the *pensionado* visa for retirees and we are full-time residents.

What do you enjoy about living in Volcán that you can't find in another part of the world, or in your home country?

The weather here for at least six months of the year is as good as or better than anywhere we have lived or traveled to. Our benchmark places are Hawaii and France.

Do you find it expensive to live in Volcán?

No. We are fortunate to have the best family restaurant in Panama

David Dell

© LYDIA DELL

What is referred to as Boquete is the main street surrounding a plaza comprising small homes with front porches, small businesses, two banks, and novelty shops scattered throughout the district. Residents might live on top of a restaurant or next to an Internet café. This is an ideal area for renters who need to stay in the center of town, without a car, and who do not mind settling down at night with some rowdy parties going at the locales below, or waking up to trucks loading and unloading their produce for local markets.

Alto Quiel maintains a reputation as a quiet suburb of Boquete, replete with fresh pine smell and lots of privacy from the rest of the district. With newly paved roads available, Jaramillo is now one of the best locations in the area. Located above Boquete, its spectacular views of the town and the oceans below afford residents the romance of both worlds.

right at our doorstep. Coffee is US$0.40 for a bottomless cup. The average meal is about US$3. We eat out sometimes three times a day. There is no real need for either heating or air-conditioning. We also have a 20-year tax exemption on our home.

Do you own or rent your residence?

Currently we own two homes, our three-bedroom house in Volcán and a four-bedroom villa on the beach at Puerto Armuelles. We have run the Volcán home as a B&B, but we love our privacy so the B&B is not a regular feature. We did extensive renovation on the Volcán home, and it is now a wonderful, cozy, country-style house of 2,000 square feet.

How often do you go to David or Panama City?

We go to David for shopping about two or three times a week. We only travel about twice a year to Panama City. The only thing we do not have in David is a Mac (Apple) store, which is a personal requirement. David has truly First World shopping, and there is hardly anything we need that the city can't supply.

How is Volcán different than Boquete or Cerro Punta? What are the advantages and disadvantages of living farther out in the Highlands?

Boquete has more upscale restaurants and you can walk everywhere. Volcán is more spaced apart; a vehicle is really necessary. Cerro Punta is colder and rainier. Living farther out is tough on the rainy, foggy nights. Panamanians drive with total disregard for life and limb, so driving at night to and from remote locations can be nerve-racking.

What general reflections can you offer about the lifestyle you live in the Chiriquí Highlands?

After traveling the world, there is no better, safer, or more affordable place to live and retire than in the Highlands of Panama. It is not paradise, but if you work at it, you can get pretty darn close.

VOLCÁN AND CERRO PUNTA

In Volcán, life resembles more prairie and farm vignettes, and project development is rare. Some residents complain of a few cell phone towers recently erected; these eyesores are more a sign of communication access to the area than a hint at future residential construction. None of the proposed residential projects have even broken ground, and chances are they never will. Local farming communities have remained in the area; thus, foreign residents appreciate the spacious living. However, living in an open area means you need a car. Since rainy weather and dense fog are more frequent in Volcán, residents are more likely to stay put at home once the nighttime falls and driving can become dangerous. Thanks to the beautiful Quetzales Trail leading through the hills of Volcán at the entrance to La Amistad, you can find bird-watchers

Ranches and farms can be seen throughout Cerro Punta and Volcán.

and ecotourists happily loitering in the wild. Remember, Volcán is up there, and life is colder at the top. Volcán does not necessarily depend on Boquete for all its basic shopping needs: There is a small square with local banks, family restaurants, and coffee shops. However, it is distant enough from recommended neighborhoods that you will need a car to go back and forth. If you are not a fan of rainy weather, think twice about Volcán. The rainy season, in the form of light drizzles most of the time, lasts throughout the year. A local doctor comments that he treats four out of five women for depression each year, which may be due to the lack of sunshine affecting brain chemistry.

Expats in the Volcán and Cerro Punta area should be conscious of living in small communities interspersed with Panamanians natives who depend on the land for their personal well-being. The popularity of the area has brought in quite a few foreigners who are solely there for vacation, complain about the limitations of a developing nation, and perhaps have tried to change the infrastructure completely by buying and opening businesses. This makes it difficult for new expats to move in without locals prejudging their intentions. Further, it simply does not work to attempt to force a community to fit Western ideals: Indigenous peoples have been living there for centuries, and this is part of the Western Highlands beauty. However, there are many hardworking expatriates who are determined to make positive contributions, such as community potluck dinners, teaching English to locals, and teaching quilting to indigenous women who sell their textiles for local medical charities.

In Volcán, there are two neighborhoods recommended for expats. One is Brisas del Norte, known as the quieter area of town south of the center.

Another is Nueva California, named by North American settlers during the 19th century gold exploration, located north of the town center. You can get more bang for your buck here.

Bambito and Cerro Punta pull you farther up into the cold and fog, in the picturesque solitude of heaving hillsides and agricultural estates. One expat compares the views to a scene from *The Sound of Music*. The Dos Rios neighborhood has been opened up for a seven-lot development. Guadalupe has been preserved by nature-loving landowners who have invested in ecoresorts along the Los Quetzales Trail. Some residents have opened their farms to the public for sightseeing, including Finca Dracula and the Harras horse farms.

DAVID

As the community around Chiriquí's highlands becomes more popular, David, Panama's third-largest city, continues to reap the benefits. A city started as a camp for 18th-century gold-miners, David today has a population of 125,000. Foreign residents and travelers alike cannot avoid becoming familiar with it, either by way of local flights in and out of the airport or by road travel along the Pan-American Highway. Most people traveling en route to remote locations like Boca Chica or Las Lajas have no choice but to use it as stopover for gas, food, and supplies and are quick to get out the next morning. However, David is clearly taking a piece of the residential pie as of late. The conveniences of up-and-coming strip malls, gourmet delis, membership stores like Price Costco, and decent dining options are a sign of happier times. David no longer has the reputation of a border town, though it is located only 45 minutes from Costa Rica's frontier, where cheap shopping and quick passport stamps can be found. Expats are opening real estate businesses, hotels, and hostels, and doing a good job of competing with the rental markets available in other lowland areas. Since it's a good middle point between the much-desired Highlands and heavenly beaches, David is a top choice for those who need a bit of everything in western Panama.

The influx of foreigners has not caused as much of a hike in real estate here as in David's neighboring Highlands. Unlike Panama City, where new developments have been springing up along the coastal bay since 2005, David has not been subject to presale construction projects. It's a "what you see is what you get" market. Only recently, large asphalt lots are being fenced off as real estate prospects for developing apartments or commercial centers. These lots cost about US$ 0.50–0.65 per square foot (US$5–7 per square meter), or range US$1.3–1.5 million dollars for 16–28 hectares (40–70 acres). Three-, four-, and five-room homes range US$45,000–65,000, according to real

PUERTO ARMUELLES

We discovered Puerto Armuelles one of the many times we pored over nautical charts of Panama's coast looking for that ideal seamount or ledge that would spell "big fish." Five or six years ago, Panama (and its real estate market) was largely a big question mark, but the fish were a certainty. Just around the corner of Punta Burica was the famous anglers' destination of Golfito, Costa Rica. Since fish don't really respect borders, the same record-breaking catches were bound to be swimming right off the beaches at Limones and Puerto Armuelles.

A trip to the bookstore netted us one solitary guide, and we eagerly sought out a description of the little town that once housed a thriving division of the United Fruit Company's effort to corner the world's banana production.

Arriving in Puerto Armuelles via an immaculate paved road, you pass several gas stations and a couple of grocery stores, and the town is dotted with typical restaurants, clothing and sundries stores, banks, pharmacies, Internet cafés, bakeries, and pretty much whatever you might need to sustain life. Okay, basic is the watchword, but we couldn't help but wonder why this complete town was so completely ignored by even locals.

The old banana pier sits in disrepair, jutting out from the *malecón* – a sort of seaside walkway that fronts the Pacific side of the town.

There you can join the locals and jig for dinner in the clear depths. There are several places where you can sip a cold *cerveza* and one really outstanding restaurant, Don Carlos, that has served the town in good times and bad with superb fresh fish dishes and the best (and possibly the only) pizza in town. If you are lucky, the owner (a local), will stop by your table and regale you with stories, opinions, and tales of old Panama. His father started the place back in the banana heyday; the legendary Pier 3 sauce still on the menu is not to be missed. That pier is gone, but the fond culinary tribute remains a testimony to better days.

The banana company housed its employees in a tiered system. Much of that housing remains and is being lovingly restored today. You can see the middle-management area known as San Jose, where little clapboard houses line a few streets, all dressed up in tropical colors. You can explore the rattletrap workers' housing right on some of the best beach real estate in Panama. And then you can step back in time and look at Las Palmas, a neighborhood of some 45 homes laid out on rolling green lawns. This was the enclave of the privileged, the bastion of the upper management, sent down to the torpid jungle to mine the yellow gold known as Musa sapientum, or "fruit of the wise men."

There are a few places outside of the big city that speak as loudly of

© DAVID DELL

the *malecón,* the main walkway that runs into the old town of "Silver City" in Puerto Armuelles

the history of this tiny nation than the villas that dot the gentle hills of Las Palmas. In their glory days, these expansive stilt-elevated homes with their teak-slatted windows and soaring ceilings were meant to cushion spoiled foreigners from the rigors of native life. The neighborhood was endowed with a swimming pool, tennis court, and a nine-hole golf course to soothe the boredom and restlessness that must have come with being stationed at what was then the end of the earth. There was (and still is) an airstrip, oddly positioned in the middle of one of the fairways, where small planes could whisk you away to the city. Beyond, you can see the ghost go-downs where packing and production took place.

It is almost impossible not to envision ladies in wide-brimmed straw hats and gentlemen in white linen suits strolling about the winding lanes exchanging greetings at sunset as the parrots cry overhead. Aside from the occasional boat parked in a driveway, or the ubiquitous SUV, little about Las Palmas has changed over the decades since it was built. Horses still wander freely through the unfenced perimeters of generous lots, birds still populate the huge old-growth trees, and the Pacific still lends its cool breezes to the porches that open into the equatorial dusk as it descends on the undiscovered and unspoiled charm of Puerto Armuelles.

Contributed by Lisa Leuthesser,
BuyingRealEstateinPanama.com

estate brokers in the area. The homes are not new and may need repairs such as a new roof or plumbing system. Rents for these homes are affordable at US$200–600 a month.

LA BARQUETA

Developments are going up 45 minutes from David, and 15 minutes from Boca Chica beach on the Gulf Coast, with 0.4- to 2-hectare lots (1–5 acres) selling at US$59,000 preconstruction, other costs to be negotiated with the developer. Oceanfront homes along the same area are selling from US$350,000 up to US$950,000, depending on fixtures and construction materials. Another community called Las Olas, a gated community in the town of La Barqueta, is selling oceanfront lots under 0.4 hectares (one acre) for US$150,000–400,000. However, the beach is quite lonely and can be dangerous. Two- and three-bedroom pre-constructed beachfront condominiums cost US$250,000–300,000 and a four-bedroom home starts at US$500,000.

Puerto Armuelles

In the peninsula of the Chiriquí Gulf, a small community of expats has discovered the mystique of the Chiquita Banana's early 20th century history, a town called Puerto Armuelles. While this banana region closed down in 2008 due to competition from regional markets, namely Ecuador, interest in this unspoiled coastal town has revived, and for excellent reason. It is distant enough from civilization to deliver you from the complaints of tiresome city life. The area also features useful necessities as foreigners settled it long ago, while retaining its reputation as an industrial town, major tourism, aside from sport fishing. Today, new interests in the region have arisen; perhaps from the crystal blue beaches and paradise effects or interests may also be generated by opportunities created by the crude-oil pipeline route passing through this area from Alaska and the $10 million project approved by

Puerto Armuelles is a charming small community.

the Martinelli government to build an oil refinery within the next 10 years. The community has a scattered population of 55,000 people. Remaining true to its colonial English homes, Puerto Armuelles mirrors much of the same architecture as the Canal Zones of eastern Panama. Its history garnered visitors such as Albert Einstein and his wife Elsa, author Henri Charriere, and Hollywood's best-known Irish priest, Pat O'Brien, not to mention the many ex-presidents, including Manuel Noriega, who frequently visited the famous "Blair House," still standing today to represent the historical settings around the town. The area's impressive beaches and secluded gulf islands sit along the Costa Rican border, and with the increase of development, a law that limits development or residential construction to no more than 15 kilometers (9 miles) from the border with Costa Rica is being enforced. It is not clear if "Puerto," as locals call it, is ready for what the outside world has planned for the Chiriquí Gulf region, but as long as prices remain stable, there is fear we will find out. Despite the progress expected, the remaining structures of its history will hopefully stay intact.

BOCAS DEL TORO

Caribbean Sea

El Golfo de los Mosquitos

Escudos de Veraguas

Boca de Río Caña

Río Caña

Peninsula Valiente

Río Cricamola

Laguna de Chiriquí

Río Guariviara

Chiriquí Grande

FORTUNA RD

Cayo Agua

Cayos Zapatillas

Quebrada de Sal

Cayo Crawl

Parque Nacional Marino Isla Bastimentos

Isla Bastimentos

Isla Popa

Punto Róbalo

Isla Carenero

Old Bank

Isla Solarte

Bocas Town

Isla Colón

Bocas del Drago

Humedales de San San Pondsack

Isla Cristóbal

ALMIRANTE RD

ALMIRANTE RD

CHIRIQUÍ GRANDE

Almirante

BOCAS DEL TORO

Bosque Protector de Palo Seco

Río Róbalo

ALMIRANTE - GUABITO RD

Changuinola

El Silencio

Río Changuinola

Guabito

Sixaola

Manzanillo

Puerto Viejo

Bribri

Sieyik

Río Teribe

Parque Internacional La Amistad

Cordillera de Talamanca

Guadalupe

COSTA RICA

CHIRIQUÍ

0   5 mi
0   5 km

BOCAS DEL TORO

Journeying north and all the way west from Panama City leads to Bocas del Toro, a fascinating string of islands sharing the same name with its mainland province. Since its inception as a capital and important commercial trading point in the mid-1800s, this archipelago of nine major islands, approximately 50 cays, and some 200 islets, has established a unique personality from the rest of Panama. Since verdant jungle backdrops, island beauty, and marine biodiversity dominate the setting, void of urban feeling, many residents who live here feel detached from the city hassles and material desires in the rest of Panama.

A large part of the distinct Bocas persona stems from its independent history. The islands were said to have formed between 8,000 and 10,000 years ago, at the end of the Ice Age, when sea levels rose and created the archipelago and separation from Central America's mainland. The islands were inhabited by the indigenous population (Ngöbe-Buglé, Teribe, Kuna, and Bribri) until Christopher Colón stumbled across the island during his fourth voyage across

© LORETO BARCELO

the Americas. It was 1502, and looking for shelter for his damaged ships, he navigated into the island's resting waters, today called Almirante, or Admiral's Bay. He settled in what is today the village of Carinero, a quiet area to careen or repair his vessel, and moved about on the islands of Bastimentos to restock on supplies. These villages are lively areas that still house residents and commercial locations near Isla Colón, the island where Bocas Town is located.

The Spanish government had forgotten about this area, and in the mid-1800s it was the Dutch and Scottish who came to Bocas del Toro from outlying Caribbean islands they had colonized to avoid paying taxes. They came with their slaves and created settlements of cattle and chicken farms. During this time, the islands began to thrive as a large trading center. Traders, traffickers, and adventure-seekers from all over Europe and the Americas were coming to Bocas for "new commercial opportunities." In 1826, Isla Colón was founded. Later, in 1890, the Superior Banana company was founded, and in 1899 the United Fruit Company (which managed Chiquita brand bananas) moved into Bocas to run its banana plantation empire. It turned over huge tracts of land for production. The exportation of sugarcane, banana, and coconut, as well as the trading of sarsaparilla, tortoiseshell, and live turtles, made Bocas del Toro the third most important city in Panama. By this time, immigrant workers from all over the West Indies had come to live and work on these plantations, creating a thriving multilingual community with major facilities and medical care.

According to historians, in 1914 a mysterious banana pest had virtually wiped out the plantations. By 1920, operations were shut down and the archipelago long forgotten. The influence of the West Indian population can still be seen in Bocas Town today, but in a decayed form of its historical past. An English-Caribbean dialect called Juari-Juari (pronounced wari wari) is spoken widely throughout the local communities. The architecture of the Dutch colonial buildings, tall two- or three-story wood homes, and wide front porches run along the main avenue, hinting at the island's colonial history.

Lay of the Land

Foreigners tend to be confused, often hearing that the islands of Bocas del Toro are part of Costa Rica. Don't depend on a Tico (Costa Rican) to correct this misconception for you. Costa Rican nationals would like to believe it. With islands so beautiful and with such an ability to instill a sense of calm and healing to those who visit or live here, why wouldn't you want take credit for it? The archipelago is, however, very much a part of Panama, located north of the Bocas del Toro mainland, which is filled with rapid rivers and rolling hills. One can enter the islands from Panama by boat by way of Almirante.

To the west of the islands, Isla Colón is only a 45-minute boat ride from the border town of Changuinola, where you can cross into Costa Rica. Isla Colón, still the main island, is where all the main services can be found. Schools, restaurants, pharmacies, supermarkets, and specialty stores are located here. The 5,000-foot airport runway receives national flights throughout the day; it is an hour from Panama City and only 20 minutes from David, with a few flights coming in from Costa Rica each week.

On the surface Bocas has gone through a rapid change in only 30 years. In 1981, when the road from the Pan-American Highway was extended to meet Chiriquí Grande, the new accessibility allowed for the resurrection of a

PRIME LIVING LOCATIONS

© LORETO BARCELO

In Bocas, look for titled land.

bustling Isla Colón to serve the 10,000 inhabitants living on the archipelago (4,000 of whom are on Isla Colón). The island hosts one bank, one hospital, the governor's office, and offices for local representatives. The remainder of the population lives throughout the islands of Carenero, Isla Solarte, Bastimentos, Isla Cristobal, Isla Popa, and Cayo Agua.

Reminiscent of its earlier popularity among international immigrants, Bocas has been known to lure the world's newest escape artists. Since the 1990s, those wanting to leave behind the pressures of a Western lifestyle and Northern climate have targeted Bocas for both full- and part-time residences. The new international population has shifted toward a fairly young generation of adventurers, entrepreneurs, and surfers.

CLIMATE

If you've never believed in the mysteries of microclimates, living in Bocas will certainly change your mind. In Bocas, seasonal changes and weather patterns really are whimsical—rain and shine just mix and mingle throughout the day, never quite making up their minds as to who will lead the dance. The rains are powerful and are shorter in some seasons, at times only cooling down an intense day of heat and humidity, while in other months, the rains will go on for days at a time, only to suddenly clear up one fine day to swelling beaches and open blue skies. These patterns do not follow those of the rest of the country, where May to November is traditionally rainy, and the dry season tumbles in with balmy breezes from December to April. When on these islands, throw those calendars out and don't bother with the Weather Channel. Rather, close your eyes and dig in to spontaneous sun and rain. Expect daily temperatures of 27–32°C (85–90°F). Have beach clothes handy and rain boots at the front door. In Bocas, the months of August and September—a tourist low season—are when dry season kicks in and the climate becomes dry and desertlike. According to locals, you will never complain about the rain again after experiencing the high temperatures, severe sun, and drought conditions in these months.

CULTURE

Bocas, as it is lovingly known, is a very different place to tourists than it would be to residents. Once past the novice transitions, expectations start to slow, and the reality of living in a wholesome environment tends to fade into early happy hours. For business owners or artists who may work at their own pace, Bocas is perfect, as life here happens on its own schedule. Anything completed on time or as promised is often considered overwhelmingly good service. Locals tend to be so friendly and stress-free that you almost feel ashamed for complaining. What's the rush? And if you think about it, who are you going to complain to? You'll find the same easygoing attitude with the local authorities, the local tourism board, and the airlines. After all, it's Bocas—didn't you move here to just "be"?

Life in Bocas is laidback.

This all may seem very simple. But the sensation of freedom—that hustle-and-bustle weight lifting off your shoulders, an effect often referred to as being "Bocatized"—tends to manifest itself in the carefree behavior of late-night partying. This kind of social life can be exhausting, and for this reason many escape from the more populated areas to frolic in isolation.

Living in Bocas will have its stresses. You get sun and rain and balmy breezes, but you also get a rapidly changing community that the service industry simply cannot handle. The influx of crime due to the widening gap between the lifestyles of locals and expats is dealt with by just not dealing. The police address crime by augmenting the amount of paperwork you must do to actually report a situation. The number of cars on the island has doubled over the last decade, and there remains only one mechanic to service the one island, Isla Colón, that can service cars.

Water and electricity come from the mainland but can go out at random times, so plan for back-up systems in your home. With regards to food and pharmacies, most anything that you will need can be found on the island. You won't get the most prime cut of beef or a vast array of leafy greens, but your daily diet of rainbow-colored foods can easily be met. The gourmet supermarkets carry more than the local supermarkets, but you will have to pay extra for them.

Many foreigners with school-aged children opt for home-schooling. Others send their children to one of the two private schools in the area: Beth El on the island, or the Tangerine school, which serves the younger grades. Tangerine is a type of international school with teachers from other parts of the world, but it is still working on its accreditation. Changuinola hosts a school called the Bilingual, and Almirante has a high school to which many locals commute each day. Both Changuinola and Almirante are on

PRIME LIVING LOCATIONS

the mainland, so you'd have to consider the boat commute through the channel.

If reading this description tends to turn you off, let your curiosity rule and stay open-minded. There is but one golden rule: Don't go to eat at a restaurant in Bocas when you are hungry. Go before you are hungry, and then you can sit back, enjoy the crowd and the reggae music, take a swing in the community hammock by the water, and savor a beer. Next thing you know, your food will arrive and you will have forgotten you ordered it an hour earlier.

Housing

Legend has it that the real estate boom in Bocas started in 2000 when a gringo traveling through the islands offered US$10,000 and a newly constructed cement house across the road to an older island local for her humble home and beachfront property. The older woman accepted the money and new house with glee. Within a few months, the foreigner turned the land over for a half-million-dollar profit. For future off-the-cuff investors, the opportunities seemed too good to be true. Locals, of course, began to worry.

Whether the story is true or not, the message communicated to original Bocatareños is that beachfront properties are a luxury. Locals have learned this the hard way, sometimes being negotiated out of their inheritances, and at other times staying true to what is theirs despite economic temptations. Costs for renting or buying have traveled up a steady curve, and perhaps the only obstacle to it rising even further is the global economic crisis that started in 2008. Even renters are noticing prices skyrocketing for apartments in Isla Colón, at US$800–1,000 monthly depending on the amenities and security. Real estate agents will tell you that there is no set rule for a price per square meter in property sales. When comparing prices and real estate listings, you'll find that a 0.2-hectare (0.5-acre) lot of land could cost US$40,000, but a beachside property on 0.4 hectare (1 acre) could cost up to US$800,000 with title. The prices run up and down depending on land and real estate characteristics, not to mention who is selling to you. For instance, local property owners might be more willing to negotiate.

Commercial properties are also selling for big money. One of the older hotels on the main avenue of Isla Colón sold for US$800,000 in 2009. Bars and restaurants are selling for US$150,000–400,000, contingent upon the facilities, equipment, and licenses sold with it.

© LORETO BARCELO

Many adventurous expats construct their own homes in Bocas, like this one built by a Spanish-French couple.

Materials are another factor in pricing. Though many buyers treasure the colonial-style homes of the banana boom days, in many other cases homes along the beach are using fine wood from local reforestations and textiles imported from abroad, once again hiking up the costs with transport and installations. Groceries and restaurant prices are now much more expensive than they were just five years ago. With two gourmet supermarkets added to the array of local ones, organic goods coming in from the mainland or even abroad, and menus displaying US$14–15 meals, bargain shopping becomes more and more challenging for long-term residents. The upside is that some investors are paying their employees correspondingly high salaries, and many Panamanian residents are also upping their standards of living and proud to have climbed that ladder. The downside is that surfers, Panamanian or otherwise, who migrate to Bocas for the great swells, easy eats, and low-budget lifestyle, are no longer cruising through so frivolously. Now they come with resumes in hand, knowing they will probably have to work for their surf.

Where to Live

BOCAS TOWN

Isla Colón is the first step for those who want to know and understand what Bocas del Toro is about and where it is going in the 21st century. While you don't quite escape from cars, buses, or supermarket lines, you *can* hang out in rustic thatched-roof huts at the same time. It is the most inhabited area of the archipelago and, if you can believe it, some long-term foreign residents have gotten to the point where they maintain two homes, one at the "beach"—one of the more isolated islands, and another in Bocas Town (the village name for Isla Colón's main center) for their "city home." There is no beach in Bocas Town, and daily life revolves more around one of two polar extremes: doing errands or sitting around drinking a cold beer in the hot sun. Instead of beaches, many "city dwellers" end up cooling off in swimming holes off restaurant or hotel docks.

For business owners, Isla Colón is the most convenient. The only bank is located there with two bank machines nearby, and supermarkets, hardware stores, bike rentals, medical care, real estate services, tourist agencies, and the few government agencies available are located sporadically throughout the main street. If you need urgent medical attention, the only hospital is on the main street, going toward the cemetery. Most expats who live in Bocas make a living in the food and beverage industry, hotel and nightlife industry, boat rentals, or artesanía (crafting). As in most "capital cities," the majority of the nightlife is centered here—and therefore the majority of the ruckus that comes with it.

In Bocas Town you'll find that the older homes built from the banana republic days are still prevalent, the colorfully painted edifices throughout the neighborhoods behind the *calle principal*. Wraparound porches, tall windows, and French doors opening up into balconies are a charming reminder of the island's history, even if they are leaning in an odd direction, giving an image of a fallen ruin. Young expatriate families who live on the main island have rented or bought some of these homes and set up picturesque little front gardens and facades, mimicking how the respected locals live. They simply want to blend in and have found out how to do it. Since 2005, construction and development are growing like wildflowers. Apartments in these new buildings rent for up to US$800 per month with amenities such as air and security.

If you take the main road going west from the center of town you'll hit Saigon, a small neighborhood built on a swamp. Homes are set back behind the main road, situated on stilts above the water, and successfully piggyback one another, with unavoidable voyeuristic neighbors. This was once a choice neighborhood for expats, who renovated the tall wooden homes, where the sound of night tides hitting up against the floorboards of your bedroom harmonize with rooster calls in the early mornings (or drunk catcalls by locals at any given time). Security is not guaranteed, though, so live here at your own risk. Saigon is an oddly comfortable neighborhood where locals and families who live in extreme conditions—without water or electricity—are side by side with renovated homes and happy-go-lucky expats.

CARENERO

A three-minute boat ride across the humble channel from Bocas Town on Isla Colón is the island of Carenero, a small key built up by Afro-Antillean and indigenous locals and home for foreigners who want to be near Bocas Town. The island is a large residential community, sans cars, where both modest homes and luxurious beachfront houses run along the coastal landscape. Nightlife has spread from Bocas Town onto Carenero as well, joining the hotel and restaurant businesses that cater to tourists. Most of the locals make a living as fishermen and boat "guys"—staying true to Christopher Colombus's original use of the same land as his careening station.

In 2009, 0.4 hectare (1 acre) of titled land was priced at US$325,000, and a luxury, top-of-the-line 7,000-square-foot home had an asking price of US$750,000. It seems like it would be more expensive, but rentals can be cheaper for long-term residents and might be a good option before jumping into any investments. Carenero is fixed with electrical and water lines coming from Bocas Town. But given the unreliability of some of the lines, real estate agents suggest that you have a power backup system, such as a generator or solar energy panels, and a rainwater collection system in case freshwater isn't available.

The biggest problem on Carenero is the *chitra* flies, those microscopic sand flies that pinch at you rather than bite. Good window screens and mosquito nets over your bedding is a must out here.

BASTIMENTOS

Moving farther along the bay before heading out to open sea is the island of Bastimentos. This western side of the island hosts the vibrant village of Bastimentos Town, a busy village of private residences and small local businesses visible from Isla Colón. Electricity and telephone lines come from Isla Colón via underwater lines, and reach as far as this western tip. Walking up from Bastimentos Town, where the cement paths give way to hillside trails, you will stumble upon foreigners who have tucked their homes into the natural landscape and attempt to live via sustainable means. Bed-and-breakfast inns and tiny restaurants have opened up beyond the beachside docks allowing for tourism near to Bocas Town.

Bastimentos Town is built with cement walking paths giving way to banana hilltops, green flowing valleys, and foot trails that lead to beaches on the other side of the island—beaches that begin the 13,200 hectares (32,600 acres) of the Bastimentos Island National Park, one of the largest marine reserves in the world. The protected area extends out to Zapatillas Cays, reachable by boat from Coral (or Crawl) Cay on the southern tip, encompassing mangroves, coral reefs, wildlife such as sloths and monkeys, and an incredibly diverse extent of aquatic life—some now endangered, like the famous red frog.

Bastimentos is one of the larger islands in area, and hiking through the bushels of rainforest across the island or taking a boat around to the eastern tip are the only ways to traverse the island and see the magical beaches. Because land is vast and the climate is wet, the hilltops are a wonderful spot for small farms and family settlements. Panama's indigenous inhabitants have been doing it for centuries.

Expats have discovered the beauty of the more desolate beaches on the southern and eastern tips of the island and have constructed homes and businesses along the shore. By employing locals, buying their materials, following their construction plans, and combining it with sassy architectural plans from elsewhere, residents have created some unique homes along Punta Vieja, the eastern tip of the island. Here a handful of ecoresorts have also settled in alongside the indigenous villages. These land sites boast incredible views of the Caribbean ocean and other islands. Efficient planning for your home and respect for the local lifestyle is essential if you expect to live out your dreams in paradise.

ISLA SOLARTE

One mile east of Bocas del Toro is Isla Solarte, boasting historically noted Hospital Point, the medical facility built in 1899 for the United Fruit Company. It was built upon a hill to capture the ocean breezes, which kept the point free of mosquitoes carrying diseases, and, with the majority of the population living in Bocas del Toro during that time, the company felt it was far enough away to keep patients healing in isolation. Hospital Point maintained 16 buildings, well-constructed sidewalks, and tidy landscaping. Facilities were shut down in 1920 with the demise of the banana republic, and many of the buildings were destroyed or left to decay, but the main building remains (now privately owned) along with the concrete sidewalks and neatly divided building lots. Today this basic infrastructure has given way to a redesign; developers selling off—as one real estate agent describes, "half rustic, half luxury homes." Today the island of approximately 1,500 residents is a combination of indigenous communities living in simple wooden homes with thatched roofs and expats living in properties that can run up to US$2 million. No matter how fancy these "gringo" homes, however, the whole community depends on wells or rainwater and solar panels. The waters surrounding the island are said to have perfect conditions for snorkeling and diving, and the rich coral reef life and diverse marine species seen through glassy turquoise waters tend to evoke their own sense of luxury among snowbird residents who really do live quite well out here. Most of the land is sold as ROP, or Rights of Possession—very different from titled land.

BOCAS DEL DRAGO, PLAYA BLUFF

Reaching around the northern and western ends of Isla Colón lie the beaches of Bocas del Drago, Playa Bluff, and Punch. Bocas del Drago is a community of mostly local and indigenous residents, and perhaps every fifth house is owned by an expat. Because this part of the island can be reached by car and is quite far by any other means, it makes living out here a serious challenge for those who don't want to invest in four-wheel-drive transportation. The drive can take 20–40 minutes depending on rain and visibility, and while roads are now paved in this direction, they are still a constant struggle to maintain. Land out in Drago is rich—a great area for forestation projects and agriculture.

Bocas del Drago has a church and a tiny schoolhouse that serves only a handful of local children, if a teacher is available. It also contains one wonderful little restaurant and bar owned by locals, who have pretty much monopolized one beach point but kept it quaint and dynamic—in fact, it is an entirely inoffensive oasis for the area's many visitors. The Smithsonian Tropical Research Institute also has facilities out here, introducing interesting personalities and studies to the area at all times. Electricity is limited, so most expats have generators and solar panels. The indigenous and locals mostly use the back stream waters to wash, but many expats have installed rainwater systems. Farther beyond Bocas del Drago are private roads that lead to elegantly designed homes built by expats.

Bocas del Drago is the epitome of Bocas del Toro life, on a smaller scale. That is, driving along from Bocas Town, you can't miss the population's diversity of Afro-Antillean locals, Ngöbe-Buglé Indians, and expats all putting their best foot forward to live together as one neighborhood.

PRIME LIVING LOCATIONS

The other communities on the back side of Isla Colón are more difficult to access, since the paved road going west along the capital island splits at a fork and continues unpaved up the north side, to Playa Bluff and Punch. The roads are tough and the shores are rougher than on the western side of the island, but surfers can't get enough of it. Hence, many swell-riding fanatics will make their way out here by bikes or even walking if necessary. The beaches are not quite for swimming, but the homes are a sight for sore eyes. A Peter Kent home on the beach (a luxury developer now offering more residences built to modern standards) runs up to half a million dollars. Most people who invest out here are looking for already-constructed homes. Land is too difficult to develop now without a road to transport materials.

Getting Around

As stated earlier, cars are exclusive to Isla Colón and even then only a good four-wheel-drive vehicle will get you through to Playa Bluff and surrounding areas. There is really no need for owning a car, however, unless you see yourself needing to lug equipment or people back and forth often. There are plenty of taxis on the island now, and many residents use ATVs or motorbikes to travel around the island. A bus runs every hour 8 A.M.–4 P.M. daily from the park in the center of Bocas Town down to Bocas del Drago, which can help you get to other parts of the island along the way. ATVs work fine along all the roads, and of course motorbikes are the new bicycles. Having stated that, if you spend most of your time cruising around Bocas Town's *calle principal* and grid streets behind it, a bicycle is all you need. Many happy pedalers strap a basket to the front, a baby seat to the back, and off they go to run their daily diligences. It's quite a joy to ride down the wide streets of this colonial Afro-Caribbean town, picking out fruits and vegetables from the tiny kiosks along the road. You will feel the aura of the colonial days riding behind you.

Of course, boats are an essential form of transportation around any archipelago and Bocas is no different. From kayaks to sailboats, catamarans, speedboats, and fishing *lanchas,* people travel to and fro however they can. Ask to see the *Barco Loco,* a handmade boat fitting under no clear category, made by a zany but successful expat named Benson. It will cure you of any fear you may have of traveling by sea.

RESOURCES

Consulates and Embassies

UNITED STATES

U.S. DIPLOMATIC REPRESENTATION, WASHINGTON DC

Ambassador: Federico António HUMBERT Arias
Embassy: 2862 McGill Terrace NW
Washington, DC 20008
tel. 202/483-1407
fax 202/387-6141

U.S. DIPLOMATIC REPRESENTATION, PANAMA

Chief of Mission: Barbara Stephenson
Embassy: Edificio 783, Avenida Demetrio Basilio Lakas, Clayton, Panama City
Mailing Address: American Embassy Panama, Unit 0945; APO AA 34002
tel. 507/207-7000
fax 507/227-1964

PERMANENT MISSION TO THE ORGANIZATION OF AMERICAN STATES (OAS)

2201 Wisconsin Ave, NW, Suite C100
Washington, DC 20007
tel. 202/965-4819
fax 202/965-4836
panama@oas.org

PERMANENT MISSION TO THE UNITED NATIONS

866 United Nations Plaza, Suite 4030
New York, NY 10017
tel. 212/421 5420
fax 212/421 2694

HOUSTON

24 Greenway Plaza, Suite 1307
Houston, TX 77046
tel. 713/622-4451
fax 713/622-4468

MIAMI

5775 Blue Lagoon Drive
Miami, FL 33126
tel. 305/447-3700
fax 305/477-4142

NEW ORLEANS

2424 World Trade Center #2, Canal St.,
New Orleans, LA 70130
tel. 504/525-3458

NEW YORK

1212 Avenue of the Americas, 6th Fl.,
New York, NY 10036
tel. 212/840-2450
fax 212/840-2469

PHILADELPHIA

124 Chestnut St., Suite 1
Philadelphia, PA 19106
tel. 215/574-2994
fax 215/574 4225

SAN DIEGO

402 West Broadway, Suite 670
San Diego, CA 92101
tel. 619/235 4441
fax 619/235 4442

TAMPA

5811 Memorial Highway, Suite 104
Tampa, FL 33615
tel. 813/886-1427

FOREIGN EMBASSIES AND CONSULATES IN PANAMA

CANADA

World Trade Center, 1st fl.
Calle 53E, Marbella, Galeria Comercial
Panama City
tel. 507/294-2500
fax 507/294-2514
www.panama.gc.ca
panam@international.gc.ca

COLOMBIA

World Trade Center Building
Office 1802,
Street 53 Urbanizacion, Marbella
Panama City
tel. 507/264-9513, 507/214-9704, or 507/264-9266
fax 507/223-1134
epanama@minrelext.gov.co
www.embajadadecolombia.org.pa

COSTA RICA

Samuel Lewis Street Omega Plaza Building, 3rd fl.
National Shrine Panama
Panama City

tel. 507/264-2980 or 507/223-4059
fax 507/264 4057
embajadacr@cwpanama.net

CONSULATE OF COSTA RICA
Frente a la Policlínica Edificio Malami
Altos Oficentro Vega Oficina No. 9
David
tel. 507/774-1923
fax 507/774-1923
vcarvajal@rree.go.cr

CONSULATE OF PANAMA
(CONSULATE EN CIUDAD DE
PANAMA)
Calle Samuel Lewis
Edificio Plaza Omega 3 Piso
Panama City
tel. 507/264-2937 or 507/223-5612
fax 507/264-6348
consulpma@cwp.net.pa

UNITED KINGDOM
MMG Tower
Calle 53

Apartado/P.O. Box 0816-07946
Panama City
tel. 507/269-0866
fax 507/223-0730
britemb@cwpanama.net
www.britishembassy.gov.uk/panama

UNITED STATES
American Embassy Panama
Building 783, Demetrio Basilio Lakas Avenue
Clayton, Panama
tel. 507/207-7000
fax 507/317-5568
mailing address from the USA:
American Embassy Panama
9100 Panama City PL
Washington DC 20521-9100
PanamaWeb@state.gov
http://panama.usembassy.govw

PANAMA DEPARTMENT OF
IMMIGRATION
www.migracion.gob.pa

Planning Your Fact-Finding Trip

TRAVEL AND TOURISM INFORMATION
PANAMA TOURISM AUTHORITY
www.atp.gob.pa
www.visitpanama.com

BOCAS TOURISM
www.bocas.com

PANAMA INFO
www.panamainfo.com

Making the Move

VISAS
U.S. STATE DEPARTMENT
www.travel.state.gov/travel
This site provides comprehensive country information, including entry/exit requirements for U.S. citizens.

SERVICIO NACIONAL DE MIGRACION (PANAMA DEPARTMENT OF IMMIGRATION)
www.migracion.gob.pa

FUTURO FORESTAL
Parker Drive 919
Clayton
Panama City, Republic of Panama
tel./fax 507/317-1431
info@futuroforestal.com
www.futuroforestal.com
Futuro Forestal is a Timber Management Investment company, which helps understand the benefits of investing in sustainable reforestation.

PANAMA LAWYERS AND IMMIGRATION SERVICES

ICAZA, GONZÁLEZ-RUIZ & ALEMÁN
Aquilino de la Guardia Street No. 8,
IGRA Building
P.O. BOX 0823-02435, Panama
Republic of Panama
tel. 507/205-6000
fax 507/269-4891
igranet@icazalaw.com
www.icazalaw.com

PANAMA IMMIGRATION SERVICES
tel. 507/227-6645
fax 507/227-7485
www.panama-immigration-services.com

PANAMA OFFSHORE LEGAL SERVICES
tel. 507/227-6645
www.panama-offshore-services.com
Panama Offshore Services is a firm offering a complete range of legal services in Panama. Its website includes accurate and up-to-date information about visas, corporations, and more.

RELOCATION AND SHIPPING

CANAL MOVERS & LOGISTICS CORP.
tel. 507/232-5189 or 507/232-8096
info@canalmovers.com
www.canalmovers.com
Canal Movers are an international moving company that services cargo moving worldwide.

IPATA INTERNATIONAL
745 Winding Trail,
Holly Lake Ranch, TX 75755 USA
tel.903/769-2267
fax 903/769-2867
inquiries@ipata.com
www.ipata.com
IPATA is an international trade association of pet moving providers and other related professionals concerned with transporting domestic animals and pets throughout the world.

MOVE TO PANAMA
www.movetopanama.com
tel. 507/223-1598, cell tel. 507/6674-1598
Move to Panama is an all-service relocation company that offers fact-finding Panama tours and complete relocation services.

PANAMA PET RELOCATION
tel. 507/6619-6964 or 507/6674-1598
office tel. 507/223-1598
fax 507/223-1217
www.panamapetrelocation.com

Housing Considerations

PROPERTY SEARCH

COMPRE O ALQUILE
www.compreoalquile.com

ENCUENTRA 24
www.encuentra24.com

LA PRENSA CLASSIFIEDS
clasificados.prensa.com

PANAMA CRAIGSLIST
www.panama.craigslist.org

REAL ESTATE AGENCIES

Panama City
ARCO PROPERTIES
tel. 507/211-2548
www.arcoproperties.com
Arco Properties specializes in real estate sales and restoration development in Casco Viejo, Panama's colonial old town. They are committed to sustainable development, while improving the lifestyles

of Casco's longtime residents and new investors.

PANAMA REALTOR
www.panamarealtor.com

ROMERO REALTY
tel. 507 /265-5210 tel. in USA 954/773-8130
www.romero-realty.com
Romero Realty has over 25 years experience in property sales and management in and around Panama City and the interior beaches and highlands.

The Western Highlands
BEYOND BOQUETE REAL ESTATE
tel. 507/6714-2487 or 507/6714-2487
www.beyondboquete.com
Three business-minded expats from North America and Denmark started a successful real estate business in Boquete that services the Chiriquí, Bocas del Toro, and Lowlands of David.

SHORT-TERM RENTALS
PANAMA CASA
tel. 507/264-5302
www.panamacasa.com

PANAMA CORPORATE LIVING
tel. 507/391-3333
www.panamacorporateliving.com

PANAMA PREMIER RENTALS
tel. 507/6781-9555
www.panamapremierrentals.com

PROPERTY TITLES
PUBLIC REGISTRY OF PANAMA
www.registro-publico.gob.pa

REAL ESTATE ASSOCIATIONS
ACOBIR
www.acobir.com

CASCO VIEJO RESTORATION FIRMS
CONSERVATORIO, S.A.
www.conservatoriosa.com

CONSTRUCTIVE SOLUTIONS INC.
Casa Testa, Avenida A entre Calle 6 y 7,
San Felipe
Panama, Republic of Panama
tel. 507/212-2630
fax 507/212-0114
info@constructivesolution.net
www.constructivesolution.net
Constructive Solutions is a construction and renovation management firm that specializes in projects in Boquete, Chiriquí, and Casco Viejo, Panama City.

INTERIOR DESIGNERS
DESIGN WORKS STUDIOS
tel. 507/270-7607
darlene@dwspty.com

NATASHA RATIA DESIGN
Panama City
natasharatia@gmail.com
Natasha Ratia is an independent contractor who relocated to Panama in 2006. She has a degree in interior design from New York University. She has management experience and has worked on everything from home renovations to high-end apartment building lobby design.

WOLF DESIGN INTERNATIONAL
tel. 507 225-1605
info@wolfdi.com
www.wolfdesigninternational.com

ELECTRIC COMPANIES
ELEKTRA NORESTE
tel. 507/323-7100
www.elektra.com.pa

UNION FENOSA
tel. 507/315-7222
www.ufpanama.com

GAS COMPANIES
TROPIGAS
tel. 507/206-0000
www.tropigas.com.pa

WATER COMPANIES
IDAAN
tel. 507/523-8575
www.idaan.gob.pa

Language and Education

SPANISH LANGUAGE SCHOOLS

Panama City

BERLITZ LANGUAGE SCHOOL CENTRAL AMERICA AND PANAMA
berlitzinfo@berlitzedu.net
www.berlitzedu.net

SPANISH PANAMA
El Cangrejo (next to the main business district)
Edificio Americana #1A
Via Argentina, El Cangrejo
above Greenhouse Restaurant
tel./fax 507/213-3121
cell tel. 507/6590-2007 or 507/6624-3302
info@spanishpanama.com
www.spanishpanama.com

Boquete

HABLA YA PANAMA
Central Avenue
Los Establos Plaza 20-22
Boquete, Chiriquí
Republic of Panama
tel. 507/720-1294
USA tel. 315/254-2331
info@hablayapanama.com
www.hablayapanama.com

SPANISH BY THE RIVER
physical address: Alto Boquete, Entrada a Palmira, 180mts a mano izquierda
mailing address: Palmira, Entrega General, Boquete, Chiriquí, Panamá.
tel./fax 507/720-3456
cell tel. 507/6759-5753

Bocas del Toro

BOCAS BY THE SEA
physical address:
Calle 4ta, justo detrás del Hotel Bahía
Bocas del Toro, Isla Colón, Bocas del Toro, Panama
mailing address:
Spanish by the Sea Corp. 0101-00005
Bocas del Toro/Isla Colón, Bocas del Toro, Panama

tel./fax 507/757-9518
cellular tel. 507/6592-0775
SKYPE spanish.by.the.sea

BILINGUAL EDUCATION

Panama City

BALBOA ACADEMY
physical address: Building 129,
City of Knowledge
Clayton, Panama City, Panama
mailing address: Balboa Academy
c/o American Embassy Panama
9100 Panama City Pl.
Washington DC 20521-9100
tel. 507/211-0035 or 507/317-1186
fax 507/211-3319
jlamb@balboa-academy.org
www.balboaacademyweb.org
Preschool through high school private American education, offering the Advanced Placement college preparatory program

INTERNATIONAL SCHOOL OF PANAMA
tel. 507/293-3000
fax 507/266-7808
www.isp.edu.pa
Preschool through high school, international education in English, offering the International Baccalaureate college preparatory program

David

COLEGIO SAN AGUSTÍN
Via Interamaricana
P.O. Box 0426-01508
tel. 507/775-4338 or 507/775-3059
fax 507/774-3272
colsadav@cwpanama.net
www.colsadav2.com
Kindergarten through high school bilingual school

SOUTHERN ACCREDITATION OF COLLEGE AND SCHOOLS (SACS)
www.sacscasi.org

UNIVERSITIES

FLORIDA STATE UNIVERSITY - PANAMA CANAL BRANCH

Calle Ernesto J. Castillero #1033
Panama 6A, Republic of Panama
tel. 507/314-0367
www.panama.fsu.edu

UNIVERSITY OF LOUISVILLE

Calle 45 Bella Vista
Panama City, Panama

tel. 507/264-0777
fax 507/264-7962
reclutar@louisville.com.pa
www.louisville.com.pa

UNIVERISTY OF PANAMA

Panama City
tel. 507/523-5000 or 507/523-5001 or 507/523-5600
www.up.ac.pa

Health

PUBLIC HEALTH AGENCIES

MINISTRY OF HEALTH

www.minsa.gob.pa

PRIVATE HEALTH INSURANCE

AMERICAN LIFE INSURANCE CO.

Calle 50, Edificio Lizak 3er. Piso
tel. 507/208-8000
fax : 507/208-8001
alico@alicopan.com
www.alicopan.com

ANCON

Avenida Samuel Lewis y Calle 54
Urbanización Obarrio, Edificio AFRA
tel. 507/210-8700
fax 507/210-8799
ancon@asegurancon.com
www.asegurancon.com

ASEGURADORA MUNDIAL

Venida Balboa y Calle 41, Edificio Mundial
tel. 507/207-8700
fax 507/207-8787
info@amundial.com
www.amundial.com

ASSA

Calle 50, Edificio ASSA, Companía de Seguros
tel. 507/300-2772
fax 507/300-2729
assamercadeo@assanet.com
www.assanet.com

BRITISH AMERICAN

Calle Elvira Méndez, Edificio Vallarino - Mezzanine
tel. 507/269-8455 /269-0515
fax: 507/269-0790

GENERALI

El Cangrejo, Calle 49-B
tel. 507/206-9100
fax 507/206-9101
generali@generali.com.pa
www.generali.com

MEDISALUD

tel. 507/209-5995
www.medisalud.com.pa

INSURANCE BROKERS

FORLACOL INSURANCE BROKERS

Ursula Keiner
Panama City and Chiriquí
tel. 507/214-6939
cell tel. 507/6676-5151
www.insuranceinpanama.com/about-forlacol

VICTORIA ARIAS

PanAmerican Trust Group
Victoria Arias
Panama City
tel. 507/2084287
cell tel. 507/6747-7753
vitoarias103@gmail.com

PRIVATE HOSPITALS AND CLINICS

Panama City
CENTRO MEDICO PAITILLA
tel. 507/265-8800

HOSPITAL NACIONAL
tel. 507/2078136

HOSPITAL PUNTA PACIFICA-JOHNS HOPKINS AFFILIATE
tel. 507/204-8000
fax 507/204-8010
www.hospitalpuntapacifica.com

HOSPITAL SAN FERNANDO
tel. 507/278-6300

HOSPITAL SANTA FE
tel. 507/227-4733

PUBLIC HOSPITAL
HOSPITAL DEL NINO
tel. 507/512-9808; 512-9813

HOPSITAL SANTO TOMÁS
507/507-5600; 507-5700

EMERGENCY SERVICES
ALERTA AMBULANCE SERVICES
tel. 507/269-1111

CIVIL PROTECTION PANAMA CITY
tel. 507/316-0080

PANAMA FIRE DEPARTMENT
tel. 103

PANAMA POLICE DEPARTMENT
tel. 104 or 507/511-7700

RED CROSS PANAMA AMBULANCE
tel. 507/228-2187

SEMM AMBULANCE SERVICES
tel. 507/264-4122

ALTERNATIVE HEALTH INFORMATION
VINONI
Melissa Arauz
tel. 507/6618-3290
ma@vinoni.com,
www.vi-noni.com
ViNoni is a Panama company that produces and distributes health food products made from the noni fruit.

Employment

AMERICAN CHAMBER OF COMMERCE (PANAMA)
www.panamcham.com
A division of the American Chamber of Commerce, this Panama organization offers information, research, and economic studies on the market in Panama and investment ideas for Panama.

DIRECTORY OF DEVELOPMENT ORGANIZATIONS
www.devdir.org
Internet resources for directory of international development organizations, including for Panama.

UNITED NATIONS DEVELOPMENT PROGRAM
www.undp.org.pa
The UNDP can lead you to jobs and other programs run by the United Nations in Panama and the Central American Region.

VOLUNTEER ORGANIZATIONS
AMIGOS DE LAS AMERICAS
www.amigoslink.org
Amigos de Las Americas work in the regions of Cocle and Veraguas. Volunteers work with children, teaching health and environmental classes.

FUNDACION AMIGOS DE NINOS CON LUCEMIA Y CANCER (FANLYC)

Friends of Children with Leukemia and Cancer Foundation
Avenida México y Calle 33, Calidonia
tel. 227-7826, 225-5986, 227-7535
fax 225-5991
P.O. Box 0823-04321
Panamá, Ciudad de Panamá
www.fanlyc.org.pa

This is a well-established organization in Panama City that gives hospice space to children diagnosed with cancer and their families. The children and their families are usually from other parts of the country and would otherwise have difficulty traveling to the city and finding accommodations due to economic limitations. FANLYC offers day care services, a cafeteria, and family support. The accommodations are comfortable and the administration is always looking for volunteers and donations.

GLOBAL VISION INTERNATIONAL - PANAMA TURTLE CONSERVATION PROJECT

www.gviusa.com/projects/centralamerica/
Panama.com

This organization helps to coordinate volunteers throughout Central America. Their Panama Turtle Conservation project is located in the archipelago of Bocas del Toro. Project volunteers live and work on the beaches, patrolling and searching for the endangered leatherback turtles, which tend to be hunted. Volunteers live in huts and work to tag and monitor the turtles' behavior, relocating them if necessary. Volunteer fees incur donations toward the charity.

GLOBAL VOLUNTEER NETWORK

www.volunteer.org.nz/panama.com

Volunteers can choose from a number of programs and be placed in various communities throughout Panama. Programs include children's programs, working with orphanages and low income families, literacy programs, animal refugee projects, and nutrition projects. A woman's empowerment project called GEM, looks for professional jewelry makers to help train women in design and creation techniques.

VOLUNTEER ABROAD PANAMA

www.volunteerabroad.com/Panama

This website offers a comprehensive list of 21 volunteer programs throughout Panama that include working with children, organic farming, helping to save the rainforest, and volunteering in orphanages, among many others. Some of these programs cannot be contacted directly, and Volunteer Abroad Panama serves as a median entity to help connect volunteers with programs of interest.

Communications

INTERNET PROVIDERS

CABLE & WIRELESS
tel. 507/224-2123
www.cwpanama.com

CABLE ONDA
tel. 507/390-7555
www.cableonda.com

OPTYNEX
tel. 507/380-0000
info@optynex.com
www.optynex.com

TELECARRIER
tel. 507/300-8888
www.telecarrier.com

WIPET
tel. 507/305-7777
www.wipet.com

CELLULAR PHONE PROVIDERS

CABLE & WIRELESS
tel.507/224-6161
www.cwmovil.com

RESOURCES

CLARO
tel. 507/800-9100
www.claro.com.pa

DIGICEL
tel. 507/306-0688
www.digicelpanama.com

MOVISTAR
tel. 507/304-7000
www.movistar.com.pa

VOIP PROVIDERS

ADVANCED COMMUNICATIONS NETWORK
tel. 507/209-9999 or 507/209-0099
www.advanced099.com

CLAROCOM
tel. 507/200-5555
www.clarocom.com

CYBER CAST INTERNATIONAL
tel. 507/264-0852
info@voipunity.com
www.voipunity.com

SKYPE
www.skype.com

TELECARRIER
tel. 507/300-8888
www.telecarrier.com

MAIL FORWARDING SERVICES

AIRBOX EXPRESS
tel. 507/269-9774
www.aeropost.com

MAIL BOXES, ETC.
www.mbe.com

MIAMI EXPRESS
tel. 507/207-1155
www.miamiexpress.com

DOMESTIC COURIER SERVICES

AEROPERLAS
tel.507/315-7570
www.aeroperlas.com

AIR PANAMA
tel. 507/316-9016
www.flyairpanama.com

COPA COURIER
tel. 507/304-2660
www.copacourier.com

FLETES CHAVALES
tel. 507/261-7016

UNO EXPRESS
tel. 507/214-6279 /800-2122
www.unoexpresspanama.com

NEWSPAPERS

EL PANAMÁ AMÉRICA
www.epasa.com

LA ESTRELLA DE PANAMÁ
www.laestrella.com.pa

LA PRENSA
www.prensa.com

THE PANAMA NEWS
www.thepanamanews.com

CABLE/SATELLITE TV PROVIDERS

CABLE ONDA
tel. 507/390-7555
www.cableonda.com

SKY TV
tel. 507/207-0707
www.sky.com/mx/centroamerica

Finance

PANAMA TAXES
PANAMA OFFSHORE LEGAL SERVICES
www.panama-offshore-services.com

SOCIAL SECURITY
CAJA DE SEGURO SOCIAL
www.css.org.pa

TAXES AT HOME
THE HERITAGE FOUNDATION
www.heritage.org
Annually, the Heritage Foundation produces the Index of Economic Freedom, which details each country's investment freedoms and levels of corruption.

OFFSHORE ASSET PROTECTION
www.offshorepress.com

PANAMA EMPRENDE
www.panamaemprende.gob.pa
Panama Emprende is a government initiative started in 2008 that allows the creation of companies online within less than 48 hours.

PANAMANIAN TOURISM AUTHORITY (AUTORIDAD DE TURISMO DE PANAMÁ)
tel. 507/526-7000
www.ipat.gob.pa

PANAMA PACIFICO
www.panamapacifico.com
Panama Pacifico, a mixed-use, business, residential and recreational center, will be created over 40 years by renowned developer London & Regional Panama in conjunction with the government of Panama.

TRANSPARENCY INTERNATIONAL
www.transparency.org
Transparency International is a global organization leading the fight against corruption. It publishes an annual list of the countries in the world, ranked by levels of perceived corruption.

Travel and Transportation

AIRLINES
AEROPERLAS
tel.507/315-7570
www.aeroperlas.com

AIR PANAMA
tel. 507/316-9016
www.flyairpanama.com

COPA AIRLINES
tel. 507/217-COPA
U.S. tel. 800/FLY-COPA
www.copaair.com

INTERNATIONAL BUS TRAVEL
PANALINE
www.Panalinecr.com
Bus travel between Costa Rica and Panama only

TICA BUS
www.ticabus.com
Bus transportation from Panama to other Central American cities in Costa Rica, Nicaragua, Honduras, El Salvador, Guatemala, and Tapachula, Mexico

BY TRAIN
PANAMA RAILWAY COMPANY
Bldg. T-376, Corozal West
P.O. Box 2669 Balboa - Ancon, Panama, Republic of Panama
tel. 507/317-6070
fax 507/317-6061
info@panarail.com

www.panarail.com
Train travel between Panama City and Colón only

BY BOAT AND FERRY

Panama City and Vicinity

PANAMA CALYPSO
Amador Causeway behind Mi Ranchito Restaurant
tel. 507/314-1730
fax 507 314-1729
Panama ferry between the Amador Causeway in Panama City and Isla Taboga

Bocas Boat and Ferry

BOCAS MARINE & TOURS
Calle 3, at Av. C.
tel. 507/757-9033

JAM PAN TOURS
Calle 2, at Av D.
tel. 507/757-9619

TAXI 25
Calle 1, at Av. Central
tel. 507/757-9028

TRASBORDADORES MARINOS
Town Port, Almirante
tel. 507/6615-6674

ONLINE TRAVEL INFORMATION

ALMANAQUE AZUL
www.almanaqueazul.com
Almanaque Azul is a eco-conscious travel guide that helps you visit the best beaches and parks in Panama, while providing you with information about conservation issues relating to each area and practical information about how to visit many off-the-beaten-path locations.

TRANSPANAMA
www.transpanama.org
TransPanama is a volunteer project that is mapping and citing known trails across Panama. New volunteers are welcome.

PANAMA EXPLORERS CLUB
Edificio El Virrey, Planta Baja
Vía Italia, Punta Paitilla
tel. 507/215-2330
fax 507/215-2329
PEX Adventure Center
Vía Ranita Dorada, Capirita
telefax 507/983-6942
www.pexclub.com
Panama Explorers Club offers adventure sports for those who want to see Panama through the exciting lens of mountain peaks, rapid waters, and jungle hikes.

SECURITY AND CUSTOMS REGULATIONS

INTERNATIONAL AIR TRAVEL (IATA)
www.iata.org

PANAMA NATIONAL CUSTOMS AUTHORITY
Autoridad Nacional de Aduanas
tel. 507/506-6400 or 507/506-6406
http://201.225.226.44

VISA HEADQUARTERS ORGANIZATION
www.panama.visahq.com/customs

Prime Living Locations

PANAMA CITY

PANAMA CANAL AUTHORITY
www.panacanal.com
This website offers information about Panama Canal news and history, and daily Canal updates.

PANAMA CITY MUNICIPAL
www.municipio.gob.pa
This website is in Spanish only.

THE OFFICE OF CASCO ANTIGUO
www.cascoantiguo.gob.pa
The Casco Antiguo Office is a municipal department dedicated to the conservation and history of the colonial old town.

CENTRAL PANAMA

PANAMACENTRIC
www.panamacentric.com
This website provides news, information, and further links about Panama to expats, especially those located in Panama's central region west of Campana and in Central Highlands, the beaches of Coclé, Penonomé, Santiago, and Chitré.

PLAYA COMMUNITY
www.playacommunity.com
Playa Community is a website in English including information about Panama's many beach communities, news, expat clubs, and real estate contacts.

THE WESTERN HIGHLANDS

BAJAREQUE TIMES
www.boquete-bajareque-times.com
The Bajareque Times is a monthly newsletter, published out of Boquete, which highlights events in the Chiriquí Highlands. It is written by and for expat residents.

BOQUETE.ORG
www.Boquete.org
This website is set up to offer geographical information about Boquete and the Chiriquí Highlands. It lists community services, expat groups, personal announcements, a business directory, calendar, and local information for both expat and local residents.

BOCAS DEL TORO

THE BOCAS BREEZE
www.thebocasbreeze.com
A Bocas del Toro newspaper written in both Spanish and English for local and foreign residents who live on the islands.

BOCAS LIVING
www.bocasliving.com
Use this site to find out about daily life and resources in the archipelago of Bocas del Toro.

Glossary

ahora Literally, "now." In Panama, often ironically means "whenever."

almacenes discount department stores

bajareque mist or drizzling rain

bien ciudados freelance parking attendants who help drivers find spaces and keep an eye on your car to prevent theft and vandalism. If one helps you, you are expected to give him a few dollars.

bochinche gossip

calle principal main street

campesino farmer, country dweller

cedula Panamanian ID card

cerveza beer

chakira bead

chitra no-see-um, sand fly

choque car accident

claves ATMs

colectivo shared transportation, such as a taxi or van that picks up several people at once and charges a per-person fare

comarcas the country's indigenous regions

Diablos Rojos Red Devils, a privatized but government sanctioned service of wildly painted buses

dulcería sweets shop

jubilado retired person

la feria fair or festival

la hora gringa Western time, used to indicate punctuality is expected

la hora panameña Panama time, meaning loosely scheduled

lancha water taxi

ley law

malecón promenade or walkway

molas intricate woven fabric made by the Kuna people

mucho gusto Nice to meet you. Literally, "with pleasure."

panadería bakery

planilla payroll

rabi blanca white tail, Panama's European descendents and upper class

se vende for sale

tranquilo easygoing

un placer "My pleasure." Or "You're welcome."

white tails European descendents, the upper class of Panama

Spanish Phrasebook

You will feel more comfortable in Panama if you speak Spanish. Although Panamanians notice your foreign accent, they will appreciate your halting efforts to break the ice and transform yourself from a foreigner to a potential friend.

Panamanian Spanish sounds very different to Castellano, the traditional Spanish from Spain. The main differences are the lexicon and the accent. Panamanians invent a lot of words, so don't be shy and ask someone what they mean to say. They will also drop the letters off the end of their words. So if you know a little bit of Spanish from your school days prior, you might feel like you have to learn it all over again. Don't get intimidated. Keep speaking and listening and you will get the hang of it.

Spanish commonly uses 30 letters — the familiar English 26, plus four straightforward additions: ch, ll, ñ, and rr, which are explained in "Consonants," below.

PRONUNCIATION

Once you learn them, Spanish pronunciation rules — in contrast to English — don't change. Spanish vowels generally sound softer than in English. (*Note:* The capitalized syllables below receive stronger accents.)

Vowels

a like ah, as in "hah": *agua* AH-gooah (water), *pan* PAHN (bread), and *casa* CAH-sah (house)

e like ay, as in "may:" *mesa* MAY-sah (table), *tela* TAY-lah (cloth), and *de* DAY (of, from)

i like ee, as in "need": *diez* dee-AYZ (ten), *comida* ko-MEE-dah (meal), and *fin* FEEN (end)

o like oh, as in "go": *peso* PAY-soh (weight), *ocho* OH-choh (eight), and *poco* POH-koh (a bit)

u like oo, as in "cool": *uno* OO-noh (one), *cuarto* KOOAHR-toh (room), and *usted* oos-TAYD (you); when it follows a "q" the **u** is silent; when it follows an "h" or has an umlaut, it's pronounced like "w"

Consonants

b, d, f, k, l, m, n, p, q, s, t, v, w, x, y, z, and ch   pronounced almost as in English; **h** occurs, but is silent – not pronounced at all.

c like k as in "keep": *cuarto* KOOAR-toh (room), Tepic tay-PEEK (capital of Nayarit state); when it precedes "e" or "i," pronounce **c** like s, as in "sit": *cerveza* sayr-VAY-sah (beer), *encima* ayn-SEE-mah (atop).

g like g as in "gift" when it precedes "a," "o," "u," or a consonant: *gato* GAH-toh (cat), *hago* AH-goh (I do, make); otherwise, pronounce **g** like h as in "hat": *giro* HEE-roh (money order), *gente* HAYN-tay (people)

j like h, as in "has": *Jueves* HOOAY-vays (Thursday), *mejor* may-HOR (better)

ll like y, as in "yes": *toalla* toh-AH-yah (towel), *ellos* AY-yohs (they, them)

ñ like ny, as in "canyon": *año* AH-nyo (year), *señor* SAY-nyor (Mr., sir)

r is lightly trilled, with tongue at the roof of your mouth like a very light English d, as in "ready": *pero* PAY-doh (but), *tres* TDAYS (three), *cuatro* KOOAH-tdoh (four).

rr like a Spanish r, but with much more emphasis and trill. Let your tongue flap. Practice with *burro* (donkey), *carretera* (highway), and Carrillo (proper name), then really let go with *ferrocarril* (railroad).

Note: The single small but common exception to all of the above is the pronunciation of Spanish y when it's being used as the Spanish word for "and," as in *"Ron y Kathy."* In such case, pronounce it like the English ee, as in "keep": Ron "ee" Kathy (Ron and Kathy).

Accent

The rule for accent, the relative stress given to syllables within a given word, is straightforward. If a word ends in a vowel, an n, or an s, accent the next-to-last syllable; if not, accent the last syllable.

Pronounce *gracias* GRAH-seeahs (thank you), *orden* OHR-dayn (order), and *carretera* kah-ray-TAY-rah (highway) with stress on the next-to-last syllable.

Otherwise, accent the last syllable: *venir* vay-NEER (to come), *ferrocarril* fay-roh-cah-REEL (railroad), and *edad* ay-DAHD (age).

Exceptions to the accent rule are always marked with an accent sign: (á, é, í, ó, or ú), such as *teléfono* tay-LAY-foh-noh (telephone), *jabón* hah-BON (soap), and *rápido* RAH-pee-doh (rapid).

BASIC AND COURTEOUS EXPRESSIONS

Most Spanish-speaking people consider formalities important. Whenever approaching anyone for information or some other reason, do not forget the appropriate salutation — good morning, good evening, etc. Standing alone, the greeting *hola* (hello) can sound brusque.

Hello. *Hola (Panamanians often use the simple term "Buenas" as a regular greeting)*

Good morning. *Buenos días.*

Good afternoon. *Buenas tardes.*

Good evening. *Buenas noches.*

How are you? *¿Cómo está usted?*

Very well, thank you. *Muy bien, gracias.*
Okay; good. *Bien; dale*
Not okay; bad. *Mal or feo.*
So-so. *Más o menos.*
And you? *¿Y usted?*
Thank you. *Gracias.*
Thank you very much. *Muchas gracias.*
You're very kind. *Muy amable.*
You're welcome. *De nada; a la orden*
Goodbye. *Adios.*
See you later. *Hasta luego.*
please *por favor*
yes *sí*
no *no*
I don't know. *No sé.*
Just a moment, please. *Momentito, por favor.*
Excuse me, please (when you're trying to get attention). *Disculpe or Con permiso.*
Excuse me (when you've made an error). *Lo siento.*
Pleased to meet you. *Mucho gusto.*
What is your name? *¿Cómo se llama usted?*
Do you speak English? *¿Habla usted inglés?*
Is English spoken here? (Does anyone here speak English?) *¿Se habla inglés?*
I don't speak Spanish well. *No hablo bien el español.*
I don't understand. *No entiendo.*
How do you say...in Spanish? *¿Cómo se dice...en español?*
My name is... *Me llamo...*
Would you like... *¿Quisiera usted...*
Let's go to... *Vamos a...*

TERMS OF ADDRESS

When in doubt, use the formal *usted* (you) as a form of address.

I *yo*
you (formal) *usted*
you (familiar) *tu*
he/him *él*
she/her *ella*
we/us *nosotros*

you (plural) *ustedes*
they/them *ellos* (all males or mixed gender); *ellas* (all females)
Mr., sir *señor*
Mrs., madam *señora*
miss, young lady; *señorita*
young man; young woman *joven*
wife *esposa, mujer*
husband *esposo, marido*
friend *amigo* (male); *amiga* (female)
sweetheart *novio* (male); *novia* (female)
son; daughter *hijo; hija*
brother; sister *hermano; hermana*
father; mother *padre; madre*
grandfather; grandmother *abuelo; abuela*

TRANSPORTATION

Where is...? *¿Dónde está...?*
How far is it to...? *¿A cuánto está...?*
from...to... *de...a...*
How many blocks? *¿Cuántas cuadras?*
Where (Which) is the way to...? *¿Dónde está el camino a...?*
the bus station *la terminal de autobuses*
the bus stop *la parada de autobuses*
Where is this bus going? *¿Adónde va este autobús?*
the taxi stand *la parada de taxis*
the train station *la estación de ferrocarril*
the boat *el barco*
the launch *lancha; tiburonera*
the dock *el muelle*
the airport *el aeropuerto*
I'd like a ticket to... *Quisiera un boleto a...*
first (second) class *primera (segunda) clase*
roundtrip *ida y vuelta*
reservation *reservación*
baggage *equipaje*
Stop here, please. *Pare aquí, por favor.*
the entrance *la entrada*
the exit *la salida*
the ticket office *la oficina de boletos*
(very) near; far *(muy) cerca; lejos*

to; toward *a*
by; through *por*
from *de*
the right *la derecha*
the left *la izquierda*
straight ahead *derecho; directo*
in front *en frente*
beside *al lado*
behind *atrás*
the corner *la esquina*
the stoplight *la semáforo*
a turn *una vuelta*
right here *aquí*
somewhere around here *por acá*
right there *allí*
somewhere around there *por allá*
road *el camino*
street; boulevard *calle; bulevar*
block *la cuadra*
highway *carretera*
kilometer *kilómetro*
bridge; toll *puente; cuota*
address *dirección*
north; south *norte; sur*
east; west *este; oeste*

ACCOMMODATIONS

hotel *hotel*
Is there a room? *¿Hay cuarto?*
May I (may we) see it? *¿Puedo (podemos) verlo?*
What is the rate? *¿Cuál es el precio?*
Is that your best rate? *¿Es su mejor precio?*
Is there something cheaper? *¿Hay algo más económico?*
a single room *un cuarto sencillo*
a double room *un cuarto doble*
double bed *cama matrimonial*
twin beds *camas gemelas*
with private bath *con baño*
hot water *agua caliente*
shower *ducha*
towels *toallas*
soap *jabón*
toilet paper *papel higiénico*
blanket *manta*
sheets *sábanas*
air-conditioned *aire acondicionado*
fan *abanico; ventilador*

key *llave*
manager *gerente*

FOOD

Bon apetít *Buen Provecho*
I'm hungry *Tengo hambre.*
I'm thirsty. *Tengo sed.*
menu *carta; menú*
order *orden*
glass *vaso*
fork *tenedor*
knife *cuchillo*
spoon *cuchara*
napkin *servilleta*
soft drink *refresco*
coffee *café*
tea *té*
drinking water *agua pura; agua potable*
bottled carbonated water *agua mineral*
bottled uncarbonated water *agua sin gas*
beer *cerveza*
wine *vino*
milk *leche*
juice *jugo*
cream *crema*
sugar *azúcar*
cheese *queso*
snack *merienda; algo para picar*
breakfast *desayuno*
lunch *almuerzo*
daily lunch special *el menú del día*
dinner *cena (a late-night snack)*
the check *la cuenta*
eggs *huevos*
bread *pan*
salad *ensalada*
fruit *fruta*
mango *mango*
watermelon *sandía*
papaya *papaya*
banana *guineo, banana*
apple *manzana*
orange *naranja*
lime *limón*
fish *pescado*
shellfish *mariscos*
shrimp *camarones*

meat (without) (sin) carne
chicken pollo
pork puerco
beef; steak res; bistec
bacon; ham tocino; jamón
fried frito
roasted asada
barbecue; barbecued barbacoa; al carbón

SHOPPING

money dinero; plata
cash efectivo
money-exchange bureau casa de cambio
What is the exchange rate? ¿Cuál es el tipo de cambio?
How much is the commission? ¿Cuánto cuesta la comisión?
Do you accept credit cards? ¿Aceptan tarjetas de crédito?
money order giro
How much does it cost? ¿Cuánto cuesta?
What is your final price? ¿Cuál es su último precio?
expensive caro
cheap barato; económico
more más
less menos
a little un poco
too much demasiado

HEALTH

Help me please. Ayúdeme por favor.
I am ill. Estoy enfermo.
Call a doctor. Llame un doctor.
Take me to... Lléveme a...
hospital hospital; sanatorio
drugstore farmacia
pain dolor
fever fiebre
headache dolor de cabeza
stomach ache dolor de estómago
burn quemadura
cramp calambre
nausea náusea

vomiting vomitar
medicine medicina
antibiotic antibiótico
pill; tablet pastilla
aspirin aspirina
ointment; cream pomada; crema
bandage venda
cotton algodón
sanitary napkins use brand name, e.g., Kotex
birth control pills pastillas anticonceptivas
contraceptive foam espuma anticonceptiva
condoms preservativos; condones
toothbrush cepillo dental
dental floss hilo dental
toothpaste crema dental
dentist dentista
toothache dolor de muelas

POST OFFICE AND COMMUNICATIONS

long-distance telephone teléfono larga distancia
I would like to call... Quisiera llamar a...
collect por cobrar
station to station a quien contesta
person to person persona a persona
credit card tarjeta de crédito
post office correo
general delivery lista de correo
letter carta
stamp estampilla, timbre
postcard tarjeta
aerogram aerograma
air mail correo aereo
registered registrado
money order giro
package; box paquete; caja
string; tape cuerda; cinta

AT THE BORDER

border frontera
customs aduana
immigration migración
tourist card tarjeta de turista

inspection *inspección; revisión*
passport *pasaporte*
profession *profesión*
marital status *estado civil*
single *soltero*
married; divorced *casado; divorciado*
widowed *viudado*
insurance *seguros*
title *título*
driver's license *licencia de conducir*

AT THE GAS STATION

gas station *gasolinera*
gasoline *gasolina*
unleaded *sin plomo*
full, please *lleno, por favor con...*(the
  type of gas)
tire *llanta*
tire repair shop *taller de llantas*
air *aire*
water *agua*
oil (change) *aceite (cambio)*
grease *grasa*
My...doesn't work. *Mi...no sirve.*
battery *batería*
radiator *radiador*
alternator *alternador*
generator *generador*
tow truck *grúa*
repair shop *taller mecánico*
tune-up *afinación*
auto parts store *refaccionería*

VERBS

Verbs are the key to getting along in
Spanish. They employ mostly predictable
forms and come in three classes, which
end in *ar*, *er*, and *ir*, respectively:
to buy *comprar*
I buy, you (he, she, it) buys *compro,
  compra*
we buy, you (they) buy *compramos,
  compran*
to eat *comer*
I eat, you (he, she, it) eats *como,
  come*
we eat, you (they) eat *comemos,
  comen*

to climb *subir*
**I climb, you (he, she, it)
  climbs** *subo, sube*
we climb, you (they) climb *subimos,
  suben*
Here are more (with irregularities
indicated):
to do or make *hacer* (regular except
  for *hago*, I do or make)
to go *ir* (very irregular: *voy, va, vamos,
  van*)
to go (walk) *andar*
to love *amar*
to work *trabajar*
to want *desear, querer*
to need *necesitar*
to read *leer*
to write *escribir*
to repair *reparar*
to stop *parar*
to get off (the bus) *bajar*
to arrive *llegar*
to stay (remain) *quedar*
to stay (lodge) *hospedar*
to leave *salir* (regular except for *salgo*,
  I leave)
to look at *mirar*
to look for *buscar*
to give *dar* (regular except for *doy*, I
  give)
to carry *llevar*
to have *tener* (irregular but important:
  tengo, tiene, tenemos, tienen)
to come *venir* (similarly irregular:
  vengo, viene, venimos, vienen)

Spanish has two forms of "to be":
to be *estar* (regular except for *estoy*, I
  am)
to be *ser* (very irregular: *soy, es, somos,
  son*)
Use *estar* when speaking of location or a
temporary state of being: "I am at home."
"Estoy en casa." "I'm sick." *"Estoy enfermo."*
Use *ser* for a permanent state of being: "I
am a doctor." *"Soy doctora."*

RESOURCES

NUMBERS

zero *cero*
one *uno*
two *dos*
three *tres*
four *cuatro*
five *cinco*
six *seis*
seven *siete*
eight *ocho*
nine *nueve*
10 *diez*
11 *once*
12 *doce*
13 *trece*
14 *catorce*
15 *quince*
16 *dieciseis*
17 *diecisiete*
18 *dieciocho*
19 *diecinueve*
20 *veinte*
21 *veinte y uno or veintiuno*
30 *treinta*
40 *cuarenta*
50 *cincuenta*
60 *sesenta*
70 *setenta*
80 *ochenta*
90 *noventa*
100 *ciento*
101 *ciento y uno or cientiuno*
200 *doscientos*
500 *quinientos*
1,000 *mil*
10,000 *diez mil*
100,000 *cien mil*
1,000,000 *millón*
one half *medio*
one third *un tercio*
one fourth *un cuarto*

TIME

What time is it? *¿Qué hora es?*
It's one o'clock. *Es la una.*
It's three in the afternoon. *Son las tres de la tarde.*
It's 4 A.M. *Son las cuatro de la mañana.*
six-thirty *seis y media*
a quarter till eleven *un cuarto para las once*
a quarter past five *las cinco y cuarto*
an hour *una hora*

DAYS AND MONTHS

Monday *lunes*
Tuesday *martes*
Wednesday *miércoles*
Thursday *jueves*
Friday *viernes*
Saturday *sábado*
Sunday *domingo*
today *hoy*
tomorrow *mañana*
yesterday *ayer*
January *enero*
February *febrero*
March *marzo*
April *abril*
May *mayo*
June *junio*
July *julio*
August *agosto*
September *septiembre*
October *octubre*
November *noviembre*
December *diciembre*
a week *una semana*
a month *un mes*
after *después*
before *antes*

(Courtesy of Bruce Whipperman, author of *Moon Pacific Mexico*.)

Suggested Reading

Panama has such a rich and vivid history it is impossible to pick just a few books. However, once involved in any one of these books below, they will be sure to link you to other books of the same quality and caliber. Whether researching flora, fauna, pirates, politics or engineering greats, Panama can be found throughout the non-fiction world.

ARTS AND CULTURE

Fitzgerald Tomás, Consuelo (author), and Emiliani Núñez, Mariana (illustrator). *Pa'na'ma Quererte*. Panama: Impresora Pacifico, 2007. In Spanish only, this is worth the read. Tomás has recreated vignettes of life in the heart of Panama City, with colorful cultural releases and a solid grasp on the energy burning from the streets of everyday life. The images by Mariana Núñez are the closest thing to going out and studying the nooks and crannies of Panama yourself. Even if you can't yet read in Spanish, buy it. The images are telling enough.

Mosquera, Gerardo and Samos, Adrienne. *Multiple City: Urban Art and Global Cities: An Experiment in Context*. Amsterdam: KIT Publishers, 2004. This is a catalog of a city-wide art project that took place in Panama City in April 2003 to celebrate 100 years of Panama City. The curators Adrienne Samos and Gerardo Mosquera invited 14 international artists to participate in their celebration of the city's centennial, and documented it with this book, and a DVD catalog. The installations were the artists' gifts to city residents, and add an outsider's perspective to the graces and anomalies of Panama City. The events were a modern success.

Salvador, Mari Lyn. *The Art of Being Kuna: Layers of Meaning Among the Kuna of Panama*. Seattle, WA: University of Washington Press, 1997. A beautifully illustrated book about the life of the Kuna with colorful images of their art and clothing, and small bits of text depicting life behind their history, beliefs, and daily life.

Solarte, Tristan *El Ahogado*. Panama: 1962. Solarte is one of Panama's most celebrated authors and a known poet and essayist. He was born in Bocas Town by the name of Guillermo Sánchez Borbón. This book is the fictional story of a Panamanian adolescent who died by drowning and evokes the culture and demeanor Panamanian people's humility.

FLORA AND FAUNA

Angehr, George R., Engleman, Dodge, and Engleman, Lorna. *A Bird-finding Guide to Panama*. New York: Cornell University Press, 2008. This field guide is a comprehensive book for true bird lovers and those simply interested in the 970 bird species that can be found on the isthmus. The book is celebrated for its simple "Where to Find" sections, maps, conservation discussions, and trail guides. The book focuses more on text than images but is highly informational for anyone who wants to take on Panama's natural world.

Ridgely, Robert S. and Gwynne, John A. Jr. *A Guide to the Birds of Panama*. Princeton, New Jersey: Princeton University Press, 1992. This book is a must for anyone who looks wishes to identify birds by colors, sounds, and the foliage they live in. It is considered by some as the bible for Panama's bird-watchers and includes birds in neighboring regions Costa Rica, Nicaragua, and Colombia.

Ziegler, Christian (photographer) and Leigh, Egbert G. (contributor). *A Magic Web: The Forests of Barro Colorado Island*. USA: Oxford University Press,

RESOURCES

2002. This photo essay features the impressive photography of *National Geographic* contributor Christian Ziegler. Ziegler spent a year on the island capturing the exotic and irregular faces of everyday creatures in the forests and jungles of Panama in the microcosmic world of Barro Colorado Island, a world-class scientific tropical research site. The photos are illuminated with vibrant descriptions by ecologist Egbert Leigh.

HISTORY AND POLITICS

Dinges, John. *Our Man in Panama: How General Noriega Used the United States—And Made Millions in Drugs and Arms.* New York: Random House, 1990. Another book based on the biography and mysterious rise of General Manuel Antonio Noriega from the Panama slums to military dictatorship, and his involvement in major drug crimes.

Kempe, Federick. *Divorcing the Dictator: America's Bungled Affair with Noriega.* New York: G.P. Putnam's Sons, 1990. This book provides a complete anecdotal history on Noriega's relationship with the United States, from the CIA to his slow release from U.S. bond and into an embittered dictator. Kempe does the investigations as a professional foreign correspondent and expert.

Koester, Richard. M., and Sanchez, Guillermo. *In the Time of the Tyrants.* USA: W.W. Norton and Company, 1991. This book discusses the adept corruption intricately involved in the Torrijos government, setting the stage for the worst for Panama, leading up to 1990.

McCullough, David. *The Path Between the Seas: The Creation of the Panama Canal, 1870–1914.* New York: Simon and Schuster, 1977. An amazing account by a well-known historian about the creation, in both concept and design, of the Panama Canal, and the many stories of the immigrants and foreign nations involved in the project. It's virtually impossible to move to Panama without having read this book.

Murillo, Luis E. *The Noriega Mess: The Drugs, the Canal, and Why America Invaded.* Berkeley, CA: Video Books Production, 1995. Luis Murillo is an English-speaking Panamanian-born author who has written a book that discusses the years prior to Noriega's dictatorship as thoroughly as it does his reign and the after-effects of the United States' invasion in 1989. Different from other political books that analyze the roles of other foreign players and local politicians, Murrillo has written this book for the general reader, trying to include the most comprehensive of all stories that touched upon the years that involved even a hint of the dictatorship. It can be used as reference material and a general encyclopedia of topics surrounding this era. A highly recommended read, coming from a Panamanian who just wants to talk about those years as they were really seen.

Woodward, Bob. *The Commanders.* New York: Simon and Schuster, 1991. Although not solely about Panama, this book chronicles Woodward's investigations into the United States military involvement in the first Bush administration, including the account of the invasion on Panama, and Operation Just Cause in 1989 as a major catalyst for the U.S. military's center-stage attitude since then. For those interested in U.S. politics at the time of the invasion and how the United States has maintained its leading role, for better or worse, in the war on terrorism today, this is an intelligent read.

Index

Acknowledgments

This project was compiled with the help of many thoughtful and talented collaborators. I would like to thank everyone who worked to support and contribute to this book with honest insight. Thank you to Rebecca Love, Becky and Larry Thormalin, John Hurst, Tim Chopoorian, David Dell, Fred and Cynthia Bishop, Uriah Reisman, Adam Brunner, Sunanda Mehra and Vincent La Valle. Thank you to Rogelio Romero, Mandy Faircloth and Luis Juliao in Panama City and Etty in Bocas del Toro, for their real estate knowledge. Also to Melissa Arauz for her input. For information and resource work I want to thank the Office of Casco Antiguo, IPAT, INAC, and Migdalia Joseph. Thank you to David Young, Gerardo Berroa, Ted Harrison, Steven Rich and their respective publications.

I want to thank the New York Bagel Café and Pan y Canela for hosting me during long hours of writing and for filling my coffee addiction. To Loreto and Philippe who shared, their peace (and piece) of paradise to write in Bocas del Drago. *Siempre somos familia!*

Guido Bilbao, Alejo Simon, Dean Strober, Alejandro Lopez Chicheri deserve a million thanks for their advice and writer's talk. The writing process would not have been the same without them.

Much credit goes to Rebecca Love for her hard work, patience, and commitment to follow through on her collaboration. Credit is also due to contributors Russell Stayanoff, Cristina Costa, and Raul Altamar. To my first-class photographers, Sky Gilbar, Sergio Ochoa, and Alejandro Lopez, thank you for capturing Panama as we know it is.

I want to thank everyone at Avalon Travel, especially Grace Fujimoto and Jehan Seirafi, for believing in me while I worked through some difficult setbacks. Thank you to my editors, Annie Blakley and Elizabeth Hansen, and the rest of the Avalon team, Brice Ticen, Lucie Ericksen, Kevin McLain, and Jaime Andrade. Their collective patience and organization helped me to re-establish workable writing schedules, and their comprehension and guidance have been invaluable.

This book was written over the course of one year, mostly by night after long teaching days and weeks. I want to thank the faculty at Magen David Academy, and especially Sean Davis and Maria Dillon, for their professional support and for giving me the opportunity to work 100 percent at both of my passions. I also want to thank MDA's 2008–2009 fourth-grade students and their parents; they gave me the *ganas* to stay light and positive in a very loaded-down year.

Thank you to the best of friends, the Lauras, Helen Kiser, Loreto Barceló, and Mariana Nunez for their irreplaceable friendship and long talks of encouragement in a year that stood to test me the most.

I would like to dedicate this book in the loving memory of Giacomo, whose creative spirit pulled me through each word. I miss you.

Thank you to my voice for giving me another creative filter when I thought my well would run dry.

Above all I want to thank my entire family. To my parents—your constant love and support has been the fuel that allowed me to travel so far, open my eyes so wide, and believe in myself, although it sent me farther away than you'd have liked. Mom, your roots are mine, and I was determined to know them. *Un besote!* Dad, you are my agent, my friend, and my personal advisor. I am the world's luckiest daughter. Thank you for all your attention to my details.

www.moon.com

DESTINATIONS | ACTIVITIES | BLOGS | MAPS | BOOKS

MOON.COM is all new, and ready to help plan your next trip! Filled with fresh trip ideas and strategies, author interviews, informative blogs, a detailed map library, and descriptions of all the Moon guidebooks, Moon.com is all you need to get out and explore the world—or even places in your own backyard. As always, when you travel with Moon, expect an experience that is uncommon and truly unique.

MAP SYMBOLS

▭▭▭	Expressway	○	City/Town	✕	Airfield	◢	Archaeological Site
▭▭	Primary Road	◉	State Capital	✈	Airport	♠	Church
───	Secondary Road	⊛	National Capital	▲	Mountain	⛽	Gas Station
∙∙∙∙∙	Unpaved Road	★	Point of Interest	♣♣	Park		Mangrove
∙∙∙∙∙∙	Ferry	■	Other Location	✗	Skiing Area		Reef
━━━━	Railroad						Swamp

CONVERSION TABLES

°C = (°F - 32) / 1.8
°F = (°C x 1.8) + 32
1 inch = 2.54 centimeters (cm)
1 foot = 0.304 meters (m)
1 yard = 0.914 meters
1 mile = 1.6093 kilometers (km)
1 km = 0.6214 miles
1 fathom = 1.8288 m
1 chain = 20.1168 m
1 furlong = 201.168 m
1 acre = 0.4047 hectares
1 sq km = 100 hectares
1 sq mile = 2.59 square km
1 ounce = 28.35 grams
1 pound = 0.4536 kilograms
1 short ton = 0.90718 metric ton
1 short ton = 2,000 pounds
1 long ton = 1.016 metric tons
1 long ton = 2,240 pounds
1 metric ton = 1,000 kilograms
1 quart = 0.94635 liters
1 US gallon = 3.7854 liters
1 Imperial gallon = 4.5459 liters
1 nautical mile = 1.852 km

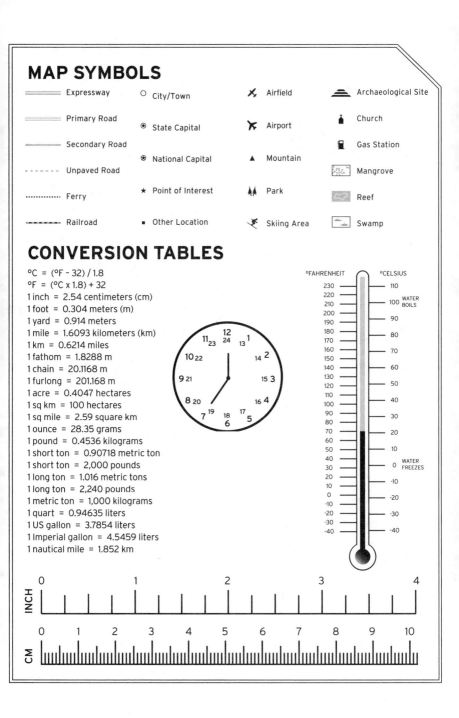

MOON LIVING ABROAD IN PANAMA

Avalon Travel
a member of the Perseus Book Group
1700 Fourth Street
Berkeley, CA 94710, USA
www.moon.com

Editor and Series Manager: Elizabeth Hansen
Copy Editor: Valerie Sellers Blanton
Graphics and Production Coordinator:
   Lucie Ericksen
Cover Designer: Lucie Ericksen
Map Editor: Brice Ticen
Cartographer: Kat Bennett
Indexer: Judy Hunt

ISBN: 978-1-59880-243-6
ISSN: 2150-2412

Printing History
1st Edition – 2009
5 4 3 2 1

Text © 2009 by Miriam Butterman.
Maps © 2009 by Avalon Travel.
All rights reserved.

Some photos and illustrations are used by permission and are the property of the original copyright owners.

Front cover photo: Chorrillo Bus Terminal, Panama City, Panama © Diane Cook and Len Jenshel/GETTYIMAGES
Title page photo: Panama City – Casco Viejo District, view of spanish colonial architecture and gardens © Holger Mette/Dreamstime.com
Interior photos: page 4 © tonisalado/iStockphoto; page 5 © Danielho/iStockphoto; pages 6 top, 7 bottom & top-right © Alejandro Chicheri; page 6 bottom © Sky Gilbar; page 7 top-left © zxvisual/iStockphoto; page 8 top & bottom-right © Miriam Butterman; page 8 bottom-left © Loreto Barcelo
Back cover photo: Hummingbird © Sky Gilbar

Printed in Canada by Friesens

KEEPING CURRENT

Although we strive to produce the most up-to-date guidebook that we possibly can, change is unavoidable. Between the time this book goes to print and the time you read it, the cost of goods and services may have increased, and a handful of the businesses noted in these pages will undoubtedly move, alter their prices, or close their doors forever. Exchange rates fluctuate – sometimes dramatically – on a daily basis. Federal and local legal requirements and restrictions are also subject to change, so be sure to check with the appropriate authorities before making the move. If you see anything in this book that needs updating, clarification, or correction, please drop us a line. Send your comments via email to feedback@moon.com, or use the address above.